FOOD&WINE

Wine Guide
2007

WINE GUIDE 2007

editor in chief **Dana Cowin**
art director **Patricia Sanchez**
editor **Lettie Teague**
volume editor **Kristen Wolfe Bieler**
assistant managing editor **Christine Quinlan**
copy editor **Anne O'Connor**
chief researcher **Colleen McKinney**
production assistant **Carl Hesler**
tastings coordinator **Fareed Rayyis**
tastings intern **Andrew Newlin**
indexer **Andrea Chesman**

produced for Food & Wine Magazine by gonzalez defino, ny
www.gonzalezdefino.com
principals **Joseph Gonzalez, Perri DeFino**

map illustrations **Ethan Cornell**

cover photography **Frances Janisch**
cover credits: Tac 02 White Wine Glass and Tac 02 Bordeaux Wine Glass
by Rosenthal Germany from Moss, www.mossonline.com, 866-888-6677.
Carafe from Michael C. Fina, www.michaelcfina.com, 800-289-3462.

AMERICAN EXPRESS PUBLISHING CORPORATION
senior vice president/chief marketing officer **Mark V. Stanich**
vice president, marketing/publisher **Marshall Corey**
senior marketing manager **Bruce Spanier**
senior fulfillment manager **Philip Black**
assistant marketing manager **Sarah Ross**
business manager **Thomas Noonan**
production manager **Stuart Handelman**

For more information on Food & Wine Cookbooks, log on to
foodandwine.com/fwbooks or call 800-284-4145.

ISSN 1522-001X

FOOD&WINE

Wine Guide 2007

by Jamal A. Rayyis

FOOD&WINE
BOOKS
American Express Publishing Corporation
New York

contents

france 24

Alsace 26
Pinot Blanc & Pinot Gris 28
Riesling &
  Gewurztraminer 29
Other Alsace Whites 31
Bordeaux 32
Whites 34
Reds 36
Burgundy 41
Chablis 44
Côte d'Or 45
Côte Chalonnaise 50
Mâconnais 52
Beaujolais 53
Loire Valley 56
Whites 57
Reds 61
Rhône Valley 63
Northern Rhône 63
Southern Rhône 67
Southern France 72
Languedoc-Roussillon 72
Provence 76
Other Southern Regions 78

italy 82

Piedmont 84
Whites 84
Reds 85
Tuscany 90
Whites 90
Reds 92
**Other Italian
Regions: North** 100
Whites 101
Reds 105
**Other Italian
Regions: Central** 108
Whites 109
Reds 111

Southern Italy 113
Whites 114
Reds 115

spain 118

Rioja 119
Ribera del Duero 122
Catalonia 123
**Other Spanish
Regions** 126

portugal 130
Whites 132
Reds 133

germany 136
Riesling 139
Other Whites 144

austria 146
Whites 147
Reds 150

greece 152
Whites 153
Reds 155

other old
world wines 156

Switzerland 156
**Central & Eastern
Europe** 158
Whites 159
Reds 160
**North Africa &
Lebanon** 161
Whites 162
Reds 163

united states 164

California 165
  Whites 167
  Rosés 177
  Reds 178

Oregon 203
  Whites 203
  Reds 206

Washington State 209
  Whites 210
  Reds 212

Other U.S. 216
  Whites & Rosés 217
  Reds 219

australia 222
  Whites 224
  Reds 228

new zealand 236
  Whites 237
  Reds 239

argentina 242
  Whites 243
  Reds 244

chile 248
  Whites 249
  Reds 250

south africa 252
  Whites 253
  Reds 255

other new world wines 258

Canada, Mexico, Uruguay 258
  Whites 259
  Reds 260

champagne & other sparkling wines 262

Champagne 263

Other Sparkling Wines 267
  France 267
  Italy 268
  Spain 269
  United States 269
  Other Countries 271

fortified & dessert wines 272

Fortified Wines 272
  Sherry 272
  Port 274
  Madeira 277

Dessert Wines 278
  Whites 278
  Reds 284

Foreword 6
How to Use This Book/
  Key to Symbols 8
The Year in Wine 9
Food & Wine's American
  Wine Awards 2006 12
Wine Tasting Guide 14
Wine Terms 16
Wine & Food 17
Food & Wine Pairings 18
Vintage Chart/Old World 20
Vintage Chart/New World 22
Grape Varieties 286
Bargain Wine Finder 294
Top Wine Websites 296
Reliable Importers 297
Index of Wines 298

foreword

The 2007 Wine Guide may be our best yet. And there are a number of reasons why. Seven, to be exact. First, there's the brilliant new design, including new typefaces and new colors—making this year's guide not only better looking but easier to read. Second, we've divided the guide into two major sections: New and Old World Wines—in recognition of the way the vinous world is divided not just geographically but stylistically too. Third, we've added even more wines—almost 200 more than last year's guide (some 1,480 recommended wines this year versus 1,300 in the 2006 edition). Fourth, fifth and sixth reasons are the new vintage charts, enhanced food and wine pairing charts and updated maps. Seventh and last (though far from least) are the twelve wine trend reports we solicited from wine experts around the world (making that twelve additional reasons why this guide is the greatest). Among those contributing their observations and expertise are Bordeaux wine authority Stephen Brook, who reports both good news (the great

2005 vintage) and bad (oversupply of wine) in that renowned region. Italian wine expert David Lynch reports he's particularly excited about developments in Piedmont, while German wine scribe Stuart Pigott takes note of that country's newest winemaking talent. Other star contributors include Madrid-based correspondent Victor de la Serna, who has found some exciting new wineries in that oldest of Spanish wine regions, Sherry; and Aussie expert Max Allen, who says look for a lot more Shiraz-Viognier blended wines on the market this year. And, of course, there's much, much more.

But whether you're looking for news on a favorite wine region or simply the name of a drinkable $10 Pinot Noir (no longer an oxymoron these days), we hope you'll find this guide not just an informative but perhaps even inspirational aid.

Dana Cowin, Editor in Chief
Lettie Teague, Executive Wine Editor
FOOD & WINE

how to use this book

All of the recommended wines in this Guide are completely up-to-date, meaning they are for sale this year. For ease of reference, each section's wines are listed alphabetically by the producer's name, followed by the vintage year in which the wine's grapes were harvested. The quality and price symbols used to rate each wine are described below.

Some wines are released within months after harvest, while others are aged for years before release. Although most wines are thoroughly drinkable when they are made available, some will taste better if they've had a few more years to age in the bottle. Tasting notes in this Guide will often suggest the optimal time for drinking a wine ("drink in 3–8 years"). For wines in this edition, the years of suggested aging begin in autumn, 2006 (not the wine's vintage).

There are certain producers who have proven over time to produce excellent wines every year. These wineries are highlighted in the "Star Producers" sections throughout the Guide. The "Best of the Best" is a list of producers that are second to none in their category. Those listed in the "Best Value" category consistently offer great wine for prices comparatively lower than wines of similar quality.

Key to Symbols

QUALITY

★★★★ **OUTSTANDING** Worth a search

★★★ **EXCELLENT** Top-notch of its type

★★ **VERY GOOD** Distinctive

★ **GOOD** Delicious everyday wine

PRICE

$$$$ **OVER $50**

$$$ **$26 TO $50**

$$ **$15 TO $25**

$ **UNDER $15**

the year
in wine

Wine Becomes America's Drink of Choice

Wine has long ranked second to beer as America's favorite alcoholic quaffer. But wine consumption has been rising steadily since the mid-1990s, and a recent Gallup poll found that a majority of Americans claim to favor it over beer. Compared to the French and Italians, who consume about 15 gallons per capita per year, American adults might seem like lightweights for tippling just under 3 gallons per person. But when it comes to the amount of wine consumed by the nation as a whole, the U.S. should become, according to analysts, the number one wine-consuming country on earth sometime in 2008.

More Wine, Fewer Rules

All those wine drinkers are likely to have more vinous choices by that time, too. One by one, state laws that had prohibited out-of-state wine shipments direct to residents are being eliminated in the wake of a 2005 U.S. Supreme Court decision which declared the bans unconstitutional. Since the writing of the previous edition of the Wine Guide, Michigan, New York, Pennsylvania, Minnesota, Florida, Texas, Ohio, Washington State and Idaho have begun to allow direct shipping of wines to their residents from out of state, and more are on their way. For information about your state's regulations, visit the website of the advocacy group Free the Grapes: www.freethegrapes.org.

Despite victory in the U.S. Supreme Court, free-trade advocates have stayed on the attack. In November 2005, a U.S. District Court judge ruled in favor of the discount retailer Costco in a suit filed against the Washington State Liquor Control Board. Costco won the right to purchase wine directly from out-of-state producers rather than being forced to go through a complex distribution system in which shops and restaurants were forced to buy products from in-

9

state middlemen. The judge also agreed with Costco that they should be allowed to strike deals directly with suppliers, enabling them to pass savings along to consumers. Washington State is appealing the decision, but it's likely that other states' distribution systems will be altered as well, bringing lower prices to more retail shelves. Good news for wine lovers.

What's In That Bottle?

Other changes in federal regulations could alter what actually goes into many bottles. Until 2006, federal law required that if a vintage year went on a bottle, 95 percent of the wine had to be made from grapes harvested that year. This requirement has fallen to 85 percent for state- and county-designated wines. Proponents of the change, who number among some of California's largest wine producers (including Ironstone Vineyards, Bronco Wine Company and Gallo, but not Kendall-Jackson), maintain that it will enable them to offer a more consistent product year after year (and allow them to blend wines purchased on the cheap during years of surplus). Plus, they argue, the 85 percent rule is consistent with regulations in competing wine-producing countries like Australia and New Zealand. The opposition protests that the point of a vintage year is to mark the distinctiveness of that particular year.

California Beats France... Again

Thirty years ago, Steven Spurrier, a respected English wine merchant, assembled a Paris tasting for a group of French wine experts and had them taste some of France's best wines alongside well-regarded, but not yet heralded wines from California, all unidentified. The results—which came to be known as the "Judgment of Paris"—shocked the world; the California wines won. Despite detractors who maintained that California wines might be good when young, but wouldn't age, California's reputation as a great wine producer was established. To commemorate this watershed event in wine history, a replay of the same tasting with the same wines (including vintages) was held simultaneously in Napa and London on May 24, 2006. While the panelists were different this time around, California again came out on top. The best of the bunch: Ridge Monte Bello 1971 Cabernet Sauvignon. It seems California wines age pretty well, after all.

France Fights Back

Unable to beat California and battered in the marketplace by other New World wine-producing countries like Australia, Argentina, Chile and South Africa, the French have decided that if they can't beat them, they might as well join them. Faced with massive surpluses of unsold wines, the French government decided this year to allow vintners to use oak chips instead of expensive oak barrels—a common New World vinification practice they once scorned—hoping to make consumer-friendly wines at a lower cost.

Could Global Warming Ruin Wine?

Changing traditions are hardly the only thing French and other wine producers have to worry about. According to reports issued by the first World Conference on Global Warming and Wine held in Barcelona at the end of March, many of the world's important wine regions, including the Chianti region in Italy, the Penedès in Spain, southern France and parts of Australia and the U.S. might be unable to produce wines at all in the coming decades. For instance, it is quite possible that the historically cool-climate region of Burgundy will no longer be able to grow the Pinot Noir that makes her reds so distinctive. And, wine regions that are able to survive might suffer from an onslaught of pests that used to die off during colder winters.

food & wine's american wine awards 2006

In the world of American wine, few honors are as important as the American Wine Awards bestowed annually by FOOD & WINE Magazine. F&W editors polled a select group of wine writers, sommeliers and past award winners, and the results are in. Here are FOOD & WINE's picks as the year's top winemaker, most promising new winery and best importer, plus the winning wines.

winemaker of the year

Bob Levy, Harlan Estate and Bond Bob Levy's winemaking philosophy is simple: "I'd like to feel that I exceed the expectations of people who know wine at the highest levels." With like-minded Bill Harlan, Levy has done just that. In 1984, the pair established a vineyard, working it differently and far more expensively than was usual at the time. Harlan Estate's Bordeaux-styled wines proved to be among the world's most seductive. This was followed by the equally superb Bond wines, crafted to express the sublime qualities of six different vineyards. What's next after making the best? Make more of it, now with talented vintner (and wife) Martha McClellan for their Levy & McClellan wines.

most promising new winery

Sea Smoke Most vintners struggle for decades to get Pinot Noir right. So it's astonishing that only seven years after planting vines in Santa Barbara County, Sea Smoke has been able to establish its Pinots as some of California's best. Sea Smoke's three distinctively styled wines show the rewards of excellent winemaking and the benefit of slope-side vineyards that provide lots of sun moderated by Pacific fogs (sea smoke) that blanket the vines at night.

best wine importer

Eric Solomon, European Cellars Confident, a bit brash, but also exuding a kind generosity, Eric Solomon is a lot like the wines he imports. In 1990, after years with one of the U.S.'s largest wine importers, Solomon started his own firm to work with small vintners, encouraging them to take a natural approach to winemaking. Solomon's portfolio today represents more than ninety wineries from five countries, including treasures like France's Domaine de la Janasse and Domaine de l'Hortus. His Spanish portfolio contains possibly the most impressive collection of Catalonian wineries in the world (his marriage to Daphne Glorian, winemaker and owner of Priorat's esteemed Clos Erasmus no doubt helps), plus gems from throughout the country.

wine awards

FOOD & WINE's expert panel of judges selected the following as the most outstanding American wines of the year:

Cliff Lede Vineyards | 2004 | SAUVIGNON BLANC UNDER $20

Rochioli Estate | 2005 | SAUVIGNON BLANC OVER $20

Saintsbury Carneros | 2004 | CHARDONNAY UNDER $20

Ramey Hyde Vineyard | 2003 | CHARDONNAY OVER $20

Saintsbury Garnet | 2004 | PINOT NOIR UNDER $20

Etude Heirloom | 2003 | PINOT NOIR OVER $20

Nelms Road | 2004 | MERLOT UNDER $20

Paloma | 2003 | MERLOT OVER $20

Boxcar | 2004 | SYRAH UNDER $20

Behrens & Hitchcock Chien Lunatique | 2003 | SYRAH OVER $20

Twenty Rows | 2003 | CABERNET SAUVIGNON UNDER $20

Merus | 2003 | CABERNET SAUVIGNON OVER $20

Plungerhead Dry Creek | 2004 | ZINFANDEL UNDER $20

Hendry Block 7 | 2003 | ZINFANDEL OVER $20

Joseph Phelps Insignia | 2002 | MERITAGE

wine tasting guide

Tasting wine is like any other acquired skill: the more you practice, the better you become. Most of us possess the necessary tools to taste wine. Our tastebuds can detect sweet, salty, bitter and sour sensations, plus "umami," the savory flavor found in mushrooms and meat. And our noses can differentiate between hundreds of aromas. The most important thing to learn is how to pay attention to the wine in your glass. Here are a few tips to help get your palate into tasting shape.

set the mood For each wine you want to taste, find a clear, stemmed glass that is comfortable to hold. Choose a well-lit place that's relatively odor-neutral. It is best not to wear perfume or scented lotion.

set the scene Pour just enough wine in the glass so it barely reaches the widest part of the bowl. This way you'll have room to swirl the wine without spilling it.

check the color A light color generally indicates a light-bodied wine; a darker color, a fuller-bodied wine. Also, white wines deepen in color with age; reds get lighter and take on a brown hue. If you've poured more than one wine, compare the colors and guess which wine will taste more concentrated. Young wines that appear browned might be the result of poor winemaking or storage.

swirl & sniff Hold the glass by its stem and swirl it gently to release the wine's aromas. Sniff. What do you smell? Sniff again. Do you smell fruit? What sort? The wine might evoke herbs, flowers, spices, vanilla or wood. Some wines smell like bell pepper, leather, roasted meat or even manure. Don't worry about cataloguing every aroma. Just articulate what you smell. Doing so will help you tell the difference between one wine and another. Sharing your impressions will help you learn and remember. Noxious smells like sulfur or must might dissipate with air. If the wine smells bad, give it a few minutes and swirl the glass to bring more contact with oxygen. If the wine still has an unappealing odor, move on to another one. If a wine smells like wet, moldy cork or cardboard, it may be "corked," meaning it has been infected by an unpleasant-smelling compound called TCA that can be found in corks. TCA is harmless, but it makes wine taste bad.

sip & swish Sip the wine and swish it around in your mouth. Try to suck air into your mouth while wine is still in it (it takes practice). This allows the wine to release more aromas. How does it feel? Does it coat your mouth? Is it light, prickly and refreshing? Does it taste bitter or sweet? Does it recall specific fruits or spices? Smell again. Does it smell like it tastes? Do you like it? There are no wrong answers; it's all about what you perceive.

to spit or swallow? If you're tasting more than a couple of wines at one sitting and want to be able to detect as much as possible from every glass (and remember your impressions tomorrow), it's important to spit.

taste in context In a horizontal tasting, you sample a range of wines that are alike in all but one way. This could be a group of wines from the same region and vintage, but made by different producers, or a group of wines from the same producer, same grape and same vintage, but from different vineyards. Comparing the differences among such similar wines will expand your knowledge. In a vertical tasting, you sample the same wine from the same producer made in different years. It's a great demonstration of how vintage can make a difference, as well as how age can change a wine's look and taste.

wine terms

You won't find much fussy wine jargon in this Guide, but it can be helpful to understand some of the terms used to describe wine. Here is a mini-glossary:

acidity The tart, tangy or zesty sensations in wine. Ideally, acidity brightens the wine's flavors much like a squeeze of lemon on fish. Wines lacking acidity taste "flabby."

balance The harmony between acidity, tannin, alcohol and sweetness in a wine.

body How heavy or thick a wine feels in the mouth.

dry A wine without perceptible sweetness. Dry wines can have powerful fruit flavors; they just don't taste sweet.

earthy An earthy wine evokes flavors like mushrooms, leather, damp straw or even manure.

fruity Wine with an abundance of fruit flavors.

mineral Flavors that reflect the minerals found in the soil in which the grapes are grown. "Steely," "flinty" and "chalky" are also words used to describe these flavors.

oaky Wines that transmit the flavors of the oak barrels in which they were aged.

powerful Wine that is full of flavor, tannin and/or alcohol.

rustic A bit rough and unsophisticated; often charming.

tannin A component of grape skins, seeds, stems and oak barrels. Mostly found in red wines, tannin gives a puckery sensation similar to that of over-steeped black tea.

terroir French term which refers to the particular attributes a wine picks up from the environment in which its grapes were grown, including such factors as climate, soil type, topography, hydrology or nearby flora.

wine & food

The old adage "White wine with fish and red with meat" has been replaced with "Drink whatever you like with whatever you want." Both approaches have advantages, but you're bound to encounter pitfalls by adhering too closely to either. The trick is to pair food and wine so that neither overwhelms or distorts the other. Some suggestions to help you on your way:

be body-conscious Delicately flavored food goes best with a light and delicate wine; heavy, full-flavored dishes call for heftier wines. The subtle flavors of sole meunière are going to get lost with a big, oaky Chardonnay.

balance extremes If a dish is rich and creamy, you need a tart, high-acid wine to cut through the fat and to cleanse your palate. A bit of sweetness in wine balances salty or spicy foods. If you can't wait to drink those young and astringent Bordeaux, Barolo or California Cabernet Sauvignons, the protein and fat of a rich cut of meat will help moderate their tannin.

pair likes Peppery meat dishes work well with spicy red wines like those from the Rhône Valley. Play fruit sauces off rich and fruity wines. Vegetal, herbal whites tend to go beautifully with green vegetables.

look to the locals Wines from a particular region often match well with foods from the same place.

mix & match The "Red with meat, white with fish" rule is a good fallback when you're unsure what to pair with a dish, but it's a rule made to be broken. Try a light, acidic red such as a Burgundy with a rich fish like salmon; or pair a rich Chardonnay with grilled chicken.

For more specific food and wine pairing recommendations, see the Food & Wine Pairings chart on page 18.

food & wine pairings

	salty or fried hors d'oeuvres	light soups	creamy or cheesy soups + pastas	shellfish
LIGHT-BODIED WHITES S. African Chenin Blanc, Muscadet, Pinot Grigio, Dry Riesling, Sauvignon Blanc, Vinho Verde	●	●		●
MEDIUM-BODIED WHITES Albariño, White Bordeaux, Unoaked Chardonnay, Loire Chenin Blanc, Off-dry Riesling, Gewürztraminer				●
FULL-BODIED WHITES Most Chardonnay, White Burgundy, Pinot Gris, Grüner Veltliner, Viognier			●	●
LIGHT-BODIED REDS Basic Beaujolais, Basic Sangiovese, Rosés			●	
MEDIUM-BODIED REDS Simple Bordeaux, Cru Beaujolais, Red Burgundy, Dolcetto, Barbera, Chianti Classico, Cabernet Franc, Grenache, Most Pinot Noir, Rioja			●	
FULL-BODIED REDS S. Italian Reds, Barbaresco & Barolo, Complex Bordeaux, Rhône Reds, Cabernet, Syrah & Shiraz, Malbec, Zinfandel				
SPARKLING Cava, Champagne, Crémant, Prosecco, Other Sparkling	●			●

light fish, like halibut or sole	richer fish, like tuna or salmon	chicken + turkey	duck + game birds	pork + veal	lamb, venison + beef	asian cuisines
●						●
	●	●				●
	●	●		●		
	●	●				
		●	●	●	●	
			●	●	●	

OLD WORLD vintage chart

REGION	YEAR 2005	2004	2003	2002	2001
BORDEAUX					
Right Bank	★★★★	★★★	★★	★★★	★★★
Left Bank (Médoc)	★★★★	★★★	★★★	★★★	★★★
Red Graves	★★★★	★★★	★★	★★★	★★
BURGUNDY					
Côte d'Or Red	★★★★	★★★	★★★★	★★★★	★★
Chablis	★★★★	★★★	★★	★★★★	★★
LOIRE					
Chenin Blanc	★★★★	★★★	★★★	★★★	★★★
Cabernet Franc	★★★★	★★	★★★	★★★	★★
RHÔNE					
Northern Red	★★★★	★★★	★★★	★	★★★
Southern Red	★★★	★★★	★★	★	★★★
ITALY					
Barolo & Barbaresco	★★	★★★	★★	★	★★★
Chianti	★★	★★★	★★	★★	★★
SPAIN					
Rioja Red	★★★	★★★	★★	★★	★★★
Ribera del Duero	★★★	★★★	★★	★	★★★
GERMANY					
Riesling	★★★★	★★★★	★★★	★★★	★★★★

● = Very bad vintage; a disaster
★ = Poor to average vintage; only the best wines are good quality
★★ = Good to very good vintage
★★★ = Excellent vintage
★★★★ = Outstanding vintage

2000	1999	1998	1997	1996	1995	1994	1993
★★★★ ★★★★ ★★★★	★★★ ★★★ ★★★	★★★★ ★★★ ★★	★★ ★★ ★★★	★★★★ ★★★★ ★★★	★★★ ★★★★ ★★★	★★★ ★★★ ★★★	★★ ★★ ★★★
★ ★★	★★★ ★★★	★★ ★★★	★★★ ★★★	★★★★ ★★★★	★★★ ★★★★	★★ ★★★	★★★ ★★
★★ ★★★	★★ ★★	★★ ★★★	● ★★★★	★★★ ★★★★	★★★ ★★★	★ ★★	★★★ ★★★
★★★ ★★★★	★★★★ ★★★	★★★ ★★★★	★★★ ★★	★★★ ★★	★★★★ ★★★★	★★★ ★★	★ ★★
★★★★ ★★★	★★★ ★★★	★★★ ★★★	★★★★ ★★★★	★★★★ ★★★	★★★ ★★★★	★★ ★★★	★★★ ★★★
★★ ★★	★★ ★★	★★★ ★★★	★★ ★★★	★★★ ★★★★	★★★★ ★★★★	★★★★ ★★★★	★★ ★★
★★	★★★★	★★★	★★★	★★★★	★★★	★★★★	★★★

NEW WORLD vintage chart

REGION	YEAR	2005	2004	2003	2002	2001
CALIFORNIA Cabernet Sauvignon		★★★	★★★	★★	★★★	★★★★
Chardonnay		★★★	★★★	★★	★★★★	★★★
OREGON Pinot Noir		★★★	★★★★	★★★	★★★	★★★
Chardonnay		★★★	★★★★	★★★	★★★	★★★
WASHINGTON STATE Bordeaux-Style Red		★★★	★★★★	★★★★	★★★★	★★★
White		★★★	★★★	★★★	★★★★	★★★
AUSTRALIA Shiraz		★★★	★★★	★★★	★★★★	★★★★
Cabernet Sauvignon		★★	★★★★	★★★	★★★	★★★
NEW ZEALAND Pinot Noir		★★	★★★	★★	★★★	★★
White		★★	★★★	★★★	★★★	★★★
SOUTH AFRICA Red		★★★	★★★	★★★★	★★★	★★★
White		★★★	★★★★	★★★	★★★	★★★
SOUTH AMERICA Argentina Red		★★★	★★★	★★★★	★★★★	★★★
Chile Red		★★★	★★★	★★★★	★★★	★★★★

● = Information on older vintages not available.
★ = Poor to average vintage; only the best wines are good quality
★★ = Good to very good vintage
★★★ = Excellent vintage
★★★★ = Outstanding vintage

2000	1999	1998	1997	1996	1995	1994	1993
★★★ ★★★	★★★ ★★★	★★ ★★	★★★ ★★★	★★★ ★★★★	★★★ ★★★★	★★★★ ★★★★	★★★ ★★
★★★★ ★★★	★★★★ ★★★★	★★★★ ★★★★	★★ ★★★	★★ ★★★	★★★ ★★★	★★★★ ★★★★	★★★ ★★★
★★★ ★★★	★★★★ ★★★	★★★ ★★★	★★ ★★★	★★★ ★★★	★★★ ★★★	★★★ ★★★	★★★ ★★★
★★★ ★★★	★★★ ★★★	★★★★ ★★★	★★★ ★★★★	★★★★ ★★★	★★★ ★★★	★★★ ★★	★★★ ★★★
★★ ★★★	★★★ ★★★	★★★★ ★★★	● ★★★	● ★★★	● ★	● ★★★	● ★
★★★ ★★★	★★★ ★★★	★★★★ ★★★	★★ ★★★	★ ★	★★★ ●	★★★ ●	★★ ●
★★★ ★★★	★★★ ★★★	★★ ★★	★★★ ★★★	★★★★ ★★★	★★★★ ★★★	★★★ ★★★	★★★★ ★★★

france

France's ancient wine industry is in the midst of a revolution. Competition from New World regions and falling domestic consumption have put French winemakers on the defensive. Some are ripping out vines, and others are making their wines in a different style. But many vintners have nothing to worry about. French wines are still the inspiration for winemaking all over the world. The good news for drinkers is that quality levels are rising and there is plenty of value coming from France.

■ Principal Wine Region

PARIS ☆
• REIMS
STRASBOURG •
Champagne
Alsace
ORLÉANS •
Loire Valley
• DIJON
NANTES
Burgundy
Atlantic Ocean
• LIMOGES
• LYON
BORDEAUX •
Rhône Valley
Bordeaux
• AVIGNON
NÎMES •
NICE
Southwest
Provence
MARSEILLE
Languedoc-Roussillon
Mediterranean Sea

France: An Overview

Many grapes are long established in France, including the best-known international varieties—Merlot, Cabernet Sauvignon, Chardonnay, Sauvignon Blanc, Syrah and Pinot Noir. But in France, regions are emphasized over individual grapes. Throughout the centuries, certain varieties were discovered to perform better in certain regions than others, and the French government made laws to regulate which grapes could be grown where. Burgundy's Pommard, for instance, must be made entirely from Pinot Noir, although you will never find the grape name listed on the bottle. French wines are crafted to evoke the region from which they come. This expression of place is referred to as *terroir*, a term that encompasses all distinguishing elements of a specific area like soil content, climate, sun exposure and surrounding plants.

French Wine Labels

French labels reflect this emphasis on terroir; in most cases they list only the regional appellation, not the grape (with the exception of Alsace). A wine that bears the name of its region is required to satisfy certain regulations designed to guarantee quality and authenticity. The system that governs these regulations is known as the Appellation d'Origine Contrôlée (AOC), or "controlled region of origin." The AOC hierarchy from top to bottom is:

• **AOC** Most French wines imported to the U.S. are AOC, which means they meet the standards of their region. Wines from Burgundy (*Bourgogne* in French), for instance, may be labeled "Appellation Bourgogne Contrôlée." Standards vary from region to region, but they typically define permitted grape varieties, winemaking practices, minimum alcohol levels (the higher the alcohol, the riper the grapes and the more intensely flavored the wine) and harvest size (overly large grape harvests are assumed to yield dilute wines).

There are AOC regions within larger AOC regions as well, and generally speaking, the more specific the subregion, the more stringent the standards. The wines of Côte de Beaune, a subregion of Burgundy, for example, must meet stricter requirements than those labeled "Bourgogne." Wines from Meursault, a subregion of Côte de Beaune, must meet even more demanding standards.

• **VIN DÉLIMITÉ DE QUALITÉ SUPÉRIEURE (VDQS)** This category's standards are sometimes a bit less strict than those for AOC wines. If enough of a VDQS region's wine-makers produce at sufficiently high quality levels, the region might be promoted to AOC status.

• **VIN DE PAYS** Literally "country wine," Vin de Pays are subject to lower standards than those for VDQS wines, but they can list the wine's place of origin and grape varieties. Many Vins de Pays are dull, but an increasing number of innovative winemakers who wish to work beyond the restraints of AOC requirements are producing some truly impressive wines.

• **VIN DE TABLE** Vin de Table translates as "table wine," and it does not meet AOC board requirements. Vintners are not allowed to mention a place of origin more specific than "France," vintages, or grape varieties on their labels. Quality is generally low, but certain iconoclasts have turned their backs on the demands of AOC and are making some stunning Vins de Table. American importers will often put stickers on these bottles with the banned information.

alsace

Alsatians are proudly French, but the influence of Germany is everywhere, from place-names to gastronomy. Many of Alsace's mostly white wines are made using German-sounding grapes, but its winemakers put a distinctly French twist on their wines. Alsatian wines are full of personality: typically high in acidity and fermented dry in the style of their French compatriots.

Alsace Grapes & Styles

Two of Alsace's most noble grapes are German in origin: Riesling and Gewurztraminer. French varieties Pinot Blanc, Pinot Gris, Muscat and Auxerrois are also widely planted. While Alsatian wines are typically bone-dry, some producers have started leaving a bit of residual sugar in their wines. Alsace is also known for its stellar dessert wines (see p. 278) and for a Champagne-style wine known as Crémant d'Alsace. Pinot Noir is the only permitted red wine here.

Alsace Wine Labels

Alsatian wines, unlike wines from other French regions, are normally labeled by grape variety. The listed grape must compose 100 percent of the bottle's contents. Blended wines are commonly known as "Edelzwicker" or "Gentil," though a few vintners choose to name their blends after the particular vineyard from which the grapes came. Fifty vineyards within Alsace have been officially declared superior to all others and are entitled to add "Grand Cru" to their labels; for example "Riesling Schlossberg Grand Cru." But the criteria for this designation are controversial, so some wineries prefer to use the name of the vineyard alone, or their own terms like "Réserve Personnelle" or "Cuvée Particulière." These names have no legal meaning but are mostly applied to premium wines.

star producers
alsace

best value
1 Bruno Hunold
2 Domaine Paul Blanck
3 Domaine Schoffit
4 J.B. Adam
5 Léon Beyer

best of the best
1 Domaine Weinbach
2 Marcel Deiss
3 Marc Kreydenweiss
4 Trimbach
5 Zind-Humbrecht

ALSACE

pinot blanc & pinot gris

Pinot Blanc and Pinot Gris are closely related, but they can make wildly different wines. Pinot Blanc is whimsical, with gentle pear, lemon and nut flavors. Pinot Gris has more weight, oozing flavors of apricot, marzipan and dry orange-zest, completely different in style from Italy's Pinot Grigio (which is the same grape). Pinot Gris often veers into the category of "off-dry." Much wine labeled "Pinot Blanc" is blended with Auxerrois. The latter is sometimes labeled as its own. Alsatian Pinot Gris has for years gone by the names of Tokay d'Alsace or Tokay Pinot Gris, but regulations now demand that it use only Pinot Gris to avoid confusion with Hungary's Tokaji wines (made from the Furmint grape).

BEST PAIRINGS Pinot Blanc is an ideal house white, easy to enjoy with simple foods like chicken Caesar salads or straightforward fish dishes. More substantial, Pinot Gris is at home with Alsatian specialties such as tarte flambée, though it's equally delicious with roast ham or game birds, especially with a fruit-based sauce.

pinot blanc recommendations

Jean Ginglinger Cuvée George | 2004 |
★ **$** Lithe lemon and ripe pear, blanched almond and stone flavors compose a lovely wine.

Lucien Albrecht Cuvée Balthazar | 2004 |
★★ **$** Soft pear, bright lemon, subtle mineral and musk flavors.

Marc Kreydenweiss Les Charmes Kritt | 2004 |
★★★ **$ $** Unlike many pale Pinot Blancs, this bold and silky wine gives salty mineral flavors with smoky pear and light lemon notes.

Martin Schaetzel Vieilles Vignes | 2004 |
★★★ **$** Old vines express concentrated flavors of stone softened by fragrant pear and floral flavors.

Trimbach | 2004 |
★★ **$** A pretty wine with light notes of lemons, pears and almonds and bright acidity.

pinot gris recommendations

Domaine Ostertag Barriques | 2004 |

★★★ $ $ $ A different take on Alsatian Pinot Gris, this was aged in small oak barrels which results in smoky, light oak notes infusing flavors of pears and white flowers. Drink now–6 years.

Domaine Weinbach Clos des Capucins Cuvée Ste. Catherine | 2004 |

★★★★ $ $ $ $ Though a bit drier than previous vintages, this still indulges with ripe pear, toasty hazelnut, earthy mushroom and sweet spice. Drink now–12 years.

Domaine Zind-Humbrecht Herrenweg de Turckheim | 2004 |

★★★★ $ $ Intensely earthy and very dry, this Pinot Gris has hypnotic aromas of chanterelles followed by succulent grapefruit and spicy, baked quince flavors. Drink in 3–15 years.

Trimbach Réserve Personnelle | 2000 |

★★★★ $ $ $ Sensational wine that seduces with ripe Asian pear, berry and pineapple flavors with precise accents of spice and smoky truffle. Drink now–20 years.

ALSACE

riesling & gewurztraminer

Riesling and Gewurztraminer are almost polar opposites in Alsace. Riesling is demure and graceful, with mineral, citrus and peach flavors, and almost always medium-bodied and dry. Gewurztraminer is fuller-bodied and overflows with potent flower and spice flavors (*Gewürz* means "spice" in German). For some, Gewurztraminer is excessively rich and flavorful. Others crave its opulence.

BEST PAIRINGS Alsatian Riesling ranks as one of the world's most flexible food wines. It's terrific with grilled snapper as well as roast duck and venison. Its high acidity can sear through cream-based sauces, and it complements ginger-laden Asian dishes. Gewurztraminer can stand up to rich or spicy foods. Try it with curry-dusted scallops or a chicken tagine with sweet and savory spices. Ripe Alsatian Munster cheese is a classic accompaniment.

riesling recommendations

Domaine Marcel Deiss Beblenheim | 2004 |
★★★ $ $ This biodynamic wine is an affordable introduction to one of France's most thoughtful winemakers. Intense flavors of peaches, pineapples, citrus and smoke come together with gracious subtlety. Drink now–10 years.

Domaine Paul Blanck Rosenbourg | 2004 |
★★★ $ $ One of the best Riesling values in the world, Rosenbourg is dry, with peachy fruit flavors brightened by minerals and acidity. Drink now–4 years.

Domaine Weinbach Clos des Capucins Cuvée Théo | 2004 |
★★★★ $ $ $ While not the highest-tier offering from the famous Domaine Weinbach, this incredibly good wine has loads of ripe pineapple, citrus and green apple flavors beautifully accented by smoky truffle and mineral notes. Drink now–12 years.

Jean Ginglinger | 2004 |
★★ $ Smoky lemon and mineral flavors nicely composed in the classic Alsatian style.

Josmeyer Le Dragon | 2004 |
★★ $ $ $ Called "Le Dragon" because the grapes hail from notably warmer soils than those of neighboring regions, this shows the ripe effects of heat with flavors of round peach, apricot and pineapple. Drink now–8 years.

Kuentz-Bas Tradition | 2004 |
★★★ $ Great wine for a very fair price, this is stuffed with peach, pineapple and fine mineral flavors.

Lucien Albrecht Cuvée Henri | 2004 |
★★★ $ $ $ Vines that are more than thirty-five years old impart unique savory mineral flavors to the ripe citrus and yellow apple notes here. Drink now–8 years.

Marc Kreydenweiss Kastelberg Le Château | 2004 |
GRAND CRU
★★★★ $ $ $ $ Superb Riesling, this is built on concentrated stone flavors, augmented by thick pineapple and tarnished pear with hints of smoky truffles. Drink in 2–20 years.

Martin Schaetzel Kaefferkopf Granit | 2004 |
★★★ $ $ $ Riesling that's a touch off-dry, with marzipan, orange, dried fruit flavors and a hint of cherry.

gewurztraminer recommendations

Domaine Zind-Humbrecht Clos Windsbuhl | 2004 |

★★★★ $ $ $ $ This oily, almost viscous Gewurztraminer is slightly off-dry and shows intensely fragrant floral, sweet spice and grapefruit flavors. Drink in 3–20 years.

Hugel et Fils Hugel | 2004 |

★★ $ $ Bone-dry, but far from austere, this conjures up roses, smoke, lime and stone.

Trimbach Cuvée des Seigneurs de Ribeaupierre | 2000 |

★★★★ $ $ $ Aromas of fresh-squeezed grapefruit make a big first impression, followed by delicious flavors of violet, cedar, sweet and savory spice and succulent pear. Drink now–20 years.

Wolfberger | 2004 |

★★ $ $ Terrific Thai-food wine, this has a touch of residual sugar and floral, fruity flavors to complement spicy fare.

other alsace whites

Single-variety wines are the norm in Alsace, however some of the region's most charming wines are blends of several different grapes. Some winemakers label these blends "Edelzwicker" or "Gentil"; others give them proprietary names. Superior Alsatian blends contain Riesling or Gewurztraminer, while simpler versions are often made with a high percentage of humble Sylvaner or Chasselas, two grape varieties that are sometimes bottled on their own. Muscat is counted among the region's noble grape varieties, making aromatic wines with flavors of honeysuckle and citrus blossom.

BEST PAIRINGS Inexpensive Alsatian blends are great on their own for casual drinking and work well as aperitifs. More complex blends pair beautifully with grilled lobster, sturgeon or roast duck. Sylvaner is a fine choice with creamy seafood bisques or milk-based chowders. Leaner Chasselas brings out the sweetness of pan-fried trout and highlights the briny, mineral notes in raw oysters or clams. Fragrant, dry Muscat is one of the few white wines that complements asparagus.

other alsace white recommendations

Domaine Marcel Deiss Engelgarten | 2002 |
★★★★ $ $ $ Thrilling "field-blend" wine, this mix of varieties serves up a fresh mélange of flavors including fruit confit, smoky truffles and stone. Drink now–20 years.

Domaine Ostertag Fronholz Muscat | 2004 |
★★★ $ $ $ One of the finest dry Muscats anywhere, with delicate citrus blossom, honeysuckle, apple and lime flavors.

Domaine Paul Blanck Vieilles Vignes Pinot Auxerrois | 2004 |
★★★ $ $ Often blended into Pinot Blanc, Pinot Auxerrois does quite well on its own. Somewhat weighty, this has peach, grapefruit and nut flavors. Drink now–4 years.

Hugel et Fils Gentil | 2004 |
★ $ A straightforward blend that brings simple pleasure in the form of graceful, light citrus and floral flavors.

Kuentz-Bas Blanc | 2004 |
★★ $ Sprightly plum, lime and stone flavors make this a refreshing warm-weather pour.

bordeaux

No region captures the imagination of wine connoisseurs like Bordeaux. Bordeaux wines are elegant, but substantial. They have inspired imitators the world over, some of which are good, but never the same as the original. Yet, Bordeaux suffers an image problem. Its top wines are so highly regarded and expensive that many wine drinkers dismiss the region outright as being out of financial reach. But since Bordeaux produces more wine than any other French region, there is no shortage of terrific wines in all price ranges.

Bordeaux Grapes & Styles

White wines from Bordeaux must be made from Sauvignon Blanc, Sémillon, Muscadelle or some combination thereof. Those from the vast area of Entre-Deux-Mers are normally light, with flavors of citrus. Whites from Graves, Pessac-Léognan and the Médoc are dry, with mineral and summer-fruit flavors augmented by oak. The sweet wines from Sauternes and its satellite regions are smoky and indulgent (see p. 279). Bordeaux red wines are made from some combination of Cabernet Sauvignon, Merlot, Cabernet Franc, Malbec, Petit Verdot and/or Carmenère. Cabernet Sauvignon excels on the Left Bank of the Gironde River, and Merlot is at its best on the Right Bank. Blending is vital to wines throughout Bordeaux, which are typically full of mouthwatering acidity.

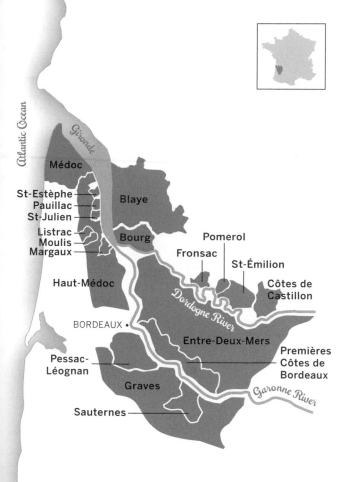

Bordeaux Wine Labels

Bordeaux wines are labeled by region. Generally, the more specific the regional designation, the higher the quality of wine. Wines labeled simply "Bordeaux" can be made with grapes coming from any part of Bordeaux. Those labeled "Bordeaux Supérieur" may come from the same region, but are required to have a slightly higher alcohol content (though they're not necessarily higher quality). Wines from the more limited Haut-Médoc region are required to meet even higher standards; those from designated communes within Haut-Médoc, such as Pauillac, St-Estèphe, St-Julien and Margaux, must meet higher standards still. In 1855, a hierarchy of wineries (or *châteaux*) was established for wineries considered superior based on the prices their wines commanded over time. Known as the "Cru Classé" system, the ranking grouped sixty-one superior wineries by *cru* (growth), from first ("Premier Cru") on top to fifth (though still very good) at the bottom. Châteaux that did not make the cut, but were still considered quite good, received the rank "Cru Bourgeois." The 1855 system is limited to châteaux in the Médoc and Sauternes, plus one in Graves. In 1955, a similar system was established to rank wines from St-Émilion, but it is subject to revision every decade. The famed wines of Pomerol are not ranked.

bordeaux whites

White Bordeaux does not receive as much attention as the region's reds, but many are excellent. The most highly regarded come from the Pessac-Léognan subregion of Graves. The vast majority of white wines come from the subregion Entre-Deux-Mers.

BEST PAIRINGS Bordeaux's maritime environs produce an abundance of foods that are ideal for the region's whites. Lemony Entre-Deux-Mers are made for raw oysters. Heavier whites from Graves are best served with more robust dishes such as baked sea bass or hearty chicken with mushrooms.

bordeaux white recommendations

Château Bonnet | 2005 | ENTRE-DEUX-MERS
★ $ Reliable from year to year, but especially good in 2005, this has snappy lemon-lime and mineral flavors.

Château de Chantegrive | 2003 | GRAVES
★★ $ High notes of bright peach, herb, lemon and stone flavors are softened by some air in the glass. Drink now–6 years.

Château Lagrange Les Arums de Lagrange | 2004 | BORDEAUX
★★★ $ $ This fabulous white wine from St-Julien's celebrated Château Lagrange deserves the same acclaim as its red. It's loaded with citrus, raspberry, almond and stone flavors. Drink now–6 years.

Château La Louvière | 2003 | PESSAC-LÉOGNAN
★★★ $ $ $ The heat of 2003 took away a bit of the magic from Bordeaux's best whites, but the luscious tropical fruit, baked quince, apricot and mineral flavors here still enchant. Drink now–10 years.

Château Lamothe de Haux | 2004 | BORDEAUX
★★ $ A terrific value for white Bordeaux; less than $12 buys this mélange of pineapple and peaches, flowers and stones.

Château Latour-Martillac Grand Cru | 2003 | PESSAC-LÉOGNAN
★★★ $ $ Surprisingly delicate for the 2003 vintage, peach and citrus blossom flavors are smoothly polished by abundant stone. Drink now–10 years.

Château Pérenne | 2004 | PREMIÈRES CÔTES DE BLAYE
★★★ $ $ $ Excellent white that tastes like a tree-ripened pear, with a squeeze of lime and touches of vanilla from oak.

Château Sainte-Marie | 2005 | ENTRE-DEUX-MERS
★★ $ Heirloom apple notes bring complexity to zippy lime flavors.

Château Smith Haut Lafitte Grand Cru | 2003 | PESSAC-LÉOGNAN
★★★ $ $ $ Typical of the château's distinctive style, this dances between elegant and funky, with stony citrus flavors intertwined with ripe pear. Drink in 2–10 years.

Château Tour de Mirambeau | 2005 | BORDEAUX
★★ $ Crisp green apple notes take on a peachy twist in this light yet succulent wine.

bordeaux reds

Bordeaux is defined by its reds. Those from Pauillac tend to be full-bodied, powerful and tannic, those from Margaux are more delicate, and those from St-Émilion are plumlike and plush. Bordeaux reds all tend to share a common earthiness and finesse. These are the wines the British fondly refer to as "claret."

BEST PAIRINGS Simple, modestly priced Bordeaux are wonderful wines to pour with steaks or grilled pork chops. More complex versions are ideal with game. Rack of lamb, roasted mushrooms and aged farmhouse Cheddar are also terrific choices.

bordeaux red recommendations

Baron Philippe de Rothschild Mouton Cadet | 2003 | BORDEAUX
★ $ Basic, widely available Bordeaux, this has a classic profile and a very fair price.

Blason d'Issan | 2003 | MARGAUX
★★★ $ $ Château d'Issan's second-tier wine deserves more than honorable mention for its toasted coffee, ripe blackberry and savory spice flavors. Drink in 2–10 years.

Château Angélus Premier Grand Cru | 2003 | ST-ÉMILION
★★★★ $ $ $ $ Marvelously indulgent, Angélus stands above most other 2003 St-Émilions, ringing with luscious blackberry, pepper, plum and stone. Drink in 2–20 years.

Château Batailley Grand Cru | 2003 | PAUILLAC
★★★ $ $ $ Very plush, very powerful, very Pauillac; this shows intensely pure, spicy cassis flavors. Drink in 2–13 years.

Château Bellevue Claribes | 2003 | BORDEAUX
★ $ There aren't many wines like this: plush, plummy, delicious Bordeaux for under $10.

Château Beychevelle | 2003 | ST-JULIEN
★★★ $ $ $ A consistent winner, Beychevelle has finesse but weight, with smoky and savory herb, spice and bright berry flavors. Drink in 2–12 years.

Château Brane-Cantenac Grand Cru | 2003 | MARGAUX
★★★ $ $ $ This producer seems to have suffered less than others from the heat of 2003, turning out a luscious wine with blueberry and blackberry flavors, spices and stone. Drink in 2–15 years.

Château Cadillac Club Merlot | 2003 | BORDEAUX
★ $ Sleek in label and name, this earthy wine offers the goodness of Bordeaux for a low price.

Château Caronne Ste-Gemme Cru Bourgeois | 2004 | HAUT-MÉDOC
★★ $ $ Typical to house style, this Caronne is wound very tight, but a couple of years will loosen the enjoyable earthy herb and juicy berry flavors. Drink in 2–12 years.

Château Chasse-Spleen | 2003 | MOULIS-EN-MÉDOC
★★ $ $ Solid, classic, good-value Médoc wine at a high level. Time will tone down the tannin and bring out aromas of herbs and berries. Drink in 3–12 years.

Château Clarke | 2003 | LISTRAC-MÉDOC
★★ $ $ Often among the least-exciting wines in the Rothschild (Lafite) portfolio, Château Clarke glows this year with pleasurable ripe cherry and sweet spice. Drink now–6 years.

Château Corbin Grand Cru | 2003 | ST-ÉMILION
★★★ $ $ The generous berry flavors and smooth, velvety texture people expect from St-Émilion are on display in this stellar example. Drink now–10 years.

Château Coufran Cru Bourgeois | 2003 | HAUT-MÉDOC
★★ $ $ Though made with an unusually high percentage of Merlot, this tastes like archetypal Médoc, with flavors of cherry, coffee and earth. Drink in 2–10 years.

Château de Candale | 2003 | HAUT-MÉDOC
★★ $ $ Cherries, spices and fine minerals make up this solid Haut-Médoc. Drink now–8 years.

Château de Cugat Cuvée Première | 2003 | BORDEAUX SUPÉRIEUR
★★ $ $ Superior to most Supérieur, this nicely weaves together cherry, chocolate, tobacco and spice flavors. Drink now–4 years.

Château de la Vieille Tour | 2003 | BORDEAUX SUPÉRIEUR
★★ $ Enjoyable, everyday claret, this offers juicy cherry, berry and stone for a bargain price.

Château de Lussac | 2002 | LUSSAC-ST-ÉMILION
★★★ $ $ Though a satellite of St-Émilion, Lussac deserves star status for wines like this: suave but earthy, with velvety black fruit and aromas of roast coffee. Drink now–12 years.

Château du Haut Caillou | 2003 | CANON-FRONSAC
★★ $ Stony wine with earthy dark fruit and maple sugar flavors. Drink now–8 years.

Château du Juge | 2003 | PREMIÈRES CÔTES DE BORDEAUX
★★ $ A tasty pepper-pot of a wine: piquant spice is cooled by smooth red fruit. Drink now–6 years.

Château Figeac Premier Grand Cru | 2003 | ST-ÉMILION
★★★ $ $ $ $ While full-bodied and heavy with cherry flavors, this has an abundance of palate-polishing stone which gives a leanness to a very fine wine. Drink now–12 years.

---

news from a wine insider
bordeaux by Stephen Brook

The 2005 Vintage
There were no debates about whether the 2005 vintage was better on the Left Bank or the Right in Bordeaux: the crop was abundant, the growing season near perfect and all regions produced great wine. Yet the news isn't all good. Bordeaux is awash in wine. All producers made too much wine, although lesser-known appellations like Fronsac, Côtes de Bourg and Lussac St-Émilion have suffered the most; many sent part of their crop to distilleries.

A Smash Success
Château d'Yquem director Pierre Lurton released the underrated 1999 wine at a modest price, then released the superlative 2001 at a much higher price, riding on the back of a perfect Parker score. It sold out immediately and demand has driven prices even higher.

An Image Makeover
A group of leading Bordeaux families has founded a new promotional organization called Bordeaux Oxygène, intended to liven up the region's staid image. In addition, a new AOC, Côtes de Bordeaux, was created to replace five Right Bank appellations: Côtes de Bourg, Côtes de Blaye, Côtes de Castillon, Côtes de Franc and Premières Côtes de Bordeaux. Vintners hope that the simpler AOC will make their wines more consumer-friendly.

Château Haut Selve | 2001 | GRAVES
★★ $ $ Evolving nicely, this Graves has benefited from age, revealing spicy black fruit, herb and stone flavors. Drink now–6 years.

Château Haut-Surget | 2003 | LALANDE DE POMEROL
★★ $ $ Pleasing cherry flavors, snippets of mint and pinches of spice mark this lovely red.

Château Labat | 2004 | HAUT-MÉDOC
★★ $ $ $ $ A high percentage of Merlot (50 percent) makes this wine more sultry than most young Haut-Médoc, but it isn't lacking any earthiness, either. Drink in 1–8 years.

Château La Bourrée | 2003 | CÔTES DE CASTILLON
★★ $ When St-Émilion gets too pricy, look for similar, well-knit wines like this berry-laden charmer. Drink now–6 years.

Château La Conseillante | 2003 | POMEROL
★★★★ $ $ $ $ Pure indulgence, this provides juicy blackberry flavors with layers of dark chocolate, violets and fine stone. Drink in 2–20 years.

Château Lafon-Rochet Grand Cru | 2003 | ST-ESTÈPHE
★★★ $ $ $ Straightforward St-Estèphe with an intense minerality joined by smoky black fruit flavors and subtle hints of dark tar. Drink in 3–12 years.

Château La Gaffelière Premier Grand Cru | 2003 | ST-ÉMILION
★★★ $ $ $ $ Big, thick and velvety smooth on the palate, this drips with succulent berry and soulful barnyard flavors. Drink in 1–15 years.

Château Lagrange Grand Cru | 2003 | ST-JULIEN
★★★ $ $ $ Consistently one of the best-value Médoc Grand Crus, Lagrange takes a hot vintage and builds a wine laden with dark berry, maple and ripe cherry flavors. Drink in 2–15 years.

Château La Pierrière | 2004 | CÔTES DE CASTILLON
★★ $ Lovely red berry flavors are framed by stone and fine tannin.

Château Lascombes Grand Cru | 2003 | MARGAUX
★★★ $ $ $ $ Smoky notes of cedar saturate black fruit in this substantial but refined wine. Drink in 2–15 years.

Château La Tour Carnet Grand Cru | 2003 | HAUT-MÉDOC
★★★ $ $ $ As is the case with many Haut-Médoc wines, this is awkward when young, but will show appealing berry, tobacco leaf and stone qualities with time. Drink in 2–10 years.

Château Lestrille Capmartin | 2003 | BORDEAUX SUPÉRIEUR
★★ $ Part rustic, part refined, this exudes forestlike flavors of leaves, smoke and wild berries, held together by fine, firming tannin. Drink now–5 years.

Château Lynch-Bages Grand Cru | 2003 | PAUILLAC
★★★★ $ $ $ $ Awe-inspiring Pauillac, with an ideal balance of fruit, acidity and tannin. Its chocolaty berry, herb and smoke flavors are ready for enjoyment now, but will only get better with a bit of age. Drink now–20 years.

Château Lyonnat | 2003 | LUSSAC-ST-ÉMILION
★★ $ $ Stock up on this lovely Lussac, offering dry cherry flavors with hints of maple and refined tannin. Drink now–5 years.

Château Malartic-Lagravière Grand Cru | 2003 | PESSAC-LÉOGNAN
★★★ $ $ $ Bordeaux for the Napa Cabernet lover, this has robust berry and pepper notes but a stoniness and high acidity that keeps it true to its French origins. Drink in 3–15 years.

Château Phélan Ségur | 2003 | ST-ESTÈPHE
★★★★ $ $ $ Superb wine that deserves the honor of a beautiful prime rib roasted with morels. Drink in 3–15 years.

Château Rousselle Cru Bourgeois | 2001 | CÔTES DE BOURG
★★ $ $ Rare in Bordeaux, a bit of Malbec is added to this blend, bringing aromatic flourishes to an otherwise austere wine.

Magrez-Fombrauge Grand Cru | 2003 | ST-ÉMILION
★★★ $ $ $ $ Sappy, syrupy, and bursting with vanilla-kissed blackberry flavors, this rich and hedonistic Bordeaux has a cleansing minerality. Drink in 2–12 years.

---

star producers
bordeaux reds

best value
1 Château Carbonnieux
2 Château La Gaffelière
3 Château Lagrange
4 Château Léoville Barton
5 Château Pontet-Canet

best of the best
1 Château Cheval Blanc
2 Château Haut-Brion
3 Château Lafite-Rothschild
4 Château Latour
5 Château Margaux

burgundy

Burgundy's wines ideally strike a perfect balance between sun-ripened fruit, minerals and smoke. At their best, they are arguably the world's finest. At their worst, they are reminders that the one who captures hearts is often the one who breaks them.

Burgundy Grapes & Styles

Almost all white Burgundy is made from Chardonnay. There are also small pockets of Pinot Blanc and Pinot Gris, but you'll never find reference to them on labels. Sauvignon Blanc, which grows in St-Bris, near Chablis, and Aligoté, mostly from the Côte Chalonnaise, are always identified by name. Red Burgundy is overwhelmingly made from Pinot Noir, except in Beaujolais, where reds are made from Gamay. Uncommon Passetoutgrains is a blend of Pinot Noir and Gamay grapes.

Burgundy Wine Labels

Burgundy wine labels list region or subregion and often the vineyard name. In most cases, the more specific the place, the better the wine. Over time, certain vineyards were recognized as being better than others, and a specific hierarchy, explained below, was established. It's important to recognize, however, that good producers can make great wines from officially unheralded vineyards, and other famous producers in celebrated locations have been known to produce dull and disappointing wines.

•**REGION** Wines produced from designated grape varieties grown in any part of Burgundy are entitled to be labeled "Bourgogne." Most regional wines are on the simple side, but in outstanding years some can be great.

•**DISTRICT** Wines made from grapes grown exclusively in one of Burgundy's major districts can take the district name (Chablis, for example). District wines appended with the word "Villages" are from more specific areas within the district, and are theoretically better.

•**VILLAGE** Wines made from grapes grown within the boundaries of a particular village may list its name on their labels: Pommard, for instance. The designation is helpful since the soil and climate are frequently consistent within a village's boundaries, and this tends to produce wines that share similarities in taste and character—or, as the French would say, a particular sense of *terroir*. However, since the boundaries of a village may have been drawn for reasons other than geology, some caution is in order.

• CHABLIS
Chablis

•**PREMIER CRU** Only 10 percent of all Burgundy's wine is classified as Premier Cru. Wines made from grapes grown in Premier Cru vineyards may add the name of the vineyard to the ranking: Meursault-Genevrières Premier Cru, for instance. Note: in Burgundy, Premier Cru ranks second to Grand Cru (below). In Bordeaux, the terms are reversed, with Premier Cru superior.

•**GRAND CRU** Fewer than 2 percent of vineyards within Burgundy are accorded the elite status of Grand Cru. Wines from these vineyards are usually the finest-quality, most concentrated and complex wines of the region, and quite often require several years or more of aging for their true potential to fully emerge. Their names are often short and simple: Montrachet, Chambertin or la Romanée. Because their reputations are so great, the words "Grand Cru" will not even appear on their label in many cases.

Be aware that a few Grand Cru vineyards traverse the borders of more than one village. In order to promote their less-illustrious wines, several villages added the name of the Grand Cru vineyard within its borders to their name. For example, the humble village of Gevrey became Gevrey-Chambertin. Many Gevrey-Chambertin wines are excellent, but they're not Chambertin.

Pairing Burgundy Wines

Serve simple Mâcon white well-chilled as an aperitif or at casual outdoor picnics. Mineral-laden Chablis is an ideal choice to highlight the brininess of oysters on the half shell. More substantial whites deserve fuller-flavored fare such as lobster with butter or roast holiday turkey. Pair them with creamy cheeses such as Epoisses or ripe Camembert. Simple red Burgundy is light enough to be served with most fish dishes, but has enough weight for red meat as well. The red wines of Beaujolais, especially when slightly chilled, are some of the world's greatest barbecue wines. Heavier, pricier Burgundies and Cru Beaujolais (see p. 54) are naturals with heartier fare such as roast lamb, duck and beef tenderloin.

BURGUNDY

chablis

Chablis is one of the world's great white wines. Imitators have tarnished the region's name with insipid wines made far from France that list "Chablis" on their labels. Chablis's distinction is the result of a cool climate, which creates high acidity, and chalky soils, which give minerality. Basic Chablis, which is rarely oaked, offers crisp green apple and citrus flavors. Premier Cru and Grand Cru wines are more intense; they are often aged in oak, which adds a smoky complexity. Petit Chablis, made from grapes grown near Chablis, is not considered as fine, though many are tasty. The village of St-Bris is known for its fragrant wines made from Sauvignon Blanc rather than Chardonnay.

chablis recommendations

A. & F. Boudin La Chantemerle | 2004 | CHABLIS
★★ $ $ A chalky Chablis classic, defined by lemon, apple and stone.

Domaine Christian Moreau Père & Fils Vaillon | 2004 |
CHABLIS PREMIER CRU
★★★ $ $ $ Summer peach flavors with citrus accents are kissed by oak in this zingy wine. Drink now–6 years.

Domaine Louis Moreau Les Clos | 2003 |
CHABLIS GRAND CRU
★★★★ $ $ $ $ Seductive, compelling wine with mixed fruit flavors offset by light, bitter herb notes and outstanding mineral flavor.

Francine et Olivier Savary | 2004 | CHABLIS
★★★ $ $ Succulent pear and peach flavors are detailed by orange zest, pineapple and smoky truffle notes. Drink now–6 years.

Jean-Claude Bessin Vieilles Vignes | 2004 | CHABLIS
★★★ $ $ Old vines pull the best from their soils; here they provide tart apple flavors with talcum-soft chalk. Drink now–8 years.

Jean-Marc Brocard Montmains | 2004 |
CHABLIS PREMIER CRU
★★★ $ $ $ Fine wine from a stellar producer; snappy green apple flavors are given a greengage plum twist and underlined by stone.

Jean-Paul & Benoit Droin Les Clos | 2004 |
CHABLIS GRAND CRU
★★★★ $ $ $ $ Les Clos is austerely mineral, but still expresses generous peach and orange blossom flavors. Drink in 3–20 years.

Joseph Drouhin Domaine de Vaudon | 2004 | CHABLIS
★★ $ $ Good-value Chablis from a respected producer. This shows citrus with almost salty mineral flavors.

Roland Lavantureux | 2004 | CHABLIS
★★★ $ $ Solid Chablis at a high level, this delivers the expected stone, grapefruit and mineral flavors.

BURGUNDY

côte d'or

The Côte d'Or (translated as the "slope of gold") is home to arguably the finest Chardonnay and Pinot Noir in the world. The Côte de Nuits comprises the region's northern half. It is celebrated for its smoke-laden, cherry- and mineral-scented reds from famous villages like Nuits-St-Georges, Gevrey-Chambertin and Fixin. The Côte d'Or's southern half, Côte de Beaune, is revered for superb whites from esteemed villages like Meursault, Chassagne-Montrachet and Santenay. District villages also make excellent red wines, including the powerful Pommard, velvety Volnay and the commanding Aloxe-Corton. North and south, the most famous wines are known only by their vineyard: La Romanée, for instance.

---

star producers
côte d'or

best value
1 Bouchard Père & Fils
2 Joseph Drouhin
3 Louis Jadot
4 Potel-Aviron
5 Verget

best of the best
1 Domaine Armand Rousseau
2 Domaine de la Romanée-Conti
3 Domaine des Comtes Lafon
4 Domaine Leflaive
5 Domaine Leroy

côte d'or recommendations

WHITES

Domaine Bernard Morey et Fils | 2004 |
BEAUNE GRÈVES PREMIER CRU

★★★ $ $ $ Deluxe, satiny wine, this is smooth, with melt-in-the-mouth, spicy baked pear flavors and fine minerals.

Domaine Chanson Les Caradeux | 2004 |
PERNAND-VERGELESSES PREMIER CRU

★★★ $ $ $ Chanson's quality renaissance is confirmed by this wine: beautiful lemony, smoky flavors are underscored by a dense minerality. Drink now–12 years.

Domaine Charles Audoin | 2004 | MARSANNAY

★★★ $ $ $ In a land full of mineral-laden whites, a ripe, succulent, fruit-driven wine like this is a lovely exception. Peach and baked quince flavors come together with herbs and minerals. Drink now–6 years.

Domaine François et Antoine Jobard Poruzots | 2004 |
MEURSAULT

★★★★ $ $ $ $ Springtime in a glass, this is an enchanting and serious wine, with complex mineral, smoke, flower and fruit flavors.

Domaine Leflaive Les Folatières | 2001 |
PULIGNY-MONTRACHET PREMIER CRU

★★★★ $ $ $ $ Though this is Premier, not Grand Cru, and doesn't come from a hallmark vintage, it still manages to offer fine flavors of stone, smoke and nut-sprinkled apples. Drink now–12 years.

Etienne Sauzet Hameau de Blagny | 2003 |
PULIGNY-MONTRACHET PREMIER CRU

★★★ $ $ $ $ Savory wine with flavors of salt-dusted orange and butterscotch. Drink now–10 years.

Faiveley Georges Faiveley Chardonnay | 2004 | BOURGOGNE

★ $ $ Clear, clean citrus and apple flavors for a nice price.

J.M. Boillot | 2003 | ST-AUBIN PREMIER CRU

★★★ $ $ $ $ Smoked pineapples and minerals are rounded out by almond flavors and oak. Drink now–8 years.

Labouré-Roi | 2003 | PULIGNY-MONTRACHET

★★★ $ $ $ Fat, indulgent, but still well-balanced, this Puligny-Montrachet is full of smoke, stone, pineapple, baked apple and toasty oak flavors. Drink now–8 years.

Michel Bouzereau et Fils Les Grands Charrons | 2004 |
MEURSAULT
★★★ $ $ $ Meursault is known for lush fruit and oak. Here, stone
leads, adding finesse to smoky, lemon, apple and olive flavors.

Michel Colin-Deléger & Fils | 2003 |
CHASSAGNE-MONTRACHET
★★★ $ $ $ $ It required a lot of skill to make balanced wines in the
warm 2003 vintage; this shows perfect equilibrium with waxy yellow
fruit, stone and zingy tropical flavors. Drink now–6 years.

Morey-Blanc | 2004 | ST-AUBIN PREMIER CRU
★★★★ $ $ $ Four-star *négociant* wine coming from an unheralded
appellation? Such is the case in this rare spicy, lemony and mineral-
laden white. Drink now–10 years.

Olivier Leflaive | 2004 | PULIGNY-MONTRACHET
★★ $ $ $ Textbook Puligny, this is full of lemon and apple flavors,
hints of smoky oak and loads of minerals. Drink now–5 years.

Thierry et Pascale Matrot Les Chevalières | 2003 |
MEURSAULT
★★★ $ $ $ Delicious orange and apricot flavors are wrapped in
minerals with licorice undercurrents. Drink now–8 years.

Vincent Girardin Vieilles Vignes | 2003 |
PULIGNY-MONTRACHET
★★★ $ $ $ $ Though not the most highly esteemed wine from this
producer's range of offerings, this is still impressive, with apple, hints
of mint and loads of stone. Drink now–8 years.

REDS

Camille Giroud | 2003 | SANTENAY
★★★ $ $ $ Substantial wine that remains lively on the palate, this
is pleasingly rustic, with earthy berry and light cherry flavors.

Charles Viénot Chaînes Carteaux | 2003 |
NUITS ST-GEORGES PREMIER CRU
★★★ $ $ $ $ Juicy, enjoyable wine, full of earthy cherry, light spice
and maple flavors laced with minerals.

Domaine Bernard Morey et Fils Clos St-Jean | 2003 |
CHASSAGNE-MONTRACHET PREMIER CRU
★★★ $ $ $ People are surprised to learn that half of Chassagne-
Montrachet's production is red. If only all of it was as good as this
spicy, toasty, smoky, red berry–infused wine. Drink in 1–10 years.

Domaine Bouchard Père & Fils Le Corton | 2004 |
CORTON GRAND CRU
★★★★ $ $ $ $ A difficult 2004 vintage shows deft handling by
Bouchard in this relatively light, but still substantial Corton with red
berry flavors and a core of stone. Drink in 2–20 years.

Domaine Chanson Clos des Fèves | 2002 |
BEAUNE PREMIER CRU
★★★ $ $ $ $ Gorgeous wine that shows off the elegance of Beaune
reds with lean, tart red berry and ironlike mineral flavors accented by
delicate herbal notes. Drink in 1–15 years.

Domaine Charles Audoin Les Favières | 2003 | MARSANNAY
★★★ $ $ $ Plush dark berry flavors are matched by heavy tannin
and fine spice in this robust, engaging wine. Drink in 2–12 years.

---

news from a wine insider
burgundy by Daniel Johnnes

The 2003/2004 Vintage

Following two decades of amazing vintages in Burgundy, the 2003 and 2004 vintages offer two very different styles. The 2003 harvest was the earliest on record and the wines show the effects of heat. Some are appealing, but others express prune flavors and hard tannins. In contrast, wines from the 2004 vintage are beautifully balanced. Whites have pure fruit flavors and good acidity; the reds are better than expected.

Notable New Wineries

In the Côte d'Or, look for: Pierre-Yves Colin of Colin-Morey, Charles Ballot at Ballot-Millot in Meursault, Thomas and Vincent Morey at Bernard Morey et Fils in Chassagne-Montrachet, Louis-Michel Liger-Belair in Vosne-Romanée, David Duband in Nuits-St-Georges, Jean-Louis Trapet in Gevrey-Chambertin, Cécile Tremblay in Vosne-Romanée and Chambolle-Musigny, and Isabelle and Alain Hasard in the Côtes du Couchois. Aubert de Villaine, co-director of Domaine de la Romanée-Conti, also makes wine in the Côte Chalonnaise; look for his Aligoté from Bouzeron and his Rully. Vincent Dureuil (Domaine Vincent Dureuil-Janthial in Rully) is another notable newcomer. In Mâcon, watch: Raphaël Sallet, Nicolas Melin of Domaine la Soufrandise, Jean Rijckaert and the Bret brothers at La Soufrandière.

Domaine d'Ardhuy Les Combottes | 2003 |
CÔTE DE BEAUNE VILLAGES
★★ $ $ Looking for an earthy, but ripe, bright berry–flavored red Burgundy for under $20? Here it is.

Domaine Gachot-Monot | 2003 | CÔTE DE NUITS VILLAGES
★★★ $ $ Rustic, but in an elegant, polished way, this is full of wild berry, smoke, stone and forest flavors, chewy tannin and finesse. Drink now–6 years.

Domaine Henri Gouges Les Chênes Carteaux | 2002 |
NUITS-ST-GEORGES PREMIER CRU
★★★ $ $ $ $ This has many of the earthy, bold fruit flavors one associates with country wine, albeit in an incredibly refined example. Drink in 2–15 years.

Domaine Lucien Boillot & Fils Les Caillerets | 2003 | VOLNAY
★★★ $ $ $ $ Dynamic, expressive Burgundy with bold cherry, wild berry, smoke and stone flavors.

Domaine Ponsot Cuvée Vieilles Vignes | 2003 |
CLOS DE LA ROCHE GRAND CRU
★★★★ $ $ $ $ There are few wines in the world as majestic and awe-inspiring as this flawless treasure. Drink in 5–20 years.

Faiveley | 2004 | LATRICIÈRES-CHAMBERTIN GRAND CRU
★★★★ $ $ $ $ A great wine that provokes tension between flavors of herb, bitter spice, stone and ripe red fruit. Time will integrate them in a beautiful way. Drink in 3–20 years.

Frédéric Magnien Seuvrées | 2004 | GEVREY-CHAMBERTIN
★★★ $ $ $ $ Delightfully floral, smoky and full of clear red berry and cherry flavors. Drink now–8 years.

Jean-Claude Boisset Les Charmes | 2002 |
CHAMBOLLE-MUSIGNY PREMIER CRU
★★★ $ $ $ $ Upfront berry, smoke and spice flavors highlighted by subtle peach notes.

Joseph Drouhin Clos des Mouches | 2003 |
BEAUNE PREMIER CRU
★★★ $ $ $ $ More intense than recent vintages of Clos des Mouches, this shows red and black cherry flavors infused with smoky minerals and spice.

Joseph Drouhin Véro Pinot Noir | 2003 | BOURGOGNE
★★ $ $ Fine Burgundy flavors without a high Burgundy price.

Labouré-Roi | 2004 | GEVREY-CHAMBERTIN

★★★ $ $ $ Peppery red berry flavors play a role, but this is more about earthy, herbal, stone-laden enjoyment. Drink now–10 years.

Louis Jadot | 2003 | NUITS-ST-GEORGES

★★★ $ $ $ More highly perfumed than most Nuits-St-Georges, this has currant and cherry flavors, flowers and spice. Drink now–8 years.

Mongeard-Mugneret | 2003 | FIXIN

★★★ $ $ $ Lovely village wine with herb and spice aromas like caraway, lavender and thyme followed by restrained red fruit flavors. Drink now–15 years.

Nicolas Potel Vieilles Vignes | 2004 | VOLNAY

★★★ $ $ $ A very modern Burgundy winemaker who doesn't ignore the old-fashioned pleasures the earth can offer. Ripe red berry flavors intermingle with enchanting aromas of smoky earth and crushed herbs. Drink in 1–10 years.

Philippe Pacalet | 2004 | POMMARD

★★★ $ $ $ $ Herbs and spices are on display in this Pommard, rich with cinnamon, clove and mint-tinted red raspberry flavors. Drink now–12 years.

Pierre Morey | 2004 | BOURGOGNE

★★★ $ $ Really lean but loaded with power, this provides a rush of smoke-saturated, piquant red fruit flavors.

Vincent Girardin La Fussière | 2003 |
MARANGES PREMIER CRU

★★★ $ $ $ Dense and hedonistic, this smoky, chewy wine needs time to soften firm tannins. Drink in 2–12 years.

BURGUNDY

côte chalonnaise

Many wines from the Côte Chalonnaise remain overlooked by all except Burgundy lovers with more sense than cash. Reds here are generally earthy and astringent compared with those from the Côte d'Or. Rully and Montagny can grow exceptional Chardonnay, but their wines fetch a lower price than many producers to the north. Keep a lookout for Aligoté, Burgundy's "other" white grape, especially those from the village of Bouzeron.

côte chalonnaise recommendations

WHITES

Château de la Saule | 2004 | **MONTAGNY PREMIER CRU**
★★★ $ $ Fascinating wine, this is salty, smoky and shows hints of animal aromas, invigorated by intense lemon flavors.

Domaine A. et P. de Villaine | 2004 | **BOUZERON**
★★ $ $ Made from Burgundy's white Aligoté grape, this gets attention for its funky herb flavors underlined by apple and stone.

Domaine du Meix-Foulot | 2004 | **MERCUREY**
★★ $ $ $ Smoky, intensely mineral-laden white with zesty orange and lemon flavors.

Faiveley Domaine de la Croix Jacquelet | 2004 | **MONTAGNY**
★★★ $ $ Ripe, mixed citrus flavors, smoke and fine stone come together in this tremendous Faiveley white.

J.M. Boillot Grésigny | 2004 | **RULLY PREMIER CRU**
★★★ $ $ $ Soft pear, bright citrus and delicate mineral flavors are accented by a light brushstroke of oak.

REDS

Danjean-Berthoux Clos du Cras Long | 2004 |
GIVRY PREMIER CRU
★★★ $ $ $ Give this lots of air in the glass to release complex and tightly wound flavors of wild red berry, appealing bitter herb and earth. Drink in 2–12 years.

Domaine Chofflet-Valdenaire Clos de Choué | 2003 |
GIVRY PREMIER CRU
★★★ $ $ Red and dark fruit flavors are joined by spicy Calvados-like apple notes in an impressive, smoky wine.

Domaine du Meix-Foulot | 2003 | **MERCUREY PREMIER CRU**
★★ $ $ $ Meix-Foulot does make more serious wines, but this has plenty of juicy, pleasurable flavors with ample stone and tannin.

Faiveley La Framboisiere | 2004 | **MERCUREY**
★★★ $ $ $ This explodes with raspberry flavors and Mercurey's typical minerals and herbs. Drink now–10 years.

Vincent Dureuil-Janthial En Guesnes | 2004 | **RULLY**
★★★ $ $ $ Ripe berry flavors and a bit of spice come together for smooth drinking.

BURGUNDY

mâconnais

The Mâconnais is often regarded as the poor country cousin of other Burgundy districts. While the vast majority of Mâcon wines are white and simple, there is a growing number of ambitious vintners who have planted in good subregions of the Mâcon and are making more complex wines. Pouilly-Fuissé is the most highly acclaimed and expensive appellation. It can produce wines just as good as those from the Côte d'Or. St-Véran offers similar quality for less money. For real value, look for wines with a village name added to the Mâcon designation, such as Mâcon-Igé.

mâconnais recommendations

Château de Beauregard Les Cras | 2004 | POUILLY-FUISSÉ
★★★★ $ $ $ Incredibly focused wine expressing the vineyard's chalky soils. Succulent pear and citrus flavors smooth out the intense minerals. Drink now–10 years.

Château Fuissé Le Clos | 2004 | POUILLY-FUISSÉ
★★★ $ $ $ From a relatively warmer region in Burgundy comes a succulent wine with citrus and pineapple flavors, peaches and stone. Drink now–8 years.

Domaine de la Croix Senaillet | 2004 | ST-VÉRAN
★★ $ $ Crushed yellow apple flavors are woven with hints of nutty marzipan in this versatile, quality wine.

Domaine de Roally | 2003 | MÂCON-MONTBELLET
★★★ $ $ Somewhat exotic, this dry, well-balanced Mâcon white shows Asian pear, sweet lemon and wild honey flavors enriched by vanilla-nut notes.

Dominique Cornin Mâcon-Chânes Les Serreudières | 2004 |
MÂCON-VILLAGES
★★ $ $ A tropical treat from the Mâconnais, this has juicy pineapple flavors and a bit of smoke.

Jean Thévenet et Fils Domaine Emilian Gillet Quintaine
| 2002 | VIRÉ-CLESSÉ
★★★ $ $ Fine Mâcon with a little age offers flavors of ripe autumn apple, honeycomb and spice.

Les Héritiers du Comte Lafon Les Maranches | 2004 |
MÂCON-UCHIZY

★★★ $ $ $ Aromatic herb and pepper notes bring charming detail to this velvety smooth grapefruit- and lemon-flavored wine.

Pierrette et Marc Guillemot-Michel Quintaine | 2004 |
MÂCON-VILLAGES

★★ $ $ $ This is just plain fun, full of the passion fruit, citrus and gooseberry exuberance of New Zealand Sauvignon Blanc, with the balance of Burgundy.

Rijckaert En Pottes Vieilles Vignes | 2004 |
MÂCON-MONTBELLET

★★★ $ $ Anyone who doubts that the Mâconnais is capable of greatness will be convinced by the honeysuckle, herb and lemon-lime flavors of this excellent wine.

Robert-Denogent Les Pommards | 2004 | ST-VÉRAN

★★★ $ $ $ Everything is in perfect harmony here; almond and lemon flavors are layered with stone and spice.

BURGUNDY

beaujolais

Beaujolais produces an abundance of inexpensive and easy-to-drink red wines as well as some whites. The region is also quite capable of superb wines that can satisfy the cravings of a light-pocketed Burgundy lover. There are a few important differences, however. Gamay, rather than Pinot Noir, rules the land. And Beaujolais has its own quality ranking system, which is explained below. Some good Chardonnay is also produced here.

• **BEAUJOLAIS NOUVEAU** These light-bodied, generally inexpensive wines hit the U.S. market around Thanksgiving time each year, released on the third Thursday of every November. Beaujolais Nouveau is fresh and light-bodied; this is as simple as wine gets.

• **BEAUJOLAIS** Wines in this category can be made from grapes grown anywhere within the region of Beaujolais. While they tend to be a bit more substantial and full-bodied than Beaujolais Nouveau, they normally lack the latter's fresh charm.

• **BEAUJOLAIS-VILLAGES** This ranking refers to wines made from grapes grown in the thirty-nine villages that occupy the rolling hills in the center of Beaujolais. They are made with more care than most simple Beaujolais, and many offer fresh fruit with an added dimension of mineral and spice flavors.

• **CRU BEAUJOLAIS** Ten hillside villages are home to the highest quality wines in Beaujolais. Cru wine tends to express concentrated berry flavors, minerals and relatively more tannin, which helps some of these wines to age well. "Beaujolais" is often not found on a Cru label. Instead, search for the following village names: Brouilly, Chénas, Chiroubles, Côte de Brouilly, Fleurie, Juliénas, Morgon, Régnié, Moulin-à-Vent and St-Amour.

BEST PAIRINGS Beaujolais natives usually chill their reds slightly—even the Cru Beaujolais. This makes even simple versions perfect picnic wines on a hot day and good pours for a party. More complex Cru Beaujolais can fill in for other red Burgundy, though they're most at home with bistro standards like boeuf bourgignon or steak frites.

beaujolais recommendations

Château de la Terrière Vieilles Vignes Cuveé Jules de Souzy | 2004 | **BROUILLY**
★★★ $ $ Old vines and a good vintage bring out pure strawberry, orange, mineral and spice flavors.

Château Fuissé Charmes | 2004 | **MORGON**
★★ $ $ This producer is best known for exemplary Pouilly-Fuissé wines, but makes stellar Beaujolais, too, as this juicy berry- and smoke-laden wine demonstrates.

Clos de la Roilette | 2004 | **FLEURIE**
★★★ $ $ Fabulous Fleurie, this is relatively light in body, but packed with herb-infused strawberry flavors.

Domaine de la Madone Le Perreon | 2005 |
BEAUJOLAIS-VILLAGES
★★ $ Cinnamon-spiced crushed strawberry flavors are bolstered by medium tannin in this solid Beaujolais-Villages.

Domaine Diochon Cuveé Vieilles Vignes | 2004 |
MOULIN-À-VENT
★★★ **$ $** Fifty-year-old vines in stony soils yield this herb- and spice-flavored wine, oozing wild berries and crushed cherries.

Domaine du Granit Cuvée Tradition | 2004 | MOULIN-À-VENT
★★★ **$ $** Stony, smoky, fresh-picked cherry flavors laced by herbs.

Domaine Manoir du Carra | 2004 | BEAUJOLAIS-VILLAGES
★★ **$** If only all Beaujolais-Villages could be like this: full of fruit, slightly earthy and high in acidity.

Domaine Piron & Lafont Quartz | 2004 | CHÉNAS
★★★ **$ $** Stone, herb and forest berry flavors are on display here.

Jean-Paul Brun Terres Dorées L'Ancien Vieilles Vignes
| 2004 | BEAUJOLAIS
★★★ **$** Though this is classified as basic Beaujolais, it delivers much more with wild berry, pine and interesting spice flavors.

Joseph Drouhin | 2005 | MOULIN-À-VENT
★★ **$ $** Dark, sappy black cherry and stone flavors make this far more impressive than simple light Beaujolais.

Louis-Claude Desvignes Javernières | 2004 | MORGON
★★★ **$ $** Granite-laden soils bring weight and added complexity to coconut-dusted strawberry flavors.

Louis Jadot Château des Lumières | 2003 | MORGON
★★★★ **$ $** Big Burgundy house Louis Jadot takes Beaujolais to a whole other level: this is full of black cherry, dark mineral, tobacco and smoke. Drink now–8 years.

Louis Tête | 2004 | BROUILLY
★★ **$** Light in body, with red cherry and lots of herb flavors, this is an ideal wine for cold cuts.

Marcel Lapierre | 2004 | MORGON
★★★★ **$ $** Beautifully aromatic and full of fragrant wild red berry and floral flavors.

Michel Tête Domaine du Clos du Fief | 2005 | JULIÉNAS
★★★ **$ $** Of all Cru Beaujolais, wines from Juliénas are often the freshest, as the juicy strawberry flavors here demonstrate perfectly.

Potel-Aviron | 2004 | MORGON CÔTE DU PY
★★★ **$ $** This finessed wine is still charmingly rustic, showing red berry flavors tangled with herb and earth.

loire valley

The Loire River cuts through hundreds of miles of France's most bountiful farmland, a region affectionately known as the *Jardin de la France*. The Loire Valley is home to some of the country's most fascinating and often the most under-appreciated wines.

Loire Valley Grapes & Styles

There is a greater diversity of grape varieties in the Loire Valley than anywhere else in France, but five grapes are most important. Muscadet, known as Melon de Bourgogne, makes dry white wines. Chenin Blanc dominates white wine production in the valley's center, yielding wines that are dry, sweet or sparkling. Cabernet Franc is the red grape of the same region. Sauvignon Blanc is responsible for the famous whites of Sancerre and Pouilly-Fumé, and Pinot Noir makes reds here. Certain regions permit blending. Valençay, for example, may be made of Sauvignon and Chardonnay.

Loire Valley Wine Labels

Loire Valley wines are labeled by appellation. Blending of grape varieties is rare, so the appellation name alone will tell you what's in the bottle. In a few cases, where a wine is made from uncommon grapes, the variety will be added to the region's name; for example, Gamay de Touraine.

Pairing Loire Valley Wines

Muscadet is nature's perfect oyster wine. Sauvignon Blanc goes beautifully with fish, chicken baked with herbs and fresh goat cheese. Weighty Chenin Blanc can stand up to roast pork, game birds and rich fish dishes. More modest versions, especially off-dry, make pleasant aperitifs and are delicious with moderately spicy Asian cuisines. Cabernet Franc is medium-bodied and high in acidity, making it a delightful pour with pâté or dry sausages. Fuller-bodied versions have the power to take on game; try one with a venison and mushroom stew. Red Sancerre can fill in for simple red Burgundy and is a good choice with salmon.

loire valley whites

The Loire Valley specializes in white wines, producing everything from light, lemony wines to profoundly earthy, mineral-laden nectars. Vineyards near the briny Atlantic produce the ultimate shellfish wine: Muscadet. Chenin Blanc ranges from insipid to absolutely enchanting here. Sauvignon Blanc makes flinty, grapefruit-scented wines. There are also many obscure varieties not seen elsewhere which are worth discovering.

LOIRE VALLEY WHITES

chenin blanc

Chenin Blanc in the Loire Valley creates some of the most exceptional white wines in the world; they offer a range of nutty, honeyed, mineral and smoky flavors, often all at once. Styles can be bone-dry or luxuriously sweet, and almost all are high in acidity. Vouvray, known mostly for its off-dry wines, is the most famous appellation, though not all wines from here are stellar. The same is true of Mont-louis across the river. Wines from the increasingly appreciated Savennières region are almost always made in a dry style and they age beautifully. Saumur Blanc, whites from Chinon and some Anjou Blanc can also be marvelous.

chenin blanc recommendations

Champalou Sec | 2005 | **VOUVRAY**
★★★ **$** Luscious spicy pear and ripe peach flavors are supported by a base of stone. Drink now–10 years.

Château d'Epiré | 2004 | **SAVENNIÈRES**
★★★ **$ $** Savennières *sec*, this seems sweet and savory at once, with flavors ranging from butterscotch to citrus, cumin seed to stone. Drink now–10 years.

Domaine Bourillon Dorléans La Coulée d'Argent Vieilles Vignes Sec | 2004 | **VOUVRAY**
★★★ **$ $** One sip of this off-dry wine's earthy, musky flavors and you'll know this is Vouvray, with added layers of almond, orange and rosewater notes.

Domaine de la Noblaie Les Chiens-Chiens | 2004 | CHINON
★★ $ $ Chenin Blanc is rarely produced in Chinon, but zesty, smoky, citrus-flavored wines like this illustrate the grape's potential here.

Domaine des Baumard Clos du Papillon | 2003 | SAVENNIÈRES
★★★ $ $ $ Ripe, spicy pear and soulful marzipan flavors are made savory by intense, salty minerals. Drink now–12 years.

Domaine Le Briseau Kharaktêr | 2004 | JASNIÈRES
★★★ $ $ Juicy, fennel-infused baked pear flavors grow positively lusty as this wine's smoky mineral notes merge with a bit of air.

Domaine Pichot Domaine Le Peu de la Moriette | 2004 | VOUVRAY
★★★ $ This lovely off-dry wine offers cinnamon-flecked applesauce and truffle flavors balanced by high acidity. Drink now–8 years.

François Chidaine Les Bournais | 2004 | MONTLOUIS-SUR-LOIRE
★★★ $ $ $ Mango- and pineapple-scented dry wine with flavors of almond and stone. Drink now–8 years.

Huet Clos du Bourg Sec | 2004 | VOUVRAY
★★★ $ $ $ Mineral-laden Vouvray, with citrus, flowers and stone flavors tinged with hints of smoke. Drink now–12 years.

Jacky Blot Domaine de la Taille aux Loups Rémus Sec | 2004 | MONTLOUIS-SUR-LOIRE
★★★ $ $ One of the best vintners in Montlouis, Blot produces a beautiful white with orange confit, peach, smoky oak notes and an abundance of mineral flavors. Drink now–8 years.

La Sansonnière La Lune | 2004 | ANJOU
★★★ $ $ $ Generous mixed fruit and spice flavors make this Anjou voluptuous; stony minerals provide firm form.

Nicolas Joly Clos de la Coulée de Serrant | 2003 | SAVENNIÈRES
★★★★ $ $ $ $ Majestic Savennières with slow-baked apple and tropical fruit flavors on top of layers of spice, smoky minerals and truffles. Drink in 2–15 years.

Thierry Germain Domaine des Roches Neuves L'Insolite | 2004 | SAUMUR
★★★ $ $ Delicate and brawny at once, this wine's perfume of peach blossoms infuses a pool of lemon, almond and stone flavors.

LOIRE VALLEY WHITES

melon de bourgogne/ muscadet

Muscadet is made from the Melon grape which yields sharp lemon, mineral and yeasty flavors. Muscadets labeled "sur lie" (on lees) are the finest; they develop complex flavors by remaining in contact with their yeasty sediment after they have fermented. The slight sparkle found in many Muscadets adds to their charm. Wines from Sèvre-et-Maine tend to be the most interesting. Muscadet is almost always served a year or two after vintage, but some well-made wines have the ability to age a decade or more.

muscadet recommendations

Château de la Fessardière Climat | 2004 | MUSCADET
★★★ $ This lemony, light-bodied wine possesses a surprisingly waxy texture and a bounty of minerals.

Château de la Ragotière (Black Label) Muscadet sur Lie
| 2004 | SÈVRE-ET-MAINE
★★ $ A pleasing bite of bitterness adds complexity to an austere, but substantial, citrus-laden wine.

Domaine de la Pépière Muscadet sur Lie | 2005 |
SÈVRE-ET-MAINE
★★★ $ Fresh and fragrant, this offers succulent peach flavors with an interesting salty edge.

Domaine de l'Ecu Expression de Granite Muscadet sur Lie
| 2004 | SÈVRE-ET-MAINE
★★★ $$ Dry, lean wine that indulges with lemon and marzipan.

Domaine La Haute Févrie Muscadet sur Lie | 2004 |
SÈVRE-ET-MAINE
★★★ $ Sweet and tart lemon and herbal notes combine with tongue-tingling minerals.

Pierre Luneau-Papin Clos des Allées Muscadet sur Lie
| 2004 | SÈVRE-ET-MAINE
★★★ $ Refined minerals highlight green fruit flavors like lime, kiwi and mango with hints of orange.

LOIRE VALLEY WHITES

sauvignon blanc

Sauvignon Blanc from the eastern Loire Valley, especially Sancerre and Pouilly-Fumé, is considered by some to be the ultimate expression of the grape. Grapefruit, goose-berry and grass flavors plus refreshing acidity are typical, but parts of the region offer wines with distinct "gunflint" aromas. Sancerre tends to be heavier, while Pouilly-Fumé is lighter and more perfumed. The latter's name (*fumé* means "smoked") refers to the wine's smoky qualities imparted by the area's flinty soil. Neighboring Quincy, Menetou-Salon and Reuilly make similar-styled wines.

sauvignon blanc recommendations

Château de Sancerre | 2004 | SANCERRE
★★ $ $ Archetypal Sancerre, this has snappy green apple and citrus flavors encrusted by stones.

Daniel Chotard | 2004 | SANCERRE
★★★ $ $ Almost defying gravity, stone flavors seem to float over the tongue, accented by delicate aromas of flowers and lemon.

Domaine de Chatenoy | 2005 | MENETOU-SALON
★★ $ $ Fresh-cut grass and white flower aromas are on display here alongside citrus blossom flavors.

Domaine Michel Brock Cuvée Cécile | 2004 | SANCERRE
★★ $ $ Fruity wine with a stony edge, this pleases with white peach, orange and berry flavors.

Domaine Vincent Delaporte Chavignol | 2004 | SANCERRE
★★ $ $ $ Creamy almond and lemon flavors add body and a gentle roundness to notes of herb and stone.

F. Tinel-Blondelet L'Arret Buffatte | 2004 | POUILLY-FUMÉ
★★★ $ $ Perfectly balanced Pouilly-Fumé that weaves together flavors of peach, lemon, almond, grass and stone.

Jean Reverdy et Fils La Reine Blanche | 2004 | SANCERRE
★★★★ $ $ Muscular but lean, this stunning Sancerre combines flavors of apples and citrus with hints of wild herbs, stones and light toasted almonds.

Jean Tatin Domaine du Tremblay | 2004 | QUINCY
★★ $ $ Earthy, herbal and full of lemon-lime flavors.

Langlois-Château Château de Fontaine-Audon | 2004 |
SANCERRE
★★ $ $ Though straightforward, this mix of citrus, yellow plum, herb and flower flavors has something quite compelling about it.

Michel Redde La Moynerie | 2003 | POUILLY-FUMÉ
★★ $ $ Delicate floral scents perfume a bed of crushed almonds, lemon and stone.

Michel Thomas Silex | 2004 | SANCERRE
★★★ $ $ Characterful Sancerre, this refreshes with minerals and is filled out by citrus and aromatic herb flavors.

Pascal Jolivet Le Château du Nozay | 2004 | SANCERRE
★★★ $ $ $ Wildly expressive herb, floral, fresh citrus and tropical aromas are followed by notes of smoke and stone.

loire valley reds

Cabernet Franc, also an important variety in Bordeaux, performs better in Loire soils than anywhere else. Some are fruity and peppery with moderate tannin meant to be enjoyed young; others are full-bodied with concentrated, smoky fruit and tannins that are suitable for long aging. The red wines of the Chinon and Saumur-Champigny regions are especially good. Pinot Noir grows in the eastern part of the region, especially in Sancerre and Menetou-Salon. These wines tend to be light-bodied, with cherry flavors and high acidity; perfectly lovely, but rarely better than basic Burgundy. Gamay and a few minor grapes also appear in the valley.

loire valley red recommendations

Bernard Baudry Franc de Pied | 2003 | CHINON
★★★ $ $ Opulent dark cherry, walnut and stone flavors are bold and assertive now, but will integrate with time. Drink in 1–10 years.

Catherine & Pierre Breton Trinch! | 2004 | BOURGUEIL
★★ $ $ Fresh and saucy, with attractive crushed black cherry and pepper notes.

Charles Joguet Cuvée Terroir | 2003 | CHINON
★★★ $ $ This less-expensive wine from one of Chinon's finest producers lacks nothing in the way of flavor—including berry, black olive, smoke and stone.

Clos Roche Blanche Gamay | 2004 | TOURAINE
★★ $ Salt-of-the-earth wine with oddly appealing pungent, earthy scents and smoky red berry flavors.

Daheuiller Domaine des Varinelles | 2002 | SAUMUR-CHAMPIGNY
★★ $ $ Cherry, spice, licorice and stone flavors in this elegant wine are shy at first, but become plush with air. Drink now–5 years.

Domaine de Bellivière Le Rouge-Gorge | 2004 | COTEAUX DU LOIR
★★★ $ $ Truly unique, this Pineau d'Aunis-based wine provides very tart, rusty red berry, herb, dill and celery seed flavors.

Domaine de Chatenoy | 2003 | MENETOU-SALON
★★ $ $ Full of red cherry and sweet, toasty oak flavors, this wine remains lean with a sheath of fine minerals.

Domaine de la Chanteleuserie Cuvée Alouettes | 2004 | BOURGUEIL
★★ $ Bright, whimsical cherry flavors are underscored by a layer of crushed wild herbs.

Frédéric Mabileau Les Rouillères | 2004 | ST-NICOLAS DE BOURGUEIL
★★★★ $ A four-star wine for $15, this gives opulent concentrated dark fruit, smoky mineral and earthy, piquant spice flavors.

Jean-Maurice Raffault Les Galuches | 2004 | CHINON
★★ $ $ Cabernet Franc's telltale peppery flavors are in full force in this easy-drinking red berry–laden wine.

Lucien Crochet La Croix du Roy | 2003 | SANCERRE
★★ $ $ Sancerre rouge often pales in comparison to Burgundy, but not this wine, with plush red fruit, spicy oak notes and the region's hallmark chalkiness.

Thierry Germain Domaine des Roches Neuves Terres Chaudes | 2004 | SAUMUR-CHAMPIGNY
★★★ $ $ Sultry Saumur, this seduces with ripe and juicy black cherry flavors spiced up by fine hints of pepper, herb and polished stone. Drink now–6 years.

rhône valley

The Rhône Valley is France's second-largest wine region. Most wine here is red and often simple, but some of the Rhône's best are among the greatest wines in all of France.

The Rhône Valley: An Overview

The Rhône Valley is home to an unusually wide range of climates, terrains and grape varieties. Along the Rhône River's path from Switzerland to the Mediterranean you'll find steep hillsides, rolling plains, stony plateaus and herb-blanketed slopes that seem like entirely different regions. But all Rhône Valley wines do share an appealing, sunny earthiness that is distinct and very charming.

RHÔNE VALLEY

northern rhône

The northern Rhône sits at the crossroads between cool continental Europe and the warmer lands that touch the Mediterranean. Its wines reflect this diversity, with a finesse that recalls Burgundy to the north and the sun-driven power of Provence to the south.

Northern Rhône Grapes & Styles

Marsanne, Roussanne and Viognier are the three grape varieties used to make northern Rhône whites. Marsanne and Roussanne are customarily blended to make the full-bodied, nutty, apricot- and baked pear–scented whites of Hermitage, Crozes-Hermitage, St-Péray and southern St-Joseph. Many of them can age a decade or more. Viognier makes the white wines of Condrieu and the minuscule neighboring appellation of Château Grillet. The Syrah grape dominates red wine production in the northern Rhône. The Cornas appellation must use Syrah alone, where it makes wines of legendary power and longevity. Other appellations permit a quantity of the region's aromatic white grapes to be blended with Syrah—up to 20 percent Viognier in Côte-Rôtie. Few winemakers take this approach, however. Of the appellation wines, St-Joseph tends to be the lightest and least tannic, followed in order of ascending strength by Crozes-Hermitage, Côte-Rôtie, Hermitage and, finally, Cornas. It is customary to age wines from the latter three appellations for years, but some maverick producers are applying winemaking techniques that make them ready to enjoy far earlier.

BEST PAIRINGS The region's substantial whites require foods that won't wither in their presence. Roast squab or quail, or chicken roasted in a clay pot with root vegetables, will certainly hold their own. Salmon steaks are another easy partner. Sweet Condrieu is divine with foie gras. For reds, pour simpler St-Joseph or Crozes-Hermitage with bistro standards like steak frites or flavorful duck confit. Save weightier, more expensive wines for equally hearty dishes like Chinese five-spice-seasoned lamb shanks, braised short ribs, venison or boar.

northern rhône recommendations

WHITES

Domaine Courbis | 2004 | ST-JOSEPH
★★ $ $ Oak-aging adds additional seasoning to this wine's baked apple and sweet spice flavors, enlivened by acidity.

Domaine des Martinelles | 2004 | CROZES-HERMITAGE
★★ $ $ This stone-flavored wine is full of mouth-coating green, snappy apple and lime flavors; a perfect summer pour.

E. Guigal | 2004 | CONDRIEU
★★★ $ $ $ A beautiful, aromatic Condrieu that demonstrates Viognier's peachy succulence with breezy floral and almond notes. Drink now–8 years.

M. Chapoutier De l'Orée | 2003 | HERMITAGE
★★★★ $ $ $ $ Decant this spectacular wine in order to coax out the subtle but spicy white peach, apple, baked quince and mineral flavors. It will become even more expressive with a few years of age. Drink in 3–15 years.

REDS

A. Clape Le Vin des Amis | 2004 | VIN DE TABLE DE FRANCE
★★★ $ $ August Clape's Cornas are legendary for their power and longevity. This unclassified red brims with flavors of blackberries, smoky pepper and spice and can be enjoyed right away.

Delas Les Bessards | 2001 | HERMITAGE
★★★★ $ $ $ $ A wine of magnificent stature, this conjures up a luxurious realm of cherry, dried rose, savory spice, earth and smoke flavors. Drink in 2–20 years.

Domaine Courbis | 2003 | ST-JOSEPH

★★ $ $ $ The pleasures of Syrah are all on display here, with crushed berry, smoke and pepper flavors finished with an appealingly bitter edge. Drink now–4 years.

Jean-Luc Colombo Les Ruchets | 2003 | CORNAS

★★★★ $ $ $ $ True to Colombo's accessible, modern style, this massive Cornas has lashes of smoky black fruit, minerals and intense spice. Time will tame the heavy oak. Drink in 2–15 years.

J.L. Chave Selection Offerus | 2003 | ST-JOSEPH

★★ $ $ $ Despite the difficult vintage, this is beautifully balanced, with flavors of stewed dark berries, some smoke and a bit of pepper. Drink now–6 years.

J.M. Gerin Champin Le Seigneur | 2004 | CÔTE-RÔTIE

★★★★ $ $ $ $ Enchanting aromas of incense, herb oil, cherry and smoky spice are bolstered by mineral flavors in this superlative wine. Drink in 3–20 years.

M. Chapoutier Les Granits | 2003 | ST-JOSEPH

★★★ $ $ $ $ A famed producer offers another delicious wine that indulges with cherry flavors, layered with notes of almonds, peppery spice, salty minerals and hints of the earth. Drink in 1–10 years.

Philippe Faury | 2004 | CÔTE-RÔTIE

★★★ $ $ $ Earthy and elegant, just like Côte-Rôtie ought to be, this shows thick berry and animal flavors accented by celery seed, cumin and light flowers. Drink in 2–15 years.

Yann Chave Le Rouvre | 2004 | CROZES-HERMITAGE

★★★ $ $ $ If only all Crozes could be so good. This brings together earthy, smoky flavors of lentils and ham with wild berry, fine minerals and mouthwatering acidity.

---

star producers
northern rhône

best value	best of the best
1 Clos des Martinets	1 A. Clape
2 E. Guigal	2 Domaine Jean-Louis Chave
3 Pascal Jamet	3 E. Guigal
4 Paul Jaboulet Aîné	4 M. Chapoutier
5 Vincent Paris	5 René Rostaing

RHÔNE VALLEY
southern rhône

The southern Rhône is distinctly a Mediterranean region. It is characterized by bright sunshine and consistently warm temperatures, and produces 95 percent of all Rhône wine. One can find sublime treasures, modest quaffers and everything in between within this vast ocean of wine.

Southern Rhône Grapes & Styles

The comparatively few whites produced in the southern Rhône are typically blends of Clairette, Grenache Blanc, Bourboulenc, Roussanne and Ugni Blanc. They tend to be medium-bodied and show apple, citrus and melon flavors. Grenache is the heart of most of the region's reds and rosés, generally blended with other grapes. Châteauneuf-du-Pape, the region's most famous appellation, allows up to thirteen varieties, both red and white, to be blended into its wines. These include Mourvèdre, Cinsault, Grenache, Roussanne, Syrah and Bourboulenc. Appellations such as Gigondas, Vacqueyras and Lirac follow similar rules. Rosés are dry, some relatively full-bodied.

Southern Rhône Wine Labels

Rhône wines are labeled by appellation. Côtes-du-Rhône is the basic designation and can be used for any wine made in the Rhône Valley, though most of these come from the south. Wines labeled Côtes-du-Rhône Villages are made in dozens of the designated villages that satisfy requirements for lower yields and higher alcohol levels (assumed to result in more intensely flavored wines). There are sixteen villages which produce wines of consistent quality and have the right to add their name to the label, for example Côtes-du-Rhône Villages Cairanne. The very best villages—Châteauneuf-du-Pape, Gigondas, Vacqueyras, Tavel and Lirac—are allowed to use the village name alone. Satellite regions such as Côtes du Lubéron, Côtes du Ventoux, Coteaux du Tricastin and Costières de Nîmes make wines similar in style and taste profile to basic Côtes-du-Rhône.

BEST PAIRINGS Pour Côtes-du-Rhône whites with bouillabaisse, Manhattan clam chowder, fish kebabs or clay-pot roasted chicken. Dry, spicy rosés make great picnic wines. Serve them also with roast ham or scallops. Earthy, berry-and-spice-flavored Côtes-du-Rhône are ideal barbecue wines and good pours for large gatherings. Pull the cork on a Côtes-du-Rhône Villages when serving hearty stews. Fuller-bodied Vacqueyras, Gigondas and Châteauneuf-du-Pape are tailor-made for herb-and-garlic-studded leg of lamb and game, particularly when they are aged.

southern rhône recommendations

WHITES

Château de la Gardine | 2003 | CHÂTEAUNEUF-DU-PAPE
★★★ $ $ $ The ashen mineral notes, citrus, herb and spicy olive oil flavors here are energized by high acidity; perfect for grilled fish.

Château La Nerthe | 2004 | CHÂTEAUNEUF-DU-PAPE
★★★ $ $ $ Full of juicy sun-ripe peach flavors highlighted by fresh lemon, herbs and stone notes.

Château St-Estève d'Uchaux Jeunes Vignes Viognier
| 2003 | CÔTES-DU-RHÔNE
★★ $ $ Pine-scented aromas bring unique refreshment to this Viognier's lime and tropical fruit flavors.

E. Guigal | 2004 | CÔTES-DU-RHÔNE
★★ $ Juicy, enjoyable wine, full of citrus and tropical fruit flavors offset by the taste of freshly cut grass.

ROSÉS

Cellier des Dauphins Prestige Rosé | 2004 |
CÔTES-DU-RHÔNE
★★ $ Straightforward and pleasing orange and strawberry flavors with a dash of fine spice.

Château d'Aqueria Rosé | 2004 | TAVEL
★★★ $ $ Tavel again reveals itself as a superior rosé. This is substantial and earthy, yet full of cherry, herb and spice flavors.

Château de Ségriès Rosé | 2005 | TAVEL
★★★ $ $ Chewy cherry, mouthwatering mango and savory spice flavors abound in this pretty but hardly insubstantial rosé.

La Vieille Ferme Rosé | 2005 | CÔTES DU VENTOUX
★ $ Rosé as it is meant to be: dry, tasty and inexpensive.

Perrin Réserve Rosé | 2004 | CÔTES-DU-RHÔNE
★★ $ Flavors of tart red berry, clementine and pine amount to lots of savory enjoyment in this fine rosé.

REDS

Alain Jaume Grande Garrigue | 2003 | VACQUEYRAS
★★ $ $ Sticky black cherry flavors are infused by notes of licorice and lavender in this tannic, full-bodied wine. Drink now–6 years.

Brunel Frères Château St-Roch | 2003 | LIRAC
★★ $ $ A lovely Lirac that offers plenty of red fruit, lavender, black tea and spice flavors. Drink now–3 years.

Cave de Rasteau Tradition | 2004 |
CÔTES-DU-RHÔNE VILLAGES RASTEAU
★★ $ Sultry wild berry, orange and spice flavors with a pinch of dry herbs bring rustic charm to this full-bodied wine. Drink now–5 years.

Cellier des Dauphins Prestige | 2003 | CÔTES-DU-RHÔNE
★ $ A sturdy, if simple, wine that expresses the region's typical strawberry and herb flavors.

Château de la Gardine | 2003 | CHÂTEAUNEUF-DU-PAPE
★★★ $ $ $ Old-fashioned Châteauneuf from a classic producer, this has earthy berry, mineral and herb flavors. Drink in 2–12 years.

Château des Tours Réserve | 2003 | VACQUEYRAS
★★★ $ $ $ From the same producer behind Châteauneuf's famed Château Rayas, this is grand and subtle at once, with flower and spice augmented by wild berry and mineral flavors. Drink in 2–10 years.

Clos de l'Hermitage | 2003 | CÔTES-DU-RHÔNE
★★ $ $ $ This intensely lusty Côtes-du-Rhône reveals wild red berry flavors intertwined with pungent herb oil, musk and earth.

Domaine de Cassan Cuvée St-Christophe | 2003 |
CÔTES-DU-RHÔNE VILLAGES BEAUMES-DE-VENISE
★★ $ Aromatic as a spice bazaar, this has crushed herb, dried flower and pepper layered with pomegranate flavors. Drink now–4 years.

Domaine de Font-Sane | 2003 | GIGONDAS
★★★ $ $ $ Fennel, caraway, camphor and meat aromas infuse this Gigondas' reservoir of delicious, mineral-laden wild berry flavors. Drink in 1–8 years.

Domaine de Grangeneuve Vieilles Vignes | 2003 |
COTEAUX DU TRICASTIN

★★ $ Vines that are more than thirty years old yield Grenache and Syrah that is wild and complex, with layers of berry, herb, tobacco and animal flavors.

Domaine de la Mordorée La Reine des Bois | 2002 |
CHÂTEAUNEUF-DU-PAPE

★★★★ $ $ $ $ Surely one of Châteauneuf's finest wines from a difficult vintage. This explodes with muscular black fruit flavors that are detailed by smoke, salt and licorice. Drink in 2–12 years.

Domaine du Banneret | 2003 | CHÂTEAUNEUF-DU-PAPE

★★★★ $ $ $ A tiny estate makes this impressively grand, old-school Châteauneuf that evokes an elegant, refined earthiness. Drink in 3–20 years.

Domaine du Vieux Télégraphe | 2003 |
CHÂTEAUNEUF-DU-PAPE

★★★★ $ $ $ One of the region's top producers makes another exceptional wine, bursting with flavors of juicy blackberry, black olive, stone and smoked herbs. Drink in 3–15 years.

Domaine Grand Veneur | 2004 | CHÂTEAUNEUF-DU-PAPE

★★★ $ $ Fresh, pure dark berry flavors are laced by aromas of smoked meat and supported by fine minerals. Drink in 2–12 years.

Domaine La Millière Cuvée Unique Merlot | 2004 |
VIN DE PAYS DE VAUCLUSE

★★ $ Should you bother with Rhône Valley Merlot? Only when it's as good as this, combining plush berry flavors with herbs and spice.

Domaine Paul Autard | 2003 | CHÂTEAUNEUF-DU-PAPE

★★★ $ $ $ Beneath this wine's surface of hedonistic sticky berry, mint and rich chocolate flavors lies a profound mineral and herbal dimension. Drink in 2–15 years.

Domaine Rabasse Charavin | 2003 |
CÔTES-DU-RHÔNE VILLAGES CAIRANNE

★★ $ $ The effects of the hot 2003 vintage are seen in this lush, corpulent wine, full of ripe fresh and baked red fruit with details of spice. Drink now–4 years.

E. Guigal | 2003 | GIGONDAS

★★ $ $ All Guigal wines are consistently good, expressive of region and vintage. This 2003 Gigondas shows especially ripe berry flavors with minerals and sweet and bitter spices. Drink now–6 years.

Féraud-Brunel | 2003 | CÔTES-DU-RHÔNE VILLAGES CAIRANNE
★★ $ $ True to Féraud-Brunel style, this is indulgent but elegant, with berry and herb flavors woven with minerals. Drink now–5 years.

Jean-Luc Colombo Les Forots | 2003 | CÔTES-DU-RHÔNE
★★ $ $ Colombo's talent for expressive Rhône reds is evident in this full-bodied, herb- and berry-scented wine. Drink now–4 years.

J. Vidal Fleury | 2004 | CÔTES DU VENTOUX
★ $ Red berry and earthy herb flavors plus a low price add up to one good barbecue wine.

Le Clos du Caillou Cuvée Unique Vieilles Vignes | 2004 |
CÔTES-DU-RHÔNE
★★★ $ $ An absolute bargain, this has the intense stoniness of some of the best Châteauneuf, with ripe red fruit, pungent herb and spice flavors. Drink in 1–6 years.

M. Chapoutier La Bernardine | 2003 | CHÂTEAUNEUF-DU-PAPE
★★★ $ $ $ Surprisingly lithe for 2003, this gives light-hearted red berry, candied violet and fine spice flavors. Drink now–10 years.

Paul Jaboulet Aîné Les Cèdres | 2003 |
CHÂTEAUNEUF-DU-PAPE
★★ $ $ $ There isn't a lot of Châteauneuf's distinctive earthiness here; it's full of plump, juicy fruit flavors instead. Drink now–6 years.

Perrin & Fils Les Christins | 2003 | VACQUEYRAS
★★★ $ $ Châteauneuf's Perrin family (of Château de Beaucastel) shows its mastery of the southern Rhône with this earthy, herbal, plush, berry-flavored wine. Drink in 2–10 years.

star producers
southern rhône

best value
1 Domaine de l'Oratoire St-Martin
2 Domaine des Grands Devers
3 Féraud-Brunel
4 Les Vignerons d'Estézargues
5 Perrin & Fils

best of the best
1 Château de Beaucastel
2 Château Rayas
3 Domaine de la Janasse
4 Domaine de la Mordorée
5 Domaine du Vieux Télégraphe

southern france

The regions of France's south—Provence, Languedoc and Roussillon, the lands collectively known as the Southwest, plus the island of Corsica—are diverse in geography and viticultural practices. They share the blessings of bright sunshine, centuries of winemaking experience and a soulfulness that is unique in France.

Southern France: An Overview

Provence, Languedoc and Roussillon are heavily influenced by the Mediterranean and are commonly referred to as the Midi. Languedoc and Roussillon are often hyphenated into one region or shortened to "Languedoc." France's rugged Mediterranean island of Corsica isn't known for welcoming foreigners, though it is sharing increasing amounts of its robust, earthy wines with the outside world.

SOUTHERN FRANCE

languedoc-roussillon

Languedoc-Roussillon was historically known for turning out vast quantities of poor-quality wine to supply the domestic table wine market. But today the region is more dedicated than ever to erasing those memories. Many of the region's vintners have cast aside appellation rules they feel inhibit quality winemaking in order to do things their own way and make better wines. Although these innovative wines have to suffer the lowly status of Vin de Pays or Vin de Table, their market performance remains high above others of their rank, as consumers all over the world recognize and pay for their quality. That said, large numbers of local wines labeled "Vin de Pays d'Oc" remain mediocre.

Languedoc Grapes & Styles

Red grapes predominate in the Languedoc, especially Carignan. When vine yields are too high, Carignan makes dull wine, but when carefully cultivated, it has the potential to provide delicious spice and berry flavors. Those from

Corbières are often best. Grapes like Syrah, Grenache and Mourvèdre are blended into the rustic, robust wines of Minervois and Fitou, while the same three grapes also turn up in the blends of the Roussillon appellation Collioure, near Spain. Plantings of Cabernet Sauvignon and Merlot are grown in the region, often for less expensive, export-oriented wines, but also for some superb, collectible wines. There is increasing interest in white varieties Grenache Blanc, Maccabéo, Muscat, Picpoul Blanc and Viognier. Chardonnay does exceptionally well around the area of Limoux. The Languedoc is also famed for its red and white dessert wines (see p. 278).

Languedoc Wine Labels

The region's most common wines are designated "Vin de Pays d'Oc," meaning they can be made with grapes grown anywhere within the Languedoc's boundaries. Some Vins de Pays come from specific areas in the Languedoc, as indicated on their labels. Such wines are governed by more restrictions than generic Vin de Pays. As elsewhere, more specific place-names require higher standards. The appellations Coteaux du Languedoc and Côtes du Roussillon are umbrellas for smaller ones. Within them, Faugères, St-Chinian, Montpeyroux, Pic-St-Loup and Collioure often show distinct local characteristics, or *terroir*. The same is true of other wines from neighboring local appellations, including the much-larger Minervois, Fitou and Corbières.

BEST PAIRINGS Simpler southern French whites are good choices when you're serving fried seafood, calamari, clams or shrimp. Limoux Chardonnay is delicious with baked white fish like cod. Pour fuller-bodied whites with roast chicken with herbs or a lightly spiced monkfish filet with creamy mushrooms. The gentle reds of Corbières and Fitou are at their best with flavorful meat dishes like roast duck, grilled lamb loin or beef tenderloin. Heavier Minervois, Côtes du Roussillon and Collioure need robust foods, like braised oxtails or lamb roasted with herbs, black olives and lots of garlic.

languedoc recommendations

WHITES

Château de Lascaux | 2005 | COTEAUX DU LANGUEDOC
★★ $ Delicious notes of spice infuse ripe pear and grapefruit flavors in one lovely white.

Château La Roque | 2004 | COTEAUX DU LANGUEDOC
★★ $ This pleases and engages at once, moving from succulent grapefruit flavors to crushed walnuts, herbs and sweet spice.

Domaine La Croix Belle Le Champ des Lys | 2004 |
VIN DE PAYS DES CÔTES DE THONGUE
★★★ $ Plush baked apple flavors are enhanced by delicate floral and spice notes and energized by minerals and good acidity.

Domaine Louise-Fabry Naoudoy | 2004 | CORBIÈRES
★★ $ A snap of acidity enlivens the spicy apple flavors in this silky-textured wine.

Hugues Beaulieu Picpoul de Pinet | 2005 |
COTEAUX DU LANGUEDOC
★★ $ Pretty wine with ripe, round flavors of pineapple and pear.

Laurent Miquel Nord Sud Viognier | 2005 | VIN DE PAYS D'OC
★★ $ A rarity from Languedoc: Viognier with real character. This delights with flower and peach flavors and tongue-tickling acidity.

Mas de Daumas Gassac | 2005 | VIN DE PAYS DE L'HÉRAULT
★★★ $ $ $ Vibrant flavors of dense stone are softened by pears, lemon curd, nuts and spice in this dry wine. Drink now–10 years.

Viognier de Campuget Cuvaumas Cuvée Prestige | 2005 |
VIN DE PAYS DU GARD
★★ $ $ Truly spectacular Viognier is often very expensive, but not here; this offers delightful peach blossom, apple and citrus flavors for a fair price.

ROSÉS

Beauvignac Syrah Rosé | 2005 | VIN DE PAYS D'OC
★★ $ Fun wine with fruity, berry and mango scents and a lemon twist on the end.

Domaine de Nizas Rosé | 2005 | COTEAUX DU LANGUEDOC
★★ $ $ The juicy cherry and subtle, savory spice flavors here are perfect by the poolside and at the dinner table.

REDS

Arrogant Frog Ribet Red | 2004 | VIN DE PAYS D'OC
★ $ To compete against Australia's kangaroos and penguins, the French offer up this critter-labeled, well-made Cabernet/Merlot blend for a competitive price.

Bernard Magrez La Passion d'une Vie | 2002 |
CÔTES DU ROUSSILLON
★★★ $$$ Bordeaux's Bernard Magrez has created this indulgent, almost dessertlike wine with seductive flower, blackberry and chocolate flavors. Drink now–6 years.

Château de Peña C Réserve | 2003 |
CÔTES DU ROUSSILLON VILLAGES
★★★ $$ 'C' stands for the often maligned Carignan grape, which is showing its best here. Pleasurable dark berry, coffee and sweet spice flavors abound.

Château de Pennautier | 2004 | CABARDÈS
★★ $ This full-bodied blend of Cabernet Sauvignon, Merlot, Syrah, Grenache and Côt (same grape as Malbec) exhibits both a robust spiciness and refined elegance.

Château des Erles Cuvée des Ardoises | 2003 | FITOU
★★★ $ Fine Fitou, the region's slate soils are on display here with minerals, herbs and red berry flavors.

Château du Donjon Grande Tradition | 2004 | MINERVOIS
★★ $ Good quaffing wine for sausages or burgers. Fresh red fruit and light floral flavors will wash things down nicely.

Château Ollieux Romanis Cuvée Classique | 2004 |
CORBIÈRES
★★ $ Terrific red that proves southern France offers some of the world's best wine bargains. Full of ripe red berry, herb and appealing animal flavors.

Château St-Jean d'Aumières | 2003 |
COTEAUX DU LANGUEDOC
★★ $ Lip-smacking red berries, tongue-tingling minerals and aromatic herbs with chewy tannin make this one serious wine for the price. Drink now–4 years.

Lulu B. Syrah | 2004 | VIN DE PAYS D'OC
★ $ Sure it's simple, but it's hard to complain about loads of spice and blueberry flavors with a French twist for not a lot of money.

provence

Provence is known more for its slow-paced rustic charm, fields of lavender and celebrity-studded beaches than for its wines, but the region has a rich and ancient viticultural tradition. From frivolous whites and refreshing dry rosés to hearty, serious reds, the wines of Provence very often represent excellent value.

Provence Grapes & Styles

Provence is recognized around the world for its charming dry rosés. They are meant to be consumed young and are generally made from a blend of Cinsault, Grenache and Mourvèdre; they are almost invariably dry. Look for those from Bandol, Coteaux de Provence and Coteaux d'Aix-en-Provence. Most whites from the region are light, crisp and lemony, typically made from local grape varieties, most famously from the seaside town of Cassis. Some heavier, mineral-rich whites come from Bandol, a region better known, however, for its full-bodied, dense reds. Bandol is the only appellation in France where the Mourvèdre grape dominates. Grenache, Carignan, Cabernet Sauvignon, Cinsault and Syrah are also planted in Provence, where each takes on various aspects of the region's distinct berry-and-herb profile. The most familiar and well-regarded of these reds come from the regions Les Baux de Provence and Coteaux d'Aix-en-Provence.

BEST PAIRINGS Provençal cuisine—heavy in rosemary, thyme, tomato, garlic and olives—is the natural partner for the region's earthy, charming wines. The flighty whites of Cassis are best with simple seafood such as oysters on the half shell and raw or fried clams. Save heavier Bandol whites for bouillabaisse or fire-roasted herb-stuffed sea bass. Provençal reds are ideal with lamb that has been heavily seasoned with herbs and garlic. Rosé works in the company of almost any food, but it's especially delicious with ratatouille and roast pork loin.

provence recommendations

WHITES

Château Ste. Roséline | 2004 | CÔTES DE PROVENCE
★★ $ $ Bright yet substantial, this offers lovely fresh herb and lemon flavors rounded out by subtle almond notes.

Clos Ste. Magdeleine | 2003 | CASSIS
★★★ $ $ Many Cassis whites are flighty, but this is waxy-textured and rich with flavors of honey and lemon confit.

ROSÉS

Bieler Père et Fils Sabine Rosé | 2005 |
VIN DE PAYS DES MAURES
★★ $ Charm your guests with this mouthwatering red cherry- and hibiscus-scented beauty.

Château de Pibarnon Rosé | 2005 | BANDOL
★★★ $ $ $ This is very dry and imbued with stones, but far from austere, with juicy berry, orange and spice flavors.

Château de Pourcieux Rosé | 2005 | CÔTES DE PROVENCE
★★ $ Palate-puckering flavors of deep minerals, cherries and bitter almonds make a refreshing aperitif.

Château de Roquefort Corail Rosé | 2005 |
CÔTES DE PROVENCE
★★ $ Peach blossom aromas and orange-apricot flavors are livened up by lemony acidity.

Château Ferry Lacombe Cuvée Lou Cascaï Rosé | 2005 |
CÔTES DE PROVENCE
★★ $ $ Hints of cedar give depth to this tart strawberry-flavored, tongue-tingling wine.

REDS

Château de Pibarnon | 2004 | BANDOL
★★★ $ $ $ A perfect expression of Bandol terroir, this is powerful and black as night, with dense blackberry and animal flavors. Drink in 2–15 years.

Château de Roquefort Les Mûres | 2003 |
CÔTES DE PROVENCE
★★★ $ $ "Les mûres" means blackberries in French, and this Provence red is indeed full of fresh-picked berry flavors with piquant spice and chewy tannin.

Château Ste. Roséline | 2004 | CÔTES DE PROVENCE
★★ $ $ Fresh and juicy with an abundance of pleasurable, spicy crushed berry flavors.

Domaine du Gros Noré | 2003 | BANDOL
★★★★ $ $ $ This wine was built for a robust stew; it's full of wild blackberry, black olive, pungent herb and appealing animal flavors. Drink in 2–10 years.

Domaine Tempier | 2003 | BANDOL
★★★ $ $ $ Tempier, one of Bandol's most stylish producers, makes this wine more velvety than normal, but the signature fragrant herb and berry flavors are still there. Drink in 1–8 years.

Le Galantin | 2003 | BANDOL
★★★ $ $ A bargain from often pricy Bandol, Le Galantin shows the broad-shouldered pleasures of black fruit, tobacco, herb and lanolin. Drink now–8 years.

Mas de Gourgonnier | 2004 | LES BAUX DE PROVENCE
★★★ $ $ This might not be "sophisticated," but for pure, delicious soulfulness, it's hard to beat this gem, rich with the scent of black-berries, herbal oil and the barnyard.

SOUTHERN FRANCE

other southern france regions

France's Southwest produces some of the brashest wines in the country, the best of which are elegant enough to be mistaken for Bordeaux. There are a few original white wines made here, too, and even some sweet ones. Off the coast from Nice, Corsica is a land of rugged beauty. Its wines were unknown to outsiders for centuries, but are increasingly appearing in the U.S.

Other Southern France Grapes & Styles
Bergerac makes wines with Bordeaux grape varietals. The wines of Cahors are based on Auxerrois (known elsewhere as Malbec), and they are full in body with berry flavors. Darker and more tannic are the wines of Madiran made from the Tannat grape. Basque country wines are crafted

from a blend of local, impossible-to-pronounce grapes, and they are hard and hearty. Jurançon is a full-bodied, spicy white wine made from Petit and Gros Manseng grapes. When dry, it is labeled Jurançon Sec. Otherwise, it is a late-harvested sweet wine (see p. 278). Monbazillac and Gaillac are similar wines, with both dry and sweet versions. Vin de Pays des Côtes de Gascogne produces light- to medium-bodied wines from local and international varieties. Wine-makers in Corsica use indigenous, Italian and international grapes to make their wines. Corsican rosés are lovely, as are many of its full-bodied, spicy reds.

BEST PAIRINGS Use Bergerac—white and red—as you would Bordeaux. Jurançon's dry whites are good for chunky country pâtés and dry, piquant sheep's milk cheeses. Sweet Jurançon is the local's choice with their superb foie gras and Roquefort cheese. Cahors is made for duck, grilled or pan-roasted. Madiran's powerful flavors are better served by braised lamb shoulder with cassoulet, or a thick, dry-aged steak. Corsican wines work similarly to those from Provence: simple whites are perfect for simple seafood, reds for meats, grilled or braised with tomatoes, herbs and garlic.

other southern france recommendations

WHITES

Charles Hours Cuvée Marie | 2004 | **JURANÇON SEC**
★★★ $ $ One of France's most engaging whites, this presents the palate with apricot, coconut and quince flavors with hints of pecan and herb.

Château Montus Sec | 2002 | **PACHERENC DU VIC-BILH**
★★★ $ $ From Madiran, land of monstrous reds, comes this fine, almost delicate white wine, with flavors of smoke, green fruit, lemon and stone.

Clos Lapeyre | 2004 | **JURANÇON SEC**
★★★ $ $ Succulent fruits from the Far East come together with sweet spice and minerals in this exotic white.

Domaine de la Salette | 2005 |
VIN DE PAYS DES CÔTES DE GASCOGNE
★★ $ Peach and light pineapple flavors provide whimsical drinking.

Domaine de Pellehaut Harmonie de Gascogne | 2005 |
VIN DE PAYS DES CÔTES DE GASCOGNE
★★★ $ Bold and assertive tropical fruit, herbs and spice flavors are honed to a sharp, delicious edge by searing acidity.

Domaine du Tariquet Chenin/Chardonnay | 2005 |
VIN DE PAYS DES CÔTES DE GASCOGNE
★★ $ Always reliable year after year, Tariquet hits the mark again with a zesty, citrus, orange spice– and anise-scented wine.

Domaine Maestracci E Prove | 2005 | CALVI
★★ $ A wonderful, inexpensive introduction to Corsica, with lime, kiwi, and appealingly smoky flavors.

Producteurs Plaimont Colombelle | 2005 |
VIN DE PAYS DES CÔTES DE GASCOGNE
★★ $ Mouthwatering peach, grapefruit and light mineral flavors come for a very gentle price.

Tour des Gendres | 2005 | BERGERAC SEC
★ $ Classic Bordeaux grapes Sémillon and Sauvignon Blanc compose this lean Bordeaux-like white with flavors of green apple, herbs and zippy lemon.

Yves Leccia Domaine d'E Croce | 2005 | PATRIMONIO
★★★ $ $ $ Silken treasure from Corsica, the Île de Beauté, this indulges with creamy pear and lemon flavors and a pinch of spice.

REDS

Château Bouissel Classic | 2004 | FRONTON
★★ $ Made from the rare Négrette grape, this delightful, medium-bodied red seems perfumed by violets and licorice and flavored by peppery red berries.

Château Bouscassé | 2002 | MADIRAN
★★★ $ A big name in Madiran, Alain Brumont forges another black and spicy red, heavy in smoke, spice and tannin. Drink now–10 years.

Château du Cèdre Le Prestige | 2003 | CAHORS
★★★ $ $ Smoky berry, black tea, dark minerals and spice make a wine that reinforces Cahors' reputation for black, concentrated wines. Drink now–8 years.

Château Lastours | 2003 | GAILLAC
★★ $ Unique, full-bodied wine that's hard to pin down: while refined and Bordeaux-like on one hand, it is rustic and wild on the other. Drink now–4 years.

Château Peyros Greenwich 43N | 2000 | MADIRAN
★★★ $ $ $ Despite six-plus years of age, this giant wine's tannins are still massive. Luckily there are plenty of fresh red berry flavors to smooth them out. Drink now–12 years.

Clos La Coutale | 2003 | CAHORS
★★ $ Not as black or dense as many of the fabled wines of Cahors past, this shows delicious wild berry and cherry flavors highlighted by earth, licorice and vanilla.

Domaine Etxegaraya | 2003 | IROULEGUY
★★★ $ $ This hard-to-pronounce Basque-country wine offers big flavors of fruit accented by bitter spice and held together with chewy tannin. Drink in 1–8 years.

Domaine Maestracci E Prove | 2003 | CALVI
★★ $ $ Charmingly rustic red from Corsica, with spicy dark berry and damp-forest aromas.

Georges Vigouroux Pigmentum Malbec | 2004 |
VIN DE PAYS DU LOT
★★ $ Spice and cherry-liqueur flavors are on display in this racy and affordable Malbec.

Heart of Darkness | 2003 | MADIRAN
★★ $ $ As the label indicates, this is dark and brooding, with robust cherry, dark chocolate and coffee flavors. Drink now–6 years.

Mounthes Le Bihan Vieillefont | 2003 | CÔTES-DE-DURAS
★★ $ $ This Bordeaux-country cousin offers some of the same re-fined red berry and spice flavors with more meat on its bones. Drink now–8 years.

Producteurs Plaimont Les Vignes Retrouvées | 2003 |
CÔTES DE ST-MONT
★★★ $ This began as a project to preserve a declining wine region and its indigenous grapes and has resulted in this deliciously earthy wine rich with mineral and berry flavors. Drink now–5 years.

italy

Italy's winemaking tradition is over three thousand years old, but its winemakers are anything but stuck in the past. Italian vintners are some of the most talented and innovative in the world, continuously working to improve their wines by applying modern techniques and experimenting with countless new and ancient grape varieties.

Lombardy
Trentino–Alto Adige
Valle d'Aosta
Friuli–Venezia Giulia
• MILAN
Veneto
VENICE
Piedmont
• GENOA
Emilia-Romagna
Liguria
FLORENCE •
Le Marche
Tuscany
Umbria
Adriatic Sea
Lazio
Abruzzi
ROME ☆
Molise
Campania
Apulia
NAPLES •
Sardinia
Basilicata
Tyrrhenian Sea
Calabria
PALERMO
Pantelleria
Sicily

■ **Principal Wine Region**

Italy: An Overview

Italian wine can be divided into regional categories that reflect dominant grapes or wine styles. Piedmont is home to truffle-scented reds like Barolo and Barbaresco which can age for decades. From the northeast come the racy whites of Trentino–Alto Adige and fruity aromatic reds like Valpolicella of the Veneto. Tuscany is the homeland of Sangiovese-based reds such as Chianti and Brunello. Central Italy is known more for easy-to-drink, forgettable wines, but some stars emerge, such as the light Umbrian white, Orvieto, the almond-scented white, Verdicchio dei Castelli di Jesi, and the dark Rosso Conero reds from Le Marche. The country's sun-drenched southern regions are currently producing some of Italy's most exciting wines from rediscovered ancient grape varieties.

Italian Wine Labels

Italian wines are almost always labeled by their place of origin. Sometimes the region is mentioned alone, such as Barolo or Chianti. Sometimes labels mention grape variety. The *Denominazione di Origine Controllata* (DOC) is Italy's regulation system; wines labeled DOC must be made in defined areas and meet specific standards. Wines designated *Denominazione di Origine Controllata e Garantita* (DOCG) are required to meet more stringent standards. For years, any wine not made according to DOC rules had to take the humble title *Vino da Tavola* (table wine). A new category, *Indicazione Geografica Tipica* (IGT), was created in 1992 to categorize an increasing number of high-quality wines that are vinified with unorthodox winemaking techniques or use unapproved grape varieties. Some vintners list the term "Classico" on a wine's label to indicate that the grapes are from a more prestigious subregion. The words "Riserva" or "Superiore" may be used when a wine meets more stringent requirements than is normal for the region.

piedmont

Piedmont (*Piemonte* in Italian) is one of the world's great wine regions. Its regal reds, Barolo and Barbaresco, are often compared to Burgundy in terms of earthy elegance, as well as their legendary ability to age. Its simpler reds, Barbera and Dolcetto, draw comparisons to Beaujolais. White and sparkling wines are also made here from a wide range of grape varieties.

piedmont whites

Piedmont's whites are secondary to its reds. Gavi di Gavi, made from the Cortese grape, is popular at home and abroad, though it is simple. Arneis, especially from the sub-region of Roero, is considerably more substantial, with peppery floral and apple flavors. Chardonnay grows well in Piedmont; the finest examples show ripe fruit flavors balanced with refreshing acidity and minerals. Semi-sweet sparkling Asti Spumante and Moscato d'Asti (see p. 268) are by far Piedmont's most popular and high-volume whites; some are uninteresting and insipid, while others are aromatic and enjoyably refreshing.

BEST PAIRINGS Gavi's high acidity and light body make it terrific with grilled or fried fish, anchovies, or pasta with pesto. Arneis is heavier, so it pairs nicely with risotto or chicken stews. Piedmont Chardonnay is a good match with heavier fish dishes or chicken.

piedmont white recommendations

Araldica La Luciana | 2005 | GAVI
★ ★ $ Grassy lemon flavors are perked up by unexpected pinches of cinnamon in this value white.

Bonny Doon Vineyard Il Circo La Funambola | 2004 | ERBALUCE DI CALUSO
★ ★ $ $ A whimsical, light-bodied white that offers waves of citrus, herb and pepper flavors.

Broglia La Meirana | 2004 | **GAVI**
★★★ **$$** The apple, pineapple and blanched almond flavors in this Gavi are finessed by fine minerals.

Bruno Giacosa | 2004 | **ROERO ARNEIS**
★★★ **$$$** This conjures up the perfume of meadow flowers, fresh-cut grass and limes.

Ceretto Blange' Arneis | 2005 | **LANGHE**
★★ **$$** A delightfully light wine with tiny bubbles that add vibrancy to citrus and grass flavors.

La Scolca Black Label | 2004 | **GAVI**
★★★ **$$$** An elegant, harmonious expression of citrus, fragrant nut and almond flavors.

Michele Chiarlo | 2004 | **GAVI**
★★★ **$$** One of Piedmont's most versatile producers makes a top-flight Gavi with fresh flavors of citrus, cherries and green almonds.

Villa Sparina Montej | 2004 | **MONFERRATO**
★★★ **$$** This attention-getter shows off a unique mélange of baked pear, lemon curd and spice flavors laced with salty minerals.

piedmont reds

Nebbiolo is Piedmont's noblest red grape. Sometimes called "Spanna," it's the grape responsible for the famed wines of Barolo and Barbaresco, plus the lesser-known Gattinara, Ghemme and Langhe. Barbera is the region's most widely planted grape. Dolcetto is the basis for many of Piedmont's easy-drinking, unpretentious reds. International varieties Cabernet Sauvignon, Merlot and Syrah have also found a home here.

BEST PAIRINGS The ultimate partner for an aged Barolo or Barbaresco is truffle-shaved risotto. Venison roasted with wild mushrooms is another delicious match. Decant wines younger than five years old for a few hours before serving them, preferably with thick steaks or braised lamb. Simpler Barbera and Dolcetto are perfect for pasta with a chunky meat ragù. More serious versions can take on thick slices of prime rib or braised lamb shoulder.

PIEDMONT REDS

barolo & barbaresco

Barolo and Barbaresco, named for two modest villages separated by a distance of less than twenty miles, are among the world's greatest wines. They're both made from the Nebbiolo grape and typically offer flavors of dry cherry, leather, truffle and smoke. These are powerful wines and some of the most ageworthy in the world. Barolo tends to be the more substantial and Barbaresco the more graceful. Regulations require Barolo to be aged three years, two in barrel, before it's released. Because of its somewhat softer profile, Barbaresco must be aged only two years, one in barrel, before release. Wines designated "Riserva" demand an extra year. These wines used to take at least a decade before being ready to drink, but modern techniques enable them to be enjoyed earlier.

barolo & barbaresco recommendations

Borgogno Riserva | 1999 | **BAROLO CLASSICO**
★★★★ $ $ $ $ Wonderfully old-fashioned, this Barolo is a rare treat. Notes of animal and mushroom infuse flavors of smoke, savory spice and dried red berries.

Boroli Villero | 2000 | **BAROLO**
★★★ $ $ $ $ Berry and earth flavors are here in equal measure, with abundant minerals and plenty of tannin. Drink in 2–20 years.

Camerano Cannubi San Lorenzo | 2001 | **BAROLO**
★★★★ $ $ $ $ A quick swirl brings forth generous flower and sweet spice aromas. Flavors of smoke, earth, truffle and spice define this pure, powerful Barolo. Drink in 2–20 years.

Cascina Bongiovanni | 2002 | **BAROLO**
★★★ $ $ $ Fans of seductive, fruit-forward wines will particularly love this Barolo with its soft, ripe red cherry and light spice flavors. Drink in 1–10 years.

Ceretto Asij | 2001 | **BARBARESCO**
★★★ $ $ $ Ceretto makes wines that are drinkable upon release yet able to age. This shows bright cherry flavors and spice, but has the stuffing to last. Drink now–12 years.

Conterno Fantino | 2002 | BAROLO
★★★ $ $ $ $ A delicious, full-bodied Barolo with ripe berry and cherry flavors, pinches of cinnamon, some tobacco, dark minerals and chewy tannins. Drink in 3–15 years.

La Spinetta | 2002 | BARBARESCO
★★★★ $ $ $ $ The best grapes from La Spinetta's best vineyards were used here, yielding an intense, smoky, savory, berry-flavored wine. Drink in 2–12 years.

Moccagatta Bric Balin | 2003 | BARBARESCO
★★★ $ $ $ Flavors ranging from cherry to vanilla and chocolate make for sensuous drinking.

Poderi Luigi Einaudi | 2002 | BAROLO
★★★ $ $ $ $ A thoroughly modern winemaker offers a wine that has lashes of ripe berry, sappy oak and spice, yet still says "Barolo." Drink now–8 years.

Renato Ratti Marcenasco | 2001 | BAROLO
★★★ $ $ $ This captivates with flavors of black currant, tea and dry herbs. It's built for lamb. Drink in 2–15 years.

Tenute Cisa Asinari dei Marchesi di Gresy Martinenga | 2001 | BARBARESCO
★★★ $ $ $ With bold aromatics of dried herbs and sweet, peppery spices, this multilayered wine delivers flavors of hibiscus and ripe red berries. Drink now–12 years.

Vietti Castiglione | 2000 | BAROLO
★★★★ $ $ $ Baked cherry, eucalyptus and mint flavors saturate this graceful, finely tannic wine. Drink now–12 years.

---

star producers
barolo & barbaresco

best value	**best of the best**
1 Beni di Batasiolo	1 Aldo Conterno
2 Luigi Pira	2 Angelo Gaja
3 Produttori del Barbaresco	3 Bruno Giacosa
4 Stefano Farina	4 Giacomo Conterno
5 Villadoria	5 Roberto Voerzio

PIEDMONT REDS
barbera & dolcetto

Barbera and Dolcetto are full of lush berry flavors. Those from Asti and Alba are plush and fruity, while Dolcetto from Dogliani and Barbera from Monferrato are smoky and laden with minerals. Most are meant for consumption soon after release, though some exceptional ones are ageworthy.

barbera & dolcetto recommendations

Bricco Mondalino | 2003 |
BARBERA DEL MONFERRATO SUPERIORE
★★ $ Earthy flavors mingle with tart red berry and lively acidity.

Bruno Porro Vigna Ribote | 2004 | DOLCETTO DI DOGLIANI
★★★ $$ Seductive Dolcetto with soft, sweet berry flavors and the smoky mineral quality typical of the region.

Ca'Viola Vilot | 2004 | DOLCETTO D'ALBA
★★★ $$ Floral aromas envelop this berry-flavored Dolcetto.

Cogno Bricco dei Merli | 2001 | BARBERA D'ALBA
★★★ $$$ See what age does to Barbera in this earthy, herbal, dry cherry– and spice-laden wine.

Damilano | 2004 | DOLCETTO D'ALBA
★★ $$ Flavors of strawberry are sprinkled with ground pepper.

Marcarini Ciabot Camerano | 2004 | BARBERA D'ALBA
★★★ $$ Sophisticated Barbera, this is lithe but still full-flavored, with fine mineral notes and firm tannin.

Marchesi di Barolo Madonna di Como | 2004 |
DOLCETTO D'ALBA
★★★ $$ Full of juicy cherry and peppery berry flavors, this comes from a well-respected Barolo producer.

Parusso Piani Noce | 2004 | DOLCETTO D'ALBA
★★ $$ Smooth and delicious strawberry, cocoa and walnut flavors are held up by fine tannin and good acidity.

Pecchenino San Luigi | 2004 | DOLCETTO DI DOGLIANI
★★★ $$ An excellent choice from a top Dolcetto producer, full of earthy black and blueberry flavors, herbs and intense mineral notes.

Poderi Colla Costa Bruna | 2003 | **BARBERA D'ALBA**

★★★ $ $ The flavors of smoke and leather, herb and berry in this lean wine make a lasting impression.

Poderi Luigi Einaudi Vigna Tecc | 2004 |
DOLCETTO DI DOGLIANI

★★★ $ $ $ Great from year to year, Vigna Tecc proves Dolcetto doesn't have to be simple. This is plush, with ripe berries, tobacco and salty mineral flavors.

Sandrone | 2004 | **BARBERA D'ALBA**

★★★ $ $ $ A bit of air brings out a complex weave of fruit, coffee, sweet spice and minerals.

Vigne Regali L'Ardì | 2004 | **DOLCETTO D'ACQUI**

★ $ Put a light chill on this wine and enjoy its simple red cherry and light berry flavors.

other piedmont reds

Piedmont's proximity to France explains the presence of French varieties Cabernet Sauvignon, Merlot and Syrah in its soils. Vintners often blend them with indigenous Italian varieties which yields intriguing results. Wines from the local variety Freisa can be charming, with a pleasing hint of sweetness and effervescence. In contrast, Ruché-based wines have an earthy, bitter appeal. Barolo lovers ought to take note of Nebbiolo wines grown in other parts of the Piedmont region, such as Gattinara, Ghemme and the Langhe hills. Nebbiolo d'Alba offers some of Nebbiolo's earthy charms in a simpler form.

other piedmont red recommendations

Bonny Doon Vineyard Il Circo La Donna Cannone | 2004 |
RUCHÉ DI CASTAGNOLE MONFERRATO

★★ $ $ No getting around the abundant minerals here, but they're nicely softened by the seductive perfume of wildflowers and round red cherry flavors.

Conterno Fantino Mon Pra' | 2003 | **LANGHE**

★★★★ $ $ $ This superb, velvety blend of Nebbiolo, Barbera and Cabernet offers power and grace, luscious berry, smoke and deep mineral flavors. Drink in 2–15 years.

OLD
WORLD

Fontanafredda Eremo Barbera e Nebbiolo | 2003 | LANGHE
★★★ $ Two great Piedmont grapes combine to beautiful effect,
creating a full-bodied, dark berry–flavored wine with undertones of
earth. Drink now–8 years.

Parusso Nebbiolo | 2003 | LANGHE
★★ $ $ $ Comparable to a good Barbaresco, this Langhe offers
earthy cherry flavors and subtle herb and spice notes.

Pro Nobis | 2004 | RUCHÉ DI CASTAGNOLE MONFERRATO
★★★ $ $ Herb, pepper and wild berry flavors emerge from a base
of minerals in this lively, medium-bodied wine.

Renato Ratti Ochetti | 2004 | NEBBIOLO D'ALBA
★★★ $ $ An important name in Barolo makes this fresh red berry–
and peach-scented Nebbiolo that is substantial and complex, but not
too serious or expensive.

Valdinera Sontuoso | 2003 | NEBBIOLO D'ALBA
★★ $ $ $ Lovely wine that expresses some of the smoky notes of
Barolo and the fresh red berry flavors of simpler Alba wines.

tuscany

Tuscany is home to some of Italy's most traditional wines,
as well as some of its most modern. Only a generation ago,
straw-covered jugs of mediocre Chianti represented a
large amount of the region's production. Today, a growing
number of quality-minded Tuscan vintners are making
spectacular wines, which range from nutty, complex
whites to elegant Chiantis and powerful, modern-styled
Super-Tuscans.

tuscany whites

Many Tuscan whites are forgettable; the uninteresting
grape Trebbiano is responsible for most of these. But the
floral-scented Vernaccia-based wines from San Gimignano
are excellent. Some producers blend them with a bit of
Chardonnay, which adds more body to the wine. Wines
made from Vermentino, full of mineral, lime and forestlike
flavors, are also worth looking for.

BEST PAIRINGS Light, fresh styles of Vernaccia di San Gimignano are delicious with salads. Serve them as well with spaghetti and grilled vegetables. Heavier examples, augmented with Chardonnay, are great with whole, roasted fish or bean soups. Simple Trebbiano is fine for washing down light luncheon fare. Tuscan Chardonnay is a good choice for roasted chicken. Pour Vermentino with seafood salads and chicken.

tuscany white recommendations

Cabreo La Pietra Chardonnay | 2003 | TUSCANY
★★★ $ $ $ Satiny butterscotch and oak flavors in this Chardonnay are balanced by notes of mango and citrus, plus good acidity.

Castello Banfi San Angelo Pinot Grigio | 2005 | TUSCANY
★ $ $ Fresh grapefruit and pine flavors make this Pinot Grigio from central Tuscany a refreshing summer pour.

Castello del Terriccio Con Vento | 2004 | TUSCANY
★★★ $ $ $ Tuscany isn't known for stand-out Sauvignon Blanc, but this peach- and grass-flavored example is a stunning exception.

Cesani | 2004 | VERNACCIA DI SAN GIMIGNANO
★★ $ Infused with strawberry and lemon flavors, this vibrant white is perfect for warm-weather drinking.

Cima Vigneto Candia Alto | 2004 | CANDIA DEI COLLI APUANI
★★★ $ $ This delicious wine is one of Tuscany's overlooked gems. Snappy green apple, lime and cherry flavors are highlighted by an appealing nuttiness.

Strozzi Titolato | 2004 | VERNACCIA DI SAN GIMIGNANO
★★ $ Salty minerals and high acidity drive this wine, combined with flavors of candied lemon peel and almond.

Tenuta di Nozzole Le Bruniche Chardonnay | 2004 | TUSCANY
★★ $ A lean, mineral-laden Chardonnay with prominent lemon and light pine flavors.

Teruzzi & Puthod Terre di Tufi | 2004 | TUSCANY
★★★ $ $ One of the most sophisticated whites in all of Tuscany. Oak-aging brings a smoky dimension to an already complex blend of four different grape varieties.

OLD
WORLD

tuscany reds

Sangiovese literally means "blood of Jove," and it is indeed the lifeline of Tuscany. It's the dominant grape in smaller subregions throughout Tuscany, either as the star grape or in an important supporting role. Sangiovese-based wines range from lean, light-bodied and astringent to indulgent and bold. Regardless of profile, these wines are high in acidity with vibrant cherry and herb flavors. In the past twenty years, French varieties Cabernet Sauvignon, Merlot and Syrah have established themselves with successful results in Tuscany, especially on the Mediterranean coastal zones of Bolgheri and Maremma.

TUSCANY REDS

chianti

Chianti is Italy's largest wine region, and it's divided into seven subdistricts of varying repute. The most famous is Chianti Classico between Florence and Siena. Chianti Rùfina, Chianti Colli Senesi and Chianti Colli Fiorentini are other well-regarded areas. Generic "Chianti," which is easy to identify because there is no subregion listed on the label, is the simplest. Less than a generation ago, vintners here were obliged to blend several indigenous grape varieties with Sangiovese and age their wines in old, large casks. Today, you'll find many modern, robust examples in the market and these are likely to be fully Sangiovese, or include up to 15 percent Cabernet Sauvignon, Merlot and Syrah. Many are also aged in small oak barrels which impart sweet vanilla flavors and concentration. Riserva wines are more dense, higher in alcohol and spend at least twenty-seven months in oak barrels.

BEST PAIRINGS Chianti is the perfect pizza wine. Non-Riserva wines from various designated subregions are fabulous wines for food; try them with chicken dishes, pot roast or pork chops. Save boldly flavored Riserva wines for thick steaks or roast game.

chianti recommendations

Badia a Coltibuono Riserva | 2000 | CHIANTI CLASSICO
★ ★ ★ ★ $ $ $ From one of Chianti's best producers, this seduces immediately with soft cherry, lavender and light leather flavors. It will also age for decades. Drink now–20 years.

Barone Ricasoli Castello di Brolio | 2001 |
CHIANTI CLASSICO
★ ★ ★ ★ $ $ $ $ Chianti as we know it started at Brolio, which still serves as the benchmark. This is powerful but restrained with berry, orange, mushroom, smoke and stone flavors. Drink in 2–20 years.

Castello dei Rampolla | 2002 | CHIANTI CLASSICO
★ ★ $ $ $ Ripe strawberry and cherry flavors are infused by smoky, tarlike aromas for an earthy, pleasurable wine.

Castello di Bossi Berardo Riserva | 2000 |
CHIANTI CLASSICO
★ ★ ★ $ $ $ Decant this massive wine to release its subtle flower and savory spice flavors intertwined with aromas of dark ripe berries and stone. Drink now–15 years.

Castello di Meleto | 2003 | CHIANTI CLASSICO
★ ★ $ $ Fresh, baked and stewed cherries are on display here, with notes of earthy herbs and minerals which bring finesse.

Giacomo Marengo | 2003 | LE TORNAIE
★ ★ $ $ This very dry, intensely earthy and tannic wine has lots of rustic charm; it will taste even better with meat.

Il Molino di Grace | 2001 | CHIANTI CLASSICO
★ ★ ★ $ $ $ A fine example of Classico, this oozes dark fruit flavors, fine spice, lots of acidity and substantial tannin. Drink now–4 years.

Il Piccolo Borgo | 2002 | CHIANTI CLASSICO
★ ★ $ $ Smoky fruit flavors here evoke the Tuscan terroir. This wine would be perfect with Italian baked beans.

Lanciola Le Masse di Greve | 2003 | CHIANTI CLASSICO
★ ★ ★ $ $ $ A luscious, smooth-textured wine brimming with cherry and berry flavors highlighted by violet and spice.

Marchesi de' Frescobaldi Castello di Nipozzano Vigneto Montesodi | 2003 | CHIANTI RÙFINA
★ ★ ★ ★ $ $ $ Exceptional Chianti. Intense cassis flavors saturate this mineral- and herb-laden wine. Drink now–12 years.

Melini Laborel Riserva | 1999 | CHIANTI CLASSICO
★★★ $ $ A bit of Cabernet gives Sangiovese a claretlike elegance in this earthy, cherry-flavored wine. Drink now–8 years.

Rocca delle Macìe Riserva | 2000 | CHIANTI CLASSICO
★★★ $ $ This classic Chianti is suave and savory, with fragrant earthiness and flavors of dark fruit, green peppercorn, bitter herb and abundant minerals. Drink now–10 years.

Rocca di Castagnoli | 2003 | CHIANTI CLASSICO
★★ $ $ Chianti goes sappy in this wine with sticky cherry, lanolin and herb oil flavors.

Ruffino Riserva Ducale Oro Riserva | 2001 |
CHIANTI CLASSICO
★★★ $ $ $ Polished mineral flavors and a kick of spicy pepper add an intriguing dimension to this silky smooth, bright berry-flavored red. Drink in 1–15 years.

San Fabiano Conti | 2004 | CHIANTI
★★ $ A longtime favorite for basic Chianti, and it's not hard to see why: ripe berry flavors are accented by notes of spice.

Spalletti | 2004 | CHIANTI
★ $ Mouthwatering acidity brings vibrancy to red berry and orange flavors; just right for a bowl of spaghetti and meatballs.

Straccali | 2004 | CHIANTI
★ $ Red cherry and bitter spice flavors plus lots of acidity make a good pizza wine.

Tenimenti Angelini San Leonino | 2002 | CHIANTI CLASSICO
★★ $ $ Chewy dry cherry, light tobacco and smoked meat flavors come to an appealingly savory end.

---

star producers
chianti

best value
1 Antinori
2 Castell'In Villa
3 Dievole
4 Fattoria Valtellina
5 Lanciola

best of the best
1 Badia a Coltibuono
2 Castell'In Villa
3 Castello di Brolio
4 Castello di Monsanto
5 Querciabella

Tenuta di Nozzole La Forra Riserva | 2001 |
CHIANTI CLASSICO
★★★★ **$ $ $** Rich, sultry and seductive, this Classico provides a sophisticated ooze of black fruit, lanolin and minerals.

Terrabianca Croce Riserva | 2001 | **CHIANTI CLASSICO**
★★★ **$ $ $** Chianti in a modern style, this is a slick, juicy wine, full of berry, lavender and sticky oak flavors. Drink now–12 years.

Toscolo Riserva | 2001 | **CHIANTI CLASSICO**
★★★ **$ $** Fans of oaky wines will enjoy this robust red. Fortunately it's perfectly balanced by plenty of fruit and salty mineral flavors.

TUSCANY REDS

montalcino

A Sangiovese subvariety, Brunello di Montalcino makes wines that are tannic, powerful and elegant, full of cherry, cedar, tobacco and leather flavors. Vintners must age Brunello wines for four years before release, two of those in barrel. Riserva wines require five years' age, three in barrel. They age beautifully. Rosso di Montalcino is referred to as "Baby Brunello"; it is released earlier and ready to drink.

BEST PAIRINGS Full-bodied Brunello requires robust fare like roast game, venison or lamb. Vegetarians should pair it with wild-mushroom lasagna or hard, pungent cheeses. Softer Rosso is perfect with tender, mild-flavored meats like filet mignon or veal scallopine.

montalcino recommendations

Argiano | 2001 | **BRUNELLO DI MONTALCINO**
★★★★ **$ $ $ $** Black fruit, chocolate and wild herb flavors flood this massive, almost waxy wine. Pair it with lamb. Drink in 3–20 years.

Camigliano | 2001 | **BRUNELLO DI MONTALCINO**
★★★ **$ $ $ $** Toned wine with bright cherry flavors tightly knit with minerals, tobacco, herb oil notes and tannin. Drink in 3–15 years.

Caparzo La Caduta | 2001 | **ROSSO DI MONTALCINO**
★★★ **$ $ $** While more powerful than many Rosso di Montalcino, this is still accessible, with loads of minerals, red fruit and peppery spice flavors. Drink now–6 years.

Caparzo Riserva | 1999 | **BRUNELLO DI MONTALCINO**
★★★★ $ $ $ $ All of Caparzo's Montalcino wines are terrific, this is just better, with peppery and savory herb, spice, animal, black cherry and bitter chocolate flavors. Drink in 3–20 years.

Castello Banfi | 2001 | **BRUNELLO DI MONTALCINO**
★★★ $ $ $ $ The best-known Brunello in America does not fall short: this is a definitive, powerful display of black fruit, tobacco and deep minerals. Drink in 2–15 years.

Castello Banfi | 2003 | **ROSSO DI MONTALCINO**
★★ $ $ $ Upfront cherry flavors, with notes of bitter herb and spice offer an appealing entrée to the world of Montalcino.

Col d'Orcia Banditella | 2002 | **ROSSO DI MONTALCINO**
★★★ $ $ $ Full of sticky lanolin and herb oil flavors and bursting with red and dark fruit, this is a serious wine built for a robust lamb stew. Drink now–8 years.

Conti Costanti | 2001 | **BRUNELLO DI MONTALCINO**
★★★ $ $ $ $ This fruit-driven Brunello offers bright red cherry and orange flavors underscored by minerals, fine tannin and high acidity. Drink now–8 years.

Il Poggione | 2003 | **ROSSO DI MONTALCINO**
★★ $ $ $ Although it isn't as big as Poggione's Brunello, this earthy, tannic wine still needs a lot of air to bring out its red fruit charms.

Palladio | 1999 | **BRUNELLO DI MONTALCINO**
★★★ $ $ $ An impressive wine with a texture as smooth as melted chocolate and generous flavors of plush berry, violet and sweet spice. Drink now–15 years.

Palladio | 2003 | **ROSSO DI MONTALCINO**
★★ $ $ Soft red berry flavors and subtle spice notes bring easy-drinking pleasure from a noble region.

Poggio Antico Altero | 2001 | **BRUNELLO DI MONTALCINO**
★★★★ $ $ $ $ Outstanding Brunello that expresses undercurrents of smoky minerals, while bright red fruit and sweet oak flavors stand front and center. Drink in 2–15 years.

Tenimenti Angelini Val di Suga | 2000 |
BRUNELLO DI MONTALCINO
★★★ $ $ $ Refined herbal, earthy flavors are in harmony with notes of red berry and minerals. Polished tannin and lots of acidity give this a long, complex finish. Drink now–15 years.

TUSCANY REDS

montepulciano, carmignano, morellino di scansano

Montepulciano is only twenty miles from Montalcino, and wines here are made from Prugnolo Gentile, a local variant of Sangiovese. Vino Nobile must be aged two years, one in oak. Riservas demand three years of age. Simpler Rosso di Montepulciano has no aging requirements. Stylistically, Vino Nobile falls somewhere between Chianti Classico and Brunello. Carmignano wines are based on Sangiovese, but they must also contain Cabernet Sauvignon. This makes them fuller-bodied and more tannic than typical Chianti. Morellino di Scansano, the "little cherry of Scansano," delivers all the charm that its whimsical name implies. It is made entirely from Sangiovese and shows bright cherry flavors, though some examples are fuller-bodied with darker fruit flavors.

BEST PAIRINGS Morellino, Carmignano and Montepulciano can be enjoyed like Chiantis of similar levels, served with pastas with meat sauces, roast game or steak.

montepulciano recommendations

Boscarelli | 2003 | **VINO NOBILE DI MONTEPULCIANO**
★★★ $ $ $ This velvety-textured Vino Nobile shows exuberant cherry flavors, grounded by a base of earthy tobacco and minerals. Drink now–10 years.

Fassati Salarco Riserva | 1999 |
VINO NOBILE DI MONTEPULCIANO
★★★ $ $ $ Benefiting from seven years of age, this Montepulcian is full of fresh berry flavors layered with hints of leather and eart Drink now–6 years.

Fattoria del Cerro | 2003 | **VINO NOBILE DI MONTEPULCIANO**
★★ $ $ Typical of the very hot 2003 vintage, this is full of fat berry flavors with an appealing bitter edge.

Tenimenti Angelini Trerose | 2001 |
VINO NOBILE DI MONTEPULCIANO
★★★ $ $ Shy at first, this relatively lean-bodied wine's red berry and herb flavors emerge boldly after some air. Drink now–8 years.

Tenimenti Ruffino Ludola Nuova | 2001 |
VINO NOBILE DI MONTEPULCIANO
★★ $ $ A full-bodied red whose sweet black cherry flavors are matched by sticky lanolin and herb notes. Drink now–6 years.

carmignano & morellino di scansano recommendations

La Doga | 2004 | **MORELLINO DI SCANSANO**
★★ $ $ Ripe cherry flavors abound here, highlighted by hints of tar.

Vittoria Contini Bonacossi Trefiano | 1996 | **CARMIGNANO**
★★★ $ $ $ The advantages of age are seen in the earthy pleasures of this truffle-scented wine, followed by flavors of cherries, leather and smoke. Drink now–8 years.

TUSCANY REDS

super-tuscans

The Italian wine revolution began in 1968 when the famed blend, Sassicaia, was released. Crafted with grapes and techniques not permitted in the region, Sassicaia soon earned international accolades and the nickname "Super-Tuscan." The movement continued and today nearly every major Tuscan winemaker makes his or her own version of a Super-Tuscan wine. Until recently these wines fell under the humble "Vino da Tavola" category, but in 1992 the classification IGT (*Indicazione Geografica Tipica*) was added to classify them (see p. 83). Most Super-Tuscans are made with a combination of French and Tuscan grapes such as Cabernet and Sangiovese; they are full-bodied, powerful, expensive wines and some of the best in Italy. Bolgheri, Sassicaia's home region, now has its own DOC.

BEST PAIRINGS Big and tannic Super-Tuscans go perfectly with a wide range of meats including grilled, dry-aged steaks and braised lamb shanks,

super-tuscan recommendations

Altesino Rosso di Altesino | 2003 | TUSCANY

★ $ $ From a famous Brunello producer, this is made in a relatively modest style, providing spicy, easy-drinking enjoyment.

Campo al Mare | 2003 | BOLGHERI

★★★ $ $ $ Juicy red berry flavors are infused by celery and cumin notes; chewy, smoky tannin holds them together. Drink in 2–10 years.

Campo di Sasso Insoglio del Cinghiale | 2004 | TUSCANY

★★ $ $ Despite its charmingly rustic label, this Bordeaux-blend is sophisticated and lithe, with peppery red berry flavors, fine tannin and high acidity. Drink now–6 years.

Castello Banfi Excelsus Sant'Antimo | 2000 | TUSCANY

★★★ $ $ $ $ Banfi's mastery of the Montalcino region extends beyond Brunello, as evidenced in this suave, substantial Cabernet/ Merlot blend. Drink now–15 years.

La Massa | 2003 | TUSCANY

★★★ $ $ $ The sultry dark berry and plum flavors here are velvet smooth. Drink now–8 years.

Lanciola Riccionero Pinot Nero | 2002 | TUSCANY

★★ $ $ $ $ This combines the acidity and spice of Tuscany with the elegance of Burgundy.

Lupicaia | 2001 | TUSCANY

★★★★ $ $ $ $ Named for wolves that tread through the vineyard, this masterfully weaves together flavors of concentrated berries with tobacco, minerals and earth. Drink in 2–15 years.

Marchesi de' Frescobaldi Castello di Nipozzano Mormoreto | 2003 | TUSCANY

★★★★ $ $ $ An intense and powerful Super-Tuscan oozing flavors of cassis, dark chocolate, anise and roast coffee. This needs age to soften its firm tannins. Drink in 3–15 years.

Ornellaia Le Volte | 2003 | TUSCANY

★★ $ $ The kid-brother of Tuscany's famed Ornellaia estate shows elegant and earthy flavors of berry and spice. Drink now–5 years.

Tenuta di Arceno Arcanum III | 2003 | TUSCANY

★★★ $ $ $ $ An unrestrained Super-Tuscan with a bold crescendo of ripe berry, toasted oak, tobacco and lavender flavors structured by firm tannin and mineral notes. Drink in 2–12 years.

Tenuta San Guido Sassicaia | 2002 | BOLGHERI

★★★★ $ $ $ $ The once-revolutionary wine that earned its place in the pantheon of the world's greatest reds, Sassicaia offers another sophisticated display of dark fruit, stone and light spice flavors with hints of lanolin. Drink in 2–20 years.

Tenuta Sette Ponti Oreno | 2003 | TUSCANY

★★★ $ $ $ $ A hedonistic nectar, revealing voluptuous dark berry, aged tobacco and polished mineral flavors. Drink in 2–15 years.

Terrabianca Campaccio Riserva | 2001 | TUSCANY

★★★★ $ $ $ $ This majestic wine shows a rare finesse; black fruit, savory spice and earthy mineral flavors are in perfect harmony. Drink now–15 years.

Villa La Selva Selvamaggio Cabernet Sauvignon | 2001 | TUSCANY

★★★ $ $ $ Beautiful Cabernet Sauvignon, this has abundant ripe flavors of cassis accented by notes of cedar and pepper, revealing the unique character of Tuscany. Drink now–12 years.

other italian regions: north

While the noble wines from Piedmont are northern Italy's most highly acclaimed, wines from other regions in the country's north are some of the most popular, such as Pinot Grigio and Soave. Northern regions are also home to some of Italy's most distinctive wines, made from local, indigenous grapes that are unknown elsewhere.

• TRENTINO–ALTO ADIGE & FRIULI–VENEZIA GIULIA
Trentino–Alto Adige (also called Südtirol) shares a border with Austria, and its Germanic influence is evident in its major grapes: Riesling, Gewürztraminer (also known as Traminer) and Müller-Thurgau. The Friuli–Venezia Giulia region (usually shortened to Friuli) has long hosted an array of international varieties such as Cabernet Franc and Merlot, as well as local varieties such as Tocai Friulano, Ribolla Gialla and Refosco.

• **VENETO** The Veneto is an immensely productive area in terms of industry and agriculture, but an emphasis on quantity over quality sullied the once fine reputation of its wines. Valpolicella and powerful variant Amarone are the best-known reds. Soave is the ubiquitous white. Today, some great vintners are making high-quality examples of both, which are well worth seeking out.

• **LOMBARDY** Between Piedmont and the northeast regions sometimes collectively called the Tre-Venezie is the region of Lombardy, home to Italy's finest sparkling wine region, Franciacorta, where vintners rely on the same grapes and techniques as those used in Champagne. Valtellina, near Switzerland, makes some good Nebbiolo. Garda, a region which Lombardy shares with Veneto, makes earthy wines from international and local grape varieties.

other northern italian whites

The most interesting whites from Trentino–Alto Adige are made primarily with Pinot Grigio, Müller-Thurgau and Pinot Blanc. Well-made versions have an exhilarating freshness to them, with robust fruit and fresh acidity. Chardonnay is also capable of making noteworthy wine here. Pinot Grigio performs well in Friuli, where aromatic Tocai Friulano, robust Ribolla Gialla and pearlike Pinot Bianco are also responsible for many distinctive wines. Sauvignon Blanc tends to be grassy in Friuli and is often outstanding, as are many blends. Veneto's great white is Soave. Unfortunately, most Soave is uninspiring, though examples from the hilly Classico zones outside of Verona are often considerably better. Most Soave is based on the Garganega grape, which expresses profound mineral, apple and almond flavors. Sauvignon Blanc, Tocai, Pinot Grigio and Pinot Bianco are also used to craft vibrant wines. Prosecco, a white grape that goes into the light sparkling wine of the same name (see Other Sparkling Wines, p. 268), is another widely grown variety in the Veneto.

BEST PAIRINGS Bring out the sweetness of shellfish with the vibrant citrus flavors of Pinot Grigio or Sauvignon Blanc. Ribolla Gialla's creamy texture makes it ideal with seafood risotto or veal. Tocai Friulano is substantial enough for pork loin or ham. Traminer's light spice flavors and high acidity make it great with Thai-spiced soups or pasta with cream sauce. Industrial Soave is best saved for punch. Higher-quality bottles from the Classico zone are great with meaty fish like sea bass or cod, and roast chicken.

other northern italian white recommendations

Allegrini Soave | 2004 | VENETO
★★ $ Incredibly talented Veneto producer makes this better-than-average Soave with lemon and nut flavors.

Alois Lageder Pinot Bianco | 2004 | ALTO ADIGE
★★★ $ The master of high-quality, moderately priced Alto Adige wines is behind this fantastic, crisp wine with mixed citrus and blanched almond flavors.

Anselmi San Vincenzo | 2004 | VENETO
★★★ $ Anselmi specializes in excellent wines like this smoky, stony, pineapple- and citrus-scented nectar.

Bertani Duè Uvè | 2004 | VENETO
★★ $ Pinot Grigio and Sauvignon Blanc are better than the sum of their parts in this nutty, citrusy, tropical fruit–laden wine.

Conti Formentini Collio Pinot Grigio | 2004 | FRIULI–VENEZIA GIULIA
★★ $ $ Balanced wine with coconut-dusted pear and lemon flavors.

Cortenova Pinot Grigio delle Venezie | 2005 | VENETO
★ $ Light and lovely, this $10 Pinot Grigio is a winning party wine.

Corte Sant'Alda Vigne di Mezzane Soave | 2004 | VENETO
★★★ $ $ Delicious single-vineyard Soave, this confected beauty is full of dried fruit, nut and sweet spice flavors that finish dry.

Damijan Ribolla Gialla | 2002 | VENEZIA GIULIA
★★★★ $ $ $ Damijan applies old winemaking techniques to craft this deeply earthy, mineral-laden, Sherry-like golden wine with dried fruit and spice flavors. Drink in 3–15 years.

Doro Princic Collio Tocai Friulano | 2004 |
FRIULI—VENEZIA GIULIA
★★ $ $ Tocai Friulano offers the unexpected, with dried apricot, wild strawberry, lemon, smoke and mineral notes.

Franz Haas Manna Vigneti delle Dolomiti | 2004 |
ALTO ADIGE
★★★ $ $ $ A heavenly blend of aromatic flower and citrus flavors with hints of blanched almond and spice.

Giovanni Puiatti Le Zuccole Isonzo del Friuli Pinot Grigio
| 2004 | **FRIULI—VENEZIA GIULIA**
★★ $ Zippy Pinot Grigio full of grapefruit and snappy apple flavors.

Girlan San Martino Pinot Bianco | 2005 | **ALTO ADIGE**
★★ $ Alive with lime and green peppercorn flavors, this lean wine will shine alongside fish.

Inama Vigneto du Lot Soave Classico | 2003 | **VENETO**
★★★★ $ $ As wild as Soave gets, this well-made white expresses intense flavors; one swirl brings forth aromas of smoke, resin, stone and unusual citrus notes.

Jermann Capo Martino | 2003 | **VENEZIA GIULIA**
★★★★ $ $ $ $ Jermann's stunning field blend of local grapes is a bit shy now. Time will soften the oak and allow the subtle autumn fruit, mineral and spice flavors to emerge. Drink in 2–13 years.

Lagaria Chardonnay | 2004 | **VENEZIA**
★ $ A high-acid Chardonnay that's simply enjoyable to drink and comes at a very fair price.

La Lot Vigneti delle Dolomiti Pinot Grigio | 2005 |
ALTO ADIGE
★★★ $ Charming, fresh-crushed apple flavors, a bit of spice and the perfume of lemon blossoms go into this terrific wine.

Livio Felluga Terre Alte Colli Orientali del Friuli | 2003 |
FRIULI—VENEZIA GIULIA
★★★ $ $ $ This beautifully composed blend of Tocai, Pinot Bianco and Sauvignon Blanc needs time to reveal its baked pear, marzipan and stone flavors. Drink in 1–8 years.

Pieropan Calvarino Soave Classico | 2003 | **VENETO**
★★★★ $ $ $ One of Italy's great white wines, this defines truly exceptional Soave, full of ripe pear and citrus flavors with subtle hints of nuts, smoke and minerals.

Pighin Collio Pinot Grigio | 2004 | FRIULI–VENEZIA GIULIA
★★★ $ $ Pighin's basic Pinot Grigio is good and this is even better. Minerals envelop flavors of pear, lemon and candied orange peel.

Plozner Grave del Friuli Tocai Friulano | 2004 | FRIULI–VENEZIA GIULIA
★★ $ An array of herbs from sage to thyme, lavender to rosemary imbue this delightfully stony wine.

Russiz Superiore Col Disôre Collio | 2003 | FRIULI–VENEZIA GIULIA
★★ $ $ Smooth from start to finish, this white blend entices with pear, white flower, light mineral and spice flavors.

Schiopetto Collio Pinot Bianco | 2004 | FRIULI–VENEZIA GIULIA
★★★ $ $ More substantial than most Pinot Bianco, this is lightly waxy, full of mineral, almond and apple flavors.

Sergio Zenato Lugana | 2003 | VENETO
★★★ $ $ Made from Trebbiano di Lugana, this absolutely lovely wine gives peach and honeysuckle flavors, a touch of light oak and lively acidity which brings everything into focus.

Suavia Soave Classico | 2005 | VENETO
★★ $ $ Lemon confit and crushed, salty almond flavors are given a lift by high acidity and a nearly sparkling texture.

Tiefenbrunner Chardonnay | 2004 | ALTO ADIGE
★★ $ Few Alto Adige Chardonnays are as good as this pear- and tropical fruit–flavored wine with vibrant acidity.

Torresella Chardonnay | 2004 | VENETO
★ $ A straightfoward and light-bodied Chardonnay perfect for good everyday drinking.

Tramin Pinot Grigio | 2005 | ALTO ADIGE
★★ $ At its best with a good chill, this Pinot Grigio offers a rich mix of enjoyable tropical fruit flavors.

Vicentini Agostino Terre Lunghe Soave | 2004 | VENETO
★★ $ $ Honeyed apple and bright lemon flavors are balanced by mouth-tingling acidity.

Villa Russiz Collio Sauvignon | 2004 | FRIULI–VENEZIA GIULIA
★★★ $ $ $ Enchantingly aromatic without going over the top, this wonderfully stony wine establishes Villa Russiz as one of the world's great Sauvignon producers.

other northern italian reds

Valpolicella from the Veneto is northeast Italy's most famous red. Made from a blend of Corvina, Rondinella and Molinara grapes, the best examples come from the hilly Classico zone. Valpolicella labeled "Superiore" are more concentrated, a reflection of superior grapes and the length of time spent in wooden barrels. Amarone della Valpolicella is a style of Valpolicella made from grapes that have been partially dried before pressing, which gives them increased intensity. Ripasso from Valpolicella is made by infusing Valpolicella wine with the must (the leftover pressed grapes) of Amarone wine. Recioto is the sweet version of Amarone (see p. 284). Light-bodied Bardolino was once widely found in American wine shops. Today, however, international varieties, such as Merlot, are more commonly exported from the region. Winemakers in other parts of northeastern Italy have a wide and fascinating array of local red varieties to work with. Refosco tends to be medium- or full-bodied, with an almost gamey bite. Pignolo and Schioppettino are dark, tannic and spicy. Lagrein is lighter in body, but peppery. Teroldego Rotaliano is a dry and savory wine. Tazzelenghe—literally "tongue cutter"—is full of tart red berry flavors and searing acidity. International grapes Merlot and Cabernet Franc tend to express somewhat more herbaceous qualities in northern Italian soils than they do in France or California.

BEST PAIRINGS Wines made from Lagrein, Refosco, Schioppettino, Tazzelenghe and Teroldego have gamey qualities that harmonize beautifully with roast meat like lamb or venison. Merlot and Pignolo are delicious with prime rib. Serve Cabernet Franc with grilled meats such as duck or chicken. Regular Valpolicella and Bardolino are good burger wines, while Classico versions go better with pasta with chunky meat ragù or sausages. Superiore and Amarone wines are intense and demand heavy, flavorful fare like braised oxtails or Moroccan lamb tagine, but will also complement aged Parmesan.

other northern italian red recommendations

Allegrini Palazzo della Torre | 2001 | VENETO
★★ $ $ A terrific entrée to Veneto reds, this is full of red berry, light herb and flower flavors with zippy acidity.

Alois Lageder Lagrein | 2003 | ALTO ADIGE
★★★ $ $ Firming acidity and tannin frame delicious flavors of ripe cherries and dark chocolate. Drink now–6 years.

Bottega Vinaia Lagrein | 2003 | TRENTINO
★★★ $ $ Lagrein's rustic notes are smoothed by oak in this sultry dark berry– and spice-flavored wine. Drink now–8 years.

Cavit Collection Vigneti delle Dolomiti Teroldego | 2004 | ALTO ADIGE
★★ $ Juicy red berry and herbs, a little spice and good acidity make a terrific everyday wine with an unusual twist.

Damijan Prelit | 2002 | VENEZIA GIULIA
★★★ $ $ $ Merlot and Cabernet may be "international" grapes, but Damijan imparts the taste of native terroir with generous stone, herb and succulent berry flavors. Drink now–12 years.

Fantinel Vigneti Sant'Helena Refosco dal Peduncolo Rosso Grave | 2002 | FRIULI–VENEZIA GIULIA
★★★ $ $ Refosco is often rough, but not here. Earthy herbal flavors are joined by suave red berry and savory spice. Drink now–8 years.

Foradori Teroldego Rotaliano | 2003 | TRENTINO
★★★ $ $ An indulgent wine from perhaps Italy's most renowned Teroldego producer; ripe berry pie flavors get a dusting of fine pepper. Drink now–6 years.

Girlan Patricia Pinot Noir | 2003 | ALTO ADIGE
★ $ $ Pinot Noir goes in an Italianate direction with bright cherry flavors, fine minerals and lots of acidity.

Jermann Mjzzu Blau & Blau | 2003 | VENEZIA
★★★ $ $ $ Blaufränkisch and Blauburgunder are woven together with velvety tannin and bring a mix of dark fruit and spice flavors. Drink now–8 years.

J. Hofstätter Lagrein | 2005 | ALTO ADIGE
★★ $ $ Fresh, spicy Lagrein, this quaffer is full of berry flavors that seem weighty and light at the same time.

Le Salette Valpolicella Classico | 2004 | VENETO
★★ $ $ This charming wine delights with spicy pepper, floral and tart red berry flavors.

Marchese Carlo Guerrieri Gonzaga San Leonardo Vigneti delle Dolomiti | 2000 | ALTO ADIGE
★★★ $ $ $ $ It isn't easy growing Bordeaux grape varieties in Trentino, but this balanced wine shows that skilled winemaking can yield beautiful, refined results. Drink now–10 years.

Masi Serego Alighieri Vaio Armaron Amarone della Valpolicella | 1999 | VENETO
★★★★ $ $ $ $ One of Amarone's greats, Masi makes a full-bodied wine, exotically spiced, and full of minerals. Drink now–20 years.

news from a wine insider

italy by David Lynch

Appellations to Watch

Vintners are up to exciting things in the Taurasi appellation of the Campania region. Aglianico, the grape of Taurasi, is rising to new heights; the dense and smoky "Selve di Luoti" Taurasi from Feudi di San Gregorio and "Cinque Querce" from Salvatore Molettieri are two of the best examples. Look also for Terredora di Paolo and Villa Raiano.

Roero in Piedmont is another appellation making news. Recently elevated to the elite status of DOCG, Roero is home to Nebbiolo-based wines that can approach the complexity of Barolo and Barbaresco, for a fraction of the price. Wines to look for include: Roero Superiore "Trinità" from Malvirà, Roero "Braja" from Deltetto, Roero "Audinaggio" from Cascina Ca' Rossa and Matteo Correggia.

Restaurants in the News

In Piedmont, the relatively new Ristorante Guido located on the Slow Food campus in Pollenzo is run by wine-savvy Piero Alciati; his mother and brother Andrea run the kitchen at the Guido da Costigliole in the Relais San Maurizio. In Alba, chef Enrico Crippa is getting lots of attention for his menu at the Ceretto wine family's bi-level Piazza Duomo. Outside Piedmont, check out Stefano Monti's wine bar Naranzaria, located on Venice's Grand Canal and the Capofaro resort on the Aeolian island of Salina.

Russiz Superiore Collio Merlot | 2001 |
FRIULI—VENEZIA GIULIA
★★ $ $ There are plenty of plush plum and berry flavors here, but the smoky tobacco notes and intense minerality are what leave a lasting impression. Drink now–6 years.

Santi Solane Ripasso Valpolicella Classico Superiore
| 2003 | **VENETO**
★★ $ The freshness of Valpolicella is complemented by the bitter charms of Amarone. Drink now–4 years.

Speri Amarone della Valpolicella Classico | 2001 | **VENETO**
★★★ $ $ $ $ Blackberry, dark chocolate and roasted meat flavors are sprinkled by spice in this hedonistic wine which remarkably stays elegant. Drink now–15 years.

Tedeschi Amarone della Valpolicella Classico | 2001 |
VENETO
★★★ $ $ $ Thick, ripe, sweet berry flavors are joined by notes of black tea, freshly ground peppercorn and savory spice in this tannic beast. Drink in 2–12 years.

other italian regions: central

Tuscany draws most of the attention, but many other regions of central Italy have their own distinct winemaking cultures dating back hundreds of years. From the frothy Lambrusca of Emilia-Romagna to the earthy, smoky Rosso Piceno of Le Marche and dark and spicy Montepulciano from Abbruzzo, there are countless red and white wines worth discovering.

• **EMILIA-ROMAGNA** Known more for its contributions to Italian culinary life (think prosciutto, parmesan cheese and Bolognese sauce) than viticulture, Emilia-Romagna still makes interesting wines. Fizzy red Lambrusca is best known, but there are good-quality whites from Chardonnay and the unusual Albana, and tasty reds from Sangiovese, Barbera and Cabernet Sauvignon.

- **LE MARCHE** Many wines from Le Marche—one of Italy's most overlooked regions—resemble those from Tuscany. Verdicchio is the region's one distinct white, rich with nutty, smoky flavors. Rosso Piceno and Rosso Cònero are Le Marche's two most noteworthy reds; both are dark, full-bodied and distinctively smoky.

- **ABRUZZI** Offering some of Italy's best wine bargains, Abruzzi is home to Trebbiano d'Abruzzo, a crisp, mineral-laden white, and Montepulciano d'Abruzzo, a red with spicy dark fruit flavors and firm tannin. Oddly, the Montepulciano grape has nothing to do with the Tuscan village of the same name (which makes wines from Sangiovese).

- **UMBRIA** Orvieto is Umbria's most important white wine. Examples made largely from bland Trebbiano are simple and inexpensive. Those that are blended together with the more flavorful Grechetto grape can be delicious. Umbria's most heralded red is Montefalco, made from the Sagrantino grape. Earthy, Sangiovese-based wines from Torgiano are also worthy of attention.

- **LAZIO** Rome's legendary *dolce vita* is fueled in part by the charmingly *frizzante* white Frascati, made in Lazio. Most are lovely, if simple wines, made from a blend of Trebbiano and Malvasia offering light, zippy citrus flavors.

other central italian whites

Albana is Emilia-Romagna's most interesting white. It is low in acidity but has a fascinating balance of baked apple, toasted nut and orange marmalade flavors. In contrast, the high acidity in Le Marche's Verdicchio adds vibrancy to the wine's unique apple and herb flavor profile. Trebbiano d'Abruzzo is often simple, but carefully cultivated, can make seductively lush wines.

BEST PAIRINGS Lazio's Frascati is delicious with baskets of fried clams. Mineral-rich Albana has a distinct nuttiness which is great with prosciutto and Parmigiano-Reggiano cheese. Enjoy Orvieto with delicate fish dishes. Verdicchio from Le Marche is at its best with fish stew.

other central italian white recommendations

Arnaldo-Caprai Grecante Grechetto dei Martani | 2004 | UMBRIA

★★ $ $ Ripe citrus and snappy apple flavors have a smoky edge in this smooth, mouthfilling wine.

Farnese Farneto Valley Trebbiano d'Abruzzo | 2004 | ABRUZZI

★★ $ Charming honeysuckle and lemon-lime flavors make this Trebbiano a delightful summer quaff.

Fattoria Nicodemi Trebbiano d'Abruzzo | 2005 | ABRUZZI

★★ $ This affordable treasure offers crisp lime and apple flavors with currents of spice and flowers.

Fazi Battaglia Verdicchio dei Castelli di Jesi Classico | 2004 | MARCHE

★★ $ Round but lively citrus and almond flavors characterize this enjoyable wine; a beautiful introduction to Verdicchio.

Lungarotti Torre di Giano Bianco di Torgiano | 2004 | UMBRIA

★★ $ Fresh ripe autumn apple flavors get a kick of spice and an uplifting zing from vibrant acidity.

Palazzone Terre Vineate Orvieto Classico | 2005 | UMBRIA

★★ $ If only all basic Orvieto was so good, full of lemon-lime, floral and almond flavors and fresh acidity. Try Palazzone's stunning Campo del Guardiano for more complexity.

Podere il Caio Grechetto | 2004 | UMBRIA

★ $ Light in body, this white shows simple and lovely lime flavors underscored by notes of wild herbs.

Sartarelli Verdicchio dei Castelli di Jesi Classico | 2004 | MARCHE

★★ $ Wines from Sartarelli are stellar at every price tier. This finely tailored Verdicchio is bursting with flavors of juicy citrus, cherry, toasted nuts and subtle stone.

Villa Bucci Riserva Verdicchio dei Castelli di Jesi Classico | 2003 | MARCHE

★★★ $ $ $ Despite the hot 2003 vintage, the masterful hands at Bucci made a beautifully balanced wine with juicy pineapple, lemon curd and intense stone flavors.

other central italian reds

Central Italy is full of simple, Sangiovese-based, Tuscan-styled wines. The most distinctive reds are Le Marche's Rosso Cònero and Umbria's Sagrantino di Montefalco. Rosso Cònero is a blend of Montepulciano and Sangiovese which yields plush, berry-flavored wines. Rosso Piceno, also from Le Marche, is similar but slightly less impressive. Sagrantino di Montefalco is a dark, brooding wine from a small corner of Umbria. Because of limited supply, it tends to be expensive. Montepulciano d'Abruzzo has long been responsible for a lot of basic table wine. It's normally pleasant, with cherry and berry flavors but some superior examples are velvety smooth, with earthy berry flavors.

BEST PAIRINGS Simple Montepulciano are perfect party wines, and good with chicken. Pour Riserva wines, either Montepulciano d'Abruzzo or Rosso Cònero, with braised lamb or beef stews. Montefalco are made for steak.

other central italian red recommendations

Arnaldo-Caprai Rosso Montefalco | 2003 | UMBRIA
★★ $ $ Sangiovese-based blend with a complex weave of bitter and sweet spice flavors augmented by cherry and minerals. For more power try Arnaldo-Caprai's Collepiano bottling.

Binomio Montepulciano d'Abruzzo | 2002 | ABRUZZI
★★★ $ $ $ This rustic and sophisticated Montepulciano has a depth that many others lack; it's savory, smoky and serious with herb, meat and roast tomato flavors. Drink in 2–15 years.

Cantina dell'Alunno Sagrantino di Montefalco | 2001 | UMBRIA
★★★ $ $ $ Robust wine full of black fruit, minerals, coffee and spice flavors wrapped up in thick tannin. Drink in 2–15 years.

Castello di Corbara Cabernet Sauvignon Lago di Corbara | 2003 | UMBRIA
★★ $ $ Some lament the presence of Bordeaux grapes in Umbria, but it's hard not to enjoy the unique herb and spice flavors that the region adds to Cabernet's standard red fruit flavors.

111

Colli Ripani Centauro Ripano Sangiovese | 2004 | MARCHE
★★ $ Juicy cherry-filled, smoky wine perfect for barbecue.

Falesco Montiano | 2001 | LAZIO
★★★ $ $ $ One of the more serious wines from the Lazio region, this is smooth with sweet spice notes and chocolaty berry flavors. Drink now–10 years.

Fattoria La Valentina Spelt Montepulciano d'Abruzzo
| 2001 | ABRUZZI
★★★ $ $ From the same producer who makes the famed Binomio wine, this isn't as complex but has plenty of fine minerals and dark berries and costs half the price. Drink now–10 years.

Il Brecciarolo Rosso Piceno Superiore | 2002 | MARCHE
★★ $ Well-priced earthy, spicy, dark berry–flavored red.

Il Feuduccio Ursonia Montepulciano d'Abruzzo | 2000 |
ABRUZZI
★★★ $ $ $ Satiny-smooth wine with ripe cherry and berry flavors on a bed of polished minerals. Drink now–10 years.

Lungarotti Vigna Monticchio Rubesco Riserva Torgiano
| 2000 | UMBRIA
★★★★ $ $ $ $ Outstanding sun-drenched wine full of spicy, earthy fruit flavors tempered by mineral notes. Drink now–15 years.

Moroder Rosso Conero | 2003 | MARCHE
★★ $ $ Bright cherry flavors give immediate, simple pleasure. Black olive, spice and smoky mineral notes add complexity.

Nicodemi Notàri Montepulciano d'Abruzzo | 2003 | ABRUZZI
★★★ $ $ An exuberant wine with flavors of blackberries, peach, flowers and spice held together with fine tannin. Drink now–4 years.

Podere il Caio | 2004 | UMBRIA
★★ $ This is a fun, affordable wine to have around; full of sassy crushed berry flavors with hints of violets.

Poggio Bertaio Stucchio Sangiovese | 2001 | UMBRIA
★★ $ $ In the right hands, Sangiovese can make great wine outside of Tuscany, too, as this smoky, berry, herb- and cumin-scented wine demonstrates. Drink now–4 years.

**Tenuta Cocci Grifoni Vigna Messieri Rosso Piceno
Superiore** | 2001 | MARCHE
★★★★ $ $ Far superior than most, this Rosso Piceno is smoky, earthy, with camphor flavors and dark fruit. Drink now–10 years.

southern italy

The abundant sunshine in southern Italy is a blessing and a curse. It easily ripens grapes but can wither balancing acidity. With improved technology, like temperature-controlled fermentation, and more careful attention paid to vineyards, wine quality in Italy's southern regions is soaring.

- **APULIA** Italy's largest producer, Apulia is responsible for an abundance of bulk wine that will never be exported to the American market. The region is capable of better wine, particularly the spicy, Negroamaro-based wines from Salice Salentino and Copertino. The Primitivo grape grown here is a relative of California's Zinfandel grape; the finest come from Manduria and exhibit a bold, fruity taste profile.
- **BASILICATA** Basilicata's Aglianico-based wines are among Italy's most enchanting reds. The vineyards are planted near the Monte Vulture volcano, and the wines express a unique minerality in addition to their floral spice flavors. Tannic versions require a few years of age.
- **CALABRIA** Italy's toe makes loads of wine, but little of it is high quality. Notable exceptions include the earth- and cherry-flavored Gaglioppo-based wines from Cirò.
- **CAMPANIA** Falanghina is Campania's most important white. The almond- and honey-scented Fiano d'Avellino and floral Greco di Tufo also earn praise. The increasingly popluar Aglianico-based wines of Taurasi are bold and sweetly spiced; they are the region's finest reds.
- **SICILY & SARDINIA** Ambitious vintners are using Sicily's indigenous grape varieties to make impressive wines. Spicy reds from Nero d'Avola and Frappatto show promise, as well as the brisk, citrusy whites from Catarratto and Grillo grapes. Merlot, Cabernet Sauvignon and Chardonnay also make graceful wines here. Sardinia's sometimes tart, sometimes tropical-tasting Vermentino is its best-known white. You will find smooth-textured, spicy red wines made from Cannonau (Grenache) and Carignano (Carignane), plus light and fruity wines from the Monica grape.

Pairing Southern Italian Wines

Greco di Tufo is a good match for spaghetti with seafood. Serve Fiano di Avellino with chicken, and Falanghina with meaty fish. Citrusy Vermentino is great with raw shellfish or grilled fish in a butter sauce. Serve Sardinian reds and full-bodied Aglianico-based wines with braised lamb. Pair Primitivo wines with kebabs or spiced stews. Simple Sicilian Nero d'Avola is perfect with deli sandwiches.

southern italian whites

Falanghina, Fiano di Avellino and Greco di Tufo are three important and distinct southern Italian whites gaining favor today, though Sardinian Vermentino and some Sicilian offerings definitely hold their own.

southern italian white recommendations

Abbazia Santa Anastasia Sinestesìa | 2004 | SICILY
★★★ $ $ $ This bottle's Art Nouveau label is as charming and original as the light peach-, flower- and spice-flavored wine itself.

Argiolas Is Argiolas Vermentino di Sardegna | 2004 | SARDINIA
★★★ $ $ An excellent Vermentino that lavishes with tropical and citrus flavors enlivened by abundant mineral notes.

Baglio di Pianetto Ficiligno | 2004 | SICILY
★★ $ $ Flavors of smoky minerals, lemon and tart cherry make this wine ideal for grilled fish.

Colosi | 2005 | SICILY
★ $ Straightforward, simple and versatile white for the price.

Feudi di San Gregorio Falanghina Sannio | 2004 | CAMPANIA
★★★ $ $ This producer sets the benchmark for Falanghina. Dark, volcanic soils impart rare mineral flavors that envelop a bouquet of citrus, peach and wild strawberry.

Mastroberardino Nova Serra Greco di Tufo | 2004 | CAMPANIA
★★★ $ $ Fragrant floral aromatics give way to flavors of luscious apple, apricot and mineral flavors.

Metiusco Salento | 2004 | **Apulia**
★★★ $ $ Dried orange peel and papaya flavors come together with a squeeze of lemon and abundant salty, peppery herb notes in this savory, uniquely delicious wine.

Mirabile Insolia | 2004 | SICILY
★★ $ Smooth and savory, this wine's tarnished ripe pear and lemon flavors are polished by minerals.

Planeta La Segreta | 2005 | SICILY
★★ $ $ A widely known Sicilian producer crafts this aromatic white; its tart grassy flavors resemble Sauvignon Blanc and its lush texture recalls Chardonnay.

Poderi Foglia Concabianco Roccamonfina | 2004 |
CAMPANIA
★★★ $ $ $ Minerals are the defining feature here, softened by apples, exotic flowers and fruit.

Santadi Cala Silente Vermentino di Sardegna | 2004 |
SARDINIA
★★ $ $ Tropical fruit flavors like mango and pineapple mark this sun-kissed Sardinian white.

Santa Maria La Palma Aragosta Vermentino di Sardegna
| 2004 | SARDINIA
★ $ Light-bodied and aromatic, this Vermentino provides refreshing summer drinking with wispy flavors of citrus and minerals.

Scilio Rubé | 2004 | SICILY
★★ $ $ Made from the indigenous Sicilian grapes Carricante and Catarratto, this lime- and almond-scented wine offers uncommon and enjoyable drinking.

Terredora Di Paolo Terre di Dora Fiano di Avellino | 2005 |
CAMPANIA
★★ $ $ Smoky minerals provide a grounding base for expressive flavors of flowers, lime, honeyed nuts and herbs.

southern italian reds

From simple, juicy quaffers to profound, spice-infused wines suitable for long aging, southern Italian reds are made from many different grape varieties not seen elsewhere. They provide abundant opportunities for discovery no matter what the occasion.

southern italian red recommendations

Abbazia Santa Anastasia Montenero | 2002 | SICILY
★★★ $ $ $ Nero d'Avola is blended with Cabernet and Merlot to yield this distinctive red, full of peppery berry flavors with exciting herbal twists. Drink now–10 years.

Albarossa Salice Salentino | 2003 | APULIA
★★ $ Strawberry flavors have an ashen edge in this simple but graceful wine.

A Mano Primitivo | 2003 | APULIA
★★ $ Primitivo's family resemblance to Zinfandel shows in this spice-scented, red berry–laden, moderately tannic wine.

Argiolas Turriga Isola dei Nuraghi | 2001 | SARDINIA
★★★ $ $ $ $ An ambitious wine that achieves true splendor, with berry, animal and spice flavors firmed by tannin. Drink in 2–12 years.

Ca'ntele Riserva Salice Salentino | 2002 | APULIA
★★ $ Robust berry and black tea flavors, plus fine minerals beg for barbecue lamb. Drink now–5 years.

Colosi | 2004 | SICILY
★ $ One of Sicily's bargains, full of tasty red berry and herb flavors.

Contini Nieddera Valle del Tirso | 2003 | SARDINIA
★★ $ $ A chewy mouthful of dried cherry, roasted meat and spice. Drink now–3 years.

Cusumano Benuara Nero d'Avola/Syrah | 2004 | SICILY
★★ $ This fun, juicy wine is full of crushed strawberry, light pepper and chocolate flavors.

Feudi di San Marzano Sessantanni Old Vines Primitivo di Manduria | 2003 | APULIA
★★★ $ $ $ From volcanic, mineral soils this black wine oozes with blackberry, bitter chocolate and smoke flavors. Drink now–8 years.

Mandra Rossa Nero d'Avola | 2004 | SICILY
★ $ A soft, easy-to-appreciate introduction to Nero d'Avola, with ripe berry flavors and a bit of spice.

Mastroberardino Radici Riserva Taurasi | 1999 | CAMPANIA
★★★★ $ $ $ $ This gargantuan red is finely detailed in fragrance, expressing the terroir of Taurasi with flavors of dense black fruit, coal, flowers and spice. Drink now–15 years.

Michele Laluce Zimberno Aglianico del Vulture | 2003 |
BASILICATA
★★★ $ $ Despite near-infernal temperatures in 2003, this wine is
still fresh, with peppery red berry flavors and fine minerals.

Orphéus Etna | 1999 | SICILY
★★★★ $ $ Indigenous Sicilian grape varieties grown on the slopes
of Mt. Etna exude black fruit, dry spice, chocolate and nut flavors in
this intriguing wine. Drink now–10 years.

Saia Nero d'Avola | 2003 | SICILY
★★★ $ $ $ Compelling, dense Nero d'Avola with sultry flavors of
black fruit infused with animal aromas. Drink in 1–8 years.

Santadi Terre Brune Carignano del Sulcis Superiore
| 2001 | SARDINIA
★★★★ $ $ $ $ One of southern Italy's most compelling wines,
Terre Brune combines sophistication and soulfulness. Full-bodied,
this brims with berry, animal and spice flavors. Drink now–12 years.

Sella & Mosca Riserva Cannonau di Sardegna | 2002 |
SARDINIA
★★★ $ Elegant but accessible; tart red berry flavors and rustic herb
and spice notes are upheld by vibrant acidity. Drink now–8 years.

Shardana Valli di Porto Pino | 2000 | SARDINIA
★★★ $ $ $ This "Super-Sardinian" tastes wild, with flavors of herb
oil, berries, lanolin and pine. Drink now–10 years.

Tasca d'Almerita Rosso del Conte Contea di Sclafani
| 2002 | SICILY
★★★★ $ $ $ An impressive wine that pairs the power of California
Cabernet, the finesse of Burgundy and the rustic flavors of Sicily.

Taurino Notarpanaro Salento | 1999 | APULIA
★★★ $ $ One can almost taste the volcanic hillside in this stunning
wine. Wild berry and flower flavors round out this surprisingly lithe
red. Drink now–10 years.

Terra dei Re Divinus Aglianico del Vulture | 2001 |
BASILICATA
★★★ $ $ $ A superb Aglianico overflowing with blackberry flavors
highlighted by ash, exotic spice and minerals. Drink now–10 years.

Torre Quarto Bottaccia Nero di Troia | 2004 | APULIA
★★★ $ $ Charmingly seductive, this well-endowed wine explodes
with enticing floral and berry flavors. Drink now–5 years.

spain

Few wine scenes are as thrilling as the one in Spain. Though Spain has more land under vine than any other country, until a decade ago, most Spanish wines were unremarkable, with the exception of some famous Rioja and the fortified wines of Jerez. But careful viticulture, talented winemaking and vintner innovation in many regions throughout the country have resulted in superb red and white wines that have thrust Spain into the international spotlight.

Bay of Biscay

Rías Baixas

Bierzo

Rioja

Navarra

Somontano

BARCELONA

Toro

Ribera del Duero

Priorat

Penedès

Rueda

Calatayud

MADRID ☆

Portugal

Spain

Utiel-Requena

VALENCIA

Ribera del Guadiana

La Mancha

Jumilla

Alicante

Mediterranean Sea

• SEVILLE

Jerez

Málaga

Atlantic Ocean

■ Principal Wine Region

Spain: An Overview

Rioja in the north and Jerez in the south are Spain's best-known regions. (For the fortified wines of Jerez, see p. 272.) Catalonia contains the plains of Penedès, responsible for fine sparkling and still wines, and the hillside vineyards of Priorat, which produce robust reds. Along the Duero River, southwest of Rioja, is Ribera del Duero, a region currently yielding some of Spain's most elegant reds. Rueda is a land of snappy whites, and Bierzo is known for minerally whites and bold reds. Albariño-based whites are made in Rías Baixas. Regions in Spain's great central plain are converting from bulk to fine wine production. Look for wines from La Mancha, Valdepeñas, Jumilla and Ribera del Guadiana.

Spanish Wine Labels

Spanish wines are labeled by region. Spain's system for designating wines is called the *Denominación de Origen* (DO) and it regulates grape varieties, harvest yields and techniques. Some regions include the name of the grape variety on the label, as well as a word like "Joven," "Crianza" or "Reserva," which indicates how long the wines have been aged in oak barrels. Laws regulating terms regarding length of age before release vary by region, though some vintners choose not to mention how long their wines have aged.

rioja

Rioja is best known for reds aged for years in oak. These wines still exist, yet many wineries are now vinifying wines differently and aging them less in order to emphasize fruit flavors. Until the last half of the 19th century, Rioja's white wines were more respected than its reds. Traditional whites were nutty and golden with baked fruit flavors; today, most are fresher, though traditional wines are worth seeking out. Look also for Rioja's dry, juicy *rosados* (rosés).

Rioja Grapes & Styles

Tempranillo is the dominant grape in Rioja. It's normally blended with Garnacha (Grenache), Cabernet Sauvignon or other local varieties, and aged in American oak, which imparts coconut and vanilla flavors. Rioja reds are given designations based on age before release. Joven wines spend little or no time in oak barrels; Crianza reds must be aged two years, one in barrel. Reservas require three years total, one in oak; Gran Reservas, five years total, two in oak. Many winemakers now believe that long aging in oak will compromise fruit flavors, and are making superb-quality wines without long oak aging. Sometimes referred to as *alta expresión* (or high expression), they are characterized by fresh, bold flavors. Rioja's *rosado* (rosé) wines are dry with appealing orange and berry flavors. Rioja whites, from Viura, Malvasia and Garnacha Blanca, are refreshing wines with apple and citrus flavors. A few vintners still make traditional, long-aged whites, with flavors of orange peel, herb and intense minerality.

Pairing Rioja Wines

Steamed mussels and pan-fried trout are perfect for fresh white Rioja. Aged whites have the weight for roast pork and flavorful cheeses. Match elegant Rioja reds according to age designations: Jovens are barbecue wines; Crianzas are delicious with lamb stews or grilled pork. Save Reservas and Gran Reservas for roast leg of lamb, ham or steak. Modern-styled Rioja works with prime rib or blue cheese.

---

star producers
rioja

best value
1 Bodegas Montecillo
2 El Coto
3 Marqués de Cáceres
4 Martínez Bujanda
5 Ramón Bilbao

best of the best
1 Bodegas Muga
2 Bodegas Roda
3 Cune
4 Marqués de Murrieta
5 R. López de Heredia

rioja recommendations

WHITES

Bodegas Bretón Loriñon | 2004 |

★★★ $ Oak-barrel aging brings exotic cinnamon and clove flavors to a stone-lined pool of apple and grapefruit.

Marqués de Cáceres | 2005 |

★ $ Served very cold, the cornucopia of fruit flavors here offer the perfect refreshment for a hot summer day.

Montecillo | 2004 |

★★ $ Grassy lemon and orange flavors make a lovely impression.

R. López de Heredia Viña Tondonia Reserva | 1988 |

★★★★ $ $ $ One of Rioja's most traditional houses proves the worth of old-style, oxidized whites, full of dried fruit, mineral and spice, with remarkably fresh acidity for its age. Drink now–15 years.

ROSÉS

El Coto Rosé | 2005 |

★★ $ Cherry and spice give interesting twists to pineapple flavors.

Marqués de Cáceres Rosé | 2005 |

★ $ Tart strawberry and ripe cherry flavors make a pretty pour.

REDS

Alba de Bretón | 2001 |

★★★★ $ $ $ $ Stunning wine made from vines over eighty years old. Fine mineral flavors bring elegance to dense, dark berry and spice flavors. Drink now–15 years.

Allende | 2003 |

★★★ $ $ Well-made, modern-style Rioja provides terrific value with smooth berry, tobacco and mineral flavors. Drink now–6 years.

Baron de Ley Finca Monasterio | 2003 |

★★★ $ $ $ Oddly appealing barnyard flavors make this velvety, smoky, blackberry-flavored wine compelling. Drink now–12 years.

Conde de Valdemar Gran Reserva | 1997 |

★★★ $ $ $ Though 1997 was not a "grand" year for Rioja, this wine-maker managed to produce a fine smoky, leathery, berry-laden wine.

El Coto Crianza | 2003 |

★ $ A kiss of oak gives a little spice to this lively, medium-bodied, berry-flavored wine.

Faustino V Reserva | 2000 |
★★ $ $ Old-fashioned, and better for it, this is earthy, smoky and full of tart, spicy red cherry flavors. Drink now–6 years.

Marqués de Cáceres Reserva | 2000 |
★★ $ $ Reliability at a high level, this red has the cherry and coconut cream flavors that made Rioja so popular. Drink now–8 years.

Ostatu Reserva | 2001 |
★★★ $ $ $ Elegant but earthy cherry and bitter chocolate flavors with hints of chalk from limestone-rich soils. Drink now–10 years.

R. López de Heredia Viña Tondonia Reserva | 1998 |
★★★ $ $ $ This Rioja wears the elegant tarnish of time on top of flavors of tart cherry, spice, leather and stone. Drink now–15 years.

San Vicente Tempranillo | 2002 |
★★★ $ $ $ Tempranillo's lusty splendor is on full display in this oak- and spice-laden, berry-saturated wine. Drink in 2–10 years.

Seis de Luberri | 2004 |
★★ $ $ Rioja on the fresh side. Exuberant berry, maple and spice flavors make this a perfect barbecue wine.

Señorío de Cuzcurrita | 2001 |
★★★ $ $ $ Aromas of violets and piquant cinnamon infuse ashy and delicious black cherry flavors. Drink now–12 years.

Valsacro | 2001 |
★★★ $ $ $ Old meets new in this beautiful wine, where red berry flavors combine with coconut-tinged, spicy oak. Drink now–10 years.

Viña Ijalba Graciano | 2001 |
★★★ $ $ The Graciano grape goes it alone in this esoteric wine full of intriguing spicy, grapey flavors.

ribera del duero

For decades, Ribera del Duero was known for a single wine only: Vega Sicilia's Unico, one of Spain's most legendary and most expensive bottlings. This all changed in the early 1980s, however, when the innovative Alejandro Fernández produced the critically acclaimed Pesquera, a wine whose success generated tremendous interest in the region. Today, Ribera del Duero is one of Spain's hottest regions.

Ribera del Duero Grapes & Styles
Ribera del Duero reds are mostly made from Tinto Fino, a local variant of Tempranillo, and some Bordeaux varieties. Similar to Rioja, they are more intense and less oaky.

Pairing Ribera del Duero Wines
Robust foods are the most appropriate partners for the red wines of Ribera del Duero. Winter stews, braised meats or thick sirloins are ideal fare.

ribera del duero recommendations

Alenza Gran Reserva | 1999 |
★★★★ $ $ $ $ Alejandro Fernández's mastery of the region comes through in this fabulous wine, packed with dark fruit, spice, herb, mushroom and profound mineral flavors. Drink now–20 years.

Alitus Reserva | 1999 |
★★★ $ $ $ $ Ripe cherry flavors are accented by spicy leather and earth in a noble, full-bodied, tannic wine. Drink in 1–15 years.

Emilio Moro | 2004 |
★★ $ $ $ This shows exuberance of youth with energetic berry and spice flavors ready to be enjoyed right away.

Montecastro | 2003 |
★★★ $ $ $ Robust yet restrained red, with berry, spice and brown sugar flavors framed by tannin and minerals. Drink in 1–10 years.

Pesquera Crianza | 2003 |
★★★ $ $ $ Pesquera ignited Ribera del Duero's renaissance; this is classic and sultry with fruit, spice and leather. Drink in 1–12 years.

Viña Sastre Pago de Santa Cruz | 2001 |
★★★ $ $ $ Red cherries are lavished by coconut cream flavors and sweet spice in this unmistakably Spanish wine. Drink now–15 years.

catalonia

Aside from the sparkling Cavas of Penedès (see p. 269), Catalonian wines were virtually ignored for centuries. They get attention today for full-bodied reds from Priorat, Montsant and Costers del Segre and blends from Somontano.

Catalonia Grapes & Styles

Catalonia is largely planted with Grenache, called *Garnatxa* in Catalan, *Garnacha* in Spanish. It composes the heart of Priorat's full-bodied reds and is the basis of reds from most subregions. As fine winemaking is new to Catalonia, its vintners are experimenting with international grapes like Cabernet, Merlot and Syrah. Garnacha Blanca makes nutty whites here. Local grapes Macabeo, Parellada and Xarel-lo make many generic and some fine whites and Cavas.

Pairing Catalonia Wines

Penedès whites are light, with mineral flavors—delicious with a wide range of fish dishes. Penedès Muscat is one of the few wines that works with asparagus. Turn to fuller-bodied whites such as those from Priorat when serving richer dishes like scallops or lobster. Reds from Penedès and Somontano are especially fine with lamb burgers or filet mignon. Powerful Priorat, Costers and Montsant demand hearty foods such as braised oxtails or lamb shanks.

catalonia recommendations

WHITES

Can Feixes Chardonnay | 2001 | **PENEDÈS**
★★ $ $ $ Well-executed Chardonnay from the land where Cava reigns, this is lightly oaked with spicy apple and citrus flavors.

René Barbier Mediterranean White | NV | **CATALONIA**
★ $ Breezy and light with charming citrus flavors.

Segura Viudas Creu de Lavit Xarel-lo | 2004 | **PENEDÈS**
★★ $ Enticing speckled pear and heirloom apple flavors are given a lively squeeze of lemon.

Torres Viña Sol | 2005 | **PENEDÈS**
★★ $ Fresh floral and lemon-lime flavors provide a delicious, light-bodied dose of sunshine.

ROSÉS

Buil & Giné Giné Rosat | 2005 | **PRIORAT**
★★★ $ $ Pink Priorat is lovely to look at, but even better to taste: this has peach, apricot and berry flavors underlaid by minerals.

Fra Guerau Rosé | 2005 | MONTSANT
★★ $ Dry but juicy orange, raspberry and spice flavors with firming minerals make a mouthwatering aperitif.

REDS

Alquézar Moristel | 2004 | SOMONTANO
★★ $ Young and spicy, this Moristel-based wine offers fun, novel drinking for your next barbecue.

Buil & Giné Pleret | 2003 | PRIORAT
★★★★ $ $ $ $ Seductive from the first sip, this entrances with fresh berry flavors, hints of minerals and spice. Drink now–15 years.

Can Blau | 2004 | MONTSANT
★★★ $ $ Smoky, spicy Montsant that veers toward the powerful style of neighboring Priorat, but with softer tannin and a softer price.

Francesc S. Bas Cellars de la Cartoixa Montgarnatx | 2002 | PRIORAT
★★★ $ $ $ Grenache with a bit of Carignane yields this medium-bodied beauty which expresses vibrant red fruit flavors, with details of violet and stone. Drink now–8 years.

Mas Estela Quindals | 2004 | EMPORDÀ
★★ $ $ A mighty red with fresh berry, spice and floral flavors.

Mas Marçal | 2004 | CATALONIA
★★ $ A delicious taste of Catalonia for a low price: nine bucks buys juicy cherry and stone flavors.

Melis | 2004 | PRIORAT
★★★ $ $ $ $ Superlative first vintage for this American/Spanish collaboration; old vines bring rich earth and stone-laden balance to luscious berry and spice flavors. Drink now–8 years.

Pasanau Finca La Planeta | 2002 | PRIORAT
★★★ $ $ $ Cabernet's peppery berry flavors are joined by earth and spice from old-vine Garnacha in this blend. Drink now–10 years.

Rotllan Torra Amadís | 2002 | PRIORAT
★★★★ $ $ $ $ Evidence of Priorat's grand reputation; this shows powerful berry, smoky minerals and tobacco. Drink in 1–10 years.

Segura Viudas Mas d'Aranyó Tempranillo Reserva | 2001 | PENEDÈS
★★ $ Luscious red berry and vanilla flavors provide a wonderful and affordable introduction to Spanish wine.

other spanish regions

Navarra has a spotty past, but its vintners are working hard to restore its good name. West of Ribera del Duero are Toro, known for bold reds; Rueda, known for snappy, aromatic whites; and Bierzo, known for fruity, structured wines. In Valencia, Utiel-Requena, Jumilla, Yecla and Alicante, vintners are moving away from bulk wine production and are making better wines. The same can be said for Valdepeñas, Ribera del Guadiana and La Mancha. The coastal region of Galicia is home to the Albariños of Rías Baixas.

Other Spanish Grapes & Styles

Spain's affinity for hearty reds continues throughout the country. Wines from La Mancha, Valdepeñas and Ribera del Guadiana can be full-bodied and graceful, made with the standard Spanish mix of grapes. Garnacha dominates in Navarra, but is sometimes blended with Tempranillo and Cabernet Sauvignon. Its dry rosados are considered among the best from Spain. Toro reds are similar to Ribera del Duero, though more concentrated. Wines from Bierzo are denser, made from Mencía. In eastern regions, Monastrell (Mourvèdre in French) rules, joined by Garnacha and the funky Bobal grape—a blend that results in black, brooding reds. Albariño provides the basis for the whites of Rías Baixas. Rueda's whites are made primarily from the Verdejo grape, augmented often by Sauvignon Blanc.

Pairing Other Spanish Wines

Albariño is good for seafood stews, seared scallops and lobster. Rueda whites have an herbal edge that makes them a match for herb-stuffed chicken breasts or spinach and goat cheese salads. Pair reds from central and eastern Spain with paella or cheeses. Serve Bierzo or Toro reds with braised pork or venison. Berry-flavored Navarra rosados are ideal with dried sausages and roast beef.

other spanish recommendations

WHITES

Bodegas Campante Gran Reboreda | 2005 | **RIBEIRO**
★★★ $ $ Made from indigenous grape varieties, this engaging wine offers a unique combination of pineapple, peach and aloe flavors.

Buil & Giné Nosis Verdejo | 2005 | **RUEDA**
★★★ $ $ Fresh as cut grass, this starts off green and lemony and finishes with flavors of peach.

Garciarevalo Casamaro | 2005 | **RUEDA**
★ $ Easy-to-enjoy summer wine; its citrus and peach flavors show their best served very cold.

Morgadío Albariño | 2005 | **RÍAS BAIXAS**
★★★ $ $ Albariño's succulence is rarely so well expressed as this; satiny-smooth and smoky with tropical fruit and peach flavors.

Naiades Verdejo | 2004 | **RUEDA**
★★★ $ $ $ Vines from the 19th century yield a special, historic wine, rich with minerals, ripe citrus, melon and pear flavors.

Nora da Neve | 2004 | **RÍAS BAIXAS**
★★★ $ $ $ Weighty, smoky wine, this combines spicy pear, peach and salty mineral flavors with rare sophistication.

Palacio de Fefiñanes Albariño | 2004 | **RÍAS BAIXAS**
★★ $ $ So light it's almost effervescent, this Rías Baixas resembles Portugal's delightful Vinho Verde. It's made for shellfish.

Txomin Etxaniz | 2005 | **GETARIAKO TXAKOLINA**
★★ $ $ Sensational wine easier to enjoy than it is to pronounce, this is loaded with crisp apple and lime zest flavors.

Valmiñor Albariño | 2004 | **RÍAS BAIXAS**
★★ $ $ One can practically taste Galicia's briny ocean breezes in this mineral-laden, lemon- and pear-scented wine.

Viñedos de Nieva Pasil Pie Franco Verdejo | 2004 | **RUEDA**
★★ $ Ripe Asian pear and dried apricot notes are given a firming frame of acidity and an appealing, bitter minerality.

ROSÉS

Vega Sindoa Rosé | 2005 | **NAVARRA**
★★ $ Delightful, full-flavored rosé with chewy texture and packed with berry and orange flavors.

REDS

Aranleón Solo | 2003 | UTIEL-REQUENA
★★ $ $ Familiar grapes Tempranillo and Syrah soften the funk of
local variety Bobal in this exuberant, full-bodied blend.

Bodegas Gutiérrez de la Vega Viña Ulises Crianza | 2002 |
ALICANTE
★★ $ $ Lusty wine from an area known more for beaches than wine,
this is saturated with mixed red berry and spice, plus firm tannin.

Cadiz Monastrell/Cabernet | 2003 | VALENCIA
★★★ $ $ Perhaps Valencia's finest wine, this oozes hedonistic ripe
berry and lanolin flavors accented by smoke. Drink now–6 years.

Casa Castillo Monastrell | 2005 | JUMILLA
★★ $ One of Jumilla's best producers makes this vibrant, fresh
expression of wild dark berry and spice.

Cenit Crianza | 2005 | TIERRA DEL VINO DE ZAMORA
★★★ $ $ $ From just outside Toro, this wine's smoky berry and
earthy flavors make it among the region's best. Drink in 1–8 years.

Dehesa La Granja Selección | 2000 |
TIERRA DEL VINO DE ZAMORA
★★★ $ $ $ This epic, smoke- and coffee-saturated wine shows
concentrated berries, licorice and lots of tannin. Drink in 3–20 years.

Dominio de Tares Bembibre | 2003 | BIERZO
★★★★ $ $ $ Bierzo proves itself as one of Spain's great wine
regions with this example; dark berry, cola and coffee flavors ooze
over a base of pure stone. Drink now–10 years.

El Nido | 2003 | JUMILLA
★★★★ $ $ $ $ Jumilla will get lots of attention for wines like this
massive, international-styled and outstanding Cabernet/Monastrell
blend. Drink now–10 years.

Finca Sandoval | 2004 | MANCHUELA
★★★★ $ $ $ Uncommonly delicious, with velvety red berry flavors,
smoky, savory cumin and white pepper notes edged with mineral.
Drink now–10 years.

Marqués de Griñón Petit Verdot | 2002 |
DOMINIO DE VALDEPUSA
★★★ $ $ $ A superior Rioja producer, Griñón works with French
grapes in Valdepusa to make a fine, deeply colored, tannic, blackberry-
and black tea–laden wine. Drink now–10 years.

Pago de Valdoneje Mencia | 2003 | BIERZO

★★ $ A red that provides a terrific low-priced introduction to the wines of Bierzo, with racy wild berry, savory spice and herb flavors for around $10.

Vega Sindoa Cabernet Sauvignon/Tempranillo | 2004 | NAVARRA

★★ $ Cabernet has a long history in the Navarra region, where it is clearly right at home. This peppery, coffee-infused red is brightened by the addition of Tempranillo.

Yonna | 2003 | CAMPO DE BORJA

★★★ $ $ Dense, meaty and concentrated berry flavors accented by nutmeg, clove and vanilla. Drink in 2–12 years.

---

news from a wine insider
spain by Victor de la Serna

The 2005 Vintage Reports

Spain's 2005 harvest took place during the driest year the country has experienced since rainfall was first recorded in 1947. Crops were down by as much as 50 percent, with the exception of Rioja. But the best producers made quality wines in spite of the challenges.

New Wines from Established Stars

One of the most consistent producers in Spain is the Rioja-based Palacios family, who continue to expand their network of high-quality, often biodynamic wine estates throughout the country. One of the newest additions to the Palacios portfolio, "As Sortes," is a dry white wine made from the Godello grape in the Valdeorras region, whose first vintage (2004) received critical acclaim. (Other Palacios labels include L'Ermita and Finca Dofí from Priorat, Corullón from the Bierzo appellation and Palacios Remondo in Rioja.) The Colet family in the Penedès region of Catalonia is achieving cultlike fame with boutique Cavas (see p. 269) that approach the quality of the top small producers in Champagne.

There are also new names in Sherry country (see p. 272) as a handful of ambitious wineries have been acquiring old soleras to craft stunning wines. Labels to look for include Tradición, El Maestro Sierra and Rey Fernando de Castilla.

portugal

Portuguese wines have been celebrated for centuries, but the sweet wines—Port and Madeira—tend to get all the attention. Today, modern facilities and new winemaking techniques have enabled Portugal to make better, cleaner and fresher dry wines from the country's wide array of indigenous grape varieties.

Vinho Verde

PORTO

Douro

Atlantic Ocean

Bairrada

Dão

Beiras

Estremadura

Ribatejo

Bucelas

LISBON ☆

Borba

Evora

Alentejo

Algarve

▨ Principal Wine Region

Portugal: An Overview

The climatically diverse regions of Portugal are home to dozens of unique grape varieties that are rarely seen elsewhere. Vinho Verde, produced in the country's northwest corner, is a light, often slightly effervescent white. The famous Port region of Douro is located along the Douro River near Spain. The region's vintners have recently been focusing on making high-quality dry, brawny reds from some of the same grape varieties that go into their acclaimed sweet wines. The resulting wines are impressive for their quality as well as value. The Bairrada and Dão regions produce firm, spicy reds. Areas around Lisbon such as Estremadura, Ribatejo and Terras do Sado make good-value wines from local and international varieties. There are also interesting reds and whites coming from Alentejo and its subregion Évora to the east.

Portuguese Grapes & Styles

Vinho Verde is one of the most refreshing white wines made anywhere. Most are low in alcohol, high in acid and possess a slight sparkle. For fuller-bodied examples, look for Vinho Verde made from Alvarinho (called Albariño in Spain) and Loureiro grapes. Other regions such as Alentejo, Dão, Douro, Bairrada and Bucelas make some whites that are well worth trying. International grapes such as Merlot and Cabernet Sauvignon have an increasing presence throughout Portugal, but the country's most compelling reds are blends made from local varieties such as Baga, Touriga Franca, Touriga Nacional and Tinta Roriz. Baga is especially important in Bairrada, where vintners use it to make dry and tannic red wines with berry flavors. The best examples can age for a decade or more. Douro reds are made from many of the same grapes as those used to make Port, and although they are dry, most offer the same flavor profile of dark fruit and sweet spice.

Portuguese Wine Labels

Most Portuguese wines found in the U.S. are labeled by region and adhere to the requirements established by the *Denominação de Origem Controlada* (DOC). Wines labeled "Reserva" must be at least half a percent higher in alcohol than the minimum set by DOC rules. Wines with the term "Garrafeira" on the label have been aged for at least two years in tanks or barrels and one more in bottle. Wines labeled by variety must be made from at least 85 percent of the named grape.

portuguese whites

Portugal is a nation of fishermen and explorers, and it boasts a wide range of fish-friendly white wines, from simple, tart Vinho Verde from the north to long-lived, relatively full-bodied whites from Alentejo in the south.

BEST PAIRINGS Pour Vinho Verde at your next clambake or alongside baskets of fried whitebait. Richer Alvarinho-based Vinho Verde is delicious with cod or crab cakes. Whites from other winegrowing regions can be served in place of Chardonnay; try older examples with pork with clams, a unique Portuguese specialty.

portuguese white recommendations

Adega de Monção Muralhas de Monção | 2004 |
VINHO VERDE
★★ **$** Tropical wine with pineapple and green mango flavors spiked with exotic spice and held up by lots of acidity.

Cartuxa | 2003 | **ALENTEJO**
★★★ **$ $** Peach and pear flavors are delicious now, but will become even more interesting with time as they develop mineral and nutty aromas. Drink now–6 years.

Encostas do Lima Medium Dry | 2005 | **VINHO VERDE**
★★ **$** Perfectly constructed Vinho Verde: light, lively and crisp with loads of minerals and ripe apple flavors.

Eugénio de Almeida E.A. | 2003 | **ALENTEJO**
★★ **$** Waxy-textured white with peach and mineral flavors.

Luis Pato Vinha Formal | 2002 | BEIRAS
★★★★ $ $ This could easily be compared to a fine Premier Cru Meursault. Heavy with minerals and flavors of smoky oak, flowers and fruit. Drink now–8 years.

Monte Velho | 2005 | ALENTEJO
★★ $ Fragrant floral notes add depth to a pool of pear and lemon flavors in this plush-textured wine.

Quinta de Cabriz Colheita Seleccionada | 2005 | DÃO
★ $ Serve this pale-colored, light and lemony wine very cold; it is a perfect quaff for warm summer nights.

Reguengo de Melgaço Alvarinho | 2005 | VINHO VERDE
★★ $ $ A ribbon of smoke is woven throughout the tongue-tingling white peach and lemon flavors in this medium-bodied white; mouth-watering acidity keeps it vibrant.

portuguese reds

Portuguese red wines are fascinating yet underappreciated. Many have a rustic charm and are especially appealing for the price. Others have the complexity and grace of some of the world's best reds. They all provide the perfect warm-up to a great bottle of Port at the end of a meal.

BEST PAIRINGS Aromatic, spicy reds such as those from Dão, Bairrada, Douro and Ribatejo need full-flavored foods; they are particularly delicious with braised butt of pork or garlicky roast leg of lamb. Wines labeled "Garrafeira" can be high in acid with flavors of earth and smoke; pair them with roast duck or suckling pig. Simple under-$10 reds are made for casual drinking with grilled sausages or burgers.

portuguese red recommendations

Campo Ardosa | 2003 | DOURO
★★★ $ $ $ Elegant red berry flavors, intense minerality and a Port-like spiciness mark this delicious wine. Drink in 2–15 years.

Casa dos Zagalos Reserva | 2002 | ALENTEJO
★★★ $ $ Impressive, full-bodied red with plush blackberry and spice flavors burnished by notes of lanolin and abundant minerals. Drink now–8 years.

Casa Ermelinda Freitas Dona Ermelinda | 2004 | PALMELA
★★ $ Good, cheap, full-bodied red wine with a spicy edge.

Casa Ferreirinha Reserva | 1996 | DOURO
★★★ $ $ $ $ Ten years of age have done good things to this wine, bringing a seductive smokiness to red fruit flavors and adding hints of leather. Drink now–5 years.

Casa Santos Lima Palha-Canas | 2004 | ESTREMADURA
★★ $ Fresh and fragrant, this tart, dark, berry-laden wine is alive with fresh herbs and dried flowers and spice.

Cortes de Cima | 2001 | ALENTEJO
★★ $ $ French and Portuguese varieties are seamlessly blended in this lean, astringent wine with tasty berry and spice flavors.

---

news from a wine insider
portugal by Jamie Goode

The Vintage Report

Portugal's winemakers have experienced a string of challenging vintages. Like most of Europe, Portugal had a wet summer in 2002, and then a torrid 2003. While the Alentejo region did relatively well in 2002, it was a difficult vintage for the Douro. Fortunately, most Douro vintners were able to produce much better wines in 2003 and both regions were blessed with a favorable 2004 vintage. Wines from the 2005 vintage are evolving beautifully, although yields were down as a result of a terrible drought.

Notable New Winemakers

In the Alentejo region, top vintners like Mouchão, Cortes de Cima, Quinta do Mouro, Esporão, Quinta do Carmo and João Portugal Ramos are being joined by newcomers well worth watching such as Herdade Grande, Monte Novo e Figueirinha and Quinta do Zambujeiro. The most thrilling of the Alentejo's new wine-makers is Malhadinha Nova.

In the Douro region, the table wine revolution continues to gain momentum, led by an unofficial consortium of top producers, known as the Douro Boys. Look for the following producers and wines: Niepoort, Quinta do Vale Meão, Quinta do Vale D. Maria, Lavradores de Feitoria, Quinta de Macedos, Chryseia, Quinta de Roriz, Poeira, Quinta de la Rosa, Churchill Estates and Pintas.

Dow Vale do Bomfim Reserva | 2004 | DOURO
★★ $ The Douro is fortunately making more and more wines like this fairly priced, full-bodied red with the berry and spice flavors that any Port lover will recognize.

Frei João Reserva | 2001 | BAIRRADA
★★ $ $ Anti-modernists will be pleased to find this old-fashioned wine: some fruit, some spice and a lot of funky, earthy charm.

Herdade do Esporão Vinha da Defesa | 2003 | ALENTEJO
★★ $ This bargain is plenty lush with ripe berry and spice flavors.

José Maria da Fonseca Periquita | 2002 | TERRAS DO SADO
★ $ Inexpensive, enjoyable wine with tart, earthy red berry flavors and an astringency that makes it particularly food-friendly.

Luis Pato Vinha Barrosa Vinha Velha | 2001 | BEIRAS
★★★★ $ $ $ Exceptional wine made from eighty-year-old vines and full of savory spice, smoky minerals, dark fruit and high acidity. Drink in 2–20 years.

Quinta das Baceladas Single Estate | 2001 | BEIRAS
★★★ $ $ Composed by the famous, jet-setting enologist Michel Rolland, this sophisticated blend of Merlot, Cabernet and local Baga shows dark berries and spice. Drink now–12 years.

Quinta da Terrugem Single Estate | 2001 | ALENTEJO
★★★ $ $ This robust, polished wine is made in an international style, yet still remains firmly rooted in Portugal with a unique array of wild berry, flower and spice notes. Drink now–10 years.

Quinta do Crasto Old Vines Reserva | 2003 | DOURO
★★★★ $ $ $ Savory spice and stone frame concentrated black fruit flavors in this superb, luxurious Douro red. Drink in 2–20 years.

Vértice | 2002 | DOURO
★★★ $ $ Slow-stewed red and dark berry flavors with a big dash of sweet spice and minerals. Drink now–6 years.

germany

German white wines, full of vibrant fruit, intense minerality and zingy acidity, are some of the world's finest. For many years, they were underappreciated in the U.S., but their sales have been increasing, thanks to a more adventurous wine-drinking public, enthusiastic sommeliers and a string of great vintages.

Principal Wine Region

Germany: An Overview

Germany's winegrowing regions are concentrated in the southwest portion of the country. Riesling is the country's most prominent grape, and it appears in different styles that vary significantly from region to region. From the dangerously steep vineyards along the banks of the Mosel River and tributaries Saar and Ruwer come delicate wines with pronounced citrus and mineral flavors. The Rheingau is known for drier, fuller-bodied Rieslings. The hilly country of the Rheinhessen is responsible for many low-quality sweet wines that gave Germany a poor reputation in the international market for decades, but wines from the steep slopes of its Rheinterrassen subregion can be outstanding. The comparatively warm Pfalz, Nahe and Baden regions produce spicier, richer, dry Rieslings, as well as a range of wines from other noble grape varieties, including Pinot Blanc and Pinot Gris. The Franken region is known for bone-dry wines made with the Kerner, Silvaner, Bacchus and Müller-Thurgau grapes, as well as for its distinctive, squat, flat bottles called "bocksbeutel."

German Grapes & Styles

Riesling is Germany's most important grape variety, both in terms of quality and quantity. Wines made with it range from bone-dry to very sweet and nectarlike, though the predominant profile is off-dry. Regardless of sweetness, nearly all Rieslings have engaging minerality and bracing acidity. Müller-Thurgau is Germany's second-most planted grape, but it normally goes into undistinguished blends. A few blends based largely on Silvaner are noteworthy, but Gewürztraminer, Muskateller (Muscat), Grauburgunder (Pinot Gris), Weissburgunder (Pinot Blanc), Bacchus, Kerner and Scheurebe are far more interesting. Germany makes some red wines, generally from Spätburgunder (Pinot Noir) and Dornfelder.

German Wine Labels

Traditional German labels are hard to read. But they are very informative, listing the winery, region, village and some-times the vineyard where the grapes were grown, plus lot and cask numbers. Grapes are usually mentioned, though in some regions, like the Rheingau, Riesling is just assumed.

German wines are classified by quality. Basic, "quality" wine is classified *Qualitätswein bestimmter Anbaugebiete* (QbA), often simply called "Qualitätswein." At a higher level are *Qualitätswein mit Prädikat* (QmP) wines, often called "Prädikatswein." QmP wines are categorized by grape ripe-ness at harvest, from Kabinett to Spätlese, Auslese, Beere-nauslese (BA) and Trockenbeerenauslese (TBA) in ascending order of ripeness. The minimum ripeness for each level is regulated by law.

Here's the tricky part: ripeness does not necessarily indicate a wine's sweetness. Depending on the balance between acidity and sugar, or how much sugar was allowed to ferment into alcohol, a Kabinett can taste sweeter than an Auslese. Some vintners put *trocken* (dry) or *halbtrocken* on their labels to indicate that the wine is dry. "Spätlese trocken," for example, means the wine is dry and made from grapes harvested at Spätlese levels of ripeness.

From the 2000 vintage forward, a parallel system was established to supposedly simplify matters. Wines that are designated "Classic" and "Selection" are high-quality wines that are theoretically dry.

Pairing German Wines

Off-dry German Rieslings are among the few wines that can take the sting off hot and spicy foods like chili-laden soft shell crabs, or chicken curry. Full-bodied dry versions beautifully accompany meaty fish and are sturdy enough for pork, duck or even venison. The searing acidity of sweet versions is ideal for foie gras. Enjoy Grauburgunder like Alsatian Pinot Gris, with turkey or ham. The spicy flavors of Scheurebe, Muskateller and Gewürztraminer make them good choices for Indian or Thai dishes. Franken's stone-dry wines match well with sole or shrimp.

riesling

For many wine lovers, Riesling is the noblest of all white wine grapes. Germany's cool climate and slate soils make for wines that are full of tropical fruit, citrus and ripe peach flavors held together with vibrant acidity and minerality. Riesling is delightfully fresh in its youth and also has the ability to age well, developing more complex mineral notes—even oddly appealing petrol flavors—over time. The best can last for decades.

riesling recommendations

Artur Steinmann Pastorius Sommerhäuser Steinbach
| 2004 | FRANKEN
★★★ $ $ $ In many ways a minimalist wine with clean minerals and defining acidity, this still possesses round, smoky pineapple and peach flavors. Drink now–10 years.

Baron Knyphausen Estate | 2005 | RHEINGAU
★★ $ Good-quality Rheingau that offers bright apple flavors with touches of ripe pear, lime and stone flavors for a very good price.

Baron von Heyl Estate | 2005 | RHEINHESSEN
★★ $ The Baron shows his sprightly side in this off-dry treat with lively lemon-lime and spice flavors.

Bassermann-Jordan Deidesheimer Paradiesgarten Kabinett | 2005 | PFALZ
★★★ $ $ Delicious full-bodied, off-dry wine, this is a flavor mélange of peach, apple and pear tarts. Drink now–12 years.

C.H. Berres Impulse | 2005 | MOSEL-SAAR-RUWER
★★ $ Easy-drinking, off-dry Riesling, full of summer fruit flavors and bracing acidity.

C.H. Berres Ürziger Würzgarten Kabinett | 2005 |
MOSEL-SAAR-RUWER
★★★ $ $ Loads of spices infuse an off-dry pool of apples and limes. Drink now–8 years.

Christmann Idig | 2004 | PFALZ
★★★★ $ $ $ $ Incredibly luscious, but still dry, this oozes orange and strawberry flavors, sweet spice and mouthwatering minerals. Drink now–20 years.

Dr. Bürklin-Wolf Wachenheimer Rechbächel | 2004 | PFALZ
★★★★ $ $ $ Lovers of outstanding white Burgundy will adore this superb, mineral-laden wine with notes of blanched almond and lemon. Drink now–20 years.

Dr. Thanisch Berncasteler Doctor Spätlese | 2004 |
MOSEL-SAAR-RUWER
★★★★ $ $ $ Exceptional wine from a world-class vineyard, this is profoundly stony, with off-dry lime, orange, truffle and herb flavors. Drink now–25 years.

Fritz Haag | 2004 | MOSEL-SAAR-RUWER
★★ $ $ Vibrant acidity enlivens slightly off-dry flavors of peaches and dried lime.

Georg Breuer Berg Schlossberg | 2004 | RHEINGAU
★★★★ $ $ $ $ The definition of exceptional Rheingau, this is dry, but far from austere, with a wealth of citrus blossom, apple and mango flavors kept firm by profound minerals and searing acidity. Drink now–20 years.

Georg Breuer Charm | 2004 | RHEINGAU
★★ $ $ An affordable entrée to one of Rheingau's best producers, this offers snappy apple, lime peel and mushroomlike earth flavors.

Graff Wehlener Sonnenuhr Kabinett | 2004 |
MOSEL-SAAR-RUWER
★ $ A lovely little off-dry wine with refreshing, white peach-scented flavors of limeade.

Grans-Fassian Trittenheimer Kabinett | 2005 |
MOSEL-SAAR-RUWER
★★★ $ Irresistible tropical fruit flavors of mango, guava and juicy pineapple make for one beautiful Riesling.

star producers
riesling

best value
1 Georg Breuer
2 Lingenfelder
3 Schloss Lieser
4 Selbach
5 Zilliken

best of the best
1 A. Christmann
2 Egon Müller
3 Fritz Haag
4 J.J. Prüm
5 Müller-Catoir

Gunderloch Jean-Baptiste Kabinett | 2005 | RHEINHESSEN
★★ $ $ Sprightly acidity and fresh, spicy peach and pear flavors mark this off-dry gem.

Hexamer Meddersheimer Rheingräfenberg Quarzit | 2005 |
NAHE
★★★ $ $ "Quarzit" on the label hints at the intense stoniness of this wine, but it is also fueled by racy citrus flavors with aromatic floral notes. Drink now–8 years

J. & H.A. Strub Niersteiner Kabinett | 2005 | RHEINHESSEN
★★ $ You'll find plenty of lemon, dry, savory spice and stone flavors in this light and lively wine that comes in a value-priced liter bottle.

Joh. Jos. Prüm Wehlener Sonnenuhr Kabinett | 2004 |
MOSEL-SAAR-RUWER
★★★ $ $ $ For lovers of austere but complex wines, this conjures a plush bouquet of crushed herbs, stone, citrus and smoke. Drink now–20 years.

Karlsmühle Kaseler Nies'chen Kabinett | 2004 |
MOSEL-SAAR-RUWER
★★★ $ $ An excellent Kabinett that tastes surprisingly like baklava, with layer upon layer of delicate flavors ranging from tropical fruit to lime blossom, smoke and truffles with a light dusting of nuts. Drink now–15 years.

Leitz Dragonstone | 2005 | RHEINGAU
★★★ $ $ Succulent peach and raspberry flavors are given a polish of mineral and a squeeze of lime in this terrific, bargain wine. Drink now–5 years.

Loosen Bros. Dr. L | 2005 | MOSEL-SAAR-RUWER
★ $ For casual drinking, simple is often better, as this slightly off-dry, crisp, apple- and lemon-flavored wine illustrates.

Louis Guntrum Oppenheimer Sackträger Spätlese Trocken
| 2004 | RHEINHESSEN
★★★ $ $ $ From Rheinhessen's steep and stony Rheinterrassen subregion comes this smoky, stony, peach- and almond-laden wine. Drink now–10 years.

Matheus Piesporter Goldtröpfchen Kabinett | 2005 |
MOSEL-SAAR-RUWER
★★ $ $ This tastes a bit like pear cider livened up by a squeeze of lime; spicy, off-dry and delicious. Drink now–10 years.

Maximin Grünhäuser Herrenberg Kabinett | 2005 |
MOSEL-SAAR-RUWER

★★★ $ $ Juicy grapefruit and peach flavors make this off-dry pour perfect for a bowl of spicy Thai noodles.

Mönchhof Mosel Slate Spätlese | 2004 | MOSEL-SAAR-RUWER

★★★ $ $ The "slate" on the label comes through in this wine's stony, mineral-laden taste profile, cushioned by off-dry flavors of peach blossoms and lime. Drink now–6 years.

Pfeffingen Dry | 2004 | PFALZ

★★ $ Full-bodied though almost effervescent and saturated with grapefruit and lemon flavors.

Prinz von Hessen | 2004 | RHEINGAU

★★ $ Sweet white peach and salty almond flavors come together smoothly in this dry, but very fruity wine.

Prinz von Hessen Winkeler Hasensprung Erstes Gewächs
| 2003 | RHEINGAU

★★★★ $ $ $ All the succulent fruit flavors that the very hot 2003 vintage is famous for are on display here, supported by a core of stone and unexpectedly high acidity. Drink now–2 years.

Reichsgraf von Kesselstatt RK | 2005 | MOSEL-SAAR-RUWER

★★★★ $ $ $ Palate-cleansing stone flavors are spiced up by lime zest for austere, excellent-value drinking.

Schloss Johannisberger Estate Spätlese Trocken | 2005 |
RHEINGAU

★★★★ $ $ $ One of Rheingau's definitive estates demonstrates its first-rate status with a concentrated, autumn fruit– and smoke-filled wine that finishes with a musky earthiness. Drink now–20 years.

Schloss Saarstein Spätlese | 2005 | MOSEL-SAAR-RUWER

★★★ $ $ $ From a vineyard so steep that harnesses had to be used to pick its grapes, this wine imparts succulent citrus, flowery apple and stone flavors as labor's reward. Drink now–15 years.

Schloss Wallhausen Two Princes | 2005 | NAHE

★ $ Straightforward but tasty marzipan, nut and and bright zingy lemon-lime flavors bring low-cost pleasure from this off-dry wine from the Nahe.

Selbach Dry (Fish Label) | 2005 | MOSEL-SAAR RUWER

★★ $ Zippy citrus, apple and spice flavors go swimmingly well with shrimp-filled Thai summer rolls.

Spreitzer Hattenheimer Wisselbrunnen Spätlese Trocken
| 2004 | **RHEINGAU**

★★ **$ $ $** An aromatic and finely sculpted dry Spätlese Rheingau that explodes with exotic fruit and herbs firmed up by stony minerals. Drink now–8 years.

Theo Minges Gleisweiler Hölle Spätlese | 2004 | **PFALZ**

★★ **$ $** This tickles the tongue at first with flowers, bitter herbs and pepper, then follows up with round, soft flavors of baked quince and tropical fruit. Drink now–10 years.

von Buhl Armand Kabinett | 2004 | **PFALZ**

★★★ **$ $** Smooth wine that coats the palate with orange blossom, pistachio, lime and floral flavors that are softened by a touch of sugar. Drink now–8 years.

von Buhl Maria Schneider Medium-Dry | 2005 | **PFALZ**

★★★ **$** A lot of wine for very little money, this just off-dry Riesling delights with a burst of lime, guava, apples and spice filled in with smoke and minerals. Drink now–8 years.

news from a wine insider

germany by Stuart Pigott

Notable New Wineries

Germany's young superstar winegrowers continue to make daring, nontraditional (and outrageously monikered) wines, many of which rival the country's best. Provocative Pfalz brands to look for include "Übermut," two uncommon Vintage Port–style wines made by Thomas Hensel and Markus Schneider, and "Black Print," a new-style red by Markus Schneider of Ellerstadt. Elsewhere, Martin Tesch, of Langenlonsheim in the Nahe, makes "Deep Blue," a rich, dry rosé from Pinot Noir. He also crafts the light and bone-dry "Riesling Unplugged," as well as "Five Miles Out," a Riesling fermented on its skins like a red wine. "G-Max" is a massive dry Riesling from Klaus-Peter Keller of Flörsheim-Dalsheim in the Rheinhessen. German wine conservatives still snub the young maverick winemakers, but this only draws more attention to their wines, which tend to sell out very soon after they are released.

von Hövel Oberemmeler Hütte Kabinett | 2004 |
MOSEL-SAAR-RUWER

★★★ $ $ Give this a bit of air to blow off subtle aromas of sulfur and allow its fascinating mélange of key lime, dill, almonds, aloe and stone to emerge from a wall of acidity. Drink now–10 years.

von Othegraven Maria v. O. | 2004 | **MOSEL-SAAR-RUWER**

★★★ $ $ von Othegraven's "basic" wine is anything but; rich with captivating floral, tangerine, pear and tropical fruit flavors that make a lasting impression. Drink now–6 years.

Weingüter Wegeler Rüdesheimer Berg Rottland Spätlese
| 2004 | **RHEINGAU**

★★★ $ $ $ Veering toward the sweet side of off-dry, this entrances with succulent peach and lime flavors and a light polish of minerals. Drink now–8 years.

Weingut Robert Weil Estate Dry | 2005 | **RHEINGAU**

★★★ $ $ Lithe but powerful, this is full of pineapple and stone, zapped by lightning-charged acidity. Drink now–12 years.

Weingut Schloss Lieser Kabinett | 2004 |
MOSEL-SAAR-RUWER

★★ $ $ Heavy with wild herbs, this Riesling also gives notes of aloe and intense minerals.

Zilliken Butterfly Medium-Dry | 2004 | **MOSEL-SAAR-RUWER**

★★ $ $ Juicy pineapple and ripe peach flavors are energized by an electric acidity.

other german whites

Grauburgunder (Pinot Gris) and Weissburgunder (Pinot Blanc) can make wines just as good as their counterparts in Alsace. Scheurebe expresses a combination of bright grapefruit flavors with feral aromas of black currant and herbs, and might be too funky for some, but has an alluring, seductive effect on plenty of others. Wines made from Kerner are similar to Riesling. Huxelrebe and Bacchus vaguely resemble Muscat. Muskateller (Muscat) and Gewürztraminer make deliciously fragrant wines. While most Silvaner and Müller-Thurgau produced in Germany go into lower-quality blends, both are capable of lovely, refreshing whites.

other german white recommendations

Artur Steinmann Pastorius Sommerhäuser Ölspiel Silvaner | 2004 | FRANKEN
★★★ $ $ Smoky and sultry, this goes beyond most Silvaner, giving soft tropical and pear flavors that are laced with the Franken region's telltale minerality.

Castell Frenzy Müller-Thurgau Trocken | 2004 | FRANKEN
★★ $ Nut-brittle flavors bring a hint of sweetness to this very dry and smoky wine that is lean in body.

Darting Dürkheimer Nonnengarten Gewürztraminer Kabinett | 2004 | PFALZ
★★★ $ $ Simply delicious, this slightly off-dry Pfalz Gewurz is saturated with spicy strawberry and succulent pineapple flavors that linger throughout a prolonged finish.

J.L. Wolf Villa Wolf Pinot Gris | 2004 | PFALZ
★★ $ A dandy wine; open, pour and be charmed by the citrus, pine-apple and fine mineral flavors.

Königschaffhausen Flaneur | 2005 | BADEN
★ $ A whimsical charmer, this delights with tropical fruit and herbs.

Theo Minges Gleisweiler Hölle Scheurebe Spätlese | 2004 | PFALZ
★★★ $ $ So full of fresh grapefruit flavors, this seems nearly juice-like. Fortunately, an intense minerality keeps it beautifully balanced and perfect for food.

Weingut Ch. W. Bernhard Frei-Laubersheimer Fels Gewürztraminer Spätlese | 2004 | RHEINHESSEN
★★★ $ $ Austere exuberance infects this relatively dry, intensely stony, spicy Spätlese that charms with fresh-cut herbs, lemon curd flavors and ripe pears.

Weingut Münzberg Weisser Burgunder Kabinett Trocken | 2004 | PFALZ
★★ $ $ Pinot Blanc is lean and lemony in this almond-scented, fine, mineral-laden wine.

austria

Austria has been influenced by the winemaking traditions of its neighbors— Germany, Hungary, Slovenia and Italy— but its wines are entirely unique. Austrian whites are especially impressive, with racy acidity that fuels their explosive fruit flavors. The country's reds are made from many grape varieties that are rarely found elsewhere, and while they are secondary in importance to whites, many are excellent.

Austria: An Overview

Niederösterreich (Lower Austria) is the country's largest region, made up of eight subregions: Carnuntum, Wachau, Donauland, Thermenregion, Traisental, Kamptal, Weinviertel and Kremstal. Burgenland is the sunniest region, and its subregions Neusiedlersee and Neusiedlersee-Hügelland stand out for aromatic whites, dry reds and sweet wines. Mittelburgenland and Südburgenland make the best reds. Styria (Steiermark) specializes in Welschriesling, Sauvignon Blanc, Muskateller and Chardonnay.

Austrian Grapes & Styles

Grüner Veltliner is Austria's most widely grown grape and offers flavors of green apple, citrus, mineral, smoke and even earthy, appealing lentil-like notes. Riesling makes fuller-bodied, drier whites than those common to Germany. Sauvignon Blanc strikes a fine balance of citrus and herb flavors in Styria, where you can also find some Chardonnay, sometimes called Morillon, as well as lush Pinot Blanc (Weissburgunder). Fragrant Welschriesling and Furmint have been grown here for centuries. Zweigelt, Blaufränkisch and Blauburgunder (Pinot Noir) yield the finest reds.

Austrian Wine Labels

Most Austrian wine labels list grape and region. The country uses a system similar to Germany's Prädikatswein (see p. 138), but ripeness standards are typically higher in Austria, and the wines tend to be drier. The Wachau region has its own classification: Steinfeder are light wines, Federspiel are heavier wines. Rich, dry Smaragd are capable of long aging.

austrian whites

Austrian whites are truly exceptional, full of summer fruit flavors, high acidity and palate-cleansing minerality. Grüner Veltliner and Riesling deserve the attention they get, but Austria's other whites are unique and worth seeking out.

BEST PAIRINGS Grüner Veltliner is compatible with hard-to-pair foods like artichokes and asparagus. Smaragd-level Veltliner is built for roast turkey or veal. Rieslings can stand up to pork or duck. Roast chicken with herbs is the best partner for Welschriesling and Weissburgunder.

AUSTRIAN WHITES

grüner veltliner

Most light-bodied, apple-scented Grüner Veltliner makes for pleasant, everyday drinking. Others are profound and seductive with flavors that recall grapefruit, nuts, herbs, flowers, smoke and white pepper.

grüner veltliner recommendations

Domäne Wachau Terrassen Federspiel | 2005 | WACHAU
★★ $ One of the best deals in Austrian wine—ripe tropical fruit and citrus, spice and stone for under $15.

Gritsch Mauritiushof Axpoint Federspiel | 2003 | WACHAU
★★★ $ Soft strawberry and lemon flavors are kept vibrant by herbs, pepper and minerals.

Leth Steinagrund Lagenreserve | 2004 | DONAULAND

★★★ $ Succulent pineapple, savory mineral and spice flavors show Grüner's depth and complexity for a good price. Drink now–6 years.

Machherndl Steinwand Smaragd | 2004 | WACHAU

★★★ $ $ This awakens the palate with flavors of pepper and smoke, apple and lime, and loads of salty minerals. Drink now–8 years.

Prager Hinter der Burg Federspiel | 2004 | WACHAU

★★★ $ $ Though one of Prager's entry-level wines, this seduces with an array of crushed apple, zesty citrus, almond and herb flavors underlined by fine minerals.

Rudi Pichler Wösendorfer Hochrain Smaragd | 2003 | WACHAU

★★★ $ $ $ $ A masterful Wachau producer takes advantage of a warm vintage to craft this cedar-scented wine with minerals, pear and spice flavors. Drink now–10 years.

Weingut Knoll Loibenberg Smaragd | 2005 | WACHAU

★★★★ $ $ $ Spectacular wine uniting flavors of smoke, salt, stone and lemons. Drink now–20 years.

AUSTRIAN WHITES

riesling

Austria's Riesling is no less noble than its Grüner Veltliner. It tends to be drier than those from Germany and fuller-bodied than those from Alsace.

riesling recommendations

Franz Hirtzberger Singerriedel Smaragd | 2004 | WACHAU

★★★★ $ $ $ Superlative, full-bodied Riesling, this indulges with peach, pineapple, herb and truffle flavors encased in stone.

Högl Ried Bruck Viessling Smaragd | 2004 | WACHAU

★★★★ $ $ $ An outstanding example of just how good Wachau Riesling can be, this oozes apricot and tropical flavors from a well of smoky minerals. Drink now–20 years.

Leth Wagramterrassen Lagenreserve | 2004 | WAGRAM/DONAULAND

★★★ $ $ $ Heavy flavors of ripe mango, pineapple and passion fruit are underscored by a mosslike earthiness. Drink now–15 years.

Rainer Wess Wachauer | 2004 | WACHAU
★★ $ Pineapple and lime flavors make the perfect Pad Thai wine.

Weingut Johann Donabaum Offenberg Smaragd | 2003 |
WACHAU
★★★ $ $ $ Pretty floral notes are followed by a labyrinth of mineral, guava, mushroom and smoky flavors. Drink now–10 years.

Weingut Knoll Schütt Smaragd | 2004 | WACHAU
★★★★ $ $ $ $ The blessings of sun and earth are felt in succulent pineapple, crushed nut, apples, spice and stone. Drink now–20 years.

other austrian whites

Weissburgunder (Pinot Blanc), Sauvignon Blanc (called Muskat-Sylvaner), and Chardonnay (Morillon) have been grown here for over a century. Grauburgunder (Pinot Gris), Gelber Muskateller and Welschriesling have been around even longer. Hungary's Furmint makes captivating wines in a small village within the Neusiedlersee-Hügelland region.

other austrian white recommendations

Anton Bauer Best of 04 Chardonnay & Welschriesling
| 2004 | DONAULAND
★★ $ Waxy and aromatic at once, this novel blend engages with ripe apples, flowers and hints of stone.

Erwin Sabathi Klassik Sauvignon Blanc | 2004 |
SOUTHERN STYRIA
★★ $ Put a good chill on this wine and enjoy its citrus, passion fruit and fresh grass flavors all summer long.

star producers
austrian whites

best value
1 Domäne Wachau
2 E. & M. Berger
3 Hopler
4 Huber
5 Loimer

best of the best
1 F.X. Pichler
2 Nigl
3 Rudi Pichler
4 Weingut Bründlmayer
5 Weingut Prager

Frühwirth Scheurebe | 2004 | STYRIA
★★★ $ $ Scheurebe gives a pleasing kick of earthy funk in this wine, alongside herbs, flowers, spice and limes.

Kracher Pinot Gris Trocken | 2005 | BURGENLAND
★★ $ Made by the master of Austrian sweet wines, this dry and well-balanced Pinot Gris entices with apple, spice and stone flavors.

Leo Hillinger Small Hill White | 2004 | BURGENLAND
★★ $ A charming blend of three aromatic grape varieties gives exuberant fruit, floral and herb flavors.

Strauss Welschriesling | 2005 | SOUTHERN STYRIA
★★ $ Fresh, zingy grapefruit flavors are deepened by stone.

austrian reds

Zweigelt is Austria's most planted red, offering juicy cherry flavors. Blaufränkisch (Lemberger) has peppery flavors and heavy tannin. Blauburgunder (Pinot Noir) can approach fine Burgundy. St. Laurent (often spelled Sankt Laurent) is Austria's best red, similar to Pinot Noir.

BEST PAIRINGS Serve Zweigelt with steaks, lamb burgers or roast chicken. Blaufränkisch is fuller-bodied and spicier; it's better with goulash or any braised red meat. Blauburgunder and St. Laurent are superb choices for duck.

austrian red recommendations

Anton Bauer Ried Wagram Cuvée No. 9 | 2003 | DONAULAND
★★★ $ $ Sultry, spicy wild berry and licorice flavors are backed by stone in this enticing blend.

Braunstein Mitterjoch Zweigelt | 2003 | BURGENLAND
★ $ Great value Austrian red, this medium-bodied quaff offers berry and savory spice flavors for around $12.

Gsellmann & Gsellmann Pinot Noir | 2002 | BURGENLAND
★★★ $ $ $ This Pinot could be compared to good Burgundy with smooth, smoky cherry, minerals and spice. Drink now–8 years.

Kollwentz Föllikberg Zweigelt | 2001 | BURGENLAND
★★ $ Zweigelt exhibits a wild side with herb oil and smoky, savory spices like coriander, cumin and celery seed, infusing dark berries.

Leo Hillinger Hill 1 | 2003 | **BURGENLAND**
★★★ $ $ $ Imperial in structure, brimming with voluptuous dark berry, exotic spice and a core of stone. Drink in 2–12 years.

Neckenmarkt Blaufränkisch | 2004 | **BURGENLAND**
★★ $ Barbecue would probably not be the first food you'd think of for Austrian wines, but this red's smoky, spicy, sappy prune flavors are a perfect match.

Pöckl Zweigelt | 2004 | **BURGENLAND**
★★ $ Incredibly smooth Burgenland red with polished fruit, tobacco and spice for a very fair price.

Zantho St. Laurent | 2004 | **BURGENLAND**
★★ $ Dominated by smoked meat flavors that would be chewy if not for the smooth tannin.

news from a wine insider
austria by Philipp Blom

2005 Vintage Report

The 2005 vintage was a struggle for most Austrian producers. Heavy fall rains and subsequent rot greatly reduced the harvest, in some cases by as much as 40 percent. Top vintners produced high-quality wines, but the less skilled suffered big losses and diminished quality levels.

One vintner who overcame these challenges was Sepp Muster, who is turning out some of the best biodynamic wines in the region of Styria. Although Muster's wines are relatively high in alcohol, they are always beautifully balanced with impressive structure and depth.

Notable New Wineries

Claus Preisinger is one of the Burgenland region's most talented winemakers, with a particular passion for Pinot Noir. His 2003 Pinot is an especially complex wine marked by both richness and a lovely finesse.

Another Pinot-focused estate worth noting is Schloss Halbturn, led by German wine director Karl-Heinz "Carlo" Wolf. Under Wolf, the estate has released several exceptional vintages including a particularly fine 2003 wine, possibly the first Pinot Noir from Austria that could rival a good Burgundian Premier Cru.

greece

A new breed of devoted, dynamic and talented winemakers is helping Greek wines revive the reputation for excellence they enjoyed centuries ago.

Greece: An Overview

Greek viticulture can be divided into four general zones: north, central, the Peloponnese and the islands. The north includes Macedonia and Thrace, with Náoussa the most famous appellation. The central zone spreads from Athens all the way north to Mt. Olympus and west to Albania. The Peloponnese, a mountainous region with warm valleys, supports a variety of wines; Mantinia, Neméa and Pátras are its most famous subregions. As for the islands, Crete boasts the largest wine industry, while the Aegean islands of Santorini and Samos stand out for dry whites and sweet whites respectively.

Greek Grapes & Styles

Greece is home to thousands of indigenous grape varieties. Savatiano is the most common white grape, typically used as the basis for Greece's pine resin–flavored wine, Retsina, though it is also capable of light, fresh wines. Roditis makes light-bodied, expressive whites with pronounced floral and mineral flavors. Pink-skinned Moscofilero is responsible for the wonderfully floral whites and spicy rosés of Mantinia. On Santorini, Assyrtiko makes powerful, mineral-laden, bone-dry wines that take on Riesling-like characteristics when they are aged. Greece's most highly regarded red grape is Xinomavro (meaning "acid-black"), which winemakers in Náoussa use to make their earthy wines. With age, these wines acquire smoky, leathery, berry flavors that echo the Nebbiolo wines of Italy's Piedmont region. The workhorse red grape of Greece is Agiorgitiko and it is responsible for copious amounts of cheap, fruity, easy-to-drink, high-acid wines as well as some elegant, complex examples. The best are from the hilly Neméa region. Wines from international grape varieties Merlot, Cabernet, Syrah and Chardonnay can be quite fine, especially when blended with indigenous grapes.

Greek Wine Labels

Wine regions take priority over grape names on most Greek wine labels. Reds from Náoussa are required by law to be made from Xinomavro, while those from Neméa use Agiorgitiko. Mantinia wines must be made from at least 85 percent Moscofilero, and Santorini wines are dominated by Assyrtiko. Grapes not traditional to particular areas, however, are usually noted on labels.

Pairing Greek Wines

Simple whites are terrific with mezes such as stuffed grape leaves, salty feta or olives. Assyrtiko was made for grilled fish or sardines drizzled with olive oil and lemon. Floral Moscofilero is delightful with spicier fare like Moroccan spiced chicken or seafood sausages. Pair fruity southern Greek reds with lamb burgers, or simply drink them on their own. More expensive Neméan wines need food—serve them with rack of lamb or roast pork loin. Náoussa and other Xinomavro-based wines match beautifully with game, slow-braised meats or grilled mushrooms.

greek whites

Greece offers countless eclectic, unique whites. Aromatic Moscofilero is somewhat reminiscent of Gewürztraminer. The whites of Santorini are intensely mineral, while the whites from Malagousia are plush and exotic. Chardonnay also does well in Greece.

greek white recommendations

Antonopoulos Vineyards Adoli Ghis | 2005 | PÁTRAS
★★★ $ $ This Pátras white has a distinct and searing acidity that cuts through dense blocks of flavors which range from smoke to bright lemon and Asian pear.

Boutari Kallisti | 2004 | SANTORINI
★★★ $ $ Citrus confit and honey-coated almond flavors drip from a beautiful, stony, slightly oaky wine.

Cooperative Cephalonia San Gerassimo Robola | 2004 | CEPHALONIA
★★ $ Nicely composed almond, lemon and stone flavors, just as Robola should be.

Domaine Gerovassiliou Malagousia | 2005 | EPANOMI
★★★ $ $ A refreshing wine that is unmistakably Mediterranean offers up succulent peach and lemon flavors perfumed by jasmine and white pepper.

Domaine Spiropoulos | 2005 | MANTINIA
★★ $ Crisp green apple flavors are given complexity and charm by a perfume of light floral aromas.

Domaine Tselepos Moscofilero | 2005 | MANTINIA
★★★★ $ Moscofilero is at its most intense here, though still shows refinement with a superb balance of ebullient floral, stone, lemon and pear flavors.

Emery Mountain Slopes Athiri | 2005 | RHODES
★★ $ Mineral-rich white with expressive stony, smoky lemon and orange flavors.

Gai'a Thalassitis | 2005 | SANTORINI
★★★ $ $ Though this is an extreme example of Santorini's high-acid and mineral hallmark profile, it's balanced and smoothed by a generous measure of ripe citrus flavors.

Lafazanis Roditis | 2005 | PELOPONNESE
★ $ Lemon-lime zest and apple flavors make for simple, refreshing poolside drinking.

Sigalas | 2005 | SANTORINI
★★★ $ $ The volcanic soils of Santorini are immediately evident in this Sigalas white; the intense minerality is accented by herbs, lemon and orange flavors.

greek reds

Greek reds range from simple to complex and ageworthy. The best wines of Náoussa can be compared to quality Barbaresco. Some reds from Neméa possess a claretlike elegance and others a chewy richness and depth of fruit. And there are plenty of others perfect for casual drinking.

greek red recommendations

Alpha Estate Xinomavro | 2004 | AMYNDEON

★★★ $ $ $ Peppery and earthy herbs seep into a bed of dried berry and cherry flavors in this refined red.

Boutari Skalani | 2003 | ARCHANES

★★★ $ $ This blend of indigenous Crete grapes is rustic in a very pleasing way, with dark berry, spice, smoke and leather, and finishing with an appealing bitterness.

Domaine Mercouri Cava | 2002 | LETRINON

★★★★ $ $ $ A black beauty oozing blackberries, carbon, dark-roasted coffee and spice.

Gai'a Estate | 2003 | NEMÉA

★★★ $ $ $ Corpulent in body and stuffed with ripe red fruit flavors, fine minerals and tannin, there are flourishes of violets that keep this sophisticated. Drink now–6 years.

Karyda | 2003 | NÁOUSSA

★★ $ $ Nicely done Náoussa in a very hot 2003 vintage that shows more juicy red fruit flavors than typical earth.

Kir-Yianni Ramnista | 2001 | NÁOUSSA

★★★ $ $ Known more for earthiness than seduction, Náoussa is rarely as sultry as it is here, with velvety berry, truffle and fine mineral flavors. Drink now–8 years.

Skouras Saint George | 2004 | NEMÉA

★★ $ Fresh and spicy cherry flavors mingle with lanolin and stone in a fun light-hearted Agiorgitiko.

Tsantali Rapsani Réserve | 1997 | EPILEGMENOS

★★★ $ $ $ An enchanting earthiness comes together with flavors of herbed black olives, ripe berries, roast meat and red cherry with hints of licorice.

other old world wines

Societies throughout the Caucasus and Middle East have been practicing viticulture since well before the Common Era. Not surprisingly, the taste for wine spread across the Old World, bringing winegrowing to climates as disparate as those of Switzerland and Morocco. Over the centuries, growers in Switzerland perfected their winegrowing tradition, while other countries, particularly in Eastern Europe, let their wine industries fall stagnant. Today, vintners in many of these countries are using modern techniques in the vineyard and the winery to make increasingly sophisticated wines that are more widely exported as international interest grows.

switzerland

Every canton in Switzerland produces wine, however the overwhelming majority of production takes place in the French-speaking western regions and the Italian-speaking southern region, Ticino. Most of Switzerland's wines are enthusiastically consumed at home. But the impeccable Swiss wines that make it to U.S. shores are worth buying when you find them for their fine-tuned balance of fruit, minerals and racy acidity.

Swiss Grapes & Styles

Chasselas is Switzerland's most common grape. It can make white wines that range in flavor from light and floral to austerely mineral, intensely citrusy or succulently pearlike. Vintners in the Valais region refer to the Chasselas grape as "Fendant." White wines from Sylvaner (locally called Johannisberg), Müller-Thurgau (a cross of Riesling and Sylvaner), Marsanne (called Ermitage here), Pinot Gris (Malvoisie), and Petite Arvine are all worth seeking out for their unique taste profiles. Pinot Noir and Gamay are the most common red wine grapes in Switzerland; they are either bottled individually or combined to make a blend called "Dôle." Merlot excels in Ticino, while Syrah prefers the Valais. Oeil de Perdrix ("partridge eye") is a dry rosé made of Pinot Noir from Neuchâtel.

Swiss Wine Labels

Swiss wines are normally labeled by grape variety, region and, if applicable, subregion. Within Switzerland, there are two exceptional subregions designated "Grand Cru." Most white wines that don't specify grape variety are likely to be made from Chasselas. Unlabeled reds are almost certainly a blend of several varieties.

Pairing Swiss Wines

Heavier versions of Chasselas, especially from the Vaud and its subregion Dézaley, match nicely with chicken in a cream sauce, smoked salmon or most soft cheeses. The Valais' mineral-rich Chasselas (Fendant) is excellent with raw shellfish, particularly oysters, as well as chalky goat cheese. Vibrant Neuchâtel Chasselas is perfect for lobster. Pinot Gris and Petite Arvine are ideal with fondue. Drink Pinot Noir as you would Burgundy, with hearty, meaty fish or grilled chicken or lamb. Merlot from Ticino and Dôle can be delicious with modest beef stews or grilled skirt steaks.

swiss recommendations

WHITES

Château d'Auvernier | 2005 | NEUCHÂTEL

★★ $ $ A subtle briny aroma is followed by a welcome rush of bright citrus and round nut flavors.

Henri Badoux Aigle Les Murailles | 2004 | AIGLE

★★★ $ $ $ Creamy almond and grapefruit flavors provide a soft cushion for the gravelly stone layered underneath.

Robert Gilliard Les Murettes Fendant | 2005 | VALAIS

★★ $ $ Light and firm at once, this is awash in smoky mineral and blanched almond flavors. Serve with oysters on the half shell.

REDS

Robert Gilliard Dôle des Monts | 2004 | VALAIS

★★★ $ $ Lovely, smoky, medium-bodied Swiss red; cherry and spice flavors make it perfect for duck.

central & eastern europe

Wine industries in Central and Eastern Europe have taken years to establish a presence in the outside world following the collapse of the crippling Iron Curtain. But the talents of local vintners combined with investment and expertise from wine professionals elsewhere have ignited a quality revolution. Results are still uneven, but there are some top-notch wines coming out of Hungary, Slovakia, Slovenia and Croatia as well as some fine bargains to be found from Bulgaria and Moldova.

Central & Eastern European Wine Labels

Central and Eastern European wine regions tend to label their wines according to grape variety, region and vintage. The famous sweet wines from Hungary's Tokaji region (see p. 280), which do not provide a list of grape varieties, are a major exception to this rule.

central & eastern european whites

Slovenia boasts some of Eastern Europe's best white wines. Made from Pinot Blanc, Pinot Grigio, Ribolla and Malvasia, many can compete with those produced across the border in Friuli, Italy. Look to Hungary for dry whites from Furmint, and to Croatia for exotic, nutty wines from Posip. Both sweet and dry Rieslings are made in various parts of Eastern Europe, as well as Welschriesling (Laski Rizling in Slovenia or Olasz Rizling in Hungary), which tastes similar but is unrelated. Chardonnay and Sauvignon Blanc also make their inevitable appearances.

BEST PAIRINGS Hungary's Furmint and Croatia's Posip are fine choices with chicken dishes, ham or turkey. Pair wines made from Pinot Grigio, Chardonnay or Riesling as you would examples from other European countries.

central & eastern european white recommendations

Dancing Man Rare Meritage | 2003 | **MARIBOR, SLOVENIA**
★★ $ Soft and approachable, this Slovenian blend offers juicy pear and grape flavors balanced by moderate acidity.

Golden Hill Chardonnay | 2003 | **MARIBOR, SLOVENIA**
★★ $ Fine minerals add complexity to the almond and lemon flavors in this well-made Chardonnay.

Kozlovic Malvazija | 2004 | **ISTRIA, CROATIA**
★★ $ $ Malvasia's fragrant, fruity charms translate well in Croatia, with an array of herb, kiwi and lime flavors.

Monarchia Cellars Zen | 2003 | **EGER, HUNGARY**
★★★ $ The obscure Hungarian Zengo grape is responsible for this lusciously nutty, lemony, spice-laden wine.

Movia Veliko | 2001 | **GORISKA BRDA, SLOVENIA**
★★★★ $ $ $ A blend of Sauvignon Blanc, Ribolla, Pinot Grigio and Chardonnay results in this outrageously good white; give it air to release the aromatic swirl of flavors. Drink now–12 years.

Royal Tokaji Furmint | 2005 | **TOKAJI, HUNGARY**
★★★ $ Sweet Tokaji is more famous, but this dry white is no less grand, with fragrant flower notes infusing succulent pears and lime.

Tibor Gal Egri Chardonnay | 2002 | **EGER, HUNGARY**
★★★ $ $ Chardonnay beautifully adapts to Hungarian soils, as this smoky, silky, mineral-laden wine illustrates.

central & eastern european reds

While elegant wines are made from Bordeaux varieties throughout Eastern Europe, the most interesting wines are those made from indigenous grapes. Hungary's colorfully named Egri Bikavér ("Bull's Blood") was once responsible for crude wines, but today it makes many sophisticated reds. Vintners craft high-quality wines from the grape Kékfrankos (known elsewhere as Blaufränkisch or Lemberger). Croatia is home to Crljenak, the parent grape of California's Zinfandel, and to Plavac Mali, a more widely grown Zinfandel relative, which shows spicy black fruit flavors.

BEST PAIRINGS Simple Bulgarian or Moldovan reds are delicious with sausages; better Croatian reds should accompany roast pork loin. Egri Bikavér matches well with roast prime rib of beef. Have a Kékfrankos with leg of lamb. Spicy Croatian reds can be enjoyed much like California Zinfandel, alongside meaty winter stews.

central & eastern european red recommendations

Damianitza Uniqato Rubin | 2003 | **TRAKIA, BULGARIA**
★★ $ $ The Rubin grape is a cross between Nebbiolo and Syrah, and in this novel wine it offers a distinct and pleasing earthiness. Drink now–5 years.

Ivo Skaramuca Vineyard Dingac | 2003 |
PELJESAC PENINSULA, CROATIA
★★ $ $ Made from Zinfandel's cousin, Plavac Mali, this has similar plush berry and spice flavors, albeit in an earthier, meatier form.

Movia Veliko | 1999 | **GORISKA BRDA, SLOVENIA**
★★★ $ $ $ Sultry blend of Merlot, Cabernet and Pinot Noir with a smooth mouthfeel and unique smokiness. Drink now–10 years.

Takler Heritage Cuvée | 2003 | **SZEKSZARD, HUNGARY**
★★★ $ $ French and Hungarian grape varieties come together with interesting results in this full-bodied, ripe, berry- and mineral-saturated wine. Drink now–8 years.

Tibor Gal Egri Bikavér | 2002 | **EGER, HUNGARY**
★★ $ $ Hungary's lusty Bull's Blood is a bit tame in this medium-bodied red, but wild flavors of herbs, berries and minerals persist.

Vini Cabernet Sauvignon | 2004 | **SLIVEN, BULGARIA**
★ $ Cabernet has a long history in Bulgarian soils, and this simple, earthy example makes a great party wine.

Vylyan Villanyi Pinot Noir | 2004 | **VILLANY, HUNGARY**
★★★ $ $ This Pinot Noir shows notes of earth like a fine Burgundy, as well as riper, rounder flavors more typical in New World versions. Drink now–5 years.

Zlatan Plavac Grand Cru | 2003 | **HVAR, CROATIA**
★★★ $ $ $ Plavac Mali has the potential for excellence, as this dark and smoky, mineral- and spice-laden red shows.

north africa & lebanon

Lebanese wines—once traded by Phoenician merchants during the classical period and celebrated throughout the Middle Ages—are enjoying renewed acclaim today. In North Africa, winemaking has existed for nearly as long, particularly during periods of Phoenician and Roman rule. France's colonization of North Africa in the 19th and mid-20th centuries greatly expanded viticulture in the region; for a time, Algeria and, to a lesser degree, Tunisia and Morocco exported huge quantities of hearty red wine to France. After independence, wine production declined considerably, but creative vintners are reestablishing the tradition with some excellent results.

North African & Lebanese Wine Labels

France's colonial influence over North Africa and Lebanon is still evidenced in the regions' wine labeling. Region names are generally emphasized over grape variety, though labels of wines made exclusively from international grapes like Chardonnay and Cabernet Sauvignon are likely to list them.

north african & lebanese whites

Lebanon grows plenty of Chardonnay and Sauvignon Blanc, but its most interesting white wines are made from indigenous varieties Merweh, which may be the same as Sémillon, and Obaideh, thought by some to be identical to Chardonnay. North African white wines are not nearly as interesting, but there are some fresh, crisp examples made from Ugni Blanc, Clairette and Muscat.

BEST PAIRINGS Serve Lebanese whites with stuffed grape leaves, hummus, grilled seafood and vegetarian fare. Fuller-bodied Lebanese whites will complement richer, heavier fish dishes. Pour a North African white with grilled sardines or crudités.

north african & lebanese white recommendations

Château Kefraya La Dame Blanche | 2004 |
BEKAA VALLEY, LEBANON
★★ $ Fresh and breezy, this Lebanese white is light, limey and ideal for herb-stuffed fish.

Les Trois Domaines Blanc | 2004 | **GUERROUANE, MOROCCO**
★ $ Green pear, lemon and grass flavors are enlivened by acidity in this softly textured, fun wine.

Musar Cuvée Blanc | 2003 | **BEKAA VALLEY, LEBANON**
★★ $ $ Made from Lebanon's indigenous Obaideh grape, this white is loaded with snappy green apple and herb flavors with earthy, mushroomlike undertones.

north african & lebanese reds

France's imprint is seen in the spicy Carignan, Cinsault and Grenache vines that are widely grown from Morocco to Lebanon. Cabernet Sauvignon, Syrah and Merlot are also popular, especially in Lebanon's Bekaa Valley. Generally speaking, Lebanese red wines tend to have a claretlike elegance with slightly fuller body. North African reds are somewhat more rustic.

BEST PAIRINGS The spicy quality of North African reds makes them perfect for lamb or chicken tagines, sausages or flavorful stews. Lebanese reds—with their refined herb-and-spice profile—are lovely with roast leg of lamb or roast chicken with herbs and spices.

north african & lebanese red recommendations

Château Kefraya | 2000 | BEKAA VALLEY, LEBANON
★★★ $ $ Sophisticated as quality Bordeaux, yet swirling with charmingly rustic herb and lanolin notes. This was made for roast leg of lamb. Drink now–8 years.

Château Musar Hochar Père et Fils | 2000 |
BEKAA VALLEY, LEBANON
★★★ $ $ Château Musar is iconic not only as a vanguard for the wines of Lebanon, but for its unique, earthy reds flavored by herbs and wild berries. This is their second wine, somewhat less complex but compelling nonetheless. Drink now–5 years.

Kahina | 2003 | GUERROUANE, MOROCCO
★★ $ $ $ Bordeaux's legendary Bernard Magrez tries his hand in Morocco, bringing some of his magic to this substantial, herb- and spice-laden wine.

Les Trois Domaines Rouge | 2003 | GUERROUANE, MOROCCO
★ $ Rich with herb and red berry flavors, this enjoyable Rhône-style wine is perfect for kebabs.

united states

Winemaking has been part of American life since the mid-1600s. Thomas Jefferson encouraged it with his own viniferous activities at Monticello and by legislation during his presidency. Each new wave of immigration from wine-producing countries abroad only strengthened viticulture's place in U.S. soils. Despite natural challenges such as climate and vine disease, and the great man-made hurdle of Prohibition, the U.S. today is the world's fourth-largest wine producer, and widely considered one of the best.

The United States: An Overview

Many people associate American wine with Californian wine, which is understandable given that 90 percent of the nation's production takes place in the Golden State. But every state has planted vineyards, though regional climatic variations limit which grape varietals succeed. In many parts of the country, vintners can grow only the native *Vitis labrusca* grape varieties, which make wines of generally lower quality. European *Vitis vinifera* grape varieties, which do thrive in many states, are responsible for the finest American wines. Regions in California and the Pacific Northwest dominate winemaking in the U.S., making wines that can rival their European models. New York State is the third-largest producer, and home to some well-crafted, cooler-climate wines. Recent attention is being paid to wines from Michigan, Missouri, Texas, Arizona and New Mexico. In the South, parts of Virginia and North Carolina are also crafting some interesting wines.

california

California is America's viticultural Eden. The state is blessed with consistent sunshine moderated by cool ocean breezes, a diversity of terrain and a growing number of the world's most talented, well-traveled winemakers. After struggling through a weak economy and an enormous wine glut, California's wine industry has emerged stronger than before with a growing presence in the domestic as well as international marketplace. As for the wines themselves, they've never been better.

Mendocino
Lake
Sierra Foothills
Sonoma Napa
SAN FRANCISCO
Contra Costa
Santa Cruz
Monterey
Pacific Ocean
San Luis Obispo
Santa Barbara
• LOS ANGELES
Temecula
SAN DIEGO

■ Principal Wine Region

California: An Overview

California produces wine from nearly every corner of the state. The most northerly of California's significant wine regions is Mendocino, a relatively cool area known mainly for elegant Chardonnay and Pinot Noir. Farther south is the Napa Valley, the state's most famed appellation, particularly for Cabernet Sauvignon. Superb Cabernet also comes from Sonoma County, Napa's neighbor to the west. Sonoma's warm Dry Creek Valley is ideal for voluptuous Zinfandel and ripe, fruity Sauvignon Blanc, whereas its cool-climate Russian River Valley is best for refined Pinot Noir, Syrah and Chardonnay. The chilly, foggy Carneros region is also home to some outstanding Pinot Noir and Chardonnay. The Central Coast region extends some 200 miles from Santa Cruz to the top of Los Angeles County and boasts a long, slow growing season which is perfect for Pinot Noir and Chardonnay. Rhône grape varieties Syrah, Grenache and Viognier also make quality wines here. To the east of San Francisco Bay, Contra Costa and the Livermore Valley, as well as Lodi and the Shenandoah Valley in the Sierra Nevada foothills, boast some of California's famous plantings of ancient, old-vine Zinfandel and Petite Sirah.

California Wine Labels

Californian labels normally give the winery's name, the region in which the grapes were grown (officially known as an AVA, or American Viticultural Area), vintage and grape variety. U.S. law permits wines that bear the name of a single grape variety to contain only 75 percent of that grape; for example, a wine labeled "Cabernet Sauvignon" might contain 25 percent Merlot. Blending isn't cheating: combining different grape varieties enables winemakers to create wines of greater complexity. In fact, some of the finest wines in California are a mélange of various Bordeaux grape varieties (see p. 178), a style that carries the legally recognized moniker "Meritage" (pronounced like "heritage"). You'll also see the term "Reserve" on the labels of some vintners' finest bottlings, but it has no regulated meaning.

california whites

California's vintners produce white wines from many international grape varieties; they range from pale, light-bodied summer quaffers to weighty, golden nectars. As it is always more challenging to make white wines in a warm climate, the state's best whites tend to come from cooler regions such as Carneros and the Russian River Valley.

CALIFORNIA WHITES

chardonnay

Chardonnay remains America's favorite pour, as well as California's most planted grape, in spite of a much-hyped backlash. As the industry matures, vintners are turning from the full-throttle tropical-fruit-and-oak profile that so many associate with the variety toward more elegant, food-friendly wines with subtle citrus and mineral notes. Fans of the former style can still find abundant examples.

BEST PAIRINGS Light, unoaked Chardonnays are terrific with lean fish and herb-marinated chicken. Buttery, oak-laden versions require robust foods like Thanksgiving turkey, roast pork or grilled fish. Wines that fall between the two extremes work well with grilled fish or baked salmon.

chardonnay recommendations

Acacia | **2004** | **CARNEROS**
★★ $ $ A well-built Chardonnay with ripe fruit, toasty oak, a little spice and good acidity.

Au Bon Climat Unity Nuits-Blanches au Bouge | 2003 |
SANTA MARIA VALLEY
★★★★ $ $ $ Full-bodied, brash, but balanced. Abundant fruit and smoky, nutty oak flavors are offset by refreshing mineral notes. Drink now–12 years.

Barnett Vineyards Sangiacomo Vineyard | 2004 | **CARNEROS**
★★★ $ $ $ A kiss of oak gives a warm glow to an otherwise steely wine, full of apple and citrus flavors. Drink now–15 years.

Cakebread Cellars | 2004 | NAPA VALLEY
★ ★ ★ $ $ $ It's not hard to see why this remains one of America's favorite Napa Chardonnays. Expressive apple, pear and a pinch of spicy oak flavors are supported by vibrant acidity.

Calera | 2002 | MT. HARLAN
★ ★ ★ $ $ $ The advantages of subtlety are revealed in this demure wine with its lacy mineral, anise and apple flavors.

Cambria Katherine's Vineyard | 2004 | SANTA MARIA VALLEY
★ ★ ★ $ $ Lemon and peach flavors are accented by toasty oak and a fine layering of minerals.

Carpe Diem Firepeak Vineyard | 2003 | EDNA VALLEY
★ ★ ★ $ $ $ Harmonious wine with lingering flavors of minerals, apples and nutty oak. Give this air or time. Drink now–8 years.

Ceàgo Vinegarden Del Lago | 2005 | MENDOCINO
★ ★ $ $ Fresh and aromatic, this organic wine comes alive in the glass with minty lime and green apple flavors.

Chalone Vineyard Estate Grown | 2004 | CHALONE
★ ★ $ $ Chalky mineral notes add an appealing dimension to this Chardonnay's apple, peach and piquant spice flavors.

Chateau St. Jean Robert Young Vineyard | 2002 |
ALEXANDER VALLEY
★ ★ $ $ The baked apple and caramel-custard flavors in this savory wine taste nearly hickory-smoked.

Clos du Bois | 2004 | NORTH COAST
★ ★ $ Solid, textbook California Chardonnay: buttery, with some pineapple, pear and citrus flavors.

Clos Du Val | 2004 | CARNEROS
★ ★ ★ $ $ Thick, though balanced, this is awash in tropical fruit and almond flavors, some oak and bright acidity. Drink now–8 years.

Crichton Hall | 2003 | NAPA VALLEY
★ ★ $ $ $ A buffet's worth of well-defined ripe fruit flavors—orange, pineapple, peach and melon—are augmented by light oak in this weighty wine. Drink now–6 years.

Davis Bynum Limited Edition | 2003 | RUSSIAN RIVER VALLEY
★ ★ ★ $ $ Subtle autumn fruit flavors with hints of toasted almond and stone emerge from this graceful white, finishing with just the right amount of oak. Drink now–8 years.

Far Niente | 2004 | NAPA VALLEY
★★★ $ $ $ $ Far Niente keeps getting better, as this beautifully balanced wine shows; each vintage brings more mineral notes to the mélange of fruit, herb and smoke flavors. Drink now–8 years.

Fess Parker Ashley's Vineyard | 2004 | SANTA RITA HILLS
★★★ $ $ $ This ebullient wine ropes together wild spicy tropical flavors with almonds and a hint of oak.

Foley Rancho Santa Rosa | 2004 | SANTA RITA HILLS
★★★ $ $ $ Cherry and citrus flavors are boldly on display in this succulent, sophisticated wine.

Girard | 2004 | RUSSIAN RIVER VALLEY
★★ $ $ This Chardonnay takes a turn from typical apple flavors to reveal palate-pleasing flavors of slow-baked, cinnamon-dusted quince and date-nut bread garnished with a hint of butter.

Grgich Hills | 2003 | NAPA VALLEY
★★★ $ $ $ Apples, pears and light citrus are highlighted by floral flavors for a charming, yet serious Chardonnay. Drink now–8 years.

Handley Estate Vineyard | 2004 | ANDERSON VALLEY
★★★ $ $ Snappy apple and sweet spice flavors run throughout this mouthwatering Anderson Valley wine.

I'M | 2004 | SONOMA COUNTY
★★ $ $ A fine-drinking white with mango, green papaya and spice flavors energized by good acidity.

Jordan | 2004 | RUSSIAN RIVER VALLEY
★★ $ $ $ Fresh-pressed apple and lemon flavors, zippy acidity and a touch of oak go into this well-crafted wine.

Kalin Cellars Cuvee LD | 1994 | SONOMA COUNTY
★★★ $ $ $ Proof that whites can age: Kalin recently released this older bottling, which oozes with roasted apple, burnt orange and spice flavors kept youthful with minerals and vibrant acidity.

Kendall-Jackson Grand Reserve | 2004 | MONTEREY/SANTA BARBARA COUNTIES
★ $ $ Juicy citrus and tropical fruit flavors in a smooth package.

Kongsgaard | 2003 | NAPA VALLEY
★★★★ $ $ $ $ Masterful wine made to show a balance of fruit and minerals; Kongsgaard approaches the lushness expected from Napa Chardonnay, with an unusual elegance. Drink now–12 years.

Lincourt | 2004 | SANTA BARBARA COUNTY
★★ $ $ Medium-bodied with citrus flavors, light oak and spice.

Miner Wild Yeast | 2004 | NAPA VALLEY
★★★ $ $ $ Toasted toffee, hazelnut, almond and cashew flavors run alongside a citrusy bouquet in this wildly expressive wine.

Morgan Double L Vineyard | 2004 | SANTA LUCIA HIGHLANDS
★★★ $ $ $ Morgan gets more interesting every year. Here, pear and citrus, plus sweet-spiced oak flavors are infused by minerals.

Paul Hobbs | 2004 | RUSSIAN RIVER VALLEY
★★★ $ $ $ Spicy apple flavors melt into toasty oak to create one excellent, satiny wine. Drink now–10 years.

Pepi | 2004 | CALIFORNIA
★ $ Zippy citrus and apple flavors make this a perfect poolside pour.

Peter Michael Winery Ma Belle-Fille | 2004 |
SONOMA COUNTY
★★★★ $ $ $ $ A touch of oak adds an intriguing depth to delicate citrus, green apple and mineral flavors. Drink now–12 years.

Qupé Bien Nacido Block Eleven Reserve | 2004 |
SANTA MARIA VALLEY
★★★ $ $ $ This producer's reputation was made by wines such as this: complex fruit flavors, bright acidity and enough minerals to add finesse. Drink now–10 years.

Ramey Ritchie Vineyard | 2003 | RUSSIAN RIVER VALLEY
★★★★ $ $ $ $ Big, thick, textured California Chardonnay at a high level. This is full of succulent citrus, tropical flavors and spice. Drink now–12 years.

Rideau Vineyard Reserve | 2004 | SANTA BARBARA COUNTY
★★★ $ $ $ The perfume of white flowers teases the nose, while pear, tropical fruit and light spice flavors engage the palate.

Robert Mondavi Winery Reserve | 2003 | CARNEROS
★★★ $ $ $ A broad-textured wine with soft pear, citrus and light pineapple flavors accented by notes of smoky oak. This is classic, well-executed California Chardonnay. Drink now–10 years.

Rusack Reserve | 2004 | SANTA MARIA VALLEY
★★★ $ $ $ The advantages of Santa Maria's cool climate are on display in this lovely, reserved wine. Delicate pear and citrus flavors are rounded out by wisps of oak.

Saintsbury Brown Ranch | 2003 | CARNEROS
★★★ $ $ $ This completely dry wine manages to express sweet nut-brittle, malt, lemon drop and orange custard flavors.

Sequoia Grove | 2004 | CARNEROS
★★ $ $ In this well-made, old-style wine, ripe flavors of pineapple get a spicy oak infusion.

Shafer Red Shoulder Ranch | 2004 | CARNEROS
★★★ $ $ $ Caramelized tropical fruit flavors would be clumsy in some hands, but Shafer gives them finesse. Drink now–8 years.

Silverado Vineyards Vineburg | 2004 | CARNEROS
★★ $ $ $ A suave wine, with apple blossom and ripe pear flavors augmented by smoky minerals and just a kiss of oak.

Stony Hill | 2002 | NAPA VALLEY
★★★★ $ $ $ Fifty-year-old Stony Hill has never been better; this lean, apple- and mineral-flavored wine has exuberant youthful vigor. Drink now–12 years.

Stuhlmuller Vineyards Estate | 2004 | ALEXANDER VALLEY
★★ $ $ Full-bodied Chardonnay with a satiny mouth-feel thanks to pear and pineapple flavors rounded out by smoky oak.

Talbott Cuvée Cynthia | 2002 | MONTEREY COUNTY
★★★★ $ $ $ $ The oily texture of this wine is offset by a cleansing acidity. Flavors of pear, peach and apple are softened by smoky oak. Drink now–12 years.

Trefethen | 2004 | OAK KNOLL DISTRICT
★★★ $ $ $ Sultry autumn fruit flavors combine with sweet blanched almond and subtle floral notes.

---

star producers
chardonnay

best value
1 Barefoot Cellars
2 Bogle
3 Chateau Souverain
4 Edna Valley Vineyard
5 Heitz Cellars

best of the best
1 Hanzell
2 Kistler
3 Kongsgaard
4 Peter Michael
5 Stony Hill

CALIFORNIA WHITES

sauvignon blanc

A renaissance of interest in California's "other white" has bred a range of Sauvignon Blanc styles. Some have zippy citrus, herb and grassy notes, while others are rounder and fruit-driven. Vintners use the term "Fumé Blanc" to evoke a connection to Pouilly-Fumé, one of France's celebrated Sauvignons; sometimes Fumé Blanc is aged in oak.

BEST PAIRINGS California Sauvignon Blanc, with its citrus, melon and fresh herb flavors, makes a lovely aperitif wine and is better with food than most Chardonnay. Play off the wine's grassiness with herb-infused chicken or fish. Its high acidity cuts through greasy foods like fried shrimp and calamari. Serve oaked Sauvignon with grilled salmon.

sauvignon blanc recommendations

Beckmen Vineyards Purisima Mountain Vineyard | 2004 |
SANTA YNEZ VALLEY
★★ $ $ One doesn't expect raspberry flavors from white wine, but they are oddly appealing here, alongside orange, lemon and spice.

Chalk Hill | 2004 | CHALK HILL
★★★ $ $ Reminiscent of silky white Bordeaux, this offers almond, lemon and peach flavors with firm minerals. Drink now–10 years.

Davis Bynum Fumé Blanc | 2005 | RUSSIAN RIVER VALLEY
★★★ $ An outstanding wine: stone and minerals add an engaging backdrop to citrus and unusual tropical fruit flavors.

Dry Creek Vineyard Fumé Blanc | 2004 | SONOMA COUNTY
★★★ $ A lithe, flinty wine with a subtle approach that leaves a lasting impression of fine herbs, minerals and tart citrus.

Duckhorn Vineyards | 2005 | NAPA VALLEY
★★★ $ $ Though this is more herbal than past vintages, Duckhorn's Sauvignon still has plush grapefruit, almond and light spice flavors.

Geyser Peak Winery Block Collection River Road Ranch
| 2005 | RUSSIAN RIVER VALLEY
★★★ $ $ This expressive, waxy-textured wine explodes with mixed fruit, mineral and light herbal flavors.

Grgich Hills Fumé Blanc | 2005 | **NAPA VALLEY**
★★★ $ $ Generous wild herb aromas and indulgent mango, pepper and stone flavors.

Hall | 2005 | **NAPA VALLEY**
★★★ $ $ Almond and lemon flavors soften up this wine's nearly austere, mineral-laden core.

Handley Handley Vineyard | 2004 | **DRY CREEK VALLEY**
★★ $ $ Awash in wildflower, apple and citrus flavors.

Honig | 2005 | **NAPA VALLEY**
★★ $ Light hints of honey add dimension to this wine's lemon- and melon-flavored base.

Kathryn Kennedy Winery | 2005 | **CALIFORNIA**
★★★ $ $ Kathryn Kennedy, esteemed for powerful Cabernet, is skilled with Sauvignon Blanc as well; this is lean, mineral-laden and delightfully aromatic.

Kenwood | 2005 | **SONOMA COUNTY**
★★ $ A light-hearted wine that tastes like peaches dusted with a little cinnamon and a twist of lemon.

Kunde Estate Magnolia Lane | 2004 | **SONOMA VALLEY**
★★ $ An herbal extravaganza ranging from aloe to grass to thyme, while citrus and pear flavors bring up the rear.

Mason | 2004 | **NAPA VALLEY**
★★★ $ $ Fresh-cut melon, piquant spice, mixed citrus and grass flavors add up to one indulgent wine well balanced by acidity.

Matanzas Creek Winery | 2004 | **SONOMA COUNTY**
★★ $ $ Excellent Sauvignon with light peach, almond and lemon.

Merryvale Juliana Vineyards | 2005 | **NAPA VALLEY**
★★★ $ $ The addition of Semillon and a touch of oak add weight to a wine dominated by lemon and pear flavors.

Rancho Zabaco Reserve | 2004 | **RUSSIAN RIVER VALLEY**
★★ $ Orange blossom, blanched almond, quince and citrus flavors offer an exotic angle to this Sonoma Sauvignon.

Robert Mondavi Winery To Kalon Vineyard Reserve Fumé Blanc | 2002 | **NAPA VALLEY**
★★★★ $ $ $ Mondavi coined the term "Fumé Blanc" and always produces one of the finest. This luscious wine offers fresh citrus, baked apple, nut and spicy oak flavors. Drink now–15 years.

Rochioli | 2005 | RUSSIAN RIVER VALLEY

★★★ $ $ $ Stellar Sauvignon that indulges with almond, lemon and orange flavors paved by stone.

Rudd | 2004 | NAPA VALLEY

★★★★ $ $ $ Don't let the screw cap fool you; this is top-flight wine with layers of mixed fruit, nut, spice and mineral flavors.

Sauvignon Republic Cellars | 2005 | RUSSIAN RIVER VALLEY

★★ $ $ Lovely wine full of papaya, floral and citrus flavors enlivened by a thin line of minerals.

Selene Hyde Vineyards | 2005 | CARNEROS

★★★ $ $ $ Zippy at first sip, this delicious Sauvignon reveals a rich complexity of mixed fruit and herb flavors that linger on the palate.

other california whites

California's diverse terrain can support a wide range of white grapes. Varieties from the climatically similar Rhône Valley, such as Roussanne, Marsanne and Viognier, are popular today. The latter is particularly appreciated for its succulent peach flavors and floral aromas. Plantings of Pinot Gris/Grigio (same grape) have more than doubled in the past few years. It can make wines that are luxuriously ripe, oozing apricot and spice in the style of Alsace, or show lighter, lemony flavors as it does in northern Italy. Alsatian-origin Pinot Blanc, appreciated for its pear, almond and lemon aromatics, is increasingly planted, though Riesling and Gewürztraminer, once common, are waning. Chenin Blanc makes a handful of charming wines in California, and you'll occasionally find a Muscat worth sipping.

BEST PAIRINGS California's Rhône-variety whites such as Viognier, Marsanne and Roussanne tend to be rich and aromatic—fine partners for flavorful bouillabaisse or cooked shellfish. Off-dry Riesling and Gewürztraminer are ideal for gingery, slightly spicy Asian dishes. Dry versions are great with seafood salads and pork. Serve heavier Pinot Blanc and Pinot Gris with meaty fish, like monkfish or swordfish. Save lighter examples for fish or chicken kebabs. California Chenin Blanc makes a lovely luncheon wine.

other white recommendations

Au Bon Climat Hildegard | 2003 | SANTA MARIA VALLEY
★★★★ $ $ $ Superb blend of Pinot Blanc and Pinot Gris, plus a dash of Aligoté. This offers flavors of cinnamon- and coconut-dusted pear, lemon and flowers. Drink now–6 years.

Babcock Pinot Grigio | 2005 | SANTA RITA HILLS
★★ $ Tongue-tickling pineapple, citrus and almond flavors are kept clean by zippy acidity.

Bargetto Dry Gewurztraminer | 2005 |
SANTA CRUZ MOUNTAINS
★★ $ Lithe-bodied white with aromas of flowers and green apple.

Beringer Alluvium Blanc | 2004 | KNIGHTS VALLEY
★★ $ $ Apple flavors are underlaid by stone in this smoky white.

Bonny Doon Vineyard Le Cigare Blanc | 2004 | CALIFORNIA
★★★ $ $ This terrific white is inspired by the rare, great whites of Châteauneuf-du-Pape. It's very dry, with abundant stony, floral, lime and plum flavors. Drink now–6 years.

Brassfield Estate Vineyard Pinot Grigio | 2004 | CLEAR LAKE
★★ $ $ A squeeze of lemony acidity refreshes nutty pear flavors.

Casa Nuestra Dry Chenin Blanc | 2005 | NAPA VALLEY
★★★ $ $ High-quality Chenin Blanc, full of minerals, spicy lemon and baked quince flavors.

Claiborne & Churchill Pinot Gris | 2005 |
ARROYO GRANDE VALLEY
★★★ $ $ This producer has mastered dry, Alsatian-styled wines. Baked pear and marzipan flavors here are rounded out with apricot and orange notes. Drink now–6 years.

Conundrum | 2004 | CALIFORNIA
★★★ $ $ This exquisite, multidimensional nectar has layers of flavor that run from flowers and spice to stone, smoke and oak.

Dry Creek Vineyard Dry Chenin Blanc | 2005 | CLARKSBURG
★★ $ Chenin Blanc is always in good hands at Dry Creek. This offers flavors of barely ripe pineapple with fresh herbs.

Handley Gewürztraminer | 2005 | ANDERSON VALLEY
★★ $ $ Fresh lime, spice and flower flavors are upfront in this great off-dry white, perfect for Thai food.

Kalin Cellars Semillon | 1996 | LIVERMORE VALLEY

★★★★ $ $ Not for everyone, this beautiful, though oxidized wine has grown complex with age. Dry lemon, almond and pungent herb flavors abound. Drink now–6 years.

Kendall-Jackson Vintner's Reserve Riesling | 2005 | CALIFORNIA

★ $ Slightly off-dry with citrus and peach flavors; a terrific choice for Chinese take-out.

Murrieta's Well Meritage | 2003 | LIVERMORE VALLEY

★★ $ $ The flavors of baked pear, lemon, sweet spice and stone in this Bordeaux-white blend are anything but shy. Drink now–8 years.

Rideau Vineyard Iris Estate Viognier | 2005 | SANTA YNEZ VALLEY

★★★ $ $ $ Slightly off-dry Viognier that exudes tropical, citrus, apple and pear flavors elevated by good acidity.

Robert Sinskey Vineyards Abraxas Vin de Terroir | 2004 | CARNEROS

★★★ $ $ $ An excellent, aromatic wine inspired by some of the superb blends of Alsace, this is full of citrus and pear flavors backed by hints of flowers, stones and spice.

Stony Hill Gewurztraminer | 2004 | NAPA VALLEY

★★★ $ $ One of Napa's great white wine producers makes perhaps its best Gewürztraminer. This dry wine oozes candied violet, lemon, almond and stone flavors.

St. Supéry Virtú | 2004 | NAPA VALLEY

★★★ $ $ Hints of sweet and savory spice underscore the mixed citrus and fragrant, refined mineral flavors in this beautifully balanced wine. Drink now–8 years.

Swanson Pinot Grigio | 2005 | NAPA VALLEY

★★ $ $ A perfume of lemon blossom and honeysuckle overtakes this apple- and citrus-flavored wine.

Tablas Creek Vineyard Esprit de Beaucastel | 2003 | PASO ROBLES

★★★★ $ $ $ A superb wine expressing a balance of sweet peach and pear flavors alongside savory spice notes.

Terre Rouge Enigma | 2004 | SIERRA FOOTHILLS

★★★ $ $ Nutty and full of tongue-tickling mineral flavors, this blend of three Rhône varieties expresses mixed citrus and apple aromatics.

Treana Mer Soleil Vineyard Marsanne/Viognier | 2002 |
CENTRAL COAST
★★★ $ $ There's a tremendous amount of ripe flavor here; grilled pineapple, mango, citrus and minerals are highlighted by floral notes.

Trefethen Dry Riesling | 2005 | OAK KNOLL DISTRICT
★★★ $ $ Terrific, zingy Riesling, this gives dry honey and mineral flavors with twists of orange.

Valley of the Moon Pinot Blanc | 2004 | SONOMA COUNTY
★★ $ Pineapple flavors take a surprisingly peppery turn.

Verdad Ibarra-Young Vineyard Albariño | 2005 |
SANTA YNEZ VALLEY
★★★ $ $ Northwest Spain's great white grape does just fine in California, with notes of honey, almond and lemon.

Vinum Cellars White Elephant | 2004 | CALIFORNIA
★★★ $ Infused with mineral, almond, pear and lavender-honey flavors, this uncommon blend is unusually appealing.

Westside White | 2004 | CENTRAL COAST
★★ $ $ This thick, golden-hued wine coats the mouth with waxy apricot, baked pear and sweet spice flavors.

california rosés

One might credit White Zinfandel for serving as a friendly entry point for Americans beginning to drink wine in the 1980s. One might also blame White Zinfandel for giving rosé the reputation for being sweet and insipid. While there is no reason why Zinfandel cannot make good rosé, California's best rosés are usually made from Pinot Noir, Grenache, Sangiovese and Carignane. They are incredibly versatile year-round, but ideal in warm months thanks to their dry, light berry–and-spice profile. "Blush" is simply a synonym for "rosé," but is usually applied to simpler versions.

BEST PAIRINGS Dry rosé is perfect sipped on its own on a hot summer day, but it's also supremely food-friendly. It tends to be light enough for delicate fish dishes, but with enough flavor to work with red meat dishes like lamb chops. It complements lots of foods in between, such as barbecue chicken, pastas with grilled vegetables or fish couscous.

rosé recommendations

Babcock's Big Fat Pink Shiraz | 2005 |
SANTA BARBARA COUNTY
★★ $ $ A cheeky label heralds a lovely wine, with cherry and spice.

Bonny Doon Vineyard Vin Gris de Cigare | 2005 | CALIFORNIA
★★★ $ Similar to a terrific French rosé, this has earthy aromas and
refreshing dry fruit flavors.

Fleming Jenkins Syrah Rosé | 2005 | SAN FRANCISCO BAY
★★ $ $ Fruity, peppery and a bit smoky, this slightly off-dry Syrah
rosé is best served really cold.

I'M | 2004 | NAPA VALLEY
★★ $ Irresistible flavors of strawberries, orange and a bit of spice.

Kuleto Estate Family Vineyards Rosato di Sangiovese
| 2004 | NAPA VALLEY
★★ $ A charming wine full of bright cherry, herbal, earthy flavors.

Pink Zeppelin | 2005 | PASO ROBLES
★★ $ A touch of tannin gives some bite to the red fruit and orange
flavors in this tasty wine.

Verdad | 2005 | ARROYO GRANDE VALLEY
★★★ $ A more serious rosé than most. Smoky notes add weight to
dry flavors of crushed berry and plum.

california reds

California is undeniably red wine country. The state's iconic
reds, from intense Cabernet Sauvignons to spicy Zinfandels
and smoky, herbal Rhône-style wines, secure its place
among the world's great wine-producing regions.

CALIFORNIA REDS

cabernet sauvignon &
bordeaux blends

In the pantheon of California wine, Cabernet Sauvignon is
definitely king. California's muscular Cabernet, inspired by
the legendary wines of Bordeaux, is bulging with dark berry
and earthy, herbal flavors. Though the grape exhibits

regional variation—exuding dense black fruit and smoke from mountain vineyards and lush red fruits and minerals from flatter regions—it is never shy. Many are designed to be aged for years, but are also accessible while young. Winemakers often follow Bordeaux tradition, blending Cabernet with other Bordeaux grapes like Merlot, Cabernet Franc, Petite Verdot and Malbec with the goal of adding complexity. These wines go by the term "Meritage" and many producers give them proprietary names, such as Opus One. Some of these Bordeaux varieties are bottled separately, most famously, Merlot (see p. 187). On its own, Cabernet Franc offers peppery, red berry flavors.

BEST PAIRINGS California Cabernet, with robust, peppery berry flavors and heavy tannins, cuts right through the fat of a well-marbled sirloin. The softer tannins of aged Cabernet make it excellent drinking with rack of lamb. Pour peppery Cabernet Franc with lamb kebabs or pork chops.

cabernet sauvignon recommendations

Altamura | 2002 | **NAPA VALLEY**
★★★ $ $ $ $ Succulent black and red cherry flavors are accented by peppery spice and supported by fine tannin. Drink now–8 years.

Barnett Vineyards | 2003 | **SPRING MOUNTAIN DISTRICT**
★★★ $ $ $ $ An outstanding, and distinctively Spring Mountain, Cabernet, this gushes intense blackberry flavors with almost coal-oil minerality. Drink in 2–15 years.

Beaulieu Vineyard | 2003 | **RUTHERFORD**
★★ $ $ Well-made, reliable Cabernet, this offers dark berry and chocolate flavors with moderate tannin. Drink now–5 years.

Beringer Private Reserve | 2002 | **NAPA VALLEY**
★★★★ $ $ $ $ Beringer has the means to achieve greatness, and this substantial wine does just that, showing dense berry, mineral oil, chocolate and spice flavors. Drink in 3–15 years.

Byington Bates Ranch Vineyard | 2003 |
SANTA CRUZ MOUNTAINS
★★★ $ $ $ Mountain Cabernet with layers of fragrant berry and animal-like flavors on a mineral-laden base. Drink in 2–10 years.

Caymus Vineyards | 2003 | **NAPA VALLEY**
★★★ $ $ $ $ Lush black cherry and light spice make Caymus a steakhouse favorite. Drink now–8 years.

Chateau St. Jean Cinq Cépages | 2002 | **SONOMA COUNTY**
★★★ $ $ $ $ Four other Bordeaux grapes add earthy complexity to Cabernet's bold powers in this savory blend. Drink now–10 years.

Chimney Rock | 2003 | **STAGS LEAP DISTRICT**
★★★ $ $ $ $ Fine minerals underscore an array of crushed berry and light brown sugar flavors. Drink now–10 years.

Clos du Bois | 2003 | **SONOMA COUNTY**
★★ $ $ Tasty as a raspberry crisp, this dry wine offers juicy fruit flavors highlighted by cinnamon and brown sugar notes.

Clos Du Val | 2003 | **NAPA VALLEY**
★★ $ $ $ This food-friendly wine from one of Napa's most reliable vintners offers distinct red fruit and spice flavors. Drink now–8 years.

Corison | 2002 | **NAPA VALLEY**
★★★ $ $ $ $ Velvety smooth with an underlying stoniness, this expresses fresh red cherry flavors. For more earthiness, try Corison's superlative Kronos Vineyard Cabernet. Drink in 2–10 years.

Dalla Valle Vineyards | 2003 | **NAPA VALLEY**
★★★★ $ $ $ $ An elegant wine with earthy red fruit and toasted nut flavors seasoned by spice and minerals. Drink in 2–15 years.

Dashe | 2002 | **ALEXANDER VALLEY**
★★★ $ $ $ Lovers of mineral-driven Cabernet will like this. Stony minerality shares the stage with ripe fruit; a bit of air coaxes out wild berries, chocolate and herbs. Drink in 1–10 years.

Diamond Creek Gravelly Meadow | 2003 | **NAPA VALLEY**
★★★★ $ $ $ $ One of the world's best Cabernets. Though full of cassis, berry and smoked pepper flavors, this wine shines as a result of its complex and profound stony underside. Drink in 1–20 years.

Duckhorn Vineyards Monitor Ledge Vineyard | 2002 |
NAPA VALLEY
★★★★ $ $ $ $ Violets shoot right through the tarry, peppery dark berry flavors in this beautiful wine. Drink now–10 years.

Estancia Keyes Canyon Ranches | 2003 | **PASO ROBLES**
★ $ Great-value Cabernet from a consistently good producer. Ripe fruit flavors are balanced by slightly bitter tannin.

Far Niente | 2003 | OAKVILLE
★★★ $ $ $ $ A bold, intriguing wine from one of Napa's grand cru producers. Noble dark fruit flavors are finessed by smoky mineral notes and robust tannin. Drink in 2–12 years.

Fisher Vineyards Coach Insignia | 2001 | NAPA VALLEY
★★★★ $ $ $ $ A luxurious ride of dark berry, mineral and spice, encased by velvety, mellowed tannin. Drink in 1–10 years.

Francis Coppola Diamond Collection Black Label Claret
| 2003 | CALIFORNIA
★ $ $ Dark berry flavors are balanced by chewy tannin.

Freemark Abbey Bosché | 2001 | NAPA VALLEY
★★★ $ $ $ $ A dusty, delicious wine with generous chocolate and cherry flavors bolstered by abundant minerals. Drink now–10 years.

Geyser Peak Winery Reserve | 2003 | ALEXANDER VALLEY
★★★ $ $ $ Lovers of lusty Australian reds will enjoy this California equivalent. Plush fruit, sticky lanolin and spice are held together by thick tannin. Drink now–10 years.

Grgich Hills | 2001 | NAPA VALLEY
★★★ $ $ $ $ One of the few winemakers responsible for putting Napa on the world stage, Mike Grgich is behind this classic wine, with red berry, fine minerals and spice. Drink now–10 years.

Hanna | 2003 | SONOMA COUNTY
★★ $ $ $ Finely polished, this offers the expected cassis and spicy pepper flavors, with surprising notes of laurel. Drink now–6 years.

Hess Select | 2003 | CALIFORNIA
★★ $ A consistently enjoyable, reliable wine worth buying by the case. Medium-bodied with pleasant cherry and spice flavors.

Honig Bartolucci Vineyard | 2002 | NAPA VALLEY
★★★ $ $ $ $ One of Honig's best Cabernets in years, this is full of dark berry flavors but lacy herbal, mineral and pepper notes keep things elegant. Drink in 2–10 years.

Jordan | 2002 | ALEXANDER VALLEY
★★ $ $ $ Velvety black fruit flavors surround a core of minerals and tannin. Drink now–8 years.

Joseph Phelps Vineyards | 2003 | NAPA VALLEY
★★★ $ $ $ Smile-inspiring fresh cherry flavors are brightened by vibrant acidity and pleasing spice. Drink now–8 years.

Kathryn Kennedy | 2002 | SANTA CRUZ MOUNTAINS
★★★★ $ $ $ $ Cassis and blackberry flavors, violets, chocolate and cedar are the makings of one stunning wine. Drink now–15 years.

Kendall-Jackson Grand Reserve | 2003 |
SONOMA/NAPA COUNTIES
★★ $ $ $ Chewy tannins fuse flavors of mocha, sweet spice and abundant mixed berries in this well-made wine. Drink now–6 years.

Kunde Estate Winery Reserve | 2002 | SONOMA VALLEY
★★★ $ $ $ $ Cassis flavors join apricot, orange and spice in this beautifully balanced wine. Drink now–8 years.

Lail Vineyards J. Daniel Cuvée | 2003 | NAPA VALLEY
★★★★ $ $ $ $ The dense spiced berry flavors and heavy tannins here are lightened by a ribbon of floral notes. Drink in 3–15 years.

news from a wine insider
california by Laurie Daniel

The 2005 Vintage
The 2005 harvest wasn't only huge (likely to be the state's second largest on record) but also of very high quality.

New Wines from Established Stars
Geyser Peak associate winemaker Ondine Chattan produced the 2003 XYZin 100, a ripe yet restrained wine made from century-old vines in Contra Costa County, east of San Francisco. She added two more Zins, called "50" and "10" (in reference to vine age), to her lineup in 2004, and the trio was released in January 2006.

Noted vintner David Ramey (who has worked at wineries such as Dominus and Rudd and has his own label, Ramey Wine Cellars) has signed on as consulting winemaker at the Napa Valley–based HALL Winery starting with the 2005 vintage. With vineyards in Rutherford and St. Helena, HALL specializes in Bordeaux varieties; its best wines are the concentrated, tightly knit Kathryn Hall Cabernet Sauvignon and a fresh, fragrant Sauvignon Blanc.

Restaurant News
In Santa Barbara County, Wine Cask Restaurant in Los Olivos (located in Fess Parker's Wine Country Inn & Spa) is worth a detour. Wine Cask owner Doug Margerum is a winemaker too, turning out some lovely wines under his own name, albeit in tiny quantities.

Lockwood Vineyard | 2004 | **MONTEREY**
★ $ This may be simple, but mixed berry and gentle spice flavors with moderate tannin give it some stuffing.

Markham Vineyards | 2002 | **NAPA VALLEY**
★★ $ $ Straightforward but high-quality, this shows violet, sweet tobacco and minerals accented with berry notes. Drink now–6 years.

Mayacamas Vineyards | 2001 | **MT. VEEDER**
★★★ $ $ $ $ A wall of chewy tannin supports exuberant red fruit and loads of dense minerals. Drink now–10 years.

Mazzocco Reserve | 2002 | **DRY CREEK VALLEY**
★★★ $ $ $ Perfumed, incenselike aromas infuse generous black fruit flavors. Drink in 1–8 years.

Merryvale Beckstoffer Vineyards Vineyard X | 2003 | **OAKVILLE**
★★★ $ $ $ Intense coffee and toasted oak flavors augment thick berries in this brash, tannic wine. Give it time. Drink in 2–10 years.

Murphy-Goode Sarah Block | 2003 | **ALEXANDER VALLEY**
★★★ $ $ $ Of all Murphy-Goode's Cabernets, this stands out for its berry and mineral flavors and chewy tannin. Drink in 2–8 years.

Oakville Ranch | 2003 | **NAPA VALLEY**
★★★ $ $ $ $ Not light, but not a bruiser either. Mixed fruit, spice and animal notes are integrated with finesse. Drink now–8 years.

Paul Hobbs | 2003 | **NAPA VALLEY**
★★★★ $ $ $ $ One of Paul Hobbs' darkest wines, this is full of blackberry and currant, black olive, bitter chocolate and black pepper flavors. Drink in 3–15 years.

Peju Province | 2003 | **NAPA VALLEY**
★★★ $ $ $ Cabernet is not a Mediterranean grape, but with the abundant herb, wild red berry and orange-spice flavors here, you might be fooled into thinking so. Drink now–6 years.

Pine Ridge | 2003 | **RUTHERFORD**
★★★ $ $ $ There is a smoky pinelike edge to the dark fruit flavors in this red, framed by minerals and tannin. Drink in 2–10 years.

PlumpJack Reserve | 2002 | **OAKVILLE**
★★★★ $ $ $ $ Dense red fruit, carbon and stony mineral flavors are held together by substantial tannin, which will soften beautifully with time. Drink in 2–15 years.

Riverside by Foppiano | 2004 | CALIFORNIA

★ $ Nothing complicated here, just tasty, fresh red berry flavors.

Robert Mondavi Winery Reserve | 2002 | NAPA VALLEY

★★★★ $ $ $ $ Mondavi focuses on earth rather than plush berry flavors. This still has plenty of ripe fruit, but is awash in stone, leather, pepper and animal flavors, too. Drink in 2–20 years.

Robert Sinskey Vineyards RSV SLD Estate | 2002 |
STAGS LEAP DISTRICT

★★★ $ $ $ $ Mineral and spice flavors are enveloped by luscious black cherry. Drink now–10 years.

Rudd | 2003 | OAKVILLE

★★★★ $ $ $ $ This brawny wine ripples with berry flavors and fine minerals and is kept delicate by spice. Drink now–12 years.

Rutherford Hill | 2003 | NAPA VALLEY

★★★ $ $ $ A lusty, dark fruit–driven wine lathered with molasses and tar flavors from toasted oak. Drink in 1–8 years.

Seavey | 2003 | NAPA VALLEY

★★★ $ $ $ $ This graceful, sultry Cabernet shows expressive dark berry flavors seasoned by minerals and tannin. Drink now–8 years.

Sequoia Grove | 2002 | NAPA VALLEY

★★★ $ $ $ A bit old-fashioned, in a good way. This is archetypal Napa Cabernet, with solid cassis, pepper and coffee flavors bolstered by firm tannin. Drink now–6 years.

Shafer | 2003 | NAPA VALLEY

★★★ $ $ $ $ Though not the biggest gun in Shafer's armory, this still offers intense black fruit, celery seed, smoke and bold mineral oil flavors. Drink in 2–12 years.

Silverado Vineyards Limited | 2002 | NAPA VALLEY

★★★ $ $ $ $ Excellent Cabernet bursting with flavors of currant, chocolate and violets, minerals and tannin. Drink now–12 years.

Simi | 2003 | ALEXANDER VALLEY

★★ $ $ $ Lush, juicy berry flavors have Alexander Valley's common signature of pepper in this well-composed wine. Drink now–5 years.

Spottswoode | 2003 | ST. HELENA

★★★★ $ $ $ $ An exquisitely detailed wine. Velvety dark fruits are layered with floral and exotic spice, salty minerals and smoke, roasted coffee and dark chocolate. Drink in 2–15 years.

Staglin Family Vineyard | 2003 | **Rutherford**
★★★★ $$$$ Masterfully sculpted, this weighty wine gives mounds of dark fruit flavors with contours of pepper, tobacco and light notes of minerals. Drink in 2–10 years.

St. Supéry Limited Edition Dollarhide | 2001 | **NAPA VALLEY**
★★★ $$$$ A Cabernet defined by dense, smoky, meaty, dark berry flavors and heavily laden with salty minerals. Serve this with roast meat. Drink in 2–10 years.

The Terraces | 2002 | **NAPA VALLEY**
★★★ $$$ This intensely stony wine is beautifully softened by an array of red and dark berry flavors. Drink now–10 years.

Terra Valentine Wurtele Vineyard | 2003 |
SPRING MOUNTAIN DISTRICT
★★★★ $$$$ Sensational Spring Mountain wine that illustrates what the district can do with Cabernet. Bold fruit flavors are elevated by tongue-tingling minerals and spice. Drink in 2–12 years.

Trefethen Halo | 2001 | **OAK KNOLL DISTRICT**
★★★★ $$$$ This robust wine is grounded by dense black fruit, carbon, smoke and fine tannin. Drink now–12 years.

Wente Vineyards Charles Wetmore Reserve | 2003 |
LIVERMORE VALLEY
★★ $$ From one of the older names in California winemaking comes this Cabernet, rich with coffee, toffee and red berry flavors.

Wild Horse | 2003 | **PASO ROBLES**
★★ $$ Exuberant cherry flavors and high acidity make for good drinking with grilled steaks.

star producers
cabernet sauvignon

best value
1 Fish Eye
2 Gallo of Sonoma
3 Hess Select
4 Laurel Glen
5 Miner Family Vineyards

best of the best
1 Colgin
2 Dalla Valle
3 Diamond Creek
4 Harlan Estate
5 Ridge

bordeaux blend recommendations

Bernardus Marinus | 2002 | **CARMEL VALLEY**
★★★ $ $ $ A core of wild red berry flavors is accented with notes of animal and earthy spice. A lovely, refined wine. Drink now–8 years.

Clos du Bois Marlstone | 2002 | **ALEXANDER VALLEY**
★★★ $ $ $ A longtime favorite, Marlstone oozes flavors of cassis, herbs, chocolate and pepper spice with fine minerals and tannin. Drink now–12 years.

Dominus | 2003 | **NAPA VALLEY**
★★★★ $ $ $ $ The powers behind Pomerol's Pétrus deliver what is surely the most Bordeaux-like wine from Napa. Supremely elegant, this reflects stunning fruit and terroir. Drink in 2–20 years.

Estancia Meritage | 2003 | **PASO ROBLES**
★★ $ $ $ As prices for California Bordeaux blends keep climbing, it's good to rely on well-made, reasonably priced wines like this.

Harlan Estate | 2002 | **NAPA VALLEY**
★★★★ $ $ $ $ This rare wine exhibits power and grace at once, with perfectly balanced fruit and mineral flavors. It's worth the search and the small loan you might need to pay for it. Drink in 3–20 years.

Métisse | 2003 | **NAPA VALLEY**
★★★ $ $ $ $ An intriguing mélange of aromas and flavors, ranging from mixed berries to flowers, minerals and spice. Drink in 1–8 years.

Miner The Oracle | 2003 | **NAPA VALLEY**
★★★★ $ $ $ $ Ripe berry and roasted coffee flavors are followed by polished minerals and spice. Drink in 2–15 years.

Mount Veeder Winery Reserve | 2002 | **NAPA VALLEY**
★★★ $ $ $ $ Black and tannic, this brims with dark berry, bitter chocolate, cumin and mineral flavors. Drink in 3–12 years.

Murphy-Goode Wild Card Claret | 2003 | **ALEXANDER VALLEY**
★★ $ $ This blend reliably gives crushed berry and spice flavors.

Opus One | 2002 | **NAPA VALLEY**
★★★★ $ $ $ $ One of the best Opus wines in years. Spice and minerals balance rich dark fruit and chocolate. Drink in 2–25 years.

Peju Province Cabernet Franc | 2003 | **NAPA VALLEY**
★★ $ $ $ Unusually aromatic, this wine is alive with herb and flower flavors, some pepper and bright red berries. Drink now–6 years.

Peter Michael Winery Les Pavots | 2003 | KNIGHTS VALLEY
★★★★ $ $ $ $ It's appropriate that California's state flower, the poppy (pavot), should grace one of its greatest clarets. This is full of dark fruit, mineral and smoke flavors. Drink in 2–15 years.

Ridge Monte Bello | 2003 | SANTA CRUZ MOUNTAINS
★★★★ $ $ $ $ This exceptional bottling belongs in the company of the world's finest wines. Its labyrinth of berry, animal, stone and spice flavors is simply captivating. Drink in 3–25 years.

Sebastiani Secolo | 2003 | SONOMA COUNTY
★★★ $ $ $ Cherry and berry flavors are nuanced with smoky tea and chocolate in this stellar blend. Drink now–10 years.

Spring Mountain Vineyard Elivette Reserve | 2002 | NAPA VALLEY
★★★★ $ $ $ $ One sip reveals this as wine made from mountain-grown fruit; it's full of intense berry flavors and profound, smoky minerals. Give it time. Drink in 3–15 years.

St. Supéry Élu | 2001 | NAPA VALLEY
★★★ $ $ $ $ Earthy chocolate, berry and mineral flavors get a spice kick. Drink now–10 years.

Trefethen Cabernet Franc | 2003 | OAK KNOLL DISTRICT
★★ $ $ $ Cabernet Franc's telltale peppery notes come through in this relatively light, cherry-kissed wine. Drink now–5 years.

Vinum Cellars The Scrapper Cabernet Franc | 2003 | EL DORADO COUNTY
★★ $ $ $ Savory, spiced chocolate, almond and pepper flavors flow together in this fascinating wine. Drink now–8 years.

CALIFORNIA REDS

merlot

Merlot is responsible for some of the most exceptional wines in California. Fueled in part by anti-Merlot ramblings in the movie *Sideways*, a Merlot backlash currently has some consumers turning their back on the grape. Merlot was the house pour of choice in the mid-nineties, thanks to its velvety texture, plumlike flavors and violet aromatics. And it remains one of the world's most noble grapes as well as the backbone of some of the state's best bottlings.

BEST PAIRINGS Merlot is generally less tannic than Cabernet, but has enough body to be served similarly—steaks, roasted lamb or venison. It is particularly good with duck. Simple Merlot is a fine choice for burgers and ribs.

merlot recommendations

Atalon | 2003 | NAPA VALLEY
★★ $ $ $ Dark fruit and chocolate flavors are expertly framed by chewy tannin and good acidity. Drink now–6 years.

Cakebread Cellars | 2003 | NAPA VALLEY
★★ $ $ $ Classic Napa Merlot, with voluptuous plum and light spice flavors framed by fine tannin. Drink now–6 years.

Clos du Bois Reserve | 2003 | ALEXANDER VALLEY
★★ $ $ Plum and berry flavors take a peppery, chocolaty turn in a wine that is consistently tasty year after year.

Crichton Hall Vineyard | 2001 | NAPA VALLEY
★★★ $ $ $ Harmonious wine with indulgent black cherry and plum flavors that coat the mouth with each sip. Drink now–6 years.

Duckhorn Vineyards Estate Grown | 2003 | NAPA VALLEY
★★★★ $ $ $ $ One of California's finest Merlots, this is full of red and black fruit flavors, spicy oak and refined minerals, yet it remains remarkably restrained. Give it time. Drink in 2–15 years.

Foppiano Vineyards | 2002 | RUSSIAN RIVER VALLEY
★ $ Strawberry and nut flavors aren't typically Merlot-like, but they are delicious here.

J. Lohr Los Osos | 2003 | PASO ROBLES
★ $ A whimsical, cherry- and berry-laden wine.

Kendall-Jackson Vineyard Estates Taylor Peak | 2003 | BENNETT VALLEY
★★★ $ $ $ Dry, earthy red fruit flavors with a savory hint of spice make this a wine for food. Drink now–5 years.

Matanzas Creek Winery | 2003 | BENNETT VALLEY
★★★ $ $ $ There's plenty of fruit here, but the real interest is the sticky herb and earth flavors lightened by unexpected floral notes. Drink now–6 years.

Murphy-Goode | 2003 | ALEXANDER VALLEY
★★ $ $ Medium-weight with ripe, sun-drenched fruit flavors.

Nickel & Nickel Suscol Ranch | 2003 | **NAPA VALLEY**
★ ★ ★ $ $ $ $ Blackberry, herb and tarlike mineral flavors unite in this sophisticated wine. Drink now–8 years.

Ramsay | 2002 | **NAPA VALLEY**
★ ★ $ Kent Rasmussen is known more for Pinot, but he crafts this plush, plummy Merlot for a good price.

Robert Sinskey Vineyards | 2002 | **CARNEROS**
★ ★ ★ $ $ $ Made from organic grapes, this meaty wine entices with berry, plum and smoky mineral flavors. Drink now–10 years

Rutherford Hill | 2003 | **NAPA VALLEY**
★ ★ $ $ Solid Merlot with dark fruit, fine tannin and good acidity.

Silverado Vineyards | 2002 | **NAPA VALLEY**
★ ★ $ $ $ This velvety Merlot offers finely textured fruit, spice and tannin. Drink now–6 years.

Stonestreet | 2003 | **ALEXANDER VALLEY**
★ ★ ★ $ $ $ There is plenty of fruit in this spicy, tannic Merlot, but flavors of earth and stone predominate. Drink now–8 years.

Trefethen | 2002 | **OAK KNOLL DISTRICT**
★ ★ ★ $ $ $ Complex and engaging, while still easy-to-enjoy, this is full of spicy fruit flavors, minerals and tannin. Drink now–8 years.

CALIFORNIA REDS

pinot noir

Pinot Noir is difficult to grow even in its native Burgundy and represents the elusive Holy Grail for many California vintners. After decades of discouraging results, the grape today is capable of greatness, particularly from the cooler parts of California like the Russian River Valley, Carneros, Santa Barbara County, the Central Coast and Mendocino. Riper and less subtle than the Burgundian ideal, California Pinot can exude graceful cherry, smoke and spice flavors.

BEST PAIRINGS California Pinot Noir is one of the world's most flexible wines. Lighter-bodied than Cabernet or Merlot, yet richer than its Burgundy counterparts, it does just as well with meat as it does with fish. Pour it with pan-roasted salmon with wild mushrooms or leg of lamb.

pinot noir recommendations

Alderbrook | 2004 | RUSSIAN RIVER VALLEY
★★ $ $ This exuberant Pinot explodes with brash berry and apricot flavors and ends with a spicy finish.

Au Bon Climat Knox Alexander | 2003 | SANTA MARIA VALLEY
★★★★ $ $ $ One of California's great Pinot producers makes this majestic wine. Oozing spice and ripe red fruit, it remains light on the tongue. Drink now–12 years.

Babcock Grand Cuvee | 2004 | SANTA RITA HILLS
★★ $ $ $ A good, consistent producer from Santa Barbara County, Babcock offers another treat, with black cherry, stone and almost bourbon-spice flavors. Drink now–6 years.

Bargetto | 2004 | SANTA CRUZ MOUNTAINS
★★ $ $ Fine fruit and sweet spice flavors come together for simple elegance in this lighter-style Pinot.

Belle Glos Clark & Telephone Vineyard | 2004 |
SANTA MARIA VALLEY
★★★ $ $ $ Pinot Noir takes a pleasing Mediterranean twist with distinct flavors of oregano and thyme, dried orange peel and smoke. Drink now–8 years.

Byron | 2004 | SANTA MARIA VALLEY
★★ $ $ Demure wine, this has all the fruit and spice one expects from California Pinot without any flash.

Calera Reed Vineyard | 2002 | MT. HARLAN
★★★★ $ $ $ Exceptional, hypnotic Pinot Noir. Smoky, pungent herb and earth flavors swirl over a pool of dry red berries and polished minerals. Drink now–15 years.

Cambria Bench Break Vineyard | 2004 | SANTA MARIA VALLEY
★★★ $ $ $ A bouquet of roses, violets and cherry blossoms are filled out with flavors of fruit and minerals. Drink now–6 years.

Chateau St. Jean | 2004 | SONOMA COUNTY
★★ $ $ Ripe berry and coffee flavors are restrained by high acidity in this well-made, reliable red.

Claiborne & Churchill Twin Creeks | 2003 | EDNA VALLEY
★★★ $ $ $ Known for its excellent Alsatian-styled whites, this winery's Burgundian efforts are beautifully realized. Berry, herb and mineral flavors are tightly woven with fine tannin. Drink now–8 years.

Clos Pegase Mitsuko's Vineyard | 2004 | CARNEROS
★★★ $ $ $ Proof that graceful Pinot can come from California, this pleases with berry and floral flavors, a bit of spice and fine minerals.

Davis Bynum Lindleys' Knoll | 2002 | RUSSIAN RIVER VALLEY
★★★ $ $ $ $ Fans of earthy wines will enjoy this—it's packed with animal and mushroom scents softened by juicy berry and aromatic floral flavors. Drink now–6 years.

Etude | 2004 | CARNEROS
★★★ $ $ $ Though not as profound as Etude's Heirloom Pinot, this is excellent drinking nonetheless. It indulges without spoiling, with berry, lavender and minerals. Drink now–6 years.

Foley Rancho Santa Rosa | 2004 | SANTA RITA HILLS
★★ $ $ $ Sappy Pinot that charms with ripe berry flavors.

Goldeneye | 2003 | ANDERSON VALLEY
★★★ $ $ $ $ A smoky wine with berry and cherry flavors accented with salty mineral notes. Drink now–8 years.

Joseph Swan Vineyards Trenton Estate Vineyard | 2003 | RUSSIAN RIVER VALLEY
★★★★ $ $ $ Superb, multidimensional wine with layers of fruit from berry to apricot to orange, plus savory spice, herbs and intense minerality. Age it. Drink in 1–15 years.

La Crema | 2004 | ANDERSON VALLEY
★★ $ $ $ In an unusual, tasty twist, this Pinot shows flavors of crushed pears, in addition to the standard cherry flavors.

Meridian | 2004 | CENTRAL COAST
★ $ Good name for value-Pinot, this offers cherry and spice for $10.

Merry Edwards Meredith Estate | 2003 | SONOMA COAST
★★★★ $ $ $ Merry Edwards' eponymous wine digs deep into the earth, with mineral and spice flavors infusing ripe berries. Time will soften the tannin. Drink in 2–12 years.

Morgan Double L Vineyard | 2004 | SANTA LUCIA HIGHLANDS
★★★ $ $ $ Always good, Morgan is even better this year. Minerals bring out refined berry, flower and spice flavors. Drink now–8 years.

Peter Michael Winery Le Moulin Rouge | 2004 | SANTA LUCIA HIGHLANDS
★★★★ $ $ $ Indulgent, elegant Pinot showing plush dark fruit flavors finished by details of minerals and spice. Drink now–10 years.

Robert Sinskey Vineyards | 2004 | **CARNEROS**
★ ★ ★ $ $ Lovely wine with a taut body and ripples of berry, violet and sculpted minerals. Drink now–8 years.

Rochioli | 2004 | **RUSSIAN RIVER VALLEY**
★ ★ ★ $ $ $ Few wines better express the Russian River. This lean berry-and-spice-flavored wine is all about finesse. Drink now–8 years.

Rusack Reserve | 2004 | **SANTA RITA HILLS**
★ ★ ★ $ $ $ Velvety berry and expressive floral flavors would be hedonistic if not contained by fine, firm tannin in this darkly hued wine. Drink now–8 years.

Saintsbury Brown Ranch | 2003 | **CARNEROS**
★ ★ ★ $ $ $ Deeply delicious cherry and apple flavors are brought to life by palate-perking minerals. Drink now–10 years.

Sanford | 2004 | **SANTA RITA HILLS**
★ ★ ★ $ $ Sanford's basic Pinot has an earthiness that many wines strive for. It is smoky, mineral-laden and full of dark fruit.

Thomas Fogarty | 2003 | **SANTA CRUZ MOUNTAINS**
★ ★ ★ $ $ Black cherry accented by violets and maple makes for one delicious wine. Drink now–6 years.

Wild Horse | 2004 | **CENTRAL COAST**
★ ★ $ $ A classic and well-made Pinot that offers just the right amount of bright cherry and berry flavors.

Woodenhead Buena Tierra Vineyard | 2003 |
RUSSIAN RIVER VALLEY
★ ★ ★ ★ $ $ $ A lithe wine, in spite of generous dark berry and date flavors with a dusting of cocoa and minerals. Drink now–12 years.

star producers
pinot noir

best value
1 Echelon
2 Meridian Vineyards
3 Navarro Vineyards
4 Oasis
5 Pepperwood Grove

best of the best
1 Au Bon Climat
2 Calera
3 Joseph Swan Vineyards
4 Sea Smoke
5 Woodenhead

CALIFORNIA REDS

syrah

Plantings of Syrah, sometimes called Shiraz, have increased more than twelvefold in Californian soils in the past decade. Syrah is famous for making some of France's finest reds in the northern Rhône Valley, and it thrives in California's warm as well as cool regions. And it's flexible. Winemakers who honor the French style produce wines with smoky, wild berry and spice flavors. Those following the Australian model craft wines which are fuller-bodied, packed with jammy dark fruit, spice and, often, high alcohol.

BEST PAIRINGS Syrah's smoky, spicy flavors and suave texture make it perfect for flavorful meat dishes. Drink it with wine-braised oxtails or short ribs. It's also marvelous with venison, boar, duck and mushroom risotto.

syrah recommendations

Alban Vineyards Reva | 2003 | **EDNA VALLEY**
★ ★ ★ ★ $ $ $ $ One of the world's great Syrah producers makes this stunning wine, with dense berry, charcoal, pepper and animal flavors. Drink in 1–15 years.

Babcock Black Label Cuvee | 2002 | **CENTRAL COAST**
★ ★ ★ $ $ This is satiny smooth, with dark berry, light pepper, violet and polished mineral flavors. Drink now–8 years.

Beckmen Vineyards Purisima Mountain Vineyard | 2003 |
SANTA YNEZ VALLEY
★ ★ ★ $ $ $ Full-bodied tannic wine saturated with roasted coffee, blackberry and smoky earth flavors. Drink now–6 years.

Failla Phoenix Ranch | 2004 | **NAPA VALLEY**
★ ★ ★ ★ $ $ $ Excellent Rhône Valley-like Syrah, this offers a rush of wild berry, exotic spice and salty mineral flavors yet still remains graceful. Drink now–8 years.

Fess Parker Rodney's Vineyard | 2003 |
SANTA BARBARA COUNTY
★ ★ ★ $ $ $ Enticing and generous flavors of espresso, chocolate, blueberry and brown sugar. Drink now–8 years.

Fleming Jenkins Madden Ranch | 2003 | LIVERMORE VALLEY
★★★ $ $ $ This lithe, graceful wine offers dark berry and earthy coffee flavors lightened by ribbons of flowers. Drink now–5 years.

Foley Rancho Santa Rosa | 2003 | SANTA RITA HILLS
★★ $ $ $ Enchanting, peppery blueberry flavors are made even more appealing by the support of velvety tannin.

Francis Coppola Diamond Collection Green Label Syrah-Shiraz | 2004 | CALIFORNIA
★ $ Spicy, juicy and simply good drinking; an affordably priced gem perfect for barbecue.

IO | 2002 | SANTA BARBARA COUNTY
★★ $ $ $ This full-flavored and full-bodied wine offers lots of berry, spicy pleasure.

Kendall-Jackson Vintner's Reserve | 2003 | CALIFORNIA
★★ $ Smoke and earth flavors are sweetened up by ripe berries in this accessible, reliable wine.

Kuleto Estate Family Vineyards | 2002 | NAPA VALLEY
★★ $ $ $ Black cherry, smoky, savory spice and chewy tannin make for great drinking with a thick, dry-aged steak. Drink now–5 years.

M. Cosentino | 2003 | CALIFORNIA
★★ $ $ Sticky berry and light coconut flavors come together in this crowd-pleasing wine.

Miner | 2003 | NAPA VALLEY
★★★ $ $ $ A heavy bottle holds a wine of surprising delicacy, with dark fruit, cocoa, flowers and fine minerals. Drink now–8 years.

Patianna Organic Vineyards Fairbairn Ranch | 2003 | MENDOCINO
★★★ $ $ $ Big, ripe blackberries saturate a core of smoky, savory, earthy mineral flavors in this biodynamic wine. Drink now–5 years.

Qupé Bien Nacido Hillside Estate | 2002 | SANTA MARIA VALLEY
★★★★ $ $ $ One of California's Syrah pioneers shows experience has advantages. This beautifully structured wine brings an infinite array of lush fruit and earthy mineral flavors. Drink in 1–12 years.

Rabbit Ridge | 2003 | PASO ROBLES
★★ $ $ Ripe red berry flavors are given a savory twist by almost salty mineral and spice notes.

Red Zeppelin Bear Valley Ranch & O'Neill Vineyards | 2004 | CENTRAL COAST

★★ $ $ A lighter style of Syrah, this has loads of red fruit flavors, a bit of spice and uplifting acidity.

Rosenblum Cellars Rominger Vineyard | 2004 | YOLO COUNTY

★★ $ $ $ Yolo County isn't often seen on wine labels, but flavors straight from a blackberry patch make it a region worth discovering.

Rusack | 2003 | SANTA BARBARA COUNTY

★★★ $ $ Sultry Syrah with a velvet mouth-feel, this shows plush dark fruit, lanolin, tobacco and spice flavors. Drink now–5 years.

Shannon Ridge | 2003 | LAKE COUNTY

★★★ $ $ $ Ripe fruit and spice mark this stalwart Syrah from an overlooked region. Serve it with braised short ribs. Drink now–5 years.

Terre Rouge High Slopes | 2002 | SIERRA FOOTHILLS

★★★ $ $ $ A distinctively earthy wine, with mineral, herb and spice flavors highlighted by red berry notes. Drink now–6 years.

Valley of the Moon | 2002 | SONOMA COUNTY

★★ $ Rich chocolaty, minty, berry flavors flow throughout this full-bodied, enjoyable Syrah.

Viader | 2003 | NAPA VALLEY

★★★ $ $ $ $ Suave but also hedonistic, this has plush, spicy berry and orange flavors, plus fine minerals and herbs. Drink now–8 years.

Wattle Creek Shiraz | 2001 | ALEXANDER CREEK

★★ $ Called "Shiraz" for a reason, this is thick stuff in the Australian model, with berry, violet and spice flavors.

---

star producers
syrah

best value

1 Bonny Doon Vineyard
2 Concannon
3 Firestone
4 Hayman & Hill
5 Valley of the Moon

best of the best

1 Alban Vineyards
2 Copain
3 Edmunds St. John
4 Failla
5 Qupé

CALIFORNIA REDS

zinfandel

Zinfandel was once thought to be a native American grape. We now know that it descended from an obscure Croatian grape and is a cousin of the southern Italian Primitivo. But Zinfandel's long history in California still gives it an American identity. The grape is anything but shy. Some vintners exploit its hedonistic tendencies, making richly flavored wines with dizzying levels of alcohol. Others apply a subtle hand, making gracefully balanced wines similar to claret. With more than a century in the state, patches of "old vine" Zinfandel exist and are known for making wines of unique intensity. Avoid White Zinfandel, the grape's rosé version.

BEST PAIRINGS Zinfandel might not be American in origin, but it most certainly belongs in the company of some of America's favorite foods. Simpler, high-acid versions are the perfect spaghetti-red and are great with calzones, pizza and barbecue ribs. More complex styles can be enjoyed like fine Cabernet, but have a particular affinity for lamb. High-octane Zinfandels require meaty, fatty dishes to absorb the alcohol. Braised short ribs do just fine.

zinfandel recommendations

Alderbrook Old Vine | 2003 | **DRY CREEK VALLEY**
★ ★ ★ $ $ Dark berry flavors are lightened by subtle flower notes in this full-bodied, yet restrained wine. Drink now–5 years.

Bocce | 2003 | **CALIFORNIA**
★ $ Simple berry flavors offer plenty of enjoyment for casual meals.

Cline Big Break | 2004 | **CONTRA COSTA COUNTY**
★ ★ ★ $ $ $ Grapes from century-old vines bring earth, herbs, wild fruit and cigar ash notes to one impressive wine. Drink now–7 years.

Dashe Todd Brothers Ranch Old Vines | 2003 |
ALEXANDER VALLEY
★ ★ ★ $ $ $ Intense flavors of cherry brandy are further augmented by dry, bitter chocolate and coffee notes. Heavy tannins support these powerful flavors. Drink in 1–8 years.

Dry Creek Vineyard Heritage | 2003 | SONOMA COUNTY
★★ $ This berry- and herb-flavored red is nice and juicy, just like Zinfandel should be.

Easton Estate Bottled | 2002 | SHENANDOAH VALLEY
★★★ $ $ $ Aromas of incense and cedar bring a new dimension to tart, crushed red berry and mineral flavors in this engaging wine.

Edizione Pennino | 2003 | RUTHERFORD
★★ $ $ $ Thick berry flavors are accented with chocolate and spiced orange in an old-style wine with contemporary appeal.

Edmeades | 2004 | MENDOCINO COUNTY
★★ $ $ Mendocino's relatively cool climate brings out the smoke and mineral flavors of this berry- and light spice–laden wine.

Foppiano | 2002 | DRY CREEK VALLEY
★★ $ Positively Chianti-like; the tart red fruit flavors here receive a kick of sticky herbs, making for one great pizza wine.

Handley | 2003 | MENDOCINO COUNTY
★★ $ $ This tastes like springtime, with floral aromas followed by berry and mineral flavors.

Hanna Bismark Mountain Vineyard | 2002 | SONOMA VALLEY
★★★ $ $ $ $ Big, powerful blackberry flavors are wrapped around a core of ironlike minerals. Drink now–8 years.

Joseph Swan Vineyards Stellwagen Vineyard | 2002 | SONOMA VALLEY
★★★★ $ $ Joseph Swan is one of California's great, quiet wineries. This medium-bodied wine is full of finesse, with red fruit, herb and dusty rose flavors underlined by fine minerals. Drink now–12 years.

Kendall-Jackson Vintner's Reserve | 2003 | CALIFORNIA
★ $ Bright strawberry and spice flavors come together for reliable, pleasurable drinking for any occasion.

Limerick Lane Collins Vineyard | 2004 | RUSSIAN RIVER VALLEY
★★★★ $ $ $ Superbly balanced wine, full of cherry and raspberry flavors. This Zinfandel is more plush than most claret, but has the same sort of elegance. Drink now–8 years.

Rabbit Ridge Westside | 2004 | PASO ROBLES
★★ $ $ Tasty Zin that consistently delivers flavors of red cherry, hibiscus and pomegranate with notes of spice.

Rancho Zabaco Stefani Vineyard | 2004 | DRY CREEK VALLEY

★★★ $ $ Rancho Zabaco's Dancing Bull is good value, but their single-vineyard Zinfandels are truly special. This is full of ripe berry and toasted spice flavors, balanced by high acidity.

Ravenswood Dickerson | 2003 | NAPA VALLEY

★★★★ $ $ $ Famous for their basic Zin, Ravenswood's single-vineyard wines reveal the vintner's real skill: seductive aromas of chocolate, mint, spice and mineral-laced berry. Drink now–10 years.

Ridge Lytton Springs | 2004 | DRY CREEK VALLEY

★★★★ $ $ $ Impressive array of cherry, orange and peach flavors beautifully balanced by fine minerals. Drink now–15 years.

Robert Biale Vineyards Black Chicken | 2004 | NAPA VALLEY

★★★★ $ $ $ Dense, blackberry flavors with scratches of minerals and spice. Delicious. Drink now–8 years.

Rosenblum Cellars Monte Rosso Vineyard Reserve | 2004 | SONOMA VALLEY

★★★ $ $ $ This robust Zin needs a warning label, lest the berry and spice flavors make you forget its high alcohol content.

Sebastiani | 2004 | SONOMA COUNTY

★ $ This longtime California producer provides an easy-drinking, full-bodied, fruit-driven wine.

Seghesio Family Vineyards Old Vine | 2003 | SONOMA COUNTY

★★★★ $ $ $ A thick Zin infused with lanolin, wild blackberry and tobacco flavors. Profound minerality and meaty tannin give it a firm frame. Drink now–8 years.

star producers
zinfandel

best value
1 Cline Cellars
2 Dry Creek Vineyard
3 Rancho Zabaco
4 Ravenswood
5 Sobon Estate

best of the best
1 Joseph Swan Vineyards
2 Limerick Lane
3 Martinelli
4 Ridge
5 Seghesio Family Vineyards

Shannon Ridge | 2002 | **LAKE COUNTY**
★★ **$ $** Char, berries and smoky tannins make this a steak wine.

The Terraces | 2003 | **NAPA VALLEY**
★★★ **$ $** Bold mountain-fruit flavors are spiced by smoky oak in an impressive, savory wine. Drink now–8 years.

Trentadue Winery La Storia | 2003 | **ALEXANDER VALLEY**
★★★ **$ $ $** Romance in a glass, with sultry berry flavors studded with fine minerals and dusted with sweet spice. Drink now–8 years.

Turley Dusi Vineyard | 2004 | **PASO ROBLES**
★★★★ **$ $ $** When it comes to thick, indulgent Zin, this is as good as it gets. Full of black fruit and loads of spice. Drink now–8 years.

Woodenhead Martinelli Road Vineyard Old Vine | 2003 |
RUSSIAN RIVER VALLEY
★★★★ **$ $ $** Beautiful, big and mouthwatering, this is surprisingly restrained. Smoked-meat flavors combine with clove, cola, berries and mineral flavors. Drink now–8 years.

other california reds

Mediterranean grapes have thrived in California soils since legions of immigrants introduced them a century ago, but have been taken seriously by winegrowers only in the last decade. In the 1980s, a group that dubbed themselves the "Rhône Rangers" discovered southern French grapes like Grenache, Mourvèdre, Carignane and Petite Sirah could produce interesting wines here. But despite hope, Italian grapes like Sangiovese, Dolcetto and Barbera have yet to really impress, though they make some nice wines.

BEST PAIRINGS Juicy, tangy reds such as Grenache and Carignane are best bets for lamb burgers or sausages, as well as pasta salad. Sophisticated versions do better with wood-grilled lamb steaks and game. Heavier, inky Mourvèdre and Petite Sirah overwhelm most light foods. Stick to braised meats or steaks. Inexpensive fruit-forward Cal-Ital wines such as Barbera, Dolcetto or Sangiovese are great for standard Italian-American classics: spaghetti with meatballs or lasagna. Serve higher-quality wines with roasted veal chops, wild mushroom risotto or prime rib.

other red recommendations

Bargetto La Vita | 2000 | **SANTA CRUZ MOUNTAINS**
★ ★ ★ $ $ $ An engaging wine with an unusual mélange of wild red berry and animal flavors. Drink now–6 years.

Beckmen Vineyards Estate Grenache | 2004 |
SANTA MARIA VALLEY
★ ★ $ $ Sticky strawberry and cherry flavors with a hint of spice and tannin to chew on at the end.

Big House Red | 2004 | **CALIFORNIA**
★ ★ $ This wild mix of many different Mediterranean grape varieties yields an exuberant wine with flavors of red fruit, herbs and spice.

Clendenen Family Vineyards Bricco Buon Natale Nebbiolo
| 2001 | **SANTA MARIA VALLEY**
★ ★ ★ ★ $ $ $ As close to an excellent Barolo as any non-Italian Nebbiolo can come, this is powerful, elegant, earthy and expertly structured. Drink now–8 years.

Concannon Limited Release Petite Sirah | 2004 |
CENTRAL COAST
★ ★ $ This berry-laden wine is simply delicious and comes at a very gentle price. Drink now–5 years.

Dare Tempranillo | 2003 | **NAPA VALLEY**
★ ★ ★ ★ $ $ $ Beautiful, smoky wine full of blackberries, minerals and incredibly refined tannin. Drink now–8 years.

Foppiano Vineyards Bacigalupi Vineyard Petite Sirah
| 2003 | **RUSSIAN RIVER VALLEY**
★ ★ ★ $ $ Longtime Petite Sirah producer Foppiano emphasizes elegance over power with berry, smoky spice flavors and lively acidity.

Frontier Red Lot No.51 | 2004 | **CALIFORNIA**
★ $ A straightforward, full-bodied red at a great price; this is perfect for your next cookout.

Il Podere dell'Olivos Teroldego | 2002 | **CENTRAL COAST**
★ ★ ★ $ $ Teroldego, a grape from northern Italy, does interesting things in California, as illustrated by this Central Coast example full of red berry, black olive and minerals.

Jade Mountain La Provençale | 2004 | **CALIFORNIA**
★ ★ $ $ Tasty as a piece of summer blueberry pie, this provides ripe berry flavors and luscious buttery notes.

Joseph Phelps Vineyards Le Mistral | 2003 |
MONTEREY COUNTY

★★★ $ $ $ Iconic Rhône-style blend. Succulent and savory with berry flavors infused by herbs, smoke and spice. Drink now–8 years.

Joseph Swan Vineyards Côtes du Rosa | 2003 |
RUSSIAN RIVER VALLEY

★★★ $ $ Splendid wine awash with wild herb, salty mineral and peppery red berry flavors.

Kuleto Estate Family Vineyards Sangiovese | 2002 |
NAPA VALLEY

★★★ $ $ Sangiovese takes an earthy turn here, sweetened up by ripe red berry flavors that finish dry.

Lolonis Heritage Vineyards Petros | 2001 | REDWOOD VALLEY
★★★ $ $ $ "Petros" means rocks, and there is a stony, mineral core here, surrounded by berry and herb flavors. Drink now–6 years.

M. Cosentino Ol' Red | NV | CALIFORNIA
★ $ Vibrant acidity elevates dry strawberry, leather and herb flavors in this ideal barbecue pour.

Qupé Los Olivos Cuvée | 2004 | SANTA YNEZ VALLEY
★★★ $ $ A classic Rhône Valley blend; it's earthy and herbal with all the ripe berry flavors typical of California. Drink now–5 years.

Robert Biale Vineyards Thomann Station Petite Sirah
| 2003 | NAPA VALLEY

★★★ $ $ $ Intense crushed dark berry flavors take on a dusty earthiness, deep minerality and loads of tannin. Drink now–8 years.

Rosenblum Cellars Pickett Road Petite Sirah | 2004 |
NAPA VALLEY

★★ $ $ $ True to Rosenblum's model of using exceptionally ripe grapes, this is saucy wine, almost off-dry and bursting with berry and spice flavors. Drink now–6 years.

Seghesio Family Vineyards Omaggio | 2003 |
SONOMA COUNTY

★★★★ $ $ $ A "Super-Tuscan" blend of Sangiovese and Cabernet loses nothing in its Sonoma translation with spicy red cherry, tobacco and lanolin flavors. Drink in 1–10 years.

Shannon Ridge Barbera | 2003 | LAKE COUNTY
★★ $ $ Brash but friendly Barbera, this full-bodied wine has spicy berry flavors and lively acidity.

Shoestring Vineyard & Winery Sangiovese | 2003 |
SANTA YNEZ VALLEY
★★ $ $ Notes of smoky oak accent tangy cherry flavors.

Silverado Vineyards Sangiovese | 2003 | NAPA VALLEY
★★ $ $ A ribbon of dried flower flavors ties up notes of tart cherry and stone beautifully, finished by cleansing acidity.

Staglin Family Vineyard Stagliano Sangiovese | 2004 |
RUTHERFORD
★★★★ $ $ $ $ Costing more than most Italian Brunello, this had better be good—and it is, with smoky mineral and tobacco flavors in a pool of black fruit. Drink in 2–10 years.

St. Francis Winery Red | 2002 | SONOMA COUNTY
★★ $ One of St. Francis's most appealing reds, full of ripe red berry flavors with a kick of herbs and spice.

Tablas Creek Vineyard Mourvèdre | 2003 | PASO ROBLES
★★★ $ $ $ Meaty, peppery and salty, this wine has plenty of dark fruit flavors, but its earthy, animal qualities predominate.

Tamás Estates Barbera | 2003 | LIVERMORE VALLEY
★ $ $ Black cherry is infused by flavors of dark black licorice.

Trentadue Winery La Storia Petite Sirah | 2003 |
ALEXANDER VALLEY
★★★ $ $ $ Wild berries, vanilla, smoke and herbs and hearty tannin come together in perfect harmony. Drink in 1–8 years.

Verdad Tempranillo/Syrah/Grenache | 2003 |
SANTA BARBARA COUNTY
★★★ $ $ Tempranillo is supported by Syrah and Grenache in a smoky wine perfumed by red berries and herbs. Drink now–5 years.

---

star producers
other california reds

best value
1 Bedford Thompson
2 Bonny Doon Vineyard
3 Cline
4 Foppiano Vineyards
5 Rosenblum Cellars

best of the best
1 Beckmen Vineyards
2 Edmunds St. John
3 Palmina
4 Qupé
5 Tablas Creek Vineyard

oregon

The average quality of wines from Oregon is the highest of any wine-producing region in America. Oregon's secret? Specialize in vines that do best in the state's relatively cool, often damp climate. Fortunately for Oregonians, that would be one of the world's most noble grapes: Pinot Noir.

Oregon: An Overview

Oregon's viticultural backbone is the chilly, wet Willamette Valley that begins just south of Eugene and stretches up to the suburbs of Portland. Pinot Noir is finicky wherever it is grown, yet does exceptionally well here, as do related Pinot Gris and Pinot Blanc, as well as Chardonnay. The Umpqua, Rogue and Applegate Valleys grow some Pinot Noir, but dedicate most vineyard land to Bordeaux, Rhône and even Spanish varieties. Some of the finest Bordeaux- and Rhône-style wines in the U.S. are made within the Columbia Valley, Columbia Gorge and Walla Walla Valley regions, which Oregon shares with Washington.

Oregon Wine Labels

Oregon's wines are customarily labeled according to grape variety. Oregon law requires that wines labeled by variety contain at least 90 percent of that grape, rather than the 75 percent allowed by federal standards (although the lesser federally-mandated percentage is permitted for the state's Bordeaux-style blends).

oregon whites

Pinot is king when it comes to Oregonian whites as well. Pinot Gris makes graceful, almost waxy-textured wines, filled with nutty, baked pear flavors. Its cousin Pinot Blanc tends to be lighter in body, with crisp citrus and apple notes. Chardonnay is responsible for some admirable wines in the state, many closer in style to the lean flavors of Burgundy than to the luscious tropical flavors of California. Riesling, Gewürztraminer and Müller-Thurgau make some fine dry and off-dry wines as well.

BEST PAIRINGS Oregon Pinot Gris is on the heavier side, making it delicious with lobster, glazed salmon or roast ham. Lighter, mineral-laden Pinot Blanc is a good choice for your next clambake. Serve oaked Chardonnay with roast turkey or salmon. Riesling and Gewürztraminer are among the few wines that work in harmony with sushi and wasabi, and spicy Thai soups.

white recommendations

Abacela Albariño | 2004 | SOUTHERN OREGON
★★★ $ $ Abacela is Oregon's master of red and white Iberian grape varieties, as this stunning Albariño shows. Citrus and apple flavors are bolstered by racy acidity.

Adelsheim Caitlin's Reserve Chardonnay | 2004 | WILLAMETTE VALLEY
★★★ $ $ $ Oaky, spicy Chardonnay doesn't necessarily mean "fruit bomb." This is plush but also lean, with apple and citrus notes underscored by abundant minerals. Drink now–8 years.

Amity Vineyards Riesling | 2005 | WILLAMETTE VALLEY
★★ $ $ Stony, savory, almost salty, this Riesling is kept clean by pure apple and mineral flavors.

A to Z Pinot Gris | 2005 | OREGON
★★ $ Good quality for a fair price, this pleases with ripe pear and citrus flavors and lots of minerals.

Benton-Lane Pinot Gris | 2005 | WILLAMETTE VALLEY
★★★ $ $ A wonderfully indulgent style of Pinot Gris, disciplined by high acidity and minerals.

Bethel Heights Vineyard Pinot Gris | 2005 | OREGON
★★ $ Blanched almond and pear flavors are combined with notes of crushed stone and earth.

Chehalem Reserve Dry Riesling | 2005 | WILLAMETTE VALLEY
★★★ $ $ A high-quality, very dry Riesling overflowing with citrus and mineral flavors highlighted by aromatic herbal notes.

Cooper Mountain Vineyards Old Vines Pinot Gris | 2004 | WILLAMETTE VALLEY
★★ $ $ Flavors of peach melba and spice infuse this tasty Pinot Gris held up by pleasant, racy acidity.

Domaine Serene Dijon Clones Etoile Vineyard
Chardonnay | 2003 | **WILLAMETTE VALLEY**
★★★★ $ $ $ Consistently one of the finest Chardonnays in the U.S., this impresses with its finesse and power. Citrus, stone and subtle smoky oak flavors sing in great harmony. Drink now–12 years.

Elk Cove Vineyards Pinot Blanc | 2005 | **WILLAMETTE VALLEY**
★★ $ $ Pinot Blanc in a classical style, showing soft pear flavors zinged up by citrus.

The Eyrie Vineyards Pinot Blanc | 2004 | **OREGON**
★★★ $ Eyrie doesn't make a lot of Pinot Blanc, so buy it when you find it and indulge in its lean, intense mineral and light pear flavors.

Foris Pinot Gris | 2005 | **ROGUE VALLEY**
★★★ $ $ One of southern Oregon's best producers presents a wine with weighty pear and nut flavors balanced by high acidity and stone.

The Four Graces Pinot Blanc | 2004 | **WILLAMETTE VALLEY**
★★ $ $ This wine charms with gentle pear and lemon flavors with a hint of savory spice.

Maysara Pinot Gris | 2005 | **MCMINNVILLE**
★★ $ $ Key lime and soft pear flavors are underlined by minerals and zingy acidity.

Montinore Estate Gewürztraminer | 2005 |
WILLAMETTE VALLEY
★★ $ Dry, spicy Gewürz, this is floral, nutty and just plain good.

Ponzi Vineyards Pinot Gris | 2005 | **WILLAMETTE VALLEY**
★★★ $ $ Excellent Pinot Gris, full of subtle autumn fruit flavors accented by peach and lime.

RoxyAnn Pinot Gris | 2005 | **OREGON**
★★ $ $ A fun wine with a fruit cocktail's worth of flavors.

Sokol Blosser Evolution 9th Edition | NV | **AMERICA**
★★ $ $ Rambunctious fruit, flower and spice flavors are punctuated by zippy acidity in this slightly off-dry, highly enjoyable wine.

Soléna Pinot Gris | 2005 | **OREGON**
★★★ $ $ Captivating peach, pear and smoky mineral flavors in this wine make it deliciously complex.

Stoller Chardonnay | 2004 | **DUNDEE HILLS**
★★★ $ $ $ Smoky, oaky and spicy, this Chardonnay's citrus and apple flavors come together nicely with nutty notes of oak.

oregon reds

There is no question which grape takes priority in Oregon: Pinot Noir. It tends to be leaner in body and more graceful than most California versions, often compared favorably to red Burgundy. Today, many Oregon vintners are following trends toward fuller-bodied Pinots than were typical in the past. Cabernet- and Merlot-based wines from warmer parts of the state fall somewhere between California and Bordeaux in profile. Some terrific Syrah, smoky and spicy, is coming from the same regions.

BEST PAIRINGS Oregon Pinot Noir is the ideal wine for salmon and chanterelles, slow-roast lamb or venison. Serve Bordeaux-style wines with steaks, and try Syrah with herb-marinated lamb chops, game or mushroom risotto.

pinot noir recommendations

Adelsheim Elizabeth's Reserve | 2004 | **WILLAMETTE VALLEY**
★★★ $ $ $ Lovely, generous red fruit flavors intertwined with herbs and minerals roll softly across the tongue. Drink now–10 years.

Amity Vineyards Schouten Single Vineyard | 2003 |
WILLAMETTE VALLEY
★★★ $ $ $ Tension between mineral, herb, tart cherry and pink grapefruit flavors results in engaging drinking. Drink now–8 years.

Anne Amie Hawks View Vineyard | 2003 | **WILLAMETTE VALLEY**
★★★ $ $ $ This delicious wine is brimming with flavors of fresh berries and wildflowers with a mineral edge. Drink now–8 years.

Archery Summit Arcus Estate | 2003 | **WILLAMETTE VALLEY**
★★★★ $ $ $ $ Yet another standout Pinot from one of Oregon's best producers. This is concentrated and fruit-filled yet still deeply earthy and elegant. Drink now–12 years.

A to Z | 2004 | **OREGON**
★★ $ $ Terrific Pinot for a terrific price, this is lithe with smoky, ripe red cherry flavors and fine tannin.

Benton-Lane First Class | 2003 | **WILLAMETTE VALLEY**
★★★ $ $ $ Ink-black wine imbued with blackberry, plum, carbon and spice flavors with thick, but satiny tannin. Drink now–8 years.

Bethel Heights Vineyard Estate Grown | 2004 |
WILLAMETTE VALLEY
★★★ $ $ $ Intense smokiness here is filled out with wild berry and herb flavors with notes of smoldering, balanced oak.

Chehalem 3 Vineyard | 2004 | **WILLAMETTE VALLEY**
★★ $ $ $ High acidity brilliantly balances red berry, orange peel and sweet spice flavors in this finessed red.

Cooper Mountain Vineyards Faces | 2004 |
WILLAMETTE VALLEY
★★ $ $ Dedicated to growing grapes according to biodynamic principles, Cooper Mountain presents this medium-bodied, earthy, herbal wine with tart berry flavors.

Domaine Serene Evenstad Reserve | 2003 |
WILLAMETTE VALLEY
★★★★ $ $ $ $ Big and thick, this oozes dark fruit, mineral oil and earthy spice flavors while remaining nimble. Drink now–10 years.

Erath La Nuit Magique | 2004 | **WILLAMETTE VALLEY**
★★★★ $ $ $ Caraway, herb, wild red berry and animal flavors leave a lasting impression. Drink now–12 years.

Et Fille Palmer Creek Vineyards | 2004 | **OREGON**
★★★★ $ $ $ Graceful, restrained wine with berry and herb flavors that wash over the palate on a wave of smoke. Drink now–6 years.

The Eyrie Vineyards Reserve | 2001 | **WILLAMETTE VALLEY**
★★★★ $ $ $ Superb, complex wine for those seeking a Pinot that emphasizes earth over ripe fruit. Drink now–12 years.

Firesteed | 2004 | **OREGON**
★ $ Light-bodied and low-priced, this wine has tart red berry and spice flavors that will perk up any midweek salmon steak.

The Four Graces Reserve | 2003 | **WILLAMETTE VALLEY**
★★★ $ $ $ A fine line of mineral flavors runs through this wine, which is rich with dark fruit and savory spice. Drink now–7 years.

Gypsy Dancer Gary & Christine's Vineyard | 2004 | **OREGON**
★★★ $ $ $ Enticing aromas of cinnamon and cumin waft through bright cherry, pomegranate and stone flavors. Drink now–10 years.

Iris Hill | 2004 | **OREGON**
★ $ $ Sappy red cherry flavors in this engaging Pinot are lightened by charming floral notes.

King Estate | 2004 | OREGON
★★ $ $ Clean red berry and spice flavors come through clearly in this medium-weight wine of fine balance.

Maysara Jamsheed | 2004 | MCMINNVILLE
★★★ $ $ Named after the ancient Persian king Jamsheed, this is one earthy, soulful elixir.

Oak Knoll Vintage Reserve | 2001 | WILLAMETTE VALLEY
★★★ $ $ $ In spite of its age, this is still fresh with dried cherry and berry flavors, hints of coffee and lanolin. Drink now–8 years.

Panther Creek Freedom Hill Vineyard | 2003 |
WILLAMETTE VALLEY
★★★ $ $ $ This might seem simple at first, but a bit of air unveils black cherry flavors, highlighted by notes of flowers and stonelike minerals. Drink now–8 years.

Patton Valley Vineyard | 2003 | WILLAMETTE VALLEY
★★★ $ $ $ Sultry, earthy and fruit-filled Pinot that will please crowds and connoisseurs alike. Drink now–8 years.

Ponzi Vineyards | 2004 | WILLAMETTE VALLEY
★★ $ $ $ One of Oregon's pioneering vintners makes this classic Oregon Pinot, with ripe but measured fruit flavors, spice and earth.

Rex Hill Maresh Vineyard | 2003 | OREGON
★★★ $ $ $ This wine's parade of red and black cherry flavors is enhanced by dried fruit and jammy notes and a fine undercurrent of minerals. Drink now–8 years.

Sokol Blosser | 2003 | DUNDEE HILLS
★★★ $ $ $ From one of Oregon's best producers, this cornucopia of fruit and spice flavors has a slight bitter edge. Drink now–6 years.

star producers
oregon reds

best value
1 Amity Vineyards
2 A to Z
3 Cloudline
4 Evesham Wood
5 Foris

best of the best
1 Archery Summit
2 Cristom
3 Domaine Drouhin
4 Domaine Serene
5 The Eyrie Vineyards

Soléna Domaine Danielle Laurent | 2003 |

WILLAMETTE VALLEY

★★★ $ $ $ Flavors of cherry jubilee and bittersweet chocolate are kept savory with minerals and herbs. Drink now–8 years.

Torii Mor Olson Estate Vineyard | 2004 | **DUNDEE HILLS**

★★★ $ $ $ $ Reminiscent of good Burgundy, this offers smooth and bright cherry, orange and spice flavors. Drink now–10 years.

WillaKenzie Estate Triple Black Slopes | 2003 |

WILLAMETTE VALLEY

★★★ $ $ $ $ Black slopes yield a black wine. This elegant red is full of dark fruit, chocolate, smoke and ash flavors. Drink now–8 years.

Willamette Valley Vineyards Estate Vineyard | 2004 |

WILLAMETTE VALLEY

★★★ $ $ $ Perfume over power is the theme of this wine, offering aromas of forest and flowers and flavors of red cherries.

washington state

Dedicated Washingtonians have turned their state into the nation's second-largest wine producer in less than two decades' time. They've also earned a reputation for some of America's best Bordeaux-style wines. Merlot and Cabernet dominate, but Rhône varieties are gaining respect with wine enthusiasts. Among whites, Chardonnay justifies high praise, as do Viognier, Semillon and Riesling.

Washington State: An Overview

Nearly all of Washington's vineyards lie in the arid, desert-like eastern part of the state following the Columbia River. The large Columbia Valley AVA encompasses most of this area, which includes the important subregions of Yakima Valley, Red Mountain and Walla Walla Valley, the latter of which is shared with Oregon.

Washington State Wine Labels

Washington labels most of its wines by grape variety. Some Bordeaux blends are labeled "Meritage" (p. 166); many wineries use proprietary names for blends.

washington state whites

Chardonnay is Washington's most important white wine grape, alternating between a nervy, citrus-laden style and a more lavishly oaked, richer California style. However, grassy, lemony Sauvignon Blancs and off-dry Rieslings are more consistently interesting, ranking among the nation's finest. Semillon can express an orange, peach and almond profile here, and Viognier is spicy and floral-scented.

BEST PAIRINGS The delicate flavors and high acidity of many Washington whites make them easy to pair with food. Oaked Chardonnay is a natural with roast monkfish or salmon. Simpler versions do better with steamed mussels and baked fish. Washington's Semillon complements crab, smoked salmon or seared scallops in a citrus-butter sauce. Semillon-Sauvignon blends are delicious with milk-based chowders. Zesty Sauvignon Blanc and oysters on the half shell are another excellent combination. Slightly off-dry Washington Riesling is at home with a range of Southeast Asian chicken or fish dishes, and pork schnitzel.

white recommendations

Abeja Chardonnay | 2004 | **WASHINGTON STATE**
★★★ $ $ $ Chardonnay from a quality producer, this is nutty, with tropical and citrus flavors, and a smoky finish. Drink now–8 years.

The Bunnell Family Cellar Roza Bergé Vineyard Gewürztraminer | 2005 | **YAKIMA VALLEY**
★★ $ $ Very dry, earthy and spicy Gewürz; perfect for Asian fare.

Chateau Ste. Michelle & Dr. Loosen Eroica Riesling | 2005 | **COLUMBIA VALLEY**
★★★★ $ $ A collaboration between Washington's oldest winery and one of Germany's best winemakers creates this rare Riesling with racy acidity, mineral and seductive lime notes. Drink now–8 years.

Columbia Crest Grand Estates Chardonnay | 2003 | **COLUMBIA VALLEY**
★ $ A simple but satisfying Chardonnay, this pleases with creamy, oaky flavors and ripe fruit.

Cougar Crest Winery Viognier | 2005 | **WALLA WALLA VALLEY**
★ ★ ★ $ $ This is Viognier with loads of personality, in the form of lime blossom, apple and green almond flavors.

DeLille Cellars Chaleur Estate | 2004 | **COLUMBIA VALLEY**
★ ★ ★ $ $ $ Modeled after the great whites of Bordeaux, this is smoky and nutty, with peach and stone flavors. Drink now–8 years.

DiStefano Sauvignon Blanc | 2005 | **COLUMBIA VALLEY**
★ ★ ★ $ Satiny citrus and peach flavors are underlined by stone in a finely tuned Sauvignon.

Doyenne Roussanne | 2004 | **COLUMBIA VALLEY**
★ ★ ★ ★ $ $ $ Roussanne rarely does so well in American soils. This explodes with pungent floral, cinnamon and peach flavors balanced by high acidity. Drink now–6 years.

Hedges CMS | 2005 | **COLUMBIA VALLEY**
★ ★ $ Chardonnay is rarely blended with Marsanne and Sauvignon Blanc, but here the combination yields an interesting bouquet of creamy pear and almond flavors zipped up by lemon and herbs.

Hogue Reserve Chardonnay | 2003 | **COLUMBIA VALLEY**
★ ★ $ $ Though lavishly oaked Chardonnay is a bit out of style, this example has enough firming acidity to pair nicely with baked salmon.

Isenhower Snapdragon | 2005 | **COLUMBIA VALLEY**
★ ★ ★ $ $ Roussanne's heft and Viognier's flowery charms come together in a delightful, aromatic, yet weighty wine.

JM Viognier | 2005 | **COLUMBIA VALLEY**
★ ★ ★ $ $ This Viognier oozes ripe, succulent, peak-of-summer peach flavors.

L'Ecole No. 41 Fries Vineyard Semillon | 2004 |
WASHINGTON STATE
★ ★ ★ $ $ Though very dry, this wine acquires an almost dessert wine lushness with flavors resembling marzipan-pear tart. It will age beautifully. Drink now–8 years.

Matthews Klipsun Vineyard Sauvignon Blanc | 2004 |
RED MOUNTAIN
★ ★ $ $ Flavors of stone and sweet spice infuse a base of citrus and fresh-cut green apples.

Poet's Leap Riesling | 2004 | **COLUMBIA VALLEY**
★ ★ ★ $ $ An ode to Riesling's delights, this is off-dry but sprightly, with an array of peach, orange and stone flavors.

washington state reds

Many Washington producers have staked their reputation on Merlot, and with good reason. Though graceful, Merlot here tends to be earthier and sturdier than versions from California. Washington vintners also craft beautiful Cabernet Sauvignon, especially from Red Mountain. Cabernet Franc excels, too. Rhône Valley varieties such as Syrah, Grenache and Mourvèdre make reds that have both power and grace. Lemberger, known as "Blue Franc" in Washington after Austria's Blaufränkisch (the same grape), is worth trying for its unique, peppery blueberry flavors.

BEST PAIRINGS Washington Merlot is often higher in acidity and tannin than California examples, able to take on robust foods such as braised meats. Pour Cabernet with roast leg of lamb or a dry-aged steak. Peppery Cabernet Franc is better with hanger steak sliced over a bed of equally peppery arugula, or grilled portobello mushrooms. Most Lembergers are simple sausage-and-burger wines; some complex versions are delicious with rich meat stews made with pork or veal and mushrooms. Washington Syrah is perfect for braised lamb shanks.

red recommendations

Abeja Cabernet Sauvignon | 2003 | **COLUMBIA VALLEY**
★★★ $ $ $ This velvety, full-bodied wine indulges with ripe red fruit and toasted oak flavors. Drink now–10 years.

The Bunnell Family Cellar Boushey-McPherson Vineyard Syrah | 2004 | **YAKIMA VALLEY**
★★★ $ $ $ Cumin and wild herb flavors saturate this smoky Syrah, alongside notes of red berry and stone. Drink now–10 years.

Buty Rediviva of the Stones | 2003 | **WALLA WALLA VALLEY**
★★★★ $ $ $ An aptly named wine that tastes as if red berries were crushed in a mortar of stone. Drink now–8 years.

Cadence Ciel du Cheval Vineyard | 2003 | **RED MOUNTAIN**
★★★ $ $ $ A balanced mix of berry and cassis flavors, with pepper and minerals, mark this harmonious red. Drink now–10 years.

Camaraderie Cellars Cabernet Franc | 2003 |
WASHINGTON STATE
★ $ $ Sticky red fruit and pepper notes make this a steak wine.

Chateau Ste. Michelle Indian Wells Merlot | 2003 |
COLUMBIA VALLEY
★★★ $ $ One of Washington's largest wineries proves you don't have to be small to make excellent wine. This is peppery and earthy, loaded with dark fruit flavors and finesse. Drink now–8 years.

Columbia Crest Reserve Syrah | 2003 | COLUMBIA VALLEY
★★ $ $ $ Lusty blueberry and smoke flavors pour out of this full-bodied, tasty wine. Drink now–5 years.

DeLille Cellars Harrison Hill | 2003 | YAKIMA VALLEY
★★★★ $ $ $ $ A first rate red with black, velvety fruit flavors fine-tuned by minerals and speckled with pepper. Drink in 2–15 years.

DiStefano Syrah R | 2003 | COLUMBIA VALLEY
★★★ $ $ $ This Syrah beautifully expresses a complex earthy side and a ripe berry dimension with a floral twist. Drink now–8 years.

Dunham Cellars Syrah | 2003 | COLUMBIA VALLEY
★★★ $ $ $ Blueberry flavors are brought to life by spice in this outstanding Syrah. Drink now–8 years.

Feather Cabernet Sauvignon | 2003 | COLUMBIA VALLEY
★★★★ $ $ $ $ Elegant yet powerful Cabernet with red fruit flavors offset by pepper, tannin and acidity. Drink now–15 years.

Gordon Brothers Family Vineyards Tradition | 2000 |
COLUMBIA VALLEY
★★★ $ $ $ A broad, balanced wine with well-defined berry, light pepper flavors and fine tannin. Drink now–6 years.

Hedges Family Estate Three Vineyards | 2003 |
RED MOUNTAIN
★★ $ $ This Red Mountain Bordeaux blend is full of flavor, but shows a restrained, claretlike refinement. Drink now–8 years.

Hogue Merlot | 2004 | COLUMBIA VALLEY
★ $ A simple twist of the screw cap brings an array of simple but pleasing berry flavors and a bit of tannin.

Isenhower River Beauty Syrah | 2004 | HORSE HEAVEN HILLS
★★★ $ $ $ Succulent wine with flavors of blueberry-orange compote and a clean, mineral-laden underside. Drink now–8 years.

JM Tre Fanciulli | 2003 | COLUMBIA VALLEY
★★★ $ $ $ Three grape varieties—Cabernet, Merlot and Syrah—unite for a rambunctious but medium-bodied wine with nut and berry flavors and lots of minerals. Drink now–6 years.

L'Ecole No. 41 Pepper Bridge Vineyard Apogee | 2003 | WALLA WALLA VALLEY
★★★★ $ $ $ L'Ecole is among Washington's best, and this is full of ripe red fruit, light spice and stone flavors. Drink now–12 years.

Leonetti Cellar Merlot | 2004 | COLUMBIA VALLEY
★★★★ $ $ $ $ One of the finest Merlots made in America, this is graceful, with lovely red and dark fruit flavors, suave tannin and salty mineral flavors. Drink now–15 years.

Maghie Cellars Merlot | 2001 | RED MOUNTAIN
★★★ $ $ $ There's no lack of red berry flavors in this Merlot, but an intriguing minerality predominates. Drink now–8 years.

Matthews | 2002 | COLUMBIA VALLEY
★★★★ $ $ $ A tremendous depth of plush fruit, spicy tobacco and mineral flavors are on display with poise. Drink in 2–15 years.

Nelms Road Merlot | 2004 | COLUMBIA VALLEY
★★ $ $ Soft berry and plum flavors combine with light spice for a gentle, but still firm wine. Drink now–5 years.

Nicholas Cole Cellars Camille | 2003 | COLUMBIA VALLEY
★★★★ $ $ $ A fine weave of dark fruit, carbon, minerals and smoke add up to one stunning wine. Give it time. Drink in 2–12 years.

Pedestal Merlot | 2003 | COLUMBIA VALLEY
★★★ $ $ $ $ Made in collaboration with one of the world's best-known oenologists, Michel Rolland, this international-styled wine is full of ripe dark fruit flavors lavished with oak. Drink now–12 years.

Ryan Patrick Vineyards Rock Island Red | 2003 | COLUMBIA VALLEY
★★ $ Ryan Patrick delivers robust, tasty red and dark fruit flavors for under twenty bucks.

Sagelands Vineyard Four Corners Merlot | 2003 | COLUMBIA VALLEY
★ $ Juicy red fruit with hints of sweet spice for good casual sipping.

Sandhill Cabernet Sauvignon | 2001 | RED MOUNTAIN
★★★ $ $ Delicious red berry–filled wine with sweet and piquant spice flavors and hints of lavender. Drink now–8 years.

Sequel Syrah | 2003 | **COLUMBIA VALLEY**
★★★★ $ $ $ $ The former winemaker of Grange, Australia's famed Shiraz, crafts this intense Washington version with black fruit, handfuls of spice and loads of minerals. Drink in 2–12 years.

Snoqualmie Vineyards Reserve Merlot | 2003 |
COLUMBIA VALLEY
★★ $ $ Dark fruit and maple flavors imbue this dense, heavily oaked Merlot. Its chewy, thick tannins need a few years to mellow out, so give it time. Drink in 1–8 years.

Tamarack Cellars Firehouse Red | 2004 | **COLUMBIA VALLEY**
★★ $ $ An unusual blend of six rarely combined grapes (Cabernet, Syrah, Merlot, Cabernet Franc, Sangiovese and Carmenère) creates an exuberant wine with red fruit and spice notes.

Walter Dacon C'est Syrah Beaux | 2004 | **COLUMBIA VALLEY**
★★★ $ $ $ This exquisite wine unleashes flavors of fresh berries, peppery flowers and polished stone. Drink now–10 years.

Waterbrook Cabernet Sauvignon | 2003 | **COLUMBIA VALLEY**
★★ $ $ Plush cherry flavors are given a kick of cinnamon-like spice in this tasty Cabernet. Drink now–4 years.

Woodward Canyon Estate | 2003 | **WALLA WALLA VALLEY**
★★★★ $ $ $ $ Superb wine that deserves comparisons to Grand Cru Bordeaux. This is powerful but demure, confident but not at all brash. Drink in 2–15 years.

Yellow Hawk Cellar Barbera | 2004 | **COLUMBIA VALLEY**
★★ $ $ Low in tannin and high in acidity with pure, tart red berry fruit flavors; just like Barbera should be.

star producers
washington state reds

best value
1 Chateau Ste. Michelle
2 Columbia Winery
3 Covey Run
4 Gordon Brothers
5 Kiona

best of the best
1 Andrew Will
2 Buty
3 Cayuse Vineyards
4 Leonetti Cellar
5 Woodward Canyon

other united states

Wine is produced in every American state. Much of it is poor quality and only for sale at the winery where it was made. But a growing number of vintners are crafting wines on a par with the best from California and the Pacific Northwest. With the liberalization of wine shipping laws today, these wines are more available to wine lovers everywhere.

Other United States: An Overview

Many regions in the U.S. endure temperatures that are too cold for European varieties (*Vitis vinifera*) like Chardonnay and Merlot to survive. In much of the South, heat and humidity promotes mold, fungi and vine-killing diseases. Many dedicated winegrowers have had success by planting disease-resistant French-American hybrids of vinifera and labrusca. Some places in the U.S. can support only hardy native American vines (*Vitis labrusca* and *Vitis rotundifolia*) which are not known to make the finest wines. However, in the increasing number of places where the noble European grape varieties do thrive, they are responsible for some of the country's most interesting wines.

The most prominent of these places is New York State, the nation's third-largest wine-producing state. One of New York's best regions is the Finger Lakes area, where wine-makers excel with Gewürztraminer and Riesling and produce small amounts of Pinot Noir and Chardonnay. Long Island is another important region for quality. Here vintners focus on Merlot, Cabernet Franc, Chardonnay and Sauvignon Blanc. Winemakers in southern New England take advantage of the moderating influence of the Gulf Stream to produce some fine whites. Pockets of the mid-Atlantic region produce noteworthy wines as well. The most exciting of these come from Virginia, where vintners work with Chardonnay, Cabernet Franc, Merlot and Viognier, as well as Italian, Spanish and obscure French varieties. Missouri has also been a longtime producer of praiseworthy wines from hybrid varieties. Vintners in Michigan craft some impressive Riesling and delicious sparklers. Parts of Texas are staking a claim to good wines from European varieties. Though working in a desert, vintners in New Mexico and Arizona benefit from cool evening temperatures and high elevation. New Mexico's finest production comes unexpectedly from cool-climate Pinot Noir and Chardonnay, which are used to make great value sparklers. Arizona's winemakers are releasing some respectable Syrah and Mourvèdre. Wines from Idaho resemble those from Washington State; off-dry Riesling is the state's specialty.

other u.s. whites & rosés

Riesling and Gewürztraminer from New York's Finger Lakes region have been correctly compared to the wines of Alsace and Germany and are surely the finest of their type in the U.S. Chardonnay takes different forms in the state, from citrus and mineral laden in the Finger Lakes to more lush and tropical on Long Island. Some exceptional, dry, spicy rosés are also made in Long Island. Wines from hybrid grapes such as Vidal and Seyval Blanc are usually simple, but a handful can be memorably nutty, especially from New York's Hudson Valley and halfway across the country in Missouri. Viognier has recently been having success in a number of different places, from Virginia to Texas. Idaho Riesling is usually off-dry, with fine acidity.

BEST PAIRINGS Subdue the sizzle of spicy Asian fare with off-dry Riesling or Gewürztraminer. Dry Riesling is a natural with freshwater fish like trout and also works beautifully with crab cakes. Dry Gewürztraminer is a perfect match for coconut-laced seafood stews and many semi-soft cow's milk cheeses. Lean Chardonnay is ideal with grilled or pan-fried fish. Oaky versions are delicious with swordfish and monkfish as well as lobster. Serve simple Seyval Blanc well-chilled at picnics. Viognier is terrific alongside barbecue chicken, pan-roasted fish or risotto.

white & rosé recommendations

WHITES

Black Star Farms Arcturos Pinot Gris | 2005 |
OLD MISSION PENINSULA, MICHIGAN
★★ $ Stony with flavors of summer fruit and a smoky, clean finish.

Borghese Barrel Fermented Chardonnay | 2002 |
NORTH FORK OF LONG ISLAND, NEW YORK
★★ $ $ Lovers of butterscotch-laden Chardonnay should seek out this rich wine, nicely balanced by citrus and high acidity.

Chamard Estate Reserve Chardonnay | 2002 |
CONNECTICUT
★★★ $ Lean Chardonnay, with apple, light tropical and abundant mineral flavors highlighted by oak.

Comtesse Thérèse Russian Oak Chardonnay | 2004 |
NORTH FORK OF LONG ISLAND, NEW YORK
★★ $ $ Spicy oak notes harmonize with citrus and stone flavors.

Dr. Konstantin Frank Rkatsiteli | 2005 |
FINGER LAKES, NEW YORK
★★★ $ $ $ A Russian native, the Rkatsiteli grape thrives in New York, offering a mineral-laden wine full of citrus and peach flavors.

Hermann J. Wiemer Dry Riesling | 2004 |
FINGER LAKES, NEW YORK
★★★★ $ $ Wiemer makes some of America's best Rieslings. This is bone-dry with peach, tropical fruit, citrus and stone flavors.

Martha Clara Vineyards Five-O | 2004 |
NORTH FORK OF LONG ISLAND, NEW YORK
★★ $ $ An unusual mix of six grape varieties results in a light, zippy, aromatic wine for summer.

Mount Pleasant Vignoles | 2005 | **MISSOURI**
★ $ $ Off-dry and fragrant with grapey, spicy flavors.

Paumanok Chenin Blanc | 2005 |
NORTH FORK OF LONG ISLAND, NEW YORK
★★ $ $ Ripe melon and tropical fruit flavors are balanced by notes of lemon in this charming wine.

Standing Stone Vineyards Gewurztraminer | 2005 |
FINGER LAKES, NEW YORK
★★★ $ $ Dry with wildly expressive lime, apple and spice aromas.

Stone Hill Winery Vidal Blanc | 2005 | MISSOURI
★ $ The French-American hybrid Vidal Blanc is in good hands at Stone Hill; this shows intriguing flavors ranging from tart lemon to aromatic strawberry-banana.

ROSÉS

Albemarle Rosé | 2004 | VIRGINIA
★ ★ $ Merlot, Cabernet Sauvignon and Cabernet Franc make up the blend in this very dry, strawberry-flavored, pepper-sprinkled rosé.

Wölffer Rosé | 2005 | THE HAMPTONS, NEW YORK
★ ★ ★ $ This Long Island producer always makes a stunning rosé: peach and cherry flavors are spicy and tart.

other u.s. reds

Winemakers across America make wines from Bordeaux varieties Merlot, Cabernet Sauvignon and Cabernet Franc. New York's Long Island, with a maritime climate similar to Bordeaux, makes the finest examples outside the West Coast. Long Island's peppery Cabernet Franc is especially worth trying. Virginia grows some Cabernet Franc as well, but many believe Sangiovese is its most interesting red grape. It won't be confused for Chianti, but it has fine cherry and spice flavors. Norton, a hybrid grape, excels in Virginia, too, as well as in Missouri. Baco Noir is a smoky, earthy, darkly colored hybrid that makes some distinct wines in northern states near Canada. There is some surprisingly good Pinot Noir from the Finger Lakes and New Mexico. Arizona's bold yet balanced Syrahs and Mourvèdres are similar to California Zinfandel.

BEST PAIRINGS Bordeaux-variety wines can be served with beef tenderloin or garlicky leg of lamb. Cabernet Franc is ideal with strip steak and even lamb curry. Serve Virginia Sangiovese with spicy lamb dishes or a baked country ham. Baco Noir is best paired with something full of flavor—pour it with braised short ribs or game birds. Pinot Noir outside the West Coast is often lean, good with lamb or duck. Rhône-variety reds fom Arizona are made for barbecue or pulled pork.

red recommendations

Augusta Winery Chambourcin | 2002 | MISSOURI
★★ $ A bit of age in oak barrels has smoothed the funk off this unique, berry- and spice-filled, hybrid-based wine.

Black Star Farms Arcturos Pinot Noir | 2004 |
LEELANAU PENINSULA, MICHIGAN
★★ $$ Lovely Pinot, full of earthy, smoked berry flavors.

Callaghan Vineyards Claire's | 2004 | SONOITA, ARIZONA
★★★ $$$ Mourvèdre, Syrah and Petite Sirah make one big red, bursting with ripe black cherry flavors and spice. Drink now–7 years.

Dos Cabezas La Montaña | 2004 | ARIZONA
★★★ $$$ Thick, sticky Petite Sirah–Merlot blend with indulgent flavors of blackberry, molasses and plum. Drink now–8 years.

Gruet Cuvée Gilbert Gruet Pinot Noir | 2003 | NEW MEXICO
★★ $$ Best-known for its sparkling wines, Gruet makes an elegant still wine, with berry and spice flavors and fine tannin.

Holy-Field Vineyard & Winery Cynthiana | 2004 | KANSAS
★★ $$ An interesting wine from the Heartland, characterized by wild berry and pungent floral flavors with an appealing animal edge.

Jamesport Sarah's Hill Pinot Noir | 2004 |
NORTH FORK OF LONG ISLAND, NEW YORK
★★ $$$ A Pinot Noir made in a restrained style, with elegant, earthy, dry cherry and spice flavors.

Macari Estate Merlot | 2002 |
NORTH FORK OF LONG ISLAND, NEW YORK
★★ $ Fruit- and earth-filled Merlot from a stellar producer.

Martha Clara Vineyards Estate Reserve Cabernet Sauvignon | 2001 | NORTH FORK OF LONG ISLAND, NEW YORK
★★ $$$ Big berry and spicy oak flavors jump out of the glass at first, but a bit of air brings everything into focus. Drink now–7 years.

Paumanok Cabernet Sauvignon | 2003 |
NORTH FORK OF LONG ISLAND, NEW YORK
★★ $$ Elegant claret with red berry flavors and an ashen edge.

Salmon Run Meritage | 2002 | NEW YORK
★★ $ Not a terribly complicated red, but its juicy berry and floral flavors are easy to enjoy.

Schneider Roanoke Point Cabernet Franc | 2003 |
NORTH FORK OF LONG ISLAND, NEW YORK
★★★ $ $ $ This red sets the standard for Cabernet Franc in Long Island with red and blackberry flavors and abundant mineral notes.

Sherwood House Vineyards Merlot | 2001 |
NORTH FORK OF LONG ISLAND, NEW YORK
★★ $ $ Full-bodied with red berry and plum flavors, this Merlot is a perfect steak wine.

Standing Stone Vineyards Pinnacle | 2004 |
FINGER LAKES, NEW YORK
★★ $ $ One doesn't expect much from Bordeaux grapes in the Finger Lakes, but this red berry– and spice-flavored wine delivers.

Stone Hill Winery Norton | 2003 | **HERMANN, MISSOURI**
★★ $ $ This Norton shows voluptuous dark berry, chocolate and spice flavors that could satisfy any Zinfandel fan.

Vineyard 48 Reserve Merlot | 2004 |
NORTH FORK OF LONG ISLAND, NEW YORK
★★ $ $ $ Lean rather than plush, this Merlot is full of dry herb and savory spice flavors combined with tart red berry.

Wölffer Premier Cru Merlot | 2002 |
THE HAMPTONS, NEW YORK
★★★★ $ $ $ $ All Wölffer reds are special, this is just more so: beautifully balanced, full of fruit and light spice flavors, minerals and a superb finesse. Drink now–8 years.

australia

Australia has transformed the world's wine landscape more than any other region on the planet. While the wine industry may still regard European wines as benchmarks of quality, consumers everywhere have demonstrated their preference for the boldly flavored, reasonably priced wines from Australian vineyards. European producers have been steadily losing market share to the Aussies, whose red and white wines have proven to be on a par with the best anywhere.

Western Australia

PERTH

Frankland River

Margaret River

Indian Ocean

Principal Wine Region

Australia: An Overview

Australia has a wide diversity of terrain and microclimates. The plush, fruity Shiraz and Chardonnay that many identify as Australia's calling cards come largely from the southeast. Barossa is known for robust Shiraz and Cabernet. Cooler Coonawarra makes earthy Cabernet; Clare and Eden Valleys are famous for mineral-laden Rieslings. The Margaret River and Frankland River regions make elegant whites and reds.

Australian Wine Labels

Australian wine labels are among the clearest in the world. Winery, region, vintage and grape are named and exact percentages are given for blends. Some wines, such as Penfolds' Grange, are so iconic that varieties aren't listed.

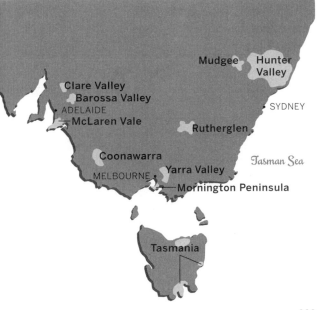

australia whites

Australia's full-bodied Chardonnay tends to get the most attention on wine shelves. But vintners are capable of much more, crafting distinctive dry Riesling, Semillon and light, lively wines from the Portuguese grape Verdelho.

AUSTRALIA WHITES

chardonnay

Chardonnay, the world's most flexible white grape, takes radically different forms here depending on region and winemaker. Fans of indulgent, tropical fruit–laden wines will find pleasure in Chardonnay from the sunny south and southeastern parts of Australia. Those who appreciate more restraint can find abundant examples from cooler areas such as Western Australia, Yarra and Clare Valleys and the island of Tasmania.

BEST PAIRINGS Think big when faced with a full-bodied Australian Chardonnay: duck à l'orange, grilled swordfish or spice-rubbed roast pork. Lighter, unoaked versions are good pours with ceviche or chicken Caesar salads.

chardonnay recommendations

Callanans Road | 2003 | **VICTORIA**
★★ $ $ Marzipan notes give lemon and apple flavors a nutty twist.

Coldstream Hills Reserve | 2003 | **YARRA VALLEY**
★★★ $ $ Perfect for those who love oaky Chardonnay that still emphasizes fresh, summer fruit flavors.

Four Sisters | 2004 | **SOUTH EASTERN AUSTRALIA**
★ $ Pleasant lime and kiwi flavors add up to lovely, simple drinking.

Giant Steps | 2003 | **YARRA VALLEY**
★★★ $ $ A terrific wine characterized by fine minerals and juicy, lightly spiced fruit.

Green Point | 2003 | **YARRA VALLEY**
★★ $ $ Kiwis, limes and green herbs are rounded out by hints of freshly sawn oak.

Indis | 2004 | **WESTERN AUSTRALIA**
★ $ Give this white a good chill and enjoy its tropical, piña-colada-like bouquet by the pool.

Rosemount Estate Hill of Gold | 2004 | **MUDGEE**
★★ $ Fresh pear and citrus join deep mineral flavors and just a hint of oak to make one classic Aussie Chardonnay.

Shaw and Smith M3 Vineyard | 2004 | **ADELAIDE HILLS**
★★★ $ $ $ Burgundy down under, this standout wine has the smoky, oaky flavors of Meursault with the minerality of Montrachet.

Tapestry | 2004 | **MCLAREN VALE**
★★ $ A solid, well-made Chardonnay that exudes graceful citrus, green apple and light floral notes.

Tyrrell's Wines Reserve | 2003 | **HUNTER VALLEY**
★★ $ $ Apples, pears and earthy flavors are bolstered by oak.

The Wishing Tree Unoaked | 2005 | **WESTERN AUSTRALIA**
★ $ Clean tropical and lemon flavors with a little snap of acidity make a fine picnic white.

Woop Woop | 2005 | **SOUTH EASTERN AUSTRALIA**
★★ $ Pineapple and mango flavors stay light and breezy here.

Yering Station | 2004 | **YARRA VALLEY**
★★★ $ $ A great value from Australia's best Chardonnay producer that is "premier cru" quality; full of minerals, citrus and apple flavors with just a kiss of oak.

other australia whites

Australia is blessed with a diverse treasury of varieties. Sauvignon Blanc does well, but its Bordeaux counterpart Semillon is often exceptional, full of marmalade and nutlike flavors when aged. Riesling can be powerful and intensely mineral when grown in the right region, and has the ability to age. Given the fame of Shiraz (Syrah) in the country, it's no surprise that other Rhône varieties such as Marsanne, Roussanne and Viognier also perform well; they are often used in blends. The Portuguese grape Verdelho was widely planted in Australia in order to make sweet, Port-style wines that were once popular. Today the grape makes some vibrant citrus-, floral- and herb-flavored wines.

BEST PAIRINGS Most Australian Riesling is dry, making it less than ideal for its usual partner: spicy Asian fare. High in acidity and aromatic, it can hold its own with less fiery dishes, such as fried shrimp or calamari, and soft-shell crab. Verdelho partners well with spinach and goat cheese salads or simple herbed chicken. Marsanne, Roussanne and Viognier are delicious with lobster or baked halibut. Pour young Semillon with sea bass; save older versions for almonds and a chunk of farmhouse Cheddar.

other white recommendations

Betts & Scholl Riesling | 2005 | EDEN VALLEY
★★ $ $ $ Peaches and cream, with a refreshing squeeze of lemon.

Cape Mentelle Sauvignon Blanc/Semillon | 2004 | MARGARET RIVER
★★ $ Margaret River's maritime climate brings cool balance to this blend's peach, pear and piquant herb flavors.

Coldstream Hills Sauvignon Blanc | 2005 | YARRA VALLEY
★★ $ $ Apple, lemon and orange flavors are sprinkled with spice and held together with a zippy acidity.

Grant Burge Thorn Riesling | 2005 | EDEN VALLEY
★★★ $ $ Known for Shiraz, Grant Burge crafts excellent Riesling, too. This one's full of mineral, citrus and spice. Drink now–6 years.

Grosset Polish Hill Riesling | 2005 | CLARE VALLEY
★★★★ $ $ $ One of the world's iconic Rieslings, Polish Hill is shy this year, showing only hints of its intense citrus, herb and mineral flavors. It will grow bold with time. Drink now–15 years.

Hewitson Mermaids Muscadel | 2005 | BAROSSA VALLEY
★★ $ Fun, light-hearted wine offering citrus, apple and fresh herb flavors that are just right for summer.

Hope Estate Verdelho | 2005 | HUNTER VALLEY
★★ $ Verdelho expresses its green side here with fresh flavors of lime, herb, aloe and pear.

Houghton Semillon/Sauvignon Blanc | 2005 | WESTERN AUSTRALIA
★★★ $ Pulling the cork on this white blend unleashes aromas of spring flowers and fresh-cut grass.

Kaesler Old Vine Semillon | 2004 | BAROSSA VALLEY
★★★ $ This succulent Semillon offers a cornucopia of tangy fruit flavors combined with a layer of fine minerals and terrific acidity. Drink now–10 years.

Keith Tulloch Semillon | 2005 | HUNTER VALLEY
★★★ $ $ Classic Hunter Valley Semillon, this exudes lemon and pear flavors that will turn almondlike with age. Drink now–8 years.

Leasingham Bin 7 Riesling | 2004 | CLARE VALLEY
★★ $ A medley of citrus, green apple, peaches and stone flavors are amplified by searing acidity.

Leeuwin Estate Art Series Riesling | 2004 | MARGARET RIVER
★★★ $ $ This Riesling seduces with subtle brush strokes of lime, almond, apple and minerals.

Mount Langi Ghiran Pinot Gris | 2004 | VICTORIA
★★ $ $ An ideal pour for those seeking the weight of Chardonnay with a bit more spice. Serve this cold.

Pike & Joyce Pinot Gris | 2005 | ADELAIDE HILLS
★★ $ $ Pinot Gris shows two personalities here: one is bright with zingy citrus flavors, while the other is waxy-textured with notes of pear, marmalade and nuts.

Primo Estate La Biondina | 2005 | ADELAIDE
★★ $ A charming little wine that delights with Asian pear, light zippy citrus and herb flavors.

Ram's Leap Semillon/Sauvignon Blanc | 2004 |
WESTERN PLAINS
★★ $ This perfect summer wine expresses the freshness and flavor of strawberry lemonade.

Screwed | 2005 | MCLAREN VALE
★ $ Chill down this cheeky-labeled wine and enjoy its creamy, pear and citrus flavors.

Shaw and Smith Sauvignon Blanc | 2005 | ADELAIDE HILLS
★★★ $ $ Simply delicious Sauvignon Blanc, awash in pear, grapefruit and light, spring-fresh herbal flavors.

Yering Station M.V.R. | 2004 | YARRA VALLEY
★★★ $ $ One of Australia's finest Chardonnay producers also treats Rhône grapes masterfully. This Marsanne, Viognier, Roussanne blend conjures toasted nut, summer fruit and floral flavors.

australia reds

Robust Shiraz, with more spicy fruit than finesse, helped put Australia on the international wine map. Both Shiraz and Cabernet Sauvignon from Australia show particular character depending on where they are grown. Mourvèdre and Grenache are other quality contenders, some from vines more than a century old. Pinot Noir is not yet big in Australia, but elegant examples from cooler parts of the country show it might have a future.

AUSTRALIA REDS

cabernet sauvignon

Some of the most exceptional Cabernets in the world hail from Australia. Bursting with dark berry, chocolate and eucalyptus flavors, they more closely resemble those from Napa than those from France. Look to Barossa Valley for Cabernet with chocolate and mint flavors; Coonawarra for those that are earthy and dense. Examples from Western Australia show a more Bordeaux-like elegance and reserve.

BEST PAIRINGS Most Australian Cabernet is intense and requires foods that can match it. Roasted or braised beef, lamb or venison are ideal. Try one of Barossa's chocolaty Cabs with goulash. Cooler-climate Cabernets are elegant, calling for loin lamb chops or bacon-wrapped filet mignon.

cabernet sauvignon recommendations

Bulletin Place | 2003 | **SOUTH EASTERN AUSTRALIA**
★ $ Juicy black cherry flavors, a bit of spice and a nice low price make this a good party pour.

Cape Mentelle | 2001 | **MARGARET RIVER**
★★★ $ $ Margaret River's temperate climate shines through suave cassis and refined pepper notes. Drink now–12 years.

d'Arenberg The Coppermine Road | 2003 | **MCLAREN VALE**
★★★ $ $ $ $ Excellent Cabernet from a top producer; packed with red fruit, minerals and sweet, peppery spice. Drink now–10 years.

Deakin Estate | 2003 | VICTORIA
★ $ An enjoyable, if simple red with defined blackberry flavors.

Grant Burge Cameron Vale | 2002 | BAROSSA
★★★ $ $ This full-bodied bruiser—oozing with sticky, minty, dark berry flavors—will taste best with braised meat. Drink now–10 years.

Katnook Estate Odyssey | 2000 | COONAWARRA
★★★ $ $ $ Ripeness gives the impression of sweetness in this sappy, black fruit– and pepper-laden wine. Drink now–15 years.

Penfolds Bin 407 | 2003 | SOUTH AUSTRALIA
★★★ $ $ Dense red fruit with hints of herbs and pepper propped up by fine tannin make this exactly the sort of exemplary red wine Penfolds is famous for. Drink now–10 years.

Penley Estate Reserve | 2002 | COONAWARRA
★★★★ $ $ $ $ Coonawarra is famous for stellar Cabernet, and this elegant but powerful wine illustrates exactly why; it exhibits abundant red fruit, dusty minerals, light floral and sweet, peppery herbal flavors. Drink now–15 years.

Shingleback | 2003 | MCLAREN VALE
★★ $ $ The plentiful red fruit flavors and fine tannin in this peppery Cabernet make it a perfect steak wine. Drink now–5 years.

Tahbilk | 1999 | NAGAMBIE LAKES
★★ $ $ Age has brought forth hints of leather and dry herb aromas to complement the flavors of red fruit and spice in this beautifully crafted Cabernet. Drink now–8 years.

AUSTRALIA REDS
shiraz

Shiraz is almost synonymous with Australia, and the grape is currently on the fast track to becoming the world's most popular red wine variety. Though it's the same grape as France's Syrah, Australian Shiraz expresses a bolder array of flavors: more dark berries, mint and chocolate, with less smoke or savory spice. Shiraz from warm-climate areas like the Barossa Valley and McLaren Vale can be even more robust. Cooler-climate Shiraz has more in common with French Syrah, but it, too, has a rambunctious quality that is particularly Australian.

BEST PAIRINGS Shiraz demands bold, flavorful dishes. Pair top-quality versions with dry-aged, roast prime rib, or with a Moroccan lamb tagine. Inexpensive and fruity Shiraz is the ultimate barbecue wine.

shiraz recommendations

Aramis The Governor Syrah | 2002 | **MCLAREN VALE**
★ ★ ★ $ $ $ Though only the first vintage for Aramis, this is robust, classic Aussie Shiraz, full of black fruit, animal and spice flavors.

Barossa Valley Estate E & E Black Pepper | 2002 |
BAROSSA VALLEY
★ ★ ★ $ $ $ $ True to its moniker, this red is packed with flavors of black pepper and black voluptuous berries. Drink in 2–15 years.

Bowen Estate | 2003 | **COONAWARRA**
★ ★ ★ $ $ $ This full-bodied Shiraz exudes exotic spice, dried berry and salty mineral flavors. Drink now–8 years.

Canonbah Bridge Drought Reserve | 2002 | **WESTERN PLAINS**
★ ★ ★ $ $ $ For those who like their Shiraz on the sticky side, this red and dark berry, coconut-cream, spice-infused wine will satisfy. Drink now–8 years.

Chateau Reynella Basket Pressed | 2003 | **MCLAREN VALE**
★ ★ ★ $ $ $ Chocolaty, minty and full of juicy blackberry flavors; a stunning wine. Drink now–10 years.

Clarendon Hills Liandra Syrah | 2003 | **CLARENDON**
★ ★ ★ ★ $ $ $ $ Outstanding wine awash in black currant and spice flavors rounded out by salty mineral notes. Drink now–20 years.

---

star producers
shiraz

best value
1 Hill of Content
2 Marquis Philips
3 Rosemount Estate
4 Wolf Blass
5 Wynns Coonawarra

best of the best
1 Clarendon Hills
2 d'Arenberg
3 Henschke
4 Mount Horrocks
5 Penfolds

Elderton Command Single Vineyard | 2002 | BAROSSA
★★★★ $ $ $ $ From an exceptional producer known for dense Shiraz, this is a spicy, oaky attention-getter. Drink now–15 years.

Final Cut Ballandown Vineyard | 2004 | LANGHORNE CREEK
★★ $ Lashes of black cherry and nut flavors make this a wine built for barbecue ribs.

Fox Creek Short Row | 2004 | MCLAREN VALE
★★★ $ $ $ This high-quality vintner never disappoints, and this wine—infused with berries, savory spice and earthy minerals—is no exception. Drink now–8 years.

Frankland Estate Isolation Ridge Vineyard | 2003 |
FRANKLAND RIVER
★★★ $ $ A savory Shiraz, rich with meaty, smoky, spicy and earthy flavors dusted with chili powder. Drink now–8 years.

Grant Burge Barossa Vines | 2004 | BAROSSA
★ $ This Barossa wine delivers flavors of herbs and berries and straightforward enjoyment for a low price.

Green Point | 2004 | VICTORIA
★★ $ $ A tasty Aussie with ripe berries and fragrant herbs.

Greg Norman Estates | 2003 | LIMESTONE COAST
★ $ An affordable crowd-pleaser characterized by simple peppery berry and toasty oak flavors.

Heathcote Estate | 2003 | HEATHCOTE
★★★ $ $ $ Robust yet remarkably demure, this wine needs age or decanting to coax the light floral, dark fruit, herb and spice flavors from the glass. Drink in 2–10 years.

Innocent Bystander Shiraz/Viognier | 2004 | VICTORIA
★★★ $ $ Fistfuls of spice and floral flavors in this meaty Shiraz offer ample guilty pleasure for a very fair price.

Kaesler The Bogan | 2004 | BAROSSA VALLEY
★★★ $ $ $ Tongue-tingling mineral notes offset this lusty wine's intense berry, herbal and spicy oak flavors; a terrific wine with finesse. Drink now–12 years.

Katnook Estate Prodigy | 2002 | COONAWARRA
★★★ $ $ Sniffing is nearly as pleasurable as sipping this wine fueled by aromatic cedar, berries and sweet spice in perfect balance. Drink now–15 years.

Long Flat | 2004 | BAROSSA
★ $ Good value Shiraz, with plush berry flavors and a little spice.

Mount Langi Ghiran Billi Billi | 2003 | VICTORIA
★ ★ $ An earthy, herb- and tart berry–flavored wine.

Nine Stones | 2004 | HILLTOPS
★ ★ $ For a moderate price, you'll get tasty quaffing with the stony, smoky and peppery berry flavors in this wine.

Penfolds Magill Estate | 2002 | SOUTH AUSTRALIA
★ ★ ★ $ $ $ One of Penfolds' more majestic wines, this is saturated with red berry flavors infused by fennel and celery seed–like notes, as well as minerals and high acidity. Drink now–12 years.

Penny's Hill Red Dot | 2004 | MCLAREN VALE
★ ★ ★ $ $ Full of wild berry, eucalyptus and stone flavors, this would be delicious with roasted meats. Drink now–5 years.

Piping Shrike | 2004 | BAROSSA VALLEY
★ ★ $ A chorus of black fruit and mineral flavors make this a fun wine for everyday drinking.

Red Knot | 2004 | MCLAREN VALE
★ $ Nothing complicated here, just juicy berry and spice flavors.

Stonehaven Winemaker's Selection | 2003 |
SOUTH AUSTRALIA
★ ★ $ A rare example of an inexpensive Shiraz that allows Syrah's peppery, smoky flavors to emerge from the blanket of berries.

Wolf Blass Platinum Label | 2001 | ADELAIDE HILLS
★ ★ ★ ★ $ $ $ $ Opulent Shiraz that offers a hedonist's delight of black fruit, tobacco, minerals and spice. Drink in 1–20 years.

Zonte's Footstep Shiraz/Viognier | 2004 | LANGHORNE CREEK
★ ★ $ $ This Shiraz is not a monster, though its mixed berry, earthy tobacco and mineral flavors do leave a big impression.

other australia reds

Mourvèdre and Grenache, two other Rhône transplants, also excel here and tend to be smokier and earthier than Shiraz. Other European grapes have had some success as well, such as Spain's Tempranillo and Italy's Sangiovese. Pinot Noir is establishing itself in Tasmania. Australia's hallmark blend is Shiraz and Cabernet Sauvignon.

BEST PAIRINGS Australia's other Rhône-variety wines are often as concentrated and fruit-driven as Shiraz and can be served similarly. Inky, dense Mourvèdre is an excellent companion to braised lamb shanks. Grenache complements chili-rubbed pork loin and anything grilled. Australian Pinot Noir is delicious with smoked pork chops, but also holds its place as a great wine for salmon.

other red recommendations

Annie's Lane Copper Trail Shiraz/Grenache/Mourvèdre
| 2001 | **CLARE VALLEY**
★★ $ $ Three Rhône varieties express their lighter, more refined side with flavors of red cherry, pomegranate, dry flower and spice balanced by high acidity.

Callanans Road Pinot Noir | 2003 | **MORNINGTON PENINSULA**
★★ $ $ A lean, graceful Pinot Noir with charming cherry, light floral and spice flavors.

Clarendon Hills Kangarilla Grenache | 2003 | **CLARENDON**
★★★★ $ $ $ $ This absolutely enchanting wine offers a generous perfume of wildflowers, citrus, honey and fresh-ground spice in a pool of fresh red berries. Drink now–12 years.

Devil's Lair | 2002 | **MARGARET RIVER**
★★★ $ $ Cabernet Sauvignon and Merlot combine to create this full-bodied, velvety-textured wine embroidered with spicy pepper and tannin. Drink now–8 years.

Grant Burge Nebuchadnezzar | 2003 | **BAROSSA**
★★★ $ $ $ This Shiraz-Cabernet blend is built to age; full of red fruit, mineral and sweet pepper flavors bolstered by heavy tannins. Drink in 2–20 years.

Hewitson Old Garden Mourvèdre | 2004 | **BAROSSA VALLEY**
★★★ $ $ Mourvèdre from vines planted in 1853 creates a delicious and complex black fruit– and olive-flavored wine with a surprisingly sprightly acidity.

Joseph Moda Cabernet Sauvignon/Merlot | 2002 |
MCLAREN VALE
★★★ $ $ $ Made using an Italian practice of partially drying grapes before pressing them, Moda is full-bodied, waxy, floral and indulgent. Drink now–12 years.

Kaesler Stonehorse Grenache/Shiraz/Mourvèdre | 2004 |
BAROSSA VALLEY
★★★ $ $ Though full-bodied, this wine's crushed berry, light herb and spice flavors dance gingerly on the palate. Drink now–6 years.

Marquis Philips Sarah's Blend | 2004 |
SOUTH EASTERN AUSTRALIA
★★ $ $ Shiraz partners with Cabernet and Merlot for a thick and spicy, sweet and savory wine with blackberry and black olive flavors.

Penfolds Koonunga Hill Cabernet/Merlot | 2003 |
SOUTH EASTERN AUSTRALIA
★★ $ Lip-smacking juicy berry and plum flavors in this blend make for delicious everyday drinking.

Peter Lehmann Clancy's | 2003 | BAROSSA
★★★ $ $ This classic Australian blend of Cabernet Sauvignon, Shiraz, plus some Merlot is robust and full of berry, plum and spice notes. Drink in 2–10 years.

Pikes Luccio | 2003 | CLARE VALLEY
★★★ $ A Super-Tuscan with an Aussie accent, this high-acid blend of Sangiovese and two Bordeaux grapes is full of lusty red fruit flavors and spice. Drink now–6 years.

Rosemount Estate GSM | 2002 | MCLAREN VALE
★★ $ $ $ An archetypal Australian wine with sticky, brambly black fruit and herbs. Drink now–6 years.

S.C. Pannell Shiraz/Grenache | 2004 | MCLAREN VALE
★★★ $ $ $ This blend yields an appealing wildness, displaying forest berries, mushrooms and spice. Drink now–10 years.

Shingleback Grenache | 2004 | MCLAREN VALE
★★ $ $ Grenache goes full steam here with rich, slow-simmered strawberry, cherry and earthy spice flavors.

Tir Na N'og Old Vines Grenache | 2003 | MCLAREN VALE
★★★ $ $ Intense minerals and spice enrobe the ripe berry flavors in this delicious wine.

Trevor Jones Boots Grenache | 2003 | SOUTH AUSTRALIA
★★ $ $ Importer Dan Philips is wild for Grenache and this sticky, spicy, fair-priced wine shows why.

Tuck's Ridge Pinot Noir | 2003 | MORNINGTON PENINSULA
★★ $ $ Red cherry and mineral flavors compose a plush, but still elegant wine held up by high acidity.

Yabby Lake Vineyard Pinot Noir | 2002 |
MORNINGTON PENINSULA
★★ $ $ $ $ The perfumed fruit aromas in this enjoyable Pinot Noir are enveloped by a bouquet of damp leaves and mushrooms. Drink now–6 years.

Yering Station Reserve Pinot Noir | 2003 | **YARRA VALLEY**
★★★★ $ $ $ Perhaps the most "Burgundian"-minded Australian producer, Yering Station offers this smoky, earthy Pinot with flavors of red berry, abundant minerals and light spice. Drink in 1–10 years.

Zonte's Footstep Cabernet/Malbec | 2003 |
LANGHORNE CREEK
★★ $ $ A charming, full-bodied wine that pleases with ripe berry and plum flavors accented by light flowers. Drink now–3 years.

news from a wine insider
australia by Max Allen

Rosé is Hot
Australia has seen enormous growth in domestic sales of rosé. (Two great ones available in the U.S.: 2005 Dominique Portet Fontaine Rosé and 2005 Charles Melton Rose of Virginia.) More Aussie vintners are adding a splash of aromatic Viognier to their Shiraz, resulting in silkier, more perfumed wines. (Clonakilla is making one of the most interesting examples of this new Shiraz style.)

Notable New Wineries
Tapanappa is a new joint venture between veteran Australian winemaker Brian Croser (Petaluma), French superstar Jean-Michel Cazes (Château Lynch-Bages) and Bollinger Champagne. It's located in the little-known region of Wrattonbully. Giaconda (Rick Kinzbrunner) and Castagna (Julian Castagna) are two new wineries in the emerging region of Beechworth.

New Wines from Established Stars
Ex-Penfolds chief winemaker John Duval has produced a delicious 2004 Shiraz/Grenache/Mourvèdre blend called Plexus, while ex-Rosemount winemaker Philip Shaw just released an array of stunning wines (some under his own name) from the New South Wales region of Orange.

new zealand

It wasn't that long ago that New Zealand's fledgling fine-wine industry was dependent on the success of a handful of iconoclastic Sauvignon Blanc producers. Today, these former rebels are joined by many others who have made Kiwi Sauvignon Blanc a model by which others are judged around the world. The country's silky Pinot Noir, smoky Syrah and refined Merlot and Cabernet-based wines have earned deserved praise as well.

■ Principal Wine Region

KUMEU
AUCKLAND
WAIHEKE ISLAND

Tasman Sea

Gisborne

Hawkes Bay

Wairarapa
Martinborough
Nelson
BLENHEIM
WELLINGTON
Marlborough

Waipara

Canterbury CHRISTCHURCH

Central
Otago
QUEENSTOWN

South Pacific Ocean

New Zealand: An Overview

New Zealand is home to a myriad of microclimates. Most of the country's viticultural action takes place on the southern end of the North Island and the northern part of the South Island. Marlborough, in the South Island, is famous for Sauvignon Blanc and Chardonnay. Central Otago, farther south on the island, makes outstanding Pinot Noir, as well as fine Riesling, Gewürztraminer and Pinot Gris. In the North Island, winemakers craft superior Pinot Noir and Syrah in Martinborough and stunning, refined Bordeaux-style red wines in Hawkes Bay.

New Zealand Wine Labels

In almost every case, New Zealand wine labels list the grape variety, vintage and region in which the grapes were grown. "Reserve" has no legal meaning, but wineries tend to apply it for their better wines. New Zealand does not yet suffer the mania for single-vineyard bottlings à la California, but some vintners do mention specific vineyard names.

new zealand whites

New Zealand whites are attention-getters for their brash fruit, pungent herb and underlying mineral flavors combined with a zingy acidity.

NEW ZEALAND WHITES

sauvignon blanc

Along with the Sancerre region of France, New Zealand sets the standard by which all other Sauvignon Blancs in the world are measured. Kiwi vintners have fine-tuned a riper style of Sauvignon that is less restrained and less mineral-laden than the French, full of expressive flavors such as citrus and lime, kiwi and gooseberry, grass and even—less flatteringly—cat pee.

BEST PAIRINGS New Zealand Sauvignon Blanc is perfect with heavily herbed dishes: rosemary roast chicken, fish with pesto. It's one of a few wines that works with asparagus and artichokes, notoriously hard to pair with wine.

sauvignon blanc recommendations

Cloudy Bay Te Koko | 2003 | MARLBOROUGH
★ ★ ★ ★ $ $ $ Proving that oak can enhance Sauvignon, this well-made treasure weaves honeysuckle with light spice, apple and citrus.

Craggy Range Winery Te Muna Road Vineyard | 2005 | MARTINBOROUGH
★ ★ ★ ★ $ $ Excellent Sauvignon that is anything but green, with ripe flavors of lemon, quince, stone and light spice.

Foxes Island | 2004 | MARLBOROUGH
★ ★ ★ $ $ $ A unique mix of flavors starts with generous tropical fruit and strawberry, finishing with a kick of peppercorn.

Mount Riley | 2005 | MARLBOROUGH
★ ★ $ Aromas of rose and peach blossom bring an exotic twist to this wine's peppery kiwi, mango and lime taste-profile.

Spy Valley | 2005 | MARLBOROUGH
★ ★ $ $ Rippling with tropical notes in the form of lime, mango and a dusting of coconut flavors.

Villa Maria Reserve | 2004 | CLIFFORD BAY
★ ★ ★ $ $ $ An indulgent Sauvignon oozing with ripe mango, lemon and light pepper flavors.

---

star producers
sauvignon blanc

best value
1 Drylands
2 Huia
3 Matua Valley
4 Spy Valley
5 Villa Maria

best of the best
1 Amisfield
2 Cloudy Bay
3 Craggy Range
4 Vavasour
5 Villa Maria

other new zealand whites

Chardonnay is responsible for many great Kiwi wines, mostly in the lean, mineral style of Chablis rather than the oak-laden, tropical fruit–driven styles of Australia. Riesling, Gewürztraminer and Pinot Gris here are flavorful and dry.

BEST PAIRINGS Unoaked Chardonnay is delicious with fish; oaked versions with salmon. Moderately spiced Asian fare and curry work well with Riesling and Gewürztraminer, while weighty Pinot Gris is ideal with roast duck breast.

other white recommendations

Clearview Estate Winery Unwooded Chardonnay | 2004 |
HAWKES BAY
★★ $ $ $ A delicious, clean, tropical fruit– and spice-laden wine.

Foxes Island Chardonnay | 2004 | MARLBOROUGH
★★ $ $ $ You will detect oak in this wine, although ripe fruit and minerals are the prominent players.

Kumeu River Pinot Gris | 2005 | KUMEU
★★ $ $ Refreshing and enjoyable Pinot Gris with flavors of nuts, pear and a squeeze of citrus.

Nobilo Icon Pinot Gris | 2005 | MARLBOROUGH
★★★ $ $ Enchantingly aromatic and slightly off-dry, this exudes flavors of spiced, baked apple, orange peel and crushed berry.

Stoneleigh Riesling | 2004 | MARLBOROUGH
★★ $ $ Austere mineral notes are softened by waves of ripe white peach and pineapple.

Voss Estate Riesling | 2004 | MARTINBOROUGH
★★★ $ $ Excellent dry Riesling awash in peaches, pineapple and pear, balanced by high acidity and minerals.

new zealand reds

New Zealand has proven itself capable of world-class Pinot Noir. Its Cabernet and Merlot deserve mention for their often Bordeaux-like taste-profiles. New Zealand Syrah, while full-bodied, is rarely as robust as the Aussie paradigm.

NEW ZEALAND REDS

pinot noir

Pinot fans are happy to add New Zealand to the small list of places in the world where the grape excels. Stylistically New Zealand Pinots fall somewhere between velvety Oregon examples and the leaner, structured wines of Burgundy.

BEST PAIRINGS New Zealand Pinot Noir is lamb's perfect partner. Try it also with seared tuna or salmon.

pinot noir recommendations

Cloudy Bay | 2004 | MARLBOROUGH
★★★ $ $ $ An elegant red, tastefully attired in a robe of fruit, ribbons of spice and garlands of minerals.

Felton Road Block 5 | 2004 | CENTRAL OTAGO
★★★ $ $ $ $ This powerful Pinot is loaded with flavors of mixed berries and spice yet maintains great finesse.

Kumeu River Village | 2004 | KUMEU
★★★ $ $ An earthy wine, with smoke, spice and an abundance of minerals accenting flavors of tart red berries.

Kupe by Escarpment | 2003 | MARTINBOROUGH
★★★ $ $ $ $ Lovers of Volnay should take note of this velvety, earthy Pinot, full of minerals, truffles and wild berries.

Main Divide | 2004 | CANTERBURY
★★★ $ $ Juicy cherry flavors and heaps of stone require food.

Matua Valley | 2004 | MARLBOROUGH
★ $ Enjoyable pepper and berry flavors make a nice everyday Pinot.

other new zealand reds

While New Zealand's cooler regions support Pinot Noir, warmer zones provide a home to Bordeaux varieties. Full-bodied Syrah shows smoke and minerals and is similar in body and style to many California expressions.

BEST PAIRINGS Like Pinot Noir, Syrah is made for lamb or venison. Bordeaux-style wines are classically paired with beef, but also work beautifully with mushroom pastas.

other red recommendations

Craggy Range Winery Gimblett Gravels Vineyard Merlot
| 2003 | **HAWKES BAY**
★★★ $ $ $ Merlot has a tough time in New Zealand, but Craggy Range manages to craft this excellent wine full of berry and stone flavors bolstered by firm tannin. Drink now–8 years.

Newton Forrest Estate Cornerstone Cabernet/Merlot/Malbec | 2002 | **HAWKES BAY**
★★★ $ $ $ A nearly black wine that tastes as dark as it looks; this oozes with black pepper, black currant and smoky, tobaccolike flavors. Drink now–6 years.

Villa Maria Cellar Selection Cabernet Sauvignon/Merlot
| 2003 | **HAWKES BAY**
★★ $ $ A purely delicious wine with clean red cherry and berry flavors accented by a pinch of spice and tannin. Drink now–3 years.

news from a wine insider
new zealand by Peter Hellman

The 2006 Vintage

New Zealand vintners expect 2006 to be the greatest vintage in the country's history. The growing season was blessed with perfect weather, unlike two unexceptional prior vintages. Exports are booming—up 64 percent in 2005—with Pinot Noir gaining in popularity.

Appellations & Grapes to Watch

In the Hawkes Bay region, Craggy Range and Esk Valley make two fantastic Bordeaux-style blends. Vintners also make impressive wines from Syrah, with the most noteworthy bottlings coming from Trinity Hill, Bilancia and Te Mata.

New Wines from Established Stars

Marlborough Sauvignon Blanc is a New Zealand calling card; two fine examples come from Cloudy Bay and Seresin. For exceptional Marlborough Pinot Noir, try the wines of TerraVin and Wither Hills.

Notable New Wineries

Clos Henri is an exciting new venture in Marlborough by Sancerre's Henri Bourgeois. Stellar Central Otago Pinot Noir producer Felton Road is joined by Mt. Difficulty, Carrick, Olssens, Amisfield, Valli and Rippon. Martinborough's best include Larry McKenna's Escarpment and Craggy Range.

argentina

Argentine wines have only recently become better known in the U.S., although Argentina has long been one of the world's largest wine-producing nations. Most of its wines are consumed domestically, but a growing number—including some of the nation's best—have found their way into wine glasses the world over.

Principal Wine Region

CHILE

South Pacific Ocean

Salta
• CAFAYATE

ARGENTINA

La Rioja

Aconcagua
VALPARAÍSO
Casablanca
Maipo ☆ SANTIAGO
Rapel
Curicó
Maule BUENOS AIRES ☆
CONCEPCIÓN

Mendoza
• LUJÁN
• TUPUNGATO

Mendoza

South Atlantic Ocean

Argentina: An Overview

Argentina's wine regions mostly skirt the eastern slopes of the Andes, where blistering sunshine is tempered by altitude, cool mountain breezes and an abundant supply of water. Mendoza is the most famous of the country's large wine regions. Within Mendoza are the subregions of Luján de Cuyo, ideally suited for growing Malbec, and Maipú, where high-quality Cabernet is produced. White grapes do well in high-altitude subregions such as Cafayate in the north, Tupungato in Mendoza, in parts of Patagonia and the high valley of Río Negro.

Argentine Wine Labels

Most bottles are easy to decipher, labeled with grape variety and region of origin. Proprietary names are given to some wines, especially those that are blends of different grape varieties. Terms such as "Reserva" and "Reserve" have no legal meaning; wineries often use them to differentiate their better wines.

argentina whites

International stars Chardonnay and Sauvignon Blanc are widely planted in Argentina, and vintners craft them in styles ranging from light and crisp to rich and buttery. Other international varieties also have a presence, such as Pinot Gris, Semillon and Viognier, but Torrontés has become the nation's emblematic white wine grape. It's grown almost exclusively in Argentine soils and produces wines that are enchantingly floral and refreshing.

BEST PAIRINGS Torrontés is light and flowery with a mineral edge—classic aperitif sipping. Rich Argentine Chardonnay requires heavier foods like spice-coated salmon filets or chicken. Pour lighter Chardonnay and Sauvignon Blanc with seafood salads or chicken empanadas.

white recommendations

Catena Chardonnay | 2004 | MENDOZA
★★ $ $ Lovers of spicy Chardonnay will enjoy this cinnamon-dusted, apple- and citrus-scented wine.

Crios de Susana Balbo Torrontés | 2005 | CAFAYATE VALLEY
★★★ $ An exceptionally seductive Torrontés, full of honeysuckle, apple blossom and citrus flavors balanced by mineral notes.

Doña Paula Los Cardos Sauvignon Blanc | 2004 | TUPUNGATO
★ $ A slightly exotic Sauvignon, with a wisp of passion fruit and guava flavors.

Finca El Portillo Sauvignon Blanc | 2005 | VALLE DE UCO
★ $ A good chill will complement the bright citrus flavors in this straightforward, refreshing white.

Luca Chardonnay | 2004 | ALTOS DE MENDOZA
★★★★ $ $ $ A weighty yet beautifully balanced Chardonnay oozing with flavors of citrus, stone, apricot and oak. This is enjoyable to drink now and will also age well.

Michel Torino Don David Reserve Torrontés | 2004 |
CAFAYATE VALLEY
★★ $ $ High-altitude vineyards bring forth a wine scented by alpine flowers, lime and fresh grass.

Terrazas de los Andes Reserva Chardonnay | 2004 |
MENDOZA
★★ $ $ Tangy orange and lemon flavors are sweetened by a succulent lick of butterscotch.

argentina reds

Malbec, a grape that originated in the southwest of France, is Argentina's alpha grape. Full of luscious dark berry and chocolate flavors with relatively soft tannins, Malbec has helped the country find its niche in the international marketplace. Cabernet Sauvignon and Merlot also have a strong presence here and are responsible for some of Argentina's most interesting reds. Increasing amounts of Syrah, Bonarda, Sangiovese and Tempranillo are also being made into noteworthy wines.

BEST PAIRINGS Argentineans frequently dine on locally raised, excellent grass-fed beef. But any flavorful cut of beef will match nicely with Argentina's robust reds. Bonarda is full of fresh fruit flavors and an earthiness that makes it ideal with lamb or braised short ribs. Vegetarians will find that a bowl of polenta smothered with a mushroom ragù will hold up to any Argentine red.

red recommendations

Bodegas Nieto Senetiner Limited Edition Bonarda | 2002 |
MENDOZA
★★★ $ $ This unusual and compelling Bonarda is rich with berry, ash and earth aromas and flavors of wild spices. Drink now–10 years.

Catena Cabernet Sauvignon | 2002 | MENDOZA
★★ $ $ Dark berry flavors and abundant tannin are lightened by a wave of lavender. Perfect with lamb. Drink now–4 years.

Cobos Malbec | 2003 | MENDOZA
★★★★ $ $ $ $ Malbec vines fifty to eighty-plus years old and one of California's greatest winemakers, Paul Hobbs, are responsible for this incredibly dense and indulgent wine. Drink now–10 years.

Crios de Susana Balbo Syrah/Bonarda | 2004 | MENDOZA
★★ $ Syrah's peppery, smoky qualities melt into Bonarda's black-berry and tobacco flavors in this delicious and affordable wine.

Domaines Barons de Rothschild (Lafite) and Nicolas
Catena Caro | 2002 | MENDOZA
★★★ $ $ $ This sophisticated Bordeaux-style wine will only grow more elegant with time. Drink in 2–10 years.

Doña Paula Estate Cabernet Sauvignon | 2004 |
LUJÁN DE CUYO
★★ $ A modest though highly enjoyable Cabernet, full of red fruit and light pepper flavors.

Don Miguel Gascón Malbec | 2004 | MENDOZA
★ $ Juicy crushed berries and spice; just the way simple Malbec should taste.

Felipe Rutini Apartado | 2002 | MENDOZA
★★★ $ $ $ Full of indulgent glazed cherries, sugared violets and dark chocolate flavors, yet remarkably balanced. Drink now–8 years.

Joffré e Hijas Reserva Merlot | 2003 | VALLE DE UCO
★★ $ $ $ A Merlot with more black olive than the typical black plum profile, this spicy, earthy red provides interesting, savory sipping. Drink in 1–6 years.

La Posta del Viñatero Pizzella Family Vineyard Malbec
| 2004 | LA CONSULTA
★★★ $ $ A hedonistic yet measured expression of what Malbec can be: full of crushed berry, flower and spice flavors balanced by high acidity. Drink now–6 years.

Mapema Tempranillo | 2004 | MENDOZA
★★ $ $ Dried cherry, spice and mineral flavors give this medium-weight wine its savory bite. Drink now–3 years.

news from a wine insider
argentina by Nick Ramkowsky

Winemakers in the News
Superstar Roberto de la Mota (Cheval des Andes and consultant at Terrazas de los Andes) has started his own winery, Mendel, which will produce two wines, both made from some of the oldest Malbec and Cabernet vines in Mendoza. And the thirty-year-old Luis Reginato is making the wines at Luca and Tikal, two of the top boutique wineries in Mendoza, owned by Laura Catena and Ernesto Catena respectively (children of Argentine winemaking legend Dr. Nicolas Catena). Look, also, for the line of single-vineyard Malbecs and Bonardas that Luis makes at La Posta del Viñatero.

Wineries to Know About
Labels to look for include: Dominio del Plata (which makes BenMarco, Susana Balbo and Crios de Susana Balbo) owned by husband-and-wife team Susana Balbo and Pedro Marchevsky; and Cuvelier Los Andes, overseen by vintner Michel Rolland and owned by Bordeaux's Cuvelier family (Château Léoville Poyferré).

Wine Country Destinations
Club Tapiz, a small new hotel and restaurant in a restored 1890 winery, offers incredible views of the Andes. Other lodging options include Cavas Wine Lodge, a luxury hotel in Mendoza, and two Postales del Plata lodges south of Mendoza.

Melipal Malbec | 2004 | MENDOZA
★★ $ $ Smooth fruit, peppery spice and high acidity get the mouth
in the mood for barbecue.

O. Fournier B Crux | 2002 | VALLE DE UCO
★★★ $ $ Lovers of modern-style Rioja will enjoy this robust Tempranillo, Malbec, Merlot blend. Drink now–8 years.

Punto Final Reserva Malbec | 2004 | PERDRIEL
★★★ $ Intense Malbec with concentrated blackberry and violet
flavors held up by fine tannin and acidity. Drink now–6 years.

Ricardo Santos La Madras Vineyard Malbec | 2004 |
MENDOZA
★★ $ $ Succulent, aromatic berries blend with earthy minerals and
spice in a sophisticated, but easy to enjoy wine. Drink now–4 years.

Salentein Syrah | 2003 | ALTO VALLE DE UCO
★★ $ $ Packed with flavors of dried fruit, orange zest and spice, this
Syrah recalls spiced fruit cake.

Tempus Alba Preludio Acorde # 1 Reserve | 2003 | MENDOZA
★★★ $ $ $ Malbec and Cabernet unite for a fruit-filled red accent-
ed by sweet spice and pepper. Drink now–8 years.

Terra Rosa Old Vine Malbec | 2003 | MENDOZA
★ $ You'll find simple but incredibly smooth drinking with this plush
berry- and nut-flavored wine.

Tikal Patriota | 2004 | MENDOZA
★★★ $ $ An homage to Bonarda and Malbec—Argentina's most
widely planted grapes—this heavyweight needs time to blossom, but
earthy berry and spice flavors will be worth it. Drink in 2–10 years.

Trapiche Broquel Cabernet Sauvignon | 2003 | MENDOZA
★★ $ Fresh, crushed berry flavors, a twist of pepper and chewy tan-
nin make one terrific barbecue wine.

Trivento Golden Reserve Malbec | 2003 | MENDOZA
★★ $ $ A core of sappy blackberry and spice flavors is rounded out
by firm tannins; this needs age, or fatty short ribs. Drink now–5 years.

Urban Uco Malbec/Tempranillo | 2003 | VALLE DE UCO
★★ $ This unique blend yields a lithe, cherry- and berry-laden wine.

Weinert Carrascal | 2003 | MENDOZA
★★ $ Lovers of old-style claret will enjoy the red berry and pepper-
corn flavors in this Malbec, Merlot and Cabernet Sauvignon blend.

chile

Chile is a grape-growing utopia. Yet, despite four centuries of experience, the country's wine industry still struggles to define itself. Chile has long been known for good wine at modest prices. A few decades ago, international investors arrived with hopes of making wines on a par with the best in the world. In a handful of cases, they succeeded, but the rest of the industry focused on increasing production rather than improving quality. In recent years, fierce international competition has forced Chilean vintners to double efforts toward quality, and many now make fine wine from regions once thought marginal.

Chile: An Overview

Chile is blessed with abundant sunshine, an ample water supply, cooling Pacific breezes and phylloxera-free vines. Most of Chile's best vineyards are located within a couple of hours of the capital, Santiago (see map p. 242). The Maipo region is famous for Cabernet; its subregion, Alta Maipo, is making wines of unique depth. Emerging fringe regions are also worth seeking out: try whites from San Antonio Valley, reds from Curicó and Syrah from Elqui Valley.

Chilean Wine Labels

Chilean wine labels list grape variety, adhering to New World convention. Some use proprietary names for blends and single-vineyard designations are appearing more frequently. One might see the English word "Reserve" on some bottles, but it, like the Spanish "Reserva," has no legal meaning.

chilean whites

Chilean whites are far less interesting than the country's reds. But white wine quality is on the rise, especially in the cool-climate, coastal regions of Casablanca and the San Antonio Valley. Chardonnay and Sauvignon Blanc make up the bulk of production, though the majority of the latter is actually Sauvignon Vert, which offers distinct, herb flavors.

BEST PAIRINGS Chile's oak- and tropical fruit–laden Chardonnay nicely complements grilled salmon. Casablanca Sauvignon Blanc pairs well with salad or chicken; serve leaner San Antonio versions with cod or snapper.

white recommendations

Aresti A Gewürztraminer | 2005 | CURICÓ VALLEY
★ $ A delightful little white with light floral and zippy lemon flavors.

Casa Silva Quinta Generación | 2004 | COLCHAGUA VALLEY
★★★ $ $ This blend of Sauvignon Gris, Viognier and Chardonnay offers a luscious treat of pear, caramel, herb and stone flavors.

Concha y Toro Terrunyo Sauvignon Blanc | 2005 |
CASABLANCA VALLEY
★★★ $ $ One of Chile's most consistently excellent Sauvignons, Terrunyo tingles the palate with mineral, citrus and smoky notes.

Errazuriz Wild Ferment Chardonnay | 2004 |
CASABLANCA VALLEY
★★ $ $ Natural yeasts bring out flavors resembling apple coffee cake in this dry, mineral-laden wine.

Garcés Silva Amayna Sauvignon Blanc | 2005 |
SAN ANTONIO/LEYDA VALLEY
★★★ $ Light-bodied yet substantial, with succulent grapefruit aromas piqued by flowers and spice.

Montes Alpha Chardonnay | 2004 | CASABLANCA VALLEY
★★★ $ $ A sultry, satiny wine that caresses with peach, passion fruit and pineapple flavors underscored by polished minerals.

chilean reds

Chilean vintners take their cue from Bordeaux when it comes to red wines. Cabernet Sauvignon and Merlot both grow well, though Cabernet is usually more impressive. Carmenère, Chile's most interesting variety, is a Bordeaux grape that has almost been forgotten in its native land. For years it was mistaken for Merlot, but today there is hope that Carmenère might provide the distinction Chile has sought for years. There's also some outstanding Chilean Syrah and Pinot Noir being made today.

BEST PAIRINGS Chile's Bordeaux-grape reds fall somewhere between California and France in style and are a good match for steak and roasted lamb. Syrah's berry and spice flavors work with roast duck, and Chilean Pinot Noir goes nicely with lamb chops or salmon steaks.

red recommendations

Altaïr | 2003 | CACHAPOAL VALLEY
★★★★ $ $ $ $ A well-bred French-Chilean collaboration crafts one of Chile's most suave, iconic wines, full of black fruit, minerals and tannin. Drink in 1–15 years.

Arboleda Merlot | 2003 | COLCHAGUA VALLEY
★ $ Modest in body and fine in tannin, this peach- and berry-flavored, easy-to-love Merlot is a perfect partner for anything off the grill.

Casa Lapostolle Clos Apalta | 2003 | COLCHAGUA VALLEY
★★★★ $ $ $ $ The top-tier wine from one of Chile's most esteemed producers is full of concentrated dark fruit, licorice, deep minerals and chewy tannin. Drink in 3–12 years.

Casa Marin Lo Abarca Hills Pinot Noir | 2003 |
SAN ANTONIO VALLEY
★★★ $ $ $ $ This remarkably lithe Pinot—full of smoky, earthy and cherry flavors—is a beautiful expression of San Antonio's cool climate and terroir. Drink now–5 years.

Chono Cabernet Sauvignon | 2004 | CENTRAL VALLEY
★ $ An affordable, claretlike gem with tart red berry, light pepper and high acidity in fine balance.

Cousiño-Macul Finis Terrae | 2003 | **MAIPO VALLEY**
★★ $ $ Heavy tannins envelop this violet, oak and wild red berry–
flavored wine. Serve this with a big steak. Drink in 3–10 years.

De Martino Gran Familia Cabernet Sauvignon | 2002 |
MAIPO VALLEY
★★ $ $ $ Sappy, sticky and tailor-made for saucy ribs.

**Domaines Barons de Rothschild (Lafite) Los Vascos
Reserve Cabernet Sauvignon** | 2003 | **COLCHAGUA**
★★★ $ $ The Bordelaise owners of Los Vascos inspire a Bordeaux-
style red, full of earthy, peppery red fruit flavors. Drink now–8 years.

Domus Aurea Cabernet Sauvignon | 2001 |
UPPER MAIPO VALLEY
★★★ $ $ $ Earthy, with licks of eucalyptus and red berries, this
distinctive Cabernet would complement any meat dish.

Errazuriz Viñedo Chadwick | 2002 | **MAIPO VALLEY**
★★★ $ $ $ $ Regal wine with earthy berry and mineral notes.

Haras de Pirque Estate Cabernet Sauvignon | 2002 |
MAIPO VALLEY
★★ $ Surely one of the best-value Cabernets in the world, offering
an indulgence of cassis, pepper and spice for around $10.

Matetic EQ Syrah | 2004 | **SAN ANTONIO**
★★★ $ $ Chile's San Antonio region conjures France's St-Joseph
with this earthy, smoky, delicious wine. Drink now–6 years.

Montes Purple Angel | 2003 | **COLCHAGUA VALLEY**
★★★★ $ $ $ Lovely for its deep purple hue and rich cedar, mineral
and exquisite wild berry flavors. Drink in 1–10 years.

Peñalolen Cabernet Sauvignon | 2003 | **MAIPO VALLEY**
★★ $ $ Flavors of cassis and pepper course through this fine red,
full of sun and earth.

Sincerity Merlot/Cabernet Sauvignon | 2003 | **COLCHAGUA**
★ $ This full-bodied blend—made according to biodynamic wine-
making principles—offers unique and enjoyable light peppery notes.

Terra Noble Gran Reserva Carmenère | 2003 | **MAULE VALLEY**
★★ $ A fine rush of wild red berries with a peppery edge.

Veramonte Primus | 2003 | **CASABLANCA VALLEY**
★★ $ $ Year after year, this is one of Chile's most consistently good,
sophisticated reds for under $20.

south africa

South Africa's wine country enjoys some of the most idyllic climatic conditions of any wine-producing country on earth. Today, South African wines are earning well-deserved international praise. Vintners are dramatically improving quality by planting better vines and using new winery technologies. And the entire industry is working hard to dispel the shameful legacy of apartheid: wine producers have signed on to a charter dedicated to increasing black ownership in the wine industry.

Atlantic Ocean

Coastal Region

Paarl

Robertson

CAPE TOWN
Constantia

Stellenbosch

Elgin

Walker Bay

Indian Ocean

■ Principal Wine Region

South Africa: An Overview

South Africa's wine regions are mostly concentrated in the southwest corner of the country, where the sun's warmth is tempered by cooling ocean breezes. The Coastal Region, which radiates outward from Cape Town, encompasses several esteemed districts. Stellenbosch and its subregion Simonsberg-Stellenbosch are noted for their aromatic, vibrant Chenin Blancs and Sauvignon Blancs, stalwart Chardonnays and fine Bordeaux-style wines. The warmer inland region of Paarl is home to more robust red wines, including Shiraz. The cooler district of Walker Bay is responsible for graceful Pinot Noirs and Chardonnays that are reminiscent of good-quality Burgundy.

South African Wine Labels

South African wine labels are straightforward, listing the name of the winery, the grape variety, the region in which the grapes were grown and the vintage. Some wineries use proprietary names for their blends, but you'll usually find the grapes listed on the back label.

south africa whites

Chenin Blanc is the country's most widely planted white grape. Sometimes called "Steen," South African Chenin Blanc offers fresh melon, citrus and mineral flavors, rather than the muskier mélange of baked apple, orange and spice notes that the grape expresses when grown in France's Loire Valley (Chenin Blanc's place of origin). Another important grape here, Sauvignon Blanc, is full of the same herbal and exotic fruit characteristics found in examples from New Zealand and California, but with more restraint. South African Chardonnay is typically medium in body, with lots of mineral flavors; those from warmer parts of the country are often full of tropical fruit flavors and are more heavily oaked, resembling California versions.

BEST PAIRINGS South African Chenin Blanc is lighter than its French counterpart and a fine choice for calamari or shrimp. Leaner, mineral-rich Chardonnay works with chicken or fish. Sauvignon Blanc is terrific with spinach and goat cheese salads or oysters on the half shell.

white recommendations

Cederberg Chenin Blanc | 2005 | CEDERBERG
★ ★ $ Spicy pear, lemon and mineral notes overlay fresh grass.

The Foundry Viognier | 2005 | COASTAL REGION
★ ★ ★ $ $ In this substantial Viognier, peach blossoms, pear and lemon smooth out smoky mineral flavors.

Glen Carlou Chardonnay | 2004 | PAARL
★ ★ $ $ Upfront apple and citrus flavors augment spicy oak notes.

Goats do Roam in Villages | 2005 | WESTERN CAPE
★ ★ $ Whimsical in name, engaging in flavor, this white has ginger and tropical fruit flavors to add exotic pleasure.

Hamilton Russell Vineyards Chardonnay | 2004 | WALKER BAY
★ ★ ★ $ $ $ The label and price might say South Africa, but the refined citrus, mineral and oak flavors in this wine say "Meursault."

Kanu Sauvignon Blanc | 2005 | STELLENBOSCH
★ ★ $ If you're moving from Margaritas to wine, the tart lime and jalapeño notes in this will ease the way.

Klein Constantia Mme. Marlbrook | 2004 | CONSTANTIA
★ ★ ★ $ $ The subtle pear, almond and grapefruit flavors here are reminiscent of a high-quality white Bordeaux.

Man Vintners Chenin Blanc | 2005 | COASTAL REGION
★ $ Put a chill on this zesty Chenin Blanc; its mixed fruit flavors make for pleasing summer sipping.

Miles Mossop Wines Saskia | 2004 | COASTAL REGION
★ ★ $ $ $ An unusual, lightly oaked Chenin Blanc/Viognier blend offers earthy apple flavors with fragrant peach. Drink now–4 years.

Neil Ellis Chardonnay | 2004 | STELLENBOSCH
★ ★ $ $ Chardonnay's expressive tropical fruit flavors are refreshed by ample minerals and mouthwatering acidity.

Nitída Semillon | 2005 | DURBANVILLE

★★ $ In the mood for something different? Drink this piquant wine with unique leafy, peachy and peppery flavors.

Plaisir de Merle Sauvignon Blanc | 2005 | COASTAL REGION

★★ $ $ Flavors of fresh citrus are on display in this tasty Sauvignon, accented by hints of ripe melon and apple.

Raats Family Wines Original Unwooded Chenin Blanc
| 2005 | COASTAL REGION

★★ $ Snappy apple and pear flavors are complemented by light minerals in this zippy wine.

Simonsig Chenin Blanc | 2005 | STELLENBOSCH

★ $ A weighty, if simple, Chenin laden with pear and apple flavors.

Spice Route Viognier | 2005 | SWARTLAND

★★ $ $ Spicy, like the label says. Peppery notes add an interesting dimension to this pear- and lemon-flavored wine.

Warwick Estate Professor Black Sauvignon Blanc | 2005 | SIMONSBERG-STELLENBOSCH

★★★ $ $ This has all the mouthwatering acidity of Sancerre with the succulent fruit flavors you expect from New World Sauvignon.

south africa reds

South Africa has its very own grape variety: Pinotage. A cross between the French-origin Cinsault and Pinot Noir, Pinotage can be funky, smoky, herbal and animal. Simpler styles resemble Beaujolais Nouveau; others are complex and full-bodied with silky tannin. Pinotage's eccentricities can become seductively charming in the hands of great winemakers. Vintners also craft full-bodied yet elegant Cabernet Sauvignon, Merlot and Shiraz. South Africa's Merlots are similar to those from Washington State, and its earthy Pinot Noirs are comparable to Oregon examples.

BEST PAIRINGS South African reds tend to be smoky and meaty, which makes them partner well with barbecue. Pinotage is excellent with roasted game birds, Merlot with pork tenderloin and veal. Shiraz and Cabernet complement venison or braised lamb shanks. Pinot Noir works with herbed rack of lamb or grilled vegetables.

red recommendations

Condé Cabernet Sauvignon | 2003 | STELLENBOSCH
★★★ $ $ $ Clean, juicy red fruit flavors are spiced up with notes of pepper and earth. Drink now–8 years.

Engelbrecht Els Vineyards | 2003 | WESTERN CAPE
★★★ $ $ $ Dark fruit flavors are accented by ashen minerals in this sophisticated red. Drink now–10 years.

Fairview Pinotage | 2004 | COASTAL REGION
★ $ Fresh crushed berries with only a touch of funk offer a gentle introduction to distinctive Pinotage.

Glen Carlou Syrah | 2004 | PAARL
★★ $ $ Syrah shows its savory side in this wine: smoked ham and barbecue bean flavors complement hints of dark berries.

Goats do Roam | 2004 | WESTERN CAPE
★ $ Crushed berries and herbs make this a fine wine at a fair price.

Hamilton Russell Vineyards Pinot Noir | 2004 | WALKER BAY
★★★ $ $ $ Just as Hamilton Russell's Chardonnay clearly says "Meursault" this earthy, Burgundian-style red says "Mercurey."

Indaba Shiraz | 2004 | WESTERN CAPE
★ $ Juicy berry flavors, a hint of smoke and a low price make for a good, crowd-pleasing barbecue wine.

Nederburg Shiraz | 2004 | WESTERN CAPE
★ $ Tarry, savory, ripe dark berry flavors take on an oddly appealing carbon note in this gently priced wine.

Sanctum Shiraz | 2003 | WESTERN CAPE
★★★★ $ $ $ Nearly black, this superb wine's flavor labyrinth shows lavender, pepper, minerals and smoke. Drink now–10 years.

Spice Route Malabar | 2002 | SWARTLAND
★★★ $ $ $ Sultry black fruit flavors are seasoned by spicy black pepper, light smoke and minerals in this stunning, dense red that will age incredibly well. Drink now–8 years.

Stark Syrah | 2003 | STELLENBOSCH
★★★ $ $ $ Great Syrah, lightly smoked and full of pepper flavors.

Thelema Cabernet Sauvignon | 2003 | STELLENBOSCH
★★★ $ $ $ Lovers of sappy, chocolate-mint, eucalyptus-flavored Cabernet will go mad for this entrancing wine. Drink now–8 years.

Tokara | 2003 | STELLENBOSCH
★★★★ $ $ $ $ This displays the New World/Old World dichotomy of South African wine; robust berry flavors combine with herbs and fine minerals. Drink now–12 years.

Vilafonté Series M | 2003 | PAARL
★★★ $ $ $ Legendary California winemaker Zelma Long teams up with South Africa's Mike Ratcliff to make this great red, with velvety black fruit, fine minerals and a backbone of tannin.

Warwick Estate Old Bush Vines Pinotage | 2004 | STELLENBOSCH
★★★ $ $ Strawberry jam, smoke, animal and tobacco flavors are framed by chewy tannin. This will remind fans of Pinotage why they love the grape. Drink now–3 years.

---

news from a wine insider
south africa by Jean-Pierre Rossouw

Appellations to Watch

Winemakers in South Africa's Cape have been experimenting successfully with terroir outside the established Constantia and Stellenbosch regions. In Cape Agulhas, Africa's southernmost tip, vintners are making striking Sauvignon Blanc. Standout producers are Agulhas Wines, Black Oystercatcher, Lomond and Springfontein. Even the desolate West Coast is making quality wine; the best examples come from Darling Cellars, Groote Post and Ormonde.

Hot Grapes

Winegrowers are discovering that the Cape has much in common with warmer wine regions, which is leading them to focus on grapes like Shiraz, Grenache, Mourvèdre and various Italian grapes, rather than the traditionally planted Bordeaux and Burgundy varieties. Vintners at the forefront of this trend include Eben Sadie, Charles Back, Alex Dale (Black Rock) and Tom Lubbe.

Notable New Wineries & Wines

M'Hudi ("harvester" in a local dialect) is one of a growing number of black-owned wineries in South Africa producing superior wines. Also, look for Grand Constance, a new wine from Groot Constantia. A blend of red and white Muscat grapes in the style of Constantia's famous sweet wines, Grand Constance was released in honor of the estate's 320th anniversary.

other new world wines

Wine production occurs throughout the Americas. Contrary to what many might believe, Canada is not too cold to grow fine wine grapes and Mexico is not too hot. In South America, you'll find interesting wines from Peru, Brazil and particularly Uruguay, where a decade or more of hard work in the vineyards and cellars has resulted in wines of exceptional quality.

Canada, Mexico, Uruguay: An Overview

Canada's most important wine regions are centered in two provinces, Ontario and British Columbia. Ontario's Niagara Peninsula and Pelee Island regions are spared potentially bitter winter temperatures by the moderating influences of Lakes Ontario and Erie. They specialize in cooler-climate grapes like Riesling and are famed for their ice wines. British Columbia has several wine subregions. The most famous is the Okanagan Valley, whose warmer southern reaches can support Bordeaux grape varieties, as well as Chardonnay, Pinot Gris and Pinot Noir. Mexico's best vineyards are in Baja California. Mexican wines tend to be full-bodied and made mostly from southern European grape varieties. Most of Uruguay's wine production is concentrated in the Canelones region, just north of the capital Montevideo, where humid subtropical conditions are cooled by breezes coming from the Atlantic. Winegrowers cultivate a number of international grape varieties, but they have their greatest success with Tannat, a grape brought to Uruguay by Basque settlers in the 19th century.

other new world whites

Grape varieties like Riesling, Gewürztraminer, Pinot Blanc and Pinot Gris excel in parts of Canada. They're generally dry in the Alsatian style. The best Chardonnays are lean and mineral-laden. Look for wines from hybrid grapes like Vidal or Seyval Blanc. Baja California makes simple, enjoyable Sauvignon Blanc, Chenin Blanc and Semillon. Uruguay's vineyards grow international grapes, as well as Torrontés, the charmingly floral grape that does well in Argentina.

BEST PAIRINGS Serve Canadian whites as you would their Alsatian counterparts. Rieslings are lovely with fish and Gewürztraminer works with spicy seafood dishes. Pour a Mexican white alongside chicken or fish tacos. Uruguay's Torrontés makes a lovely aperitif.

white recommendations

Cave Spring CSV Riesling | 2004 |
NIAGARA PENINSULA, CANADA
★ ★ ★ $ $ $ Dry and complex, this is classic Riesling, saturated with citrus, peach and deep stone flavors. Drink now–8 years.

Jackson-Triggs Proprietors' Grand Reserve
Sauvignon Blanc | 2004 | **OKANAGAN VALLEY, CANADA**
★ ★ $ $ Though a relatively full-bodied Sauvignon Blanc, this version has high acidity that brings zip to melon and citrus flavors.

Malivoire Pinot Gris | 2004 | NIAGARA PENINSULA, CANADA
★ ★ $ A weighty apple- and citrus-flavored wine with searing acidity.

Peninsula Ridge Estates Winery Vintners Private Reserve
Chardonnay | 2003 | **NIAGARA PENINSULA, CANADA**
★ ★ $ $ $ Heavy oak is balanced by lots of citrus and acidity.

Viñedo de los Vientos Angel's Cuvée Blanc de Bianco
| 2004 | **ATLANTIDA, URUGUAY**
★ ★ ★ $ $ $ This polished wine sparkles with fine minerals, light pear, citrus and floral flavors.

other new world reds

Ontario winemakers persist year after year in their quest to make good red wine, despite climatic challenges. They are most successful with Pinot Noir and Cabernet Franc. Baco Noir is a hybrid grape that makes smoky, full-bodied wines with a distinct rustic quality. It's worth trying Gamay, which is generally fresh and fruity. British Columbia's Bordeaux-style wines are similar to those from Washington State. Quality Mexican reds are full-bodied and flavorful. Northern Italy's finicky Nebbiolo does surprisingly well there, as does Syrah, Tempranillo, Cabernet and Zinfandel. Uruguay grows Merlot, Cabernet and Syrah, but its star is Tannat, the grape behind France's famously tannic Madiran. Cultivated in Uruguay since the 19th century, Tannat is full-bodied, but softer and less tannic than its French counterpart.

BEST PAIRINGS Canada's Bordeaux blends can take the place of similar wines from Washington State, alongside rack of lamb or thick sirloins. Pinot Noir is delicious with tuna. Have Baco Noir with braised meat. Mexico's Nebbiolo is a flexible wine, terrific with spice-rubbed pork or chicken. Uruguay's lusty Tannat is at its best with beef.

red recommendations

Adobe Guadalupe Kerubiel | 2003 |
GUADALUPE VALLEY, MEXICO
★ ★ ★ $ $ $ Five different grape varieties create this smooth wine, full of chocolaty berry, orange and spice flavors. Drink now–6 years.

Casa de Piedra Vino de Piedra | 2003 | **ENSENADA, MEXICO**
★ ★ ★ $ $ $ $ This is Mexico's finest wine. Full-bodied but delicate, it shows sultry berry, spice and stone flavors. Drink now–8 years.

Domaine Monte de Luz Syrah | 2005 | **SAN JOSE, URUGUAY**
★ ★ $ Fresh crushed strawberries, light spice and high acidity make up this lovely Syrah.

L.A. Cetto Private Reserve Nebbiolo | 2000 |
GUADALUPE VALLEY, MEXICO
★ ★ ★ $ $ Smoky, dark berry-flavored wine made by one of the few producers outside Italy who successfully works with Nebbiolo.

Malivoire Pinot Noir | 2003 | NIAGARA PENINSULA, CANADA
★★★ $ $ Light-bodied, yet still powerful, this offers smoke and earthy flavors, minerals and tart, spicy red fruit. Drink now–6 years.

Osoyoos Larose Le Grand Vin | 2003 |
OKANAGAN VALLEY, CANADA
★★★ $ $ $ Canada's most ambitious red, this French-Canadian collaboration displays the finesse of Bordeaux. Drink in 3–10 years.

Valmar Cabernet Sauvignon | 2000 |
BAJA CALIFORNIA, MEXICO
★★ $ $ A dry and tannic wine with peppery red berry flavors and good acidity that make it perfect for grilled meat.

Viñedo de los Vientos Tannat | 2002 | ATLANTIDA, URUGUAY
★★★ $ $ This full-bodied, smoky Tannat shows what Uruguay can do with the grape. It bursts with notes of berry, tobacco, iron and salt. Drink now–8 years.

news from a wine insider
canada by Tony Aspler

The 2005 Vintage
Making wine in Canada is often challenging, but the 2005 vintage was particularly frustrating for Ontario producers. The harsh winter damaged a large percentage of vines, resulting in a significant production decrease—as much as 60 percent. Still, many producers managed to turn out excellent wines, including Malivoire Wine Company, Daniel Lenko Estate Winery, Henry of Pelham and Peninsula Ridge.

Meanwhile, two thousand miles away in British Columbia's Okanagan Valley, vintners had an easier time with the 2005 vintage: a mild summer and fall yielded stunning wines. Top producers like Cedar Creek, Blue Mountain, Jackson-Triggs, Mission Hill Family Estate and Sumac Ridge all made worthy examples, as did up-and-comers like Black Hills, Laughing Stock, Adora and Blasted Church.

Notable New Wineries
Among the more interesting of Canada's many new wineries are: Tawse Winery, Fielding Estate Winery, Flat Rock Cellars, Stratus Vineyards, Coyote's Run Estate Winery, Le Clos Jordan and Mike Weir Estate Winery.

champagne & other sparkling wines

Whether it's a charming Prosecco from northern Italy, a crisp, fruity Cava from Spain or a decadent Grand Cru Champagne from France, sparkling wine makes any occasion more festive. But there's no need to save them for special events; fine sparklers are actually great everyday, food-friendly wines and are available in all price ranges.

Sparkling Wine: An Overview

Nearly every wine region makes some type of wine that sparkles. Most agree that the finest examples come from regions with cool climates and soils rich in minerals. Grapes from these regions usually develop complex flavor profiles while maintaining high acidity, which is essential to the production of quality sparkling wines. Champagne, a cool region with distinct chalky soils in northern France, is the world's most famous and revered region for sparkling wine. Outside of Champagne, look to the Carneros, Mendocino and Anderson Valley regions in northern California; to northern Italy and Spain, where you will often find excellent value sparklers; and to the island of Tasmania, Australia's premier sparkling wine region.

champagne

There is no sparkler as well known or esteemed as those from the Champagne region of France. While grapes from Champagne's cool climate rarely become ripe enough to produce fine still wine, they are very high in acidity, making them ideal for sparkling wine. The region's limestone-rich soils give Champagne its hallmark minerality. Only sparkling wines made in France's Champagne region are entitled to be called "Champagne."

Champagne Grapes & Styles

Champagne is almost always made from one or more of three permitted grape varieties: Chardonnay, Pinot Noir or Pinot Meunier. Wines labeled *Blanc de Blancs* ("white from whites") are 100 percent Chardonnay. *Blanc de Noirs* wines are made from Pinot Noir and/or Pinot Meunier. Rosé wines are made either by blending a little red wine into the white sparkling wine, or by soaking pigment-rich red grape skins with pressed juice. Most Champagne today is dry, but a few producers make sweeter versions.

Champagne Labels

All Champagnes say "Champagne" on the label. Most Champagnes are non-vintage (NV), that is, they are blends of wines from different years. This practice allows each Champagne house to create and maintain a consistent house style. Vintage Champagnes are only produced in years when grapes ripen especially well. Many houses offer different levels of vintage wines. Their top wines are often referred to as *Tête de Cuvée* or *Cuvée Prestige*, though the terms have no legal meaning. These wines are usually given proprietary names such as Moët's famous Dom Pérignon or Veuve Clicquot's La Grande Dame. As in other wine regions of France, vineyards that are considered superior to

others are entitled to Premier Cru status, and the very best are classified as Grand Cru. Champagne labels indicate their level of sweetness. From driest to sweetest the categories of Champagne are: *Brut Nature* (also known as *Brut Zéro, Pas Dosé* or *Sans-Dosage*), *Extra Brut, Brut, Extra Dry/Extra Sec, Sec/Dry* and *Demi-Sec*. (Oddly, wines labeled "Sec/Dry" are normally a touch sweet.) "Brut," which is dry, is the most common category on the market.

Pairing Champagne

Champagne is often enjoyed as an aperitif, but it is in fact a a fabulous food wine. Lean, mineral-laden styles are superb with oysters, while more medium-bodied Champagne is marvelous with crab, baked halibut or roast chicken. Richer styles are wonderful with smoked salmon, pork or creamy pasta dishes. Oddly, the classic pairing of Champagne and caviar is not ideal, since the wine's high acidity makes the briny, fishy flavors of caviar seem metallic.

champagne recommendations

WHITES

Charles Heidsieck Brut | 1995 |
★★★★ $ $ $ $ Though not cheap, an exotic ambrosia of flavors—including mangos, honeydew, honey and spice—make this pour an exceptional value for $65.

Delamotte Blanc de Blancs Brut | 1999 |
★★★★ $ $ $ $ This is less prestigious than its much-celebrated sibling, Salon Le Mesnil, however, flavors of fresh-squeezed grapefruit, sweet spice and almonds make it a very fine cuvée prestige.

Deutz Classic Brut | NV |
★★ $ $ $ Savory, smoky wild mushroom flavors are lightened by a squeeze of lemon and a pinch of spice in this earthy wine.

Diebolt-Vallois Cuvée Prestige Blanc de Blancs Brut | NV |
★★★ $ $ $ $ Aromas of fresh-baked bread and powdery minerals bring depth to Asian pear and citrus flavors.

Gaston Chiquet Tradition Brut | NV | PREMIER CRU
★★★ $ $ $ An unusual array of anise and herb flavors infuse this fascinating, chalky, tropical fruit–filled wine.

Georges Gardet Cuvée St-Flavy Brut | NV |
★★ $$ Ripe yellow apple flavors are accented by light berries and spiced orange in this small-production, family-made Champagne.

Gosset Grande Réserve Brut | NV |
★★★ $$$$ Clean, crisp lemon-lime and mineral flavors bring refreshment to indulgent ripe pineapple and sweet spice.

Krug Brut | 1995 |
★★★★ $$$$ Spectacular Champagne that immediately reveals exotic herbs and spice, dried lime peel and briny mineral flavors.

L. Aubry Fils Brut | NV | PREMIER CRU
★★★ $$$ Voluptuous wine saturated with succulent flavors of spicy pear, orange and minerals.

Laurent-Perrier Grand Siècle Brut | NV |
★★★ $$$$ Wonderfully rich with flavors of yeast, cherries and nuts, this brings the pleasures of aged Champagne without the wait.

Louis Roederer Premier Brut | NV |
★★ $$$$ Mouth-filling tropical fruit flavors are matched by stone in this full-bodied sparkler.

Margaine Brut | NV | PREMIER CRU
★★★ $$$ Too many complex flavors to analyze here; orange peel and autumn apples give way to hints of spiced plum and grapefruit.

Moët & Chandon Dom Pérignon Oenothèque Brut | 1990 |
★★★★ $$$$ From the depths of Dom Pérignon's treasury comes this brilliant gem full of toasted almond and smoke flavors accented by the finest mineral, lime zest and truffle notes.

Moët & Chandon White Star | NV |
★★ $$$ Pineapple, pear and apple flavors with a hint of sweetness make a fine brunch or wedding cake wine.

Nicolas Feuillatte Cuvée 225 Brut | 1997 |
★★★ $$$$ One of Feuillatte's latest cuvées shows the benefit of oak-aging, but still stays fresh, drenched by sweet and piquant spice, yellow apple flavors and lots of mouthwatering acidity.

Origine Marcel Hemard Brut | NV | PREMIER CRU
★★ $$$ Baked apple, holiday spice and toasty bread flavors.

Piper-Heidsieck Cuvée Rare | NV |
★★★ $$$$ Honeysuckle, fragrant jasmine and blanched almond flavors are coated in citrus marmalade with a hint of sweetness.

Pol Roger Brut | NV |

★★ **$ $ $** For lean, polished, mineral-laden, citrus- and apple-scented Champagne, there's no better value.

Pommery Brut Royal | NV |

★★ **$ $ $** Delicate luxury for a good price, this tickles the palate with citrus, tart peach and light floral flavors.

Serveaux Carte d'Or Brut | NV |

★★★ **$ $ $** This is loaded with an array of heirloom pear and apple flavors, kept crisp by vibrant acidity.

Trouillard Extra Sélection Brut | NV |

★★★ **$ $ $** One of Champagne's great values, less than $30 buys fine apple and citrus flavors augmented by notes of creamy, toasty nuts and underscored by minerals.

ROSÉS

Bruno Paillard Première Cuvée Rosé Brut | NV |

★★ **$ $ $ $** Beautiful pink hue and lots of ripe peach flavors.

Krug Rosé Brut | NV |

★★★★ **$ $ $ $** One of the finest wines on the planet. Flavors of summer peaches, raspberries, clementines, plus chalky mineral notes compose this flawless Krug Champagne.

Taittinger Comtes de Champagne Brut Rosé | 1999 |

★★★★ **$ $ $ $** Marvelous salmon-hued Champagne, with tart and sweet cherry, strawberry and spice flavors on a bed of minerals.

Veuve Clicquot Ponsardin Brut Rosé | NV |

★★ **$ $ $ $** New from Veuve Clicquot, this non-vintage rosé charms with a creamy texture and delicate strawberry and orange flavors.

---

star producers
champagne

best value
1 Bonnaire
2 Charles Heidsieck
3 Egly-Ouriet
4 Nicolas Feuillatte
5 Pol Roger

best of the best
1 Bollinger
2 Charles Heidsieck
3 Jacques Selosse
4 Krug
5 Salon

other sparkling wines

While no region carries the same prestige as Champagne, there are countless other sparkling wines worthy of merit, often with much gentler price tags.

france

Champagne gets the glory, but sparkling wine is produced all over France. Some of the best are from the Loire Valley, Alsace and Languedoc's Limoux. They're normally made from grapes common to their respective regions and can be excellent. Those made like Champagne are labeled *méthode classique* or *méthode traditionnelle*. You will also find sparklers called *Crémant, Brut,* or *Mousseux.*

other french sparkling wine recommendations

Antech Cuvée Elégance Brut | NV | BLANQUETTE DE LIMOUX
★★ $ Apple and lemon flavors are slightly toasted in this lovely Champagne-styled wine from the south.

Bouvet Saphir Brut | 2003 | SAUMUR
★★ $$ A touch of residual sugar rounds out the apple and citrus flavors of this dry sparkler.

Domaine du Vieux Pressoir | NV | SAUMUR
★★ $$ Zippy lemon and pear and lots of stone make up a terrific, inexpensive fill-in for Champagne.

Jaillance Cuvée Impériale Tradition | NV | CLAIRETTE DE DIE
★ $ An absolute delight; like drinking a mousse of peach blossoms.

Langlois-Château Brut | NV | CRÉMANT DE LOIRE
★★ $$ So filled with marzipan and orange flavors, this dry wine almost seems dessertlike.

Wolfberger Brut Rosé | NV | CRÉMANT D'ALSACE
★★ $$ Alsace is not known for rosés, but this example is finely executed, giving a perfume of cherry and orange.

italy

Italy makes a wide variety of *spumante* (sparkling) wines. The dry, mineral-laden examples from the Franciacorta subregion in Lombardy are made in the same manner as Champagne, using what is locally called the *metodo classico*. Some stand up to their French counterparts in quality. Moscato d'Asti is a lightly sweet and charming sparkler from Piedmont, and while many are simple, they are lovely post-meal sippers. Prosecco, made near Venice, provides affordable and fun refreshment.

italian sparkling wine recommendations

Bellavista Gran Cuvée Satèn | NV | **FRANCIACORTA**
★★★ $ $ $ $ Smoky, sophisticated and made from 100 percent Chardonnay, this is one of the few Franciacorti that is on a par with fine Champagne.

Bellenda Extra Dry | 2005 |
PROSECCO DI CONEGLIANO VALDOBBIADENE
★★ $ $ Ripe tangerine and peach flavors are nicely balanced by acidity in this silky-textured wine.

Bisol Jeio Brut | NV | **PROSECCO**
★★ $ Gingery orange and powdery mineral flavors compose this refreshing, appetite-stimulating bubbly.

Col Vetoraz Brut | NV | **PROSECCO DI VALDOBBIADENE**
★★★ $ $ Pure fun at a high level, with apple and almond flavors and a mineral edge.

Maschio M Spago | NV | **PROSECCO DEL VENETO**
★ $ Prosecco done gently, with soft bubbles and slightly sweet pear and almond flavors.

Mionetto Cartizze | NV | **PROSECCO DI VALDOBBIADENE**
★★★ $ $ More ambitious than most Prosecco, this is awash with spicy pear and light orange flavors accented by smoke.

Zardetto Zeta | 2004 | **PROSECCO CONEGLIANO**
★ $ $ Frothy orange vanilla flavors impart a nearly creamsicle-like charm to this well-made Prosecco.

spain

Spain's sparkling Cavas have been providing inexpensive alternatives to Champagne for years. While their greatest virtue had been price, they have improved tremendously in quality in the recent past. Happily, prices generally remain modest. By law, all are made from local grapes, using the Champagne method.

spanish sparkling wine recommendations

Aviñyó Reserva Brut | NV | CAVA
★★★ $$ Impressive Cava with tangerine, lime and herb flavors coating a polished core of minerals.

Buil & Giné Extra Brut | NV | CAVA
★★ $$$ The fresh flavors of early summer seep from a breezy, lemony, light and peachy Cava underlined by salty minerals.

Freixenet Cordon Negro Brut | NV | CAVA
★ $ The sort of wine you'll be glad exists: well-made, if simple, with zingy citrus flavors for a low price.

Huguet Gran Reserva Brut Nature | 2002 | CAVA
★★★ $$ Terrific value, this is lean but still offers generous flavors of Meyer lemon and smoke which soften a dense bed of minerals.

Mont Marçal Extremarium Brut | NV | CAVA
★★ $$ A full-bodied Cava, with ripe pear, lemon and spice flavors.

Segura Viudas Reserva Heredad Brut | NV | CAVA
★★★ $$ Apple- and orange-laden wine sharpened by smoky minerals and searing acidity.

united states

Producers throughout the U.S. make a variety of sparkling wines, many using Champagne's *méthode traditionnelle* or *méthode champenoise*. California's examples are the standouts, especially those made in cooler regions such as Carneros and the Anderson and Green Valleys. New York, the Pacific Northwest, Michigan and New Mexico also make some fine sparkling wines.

u.s. sparkling wine recommendations

Clinton Vineyards Seyval Naturel | NV |
HUDSON RIVER, NEW YORK

★★ $ $ Fascinating drinking from the heart of the Hudson Valley, this hybrid-grape wine offers an array of herb and key lime flavors.

Domaine Carneros by Taittinger Le Rêve Blanc de Blancs
Brut | 1999 | **CARNEROS, CALIFORNIA**

★★★★ $ $ $ $ A noble producer from Champagne crafts this California wine with both finesse and succulent tropical fruit flavors.

Gruet Brut | NV | **NEW MEXICO**

★★ $ One of America's best values for sparkling wine brings crisp, apple flavors and stone from New Mexico's high desert.

Handley Brut | 2000 | **ANDERSON VALLEY, CALIFORNIA**

★★★ $ $ $ One of Handley's best efforts to date, this explodes with orange, anise and apple flavors with a kick of spice and stone.

Iron Horse Blanc de Blanc LD | 1996 |
SONOMA COUNTY/GREEN VALLEY, CALIFORNIA

★★★★ $ $ $ $ This shows the complexity of age with seductively smoky flavors of citrus, dry apricot and truffle-scented minerals.

Mumm Napa DVX | 1999 | **NAPA VALLEY, CALIFORNIA**

★★★ $ $ $ All of Mumm Napa's sparklers represent good value; this creamy, grapefruit- and clove-scented wine is their top cuvée, with a light, appealing toastiness.

Roederer Estate Brut | NV | **ANDERSON VALLEY, CALIFORNIA**

★★ $ $ Champagne Louis Roederer makes this California sparkler, and it well represents its French breeding with flavors of lemon and minerals. For superlative drinking, try its sibling L'Ermitage.

Scharffenberger Brut | NV | **MENDOCINO COUNTY, CALIFORNIA**

★★ $ $ Lean, orange- and lime-infused bubbly that demonstrates a return to Scharffenberger's original style.

Schramsberg Brut Rosé | 2003 |
NAPA/MENDOCINO/SONOMA/MARIN COUNTIES, CALIFORNIA

★★★ $ $ $ Mouthwatering acidity brings out all the succulent goodness of tart red berry, orange and stone flavors.

Wölffer Brut | 2003 | **THE HAMPTONS, NEW YORK**

★★★ $ $ $ Rich bubbly in a hedonistic style, this indulges with a cornucopia of citrus, tropical fruit and berry flavors.

other countries

Germany and Austria make some fine (and a lot of average) sparkling Sekt from Riesling and Pinot Blanc. Portugal and Greece offer well-made sparklers at very fair prices. South Africa, Argentina, Australia and New Zealand all make Champagne-inspired sparklers. Australian offerings include a deeply red, full-bodied and tannic sparkling Shiraz (made in dry and sweeter forms).The former Soviet Republics of Georgia, Armenia and Moldova produce medium-sweet red and white sparklers, but they're rarely available in the U.S.

other countries sparkling wine recommendations

WHITES

Schlumberger Cuvée Klimt Brut | NV | **VIENNA, AUSTRIA**
★★ $ $ This walks the line between sumptuous and austere with a unique medley of apple, olive oil and bitter almond notes.

Spiropoulos Ode Panos Brut | 2003 | **PELOPONNESE, GREECE**
★ $ Nothing complex here, just straightforward apple and sweet-scented flower flavors.

Vértice Reserva Bruto | 2001 | **DOURO, PORTUGAL**
★★ $ Douro producers are famous for their sweet, fortified Ports and dark, dry reds, but they are also capable of lovely sparkling wines such as this light, apple-scented wine.

ROSÉS

Taltarni Brut Taché | NV | **VICTORIA/TASMANIA, AUSTRALIA**
★★ $ $ Fragrant but tart strawberry flavors are brushed by orange peel in this pastel pink–hued rosé.

REDS

Fox Creek Vixen | NV | **MCLAREN VALE, AUSTRALIA**
★★★ $ $ Things are different Down Under as this ruby-hued sparkler with flavors of herb, spice and dark berries shows.

Joseph Sparkling Red | NV | **ADELAIDE, AUSTRALIA**
★★★ $ $ $ Spice dominates in this sparkling red flavored by dried cherry, sandlewood, ground clove and cinnamon; a perfect partner for holiday fruitcakes.

fortified & dessert wines

From a bone-dry fino Sherry before dinner to a luxuriously sweet, late-harvest wine with dessert, fortified and dessert wines can be a memorable way to frame a repast. Fortified wines like Sherry and Madeira can be enjoyed throughout the meal, too.

fortified wines

Fortified wines are made by adding alcohol—neutral grape brandy—before bottling. The extra alcohol helps preserve the wine and, if added before the wine finishes fermenting (before its natural grape sugar has converted to alcohol), it can create a sweet wine, which is the case with many of the best-known fortified wines—Port, Sherry and Madeira.

FORTIFIED WINES

sherry

Southern Spain's Jerez region is known above all else for its Sherry. Though often overlooked by wine drinkers, Sherry is among the world's most distinctive wines, its flavors marked by the chalky soils of Jerez and the wild yeasts that ferment the grape juice. There's a Sherry for every taste, in styles ranging from completely dry to unctuously sweet.

Sherry Grapes & Styles

Most Sherry is made from Palomino grapes, though sweet styles are often made from or with the addition of Pedro Ximénez or Moscatel grapes. Sherry is usually blended from wines of different years, using a system called the "Solera." There are two basic categories of Sherry: Fino and Oloroso. Both contain several subcategories.

• **FINO SHERRY** is yeasty, floral and slightly nutty. It derives its distinct flavors from *flor,* a yeast that grows on the wine's surface and stifles oxygen while the wine matures in wooden casks. **Manzanilla Sherry** is a Fino made around Sanlúcar de Barrameda, a seaside area especially hospitable to *flor*. Fresh as the salty ocean breezes that blow over the vineyards, the wines express notes of fragrant chamomile (*manzanilla* in Spanish). **Amontillado** is a Fino that continues to age after its oxygen-inhibiting *flor* dies. Oxidation brings nutty qualities to the wine's inherent minerality. Most Amontillado is dry. **Pale Cream Sherries** are Finos sweetened by Pedro Ximénez wine or grape juice concentrate.

• **OLOROSO SHERRY** doesn't develop *flor,* so it oxidizes with age, becoming nutty, smoky and earthy as it turns a dark amber hue. Some Olorosos are dry, but most are sweet. **Cream Sherry** is an Oloroso sweetened with Pedro Ximénez wine. **Palo Cortado** is an uncommon type of Oloroso that develops *flor* later in the maturation process. It's chestnut in color, with a style between Oloroso and Amontillado.

• **PEDRO XIMÉNEZ** (or PX for short) is technically not Sherry, but several Sherry houses make it. PX gets its thick, syrupy-sweet, dried fruit flavors from grapes of the same name grown mainly in the Montilla-Moriles region outside of Jerez.

BEST PAIRINGS Dry Fino is everything a great aperitif wine should be: light, palate-stimulating and delicious on its own or with salted nuts, olives, some cheeses, as well as shellfish and other seafood tapas. Dry Oloroso Sherry is perfect with squash soups, cured ham or nutty cheeses such as Manchego. Sweeter versions are excellent with bread pudding. Pour PX over vanilla ice cream.

sherry recommendations

Barbadillo Eva Cream Sherry

★★★ $ This divine, medium-sweet wine indulges with dry fig, orange and a tinge of salty Serrano ham flavors.

Bodegas Hidalgo La Gitana Manzanilla

★★★ $ $ One of the world's most delightful wines, this chamomile-scented Manzanilla captures the freshness of a salty ocean breeze.

Bodegas Hidalgo La Gitana Pastrana Manzanilla Pasada

★★★ $ $ Compare this aged Manzanilla to Hidalgo's fresh one; the sea breeze is still there, but with toasted almonds and honey notes.

Bodegas Toro Albalá Don PX Gran Reserva | 1971 |

★★★ $ $ $ Ebony-tinged, high-acid wine with intense flavors of sweet blackberry, camphor and papaya that give this a long finish.

Gonzalez Byass Apóstoles Palo Cortado Muy Viejo

★★★ $ $ Creamy in one measure, erotically earthy in another, this entices with the perfume of truffles, dry figs, orange and sweet spice.

Gonzalez Byass Tio Pepe Palomino Extra Dry Fino

★★ $ $ $ Salty nut and apple flavors are perfect with almonds.

Lustau East India Solera

★★★ $ $ $ You won't need dessert with this wine. Fruit, nut and bitter chocolate flavors here will more than satisfy any sweet tooth.

Lustau Los Arcos Dry Amontillado

★★ $ $ Caramel-rich, but dry, with orange zest and toasted almond flavors balanced by salty minerals.

Osborne 10 RF Oloroso Medium

★★ $ A touch of sweetness joins the savory toasted nut, apricot and peppery spice flavors here; this versatile wine will pair nicely with meat empanadas as well as fruit cake.

FORTIFIED WINES

port

British wine merchants stumbled upon the sweet wines of Portugal's Douro region in the 17th century while searching for a substitute for the embargoed wines of France. Port (named for the Portuguese city Oporto) has been enjoyed by wine lovers the world over ever since.

Port Grapes & Styles

More than eighty different grapes can be used to make Port; the best are Touriga Nacional, Touriga Franca and Tinta Roriz (Tempranillo). Port is labeled by style, from off-dry White Port to tannic, sweet, ageworthy Vintage Port. There are three basic categories of Port: White, Ruby and Tawny. The latter two contain several subcategories.

• **WHITE PORT,** made from white grapes, is a refreshing aperitif with its lightly sweet, citrusy flavor. Some houses make slightly oxidized versions which are also refreshing.

• **RUBY PORT** is the most common style. Generic versions are simple, blended from young wines. More intense versions are **Reserve** or **Vintage Character Ports**, which are blends of Ruby Ports aged four to six years. These wines often carry proprietary names like Warre's Warrior or Graham's Six Grapes. **Late Bottled Vintage (LBV) Ports** are Rubies from a single vintage aged four to six years in barrels. They acquire some of the attributes of Vintage Ports without requiring further aging. **Vintage Ports** are the most precious of the Rubies, blended from the best grapes from a single vintage; they are only made in years when the harvest is exceptional. Aged in oak casks for two to three years, Vintage Port can require decades of aging before its potential is realized. **Single Quinta Vintage Ports** are made from the grapes of a single excellent vineyard (*quinta*).

• **TAWNY PORTS** are kept in barrels significantly longer than Vintage or other Ruby Ports, where they develop dried fruit and nut flavors and the tawny color that gives them their name. Generic Tawnies are blends from different years. The finest Tawnies, however, are labeled with the average age of wine in the bottle, usually five to forty years. **Colheita Ports** are Tawny Ports from a single vintage (*colheita*). All Tawnies are ready to drink upon release.

BEST PAIRINGS Chilled White Port is a refreshing aperitif. Rubies are a fine match for berry pies. Vintage Port is traditionally savored alone or with strong cheeses. Tawny Port's nutty flavors are delicious with pear tarts or pecan pies.

port recommendations

Churchill's Vintage | 2003 |

★★★ $ $ $ $ Rich, concentrated Port with dark cherry, minerals, smoke and spice that will only improve with time; this will be truly spectacular in 20 years.

Delaforce Colheita | 1986 |

★★★ $ $ $ A relatively cooler year in the Douro yielded lighter wines. This dry, Vintage Tawny is a beautiful expression of subtlety with pineapple, orange and spice flavors.

Dow's Fine Ruby

★★ $ Bright cherry and an eclectic mix of herbs and spice provide a lovely end to an evening for not a lot of money.

Ferreira Quinta do Porto 10 Year Tawny

★★ $ $ $ One often yearns for more age when tasting ten-year Tawny, but this mineral-drenched, dry cherry– and apricot-flavored wine shows the advantages of youth.

Fonseca 40 Year Tawny

★★★★ $ $ $ $ Forty years have done exceptionally well by this off-dry, truffle- and musk-scented Tawny, laden with figs and stones.

Osborne 10 Year Tawny

★★ $ $ $ Though relatively simple for an age-designated Tawny, this fruit-styled Port still gives plenty of tasty, tarnished orange and red berry flavors.

Poças 20 Year Tawny

★★★ $ $ $ Chestnut in hue, nutty and spicy in profile, with dried orange, fig and mineral flavors kept vibrant by high acidity.

star producers
port

best value
1 Delaforce
2 Gould Campbell
3 Ramos Pinto
4 Smith Woodhouse
5 Warre's

best of the best
1 Fonseca
2 Graham's
3 Niepoort
4 Quinta do Noval
5 Taylor Fladgate

Quinta do Crasto Late Bottled Vintage | 1999 |
★★★ $ $ Theoretically, you could enjoy this wine's bright cherry and smoky earth flavors now, but this is an LBV that will age well.

Quinta do Noval Vintage | 2003 |
★★★★ $ $ $ $ If you can't spring for Noval's sublime Nacional (at a staggering $800), you'll be more than satisfied to settle for this herbal, berry and flowery-spiced Port—for one-eighth the price.

Ramos Pinto Vintage | 2003 |
★★★ $ $ $ $ Funky, old-fashioned Port with an intense mix of wild berries, pungent herbs, spice, chocolate and tannin. This needs time.

Romariz Vintage | 2003 |
★★★ $ Lithe-bodied Vintage Port? Well, not quite, but this wine's strengths lie in finesse rather than power, with fine cherry, berry and spice flavors, plus a bit of tannin.

Taylor Fladgate Vintage | 2003 |
★★★★ $ $ $ $ Superlative Vintage Port, this is as lush as they come, with an impressive and complex array of fruit flavors and spice. Age for decades.

Warre's Quinta da Cavadinha Vintage | 1989 |
★★★ $ $ $ A beautiful, well-developed Vintage Port that shows generous dry and fresh cherry, flower and spice flavors.

FORTIFIED WINES

madeira

Madeira is named for the Portuguese island off the coast of Morocco where it's made. While it was the American drink of choice in the 19th century, it isn't as appreciated today. Like Sherry, it comes in styles for before, during and after a meal.

Madeira Grapes & Styles

Most Madeira wines are blends, but the best versions will carry the name of one of four grape varieties: Sercial, Verdelho, Bual and Malmsey (Malvasia). Sercial makes the driest wines, while wines from Verdelho, Bual and Malmsey (Malvasia) are progressively sweeter. "Rainwater" refers to a medium-dry blend. Madeiras with age designations, such as five-year, ten-year or fifteen-year, are blends from different years, the number referring to the youngest wine in the blend. Solera Madeiras, on the other hand, indicate the vintage of the oldest wine in the blend. Vintage-dated wines are rare but exceptional and often impressively old.

BEST PAIRINGS Madeira is a classic match for flavorful, hearty winter soups. Sercials and Verdelhos go nicely with salty nuts, dry cheeses or sautéed shellfish. The richness, sweetness and high acidity of Buals and Malmseys make them ideal for crème brûlée, baked fruit or custard tarts.

madeira recommendations

Blandy's 5 Year Rich Alvada
★★ $ $ Low-priced taste of Madeira's herbal, dried fruit pleasures.

Broadbent Colheita | 1996 |
★★★ $ $ $ Lovely and relatively light-bodied, this is full of flavor, ranging from fresh-squeezed grapefruit to herbs and walnuts.

Broadbent Rainwater
★ $ This offers sweet, if simple, dry fruit and nut flavors.

Cossart Gordon 5 Year Bual
★★★ $ $ Pungent herb qualities course through the dried orange and spice flavors in this lovely Bual.

The Rare Wine Co. Historic Series Special Reserve Charleston Sercial
★★★ $ $ $ Just off-dry, this aperitif wine recreates a style popular in 19th-century Charleston, with apple, almond and herb flavors.

dessert wines

Unfortified sweet dessert wines are among the world's most delicious things. Often quite low in alcohol, these beautifully made wines are surely the ambrosia of the gods.

white dessert wines

White dessert wines are full of entrancing flavors that range from flowers to spice, nuts, honey, truffles and smoke. They are one of the finest ways to end any meal.

White Dessert Wines Grapes & Styles

• **LATE-HARVEST** wines are made from grapes left on the vine late into fall in order to attain especially high sugar levels. They can be made from any grape variety and nearly every winemaking region produces them. Some of the most famous examples come from Germany (marked *Spätlese,* which means "late," or *Auslese,* which is even sweeter) and Alsace (where they're marked *Vendanges Tardives* or VT). California, Australia, South Africa, Chile and the Greek isle of Samos also make excellent versions.

• **PASSITO** wines are made from grapes that have been dried before pressing. A specialty of Italian vintners, passito wines are made from a myriad of grape varieties. In Tuscany and Umbria, producers use Trebbiano grapes and call the wines *Vin Santo*. The island of Pantelleria makes lush late-harvest wines from local Zibibbo, a type of Muscat. French versions are called Vin de Paille, or "straw wine."

• **BOTRYTIS** wines are considered the most noble of all sweet wines. They achieve their distinctive flavors from *Botrytis cinerea,* a mold affectionately called "noble rot." The mold sucks the water out of the grapes, concentrating their luscious fruit flavors and adding smoky, spicy, truffle-like nuances. The most famous botrytized wines are those from Bordeaux's Sauternes region and subregion Barsac, where Sémillon, Sauvignon Blanc and Muscadelle are blended to yield wines of exceptional flavor and longevity. Neighboring Loupiac and Cadillac produce similar, though less-expensive wines. The Loire Valley subregions of Quarts de Chaume, Vouvray, Coteaux du Layon, Montlouis and Bonnezeaux produce superb sweets from Chenin Blanc. Alsatian vintners use their finest grape varieties to make *Sélection de Grains Nobles* (SGN) wines. Germans and Austrians produce sublime botrytized wines from Riesling and other varieties, which they designate *Beerenauslese* (BA) or *Trockenbeerenauslese* (TBA) according to the intensity of the grapes (see p. 138). California, South Africa and Australia also produce golden wines from botrytis-affected grapes.

- **ICE WINE/EISWEIN** is made from grapes that have been left to ripen on the vine until the first freeze. The grapes are pressed while frozen, which yields small amounts of very concentrated sweet juice. Riesling makes some of the most famous ice wines, although nearly any grape variety can be used. The best ice wines come from Germany and Austria, but there are also superb examples from Canada, and even New York and Washington State. In places where it rarely freezes, some winemakers simply put especially ripe grapes in a freezer and then press them.
- **VIN DOUX NATUREL** (VDN) is a category of wines that are fortified with brandy during fermentation, preserving the grape's natural sweetness. Made primarily in the south of France, the two most noteworthy white wine examples are Muscat de Beaumes-de-Venise from France's Rhône Valley and Muscat de Rivesaltes from the Languedoc-Roussillon.
- **TOKAJI** is made in Hungary and a small part of Slovakia by a unique method that infuses a base of dry white still wine with a mash of botrytis-infected grapes (called *aszù* in Hungarian). Tokaji is graded according to the quantity of crushed grapes that are added to the base, from three to six *puttonyos*, each puttonyo equaling a bin's worth of crushed grapes. The higher the puttonyo count, the sweeter the wine. The ultimate expression of Tokaji is Eszencia, a concentrated sweet wine made from the juice that oozes from the grapes crushed only by the pressure of their own weight. At every level, Tokaji typically takes on flavors of dried apricot, orange and almond, balanced by high acidity.

BEST PAIRINGS Sauternes, Tokaji, VT or Auslese Riesling are all high in acidity yet sweet, which makes them ideal partners for foie gras or strong, piquant cheeses like Roquefort. The honeyed, floral flavors of Samos Muscats and Italy's rich and nutty Passitos are great with biscotti. Pour a Vin Doux Naturel with crème brûlée. Savor the fresh, pure flavors of ice wine with nothing more than sweet, ripe summer fruit like peaches or berries.

white dessert wine recommendations

Amity Vineyards Late Harvest Riesling | 2002 |
WILLAMETTE VALLEY, OREGON
★★ $ $ (375 ml) A bit of age has released Riesling's tendencies
toward smoke and petrol, amidst lemon and peach flavors.

Black Star Farms A Capella Riesling Ice Wine | 2004 |
OLD MISSION PENINSULA, MICHIGAN
★★★ $ $ $ $ (375 ml) Plusher in body than many ice wines, this
treat from Michigan offers an array of apricot and orange flavors.

**Bodegas Gutiérrez de la Vega Casta Diva Cosecha Miel
Muscat** | 2004 | **ALICANTE, SPAIN**
★★★ $ $ $ (500 ml) Hypnotic aromas of dried Mediterranean
herbs infuse this stunning, apple-flavored wine.

Château Coutet Premier Cru | 2003 |
SAUTERNES-BARSAC, FRANCE
★★★ $ $ $ Sweet-spiced baked quince flavors are made even
juicier by orange and pineapple, all balanced by high acidity.

Château de Jau | 2005 | **MUSCAT DE RIVESALTES, FRANCE**
★★ $ $ (500 ml) Light, lemony and floral; perfect for sorbet.

Château Gravas | 2003 | **SAUTERNES, FRANCE**
★★ $ $ (375 ml) Not the most complex wine from Sauternes, but
this wine's lovely smoky citrus confit flavors also cost a lot less.

Château Suduiraut Premier Cru | 2003 | **SAUTERNES, FRANCE**
★★★★ $ $ $ $ Thick yet delicate with peach, pineapple and spice.

**Concha y Toro Private Reserve Late Harvest
Sauvignon Blanc** | 2002 | **MAULE VALLEY, CHILE**
★★ $ (375 ml) Low-cost Sauternes-styled, smoky gem from Chile.

Dolce | 2002 | **NAPA VALLEY, CALIFORNIA**
★★★★ $ $ $ $ (375 ml) Proof that Napa's best wines don't have
to be red, this indulges with cedar, spice, fig, apricot and beeswax.

Domaine de La Pigeade | 2004 |
MUSCAT DE BEAUMES-DE-VENISE, FRANCE
★★ $ (375 ml) Abundant lime blossom, honey and lemon flavors.

Domaine des Baumard Clos de Ste-Catherine | 2004 |
COTEAUX DU LAYON, FRANCE
★★★ $ $ $ Mouthwatering and clean, this shows flavors of fresh-
squeezed Meyer lemons with a refreshing brush of pine.

Domaine Zind-Humbrecht Vendanges Tardives Brand Riesling | 2004 | ALSACE, FRANCE

★★★★ $ $ $ $ Riesling has no finer expression than this great wine. It's off-dry, full of pineapple, sweet and savory spice flavors ranging from cinnamon to cumin to celery seed.

Elderton Botrytis Semillon | 2005 | RIVERINA, AUSTRALIA

★★★ $ $ (375 ml) Sweet, grilled pineapple flavors stay remarkably balanced and fresh in this terrific Aussie Semillon.

Errazuriz Late Harvest Sauvignon Blanc | 2005 | CASABLANCA VALLEY, CHILE

★ $ (375 ml) Rich with simple citrus and melon flavors that bring plenty of pleasure.

Fazi Battaglia Arkezia Muffo di San Sisto | 2000 | MARCHE, ITALY

★★★ $ $ $ $ (500 ml) Uniquely good, this Verdicchio-based wine is dry and sweet at once, with intense mineral, dried orange and a fine line of black currant flavors.

Gsellmann & Gsellmann Beerenauslese | 2001 | BURGENLAND, AUSTRIA

★★★ $ $ (500 ml) Funky Scheurebe is blended with the more conventional Pinot Blanc for a wine with smooth pear and citrus jazzed up by exuberant herb and savory spice flavors.

Hermann J. Wiemer Select Late Harvest Johannisberg Riesling | 2003 | FINGER LAKES, NEW YORK

★★★ $ $ (500 ml) Minerals and acidity keep the sappy citrus and pear flavors here in perfect balance.

Inniskillin Oak Age Vidal Ice Wine | 2004 | NIAGARA PENINSULA, CANADA

★★★ $ $ $ (187 ml) The world's most famous maker of ice wine again establishes its reign with a spicy, succulent wine with roast-corn custard and orange flavors.

Jackson-Triggs Proprietors' Reserve Vidal Icewine | 2004 | NIAGARA PENINSULA, CANADA

★★ $ $ (187 ml) Fascinating, intensely smoky ice wine filled out by baked apple and thyme flavors.

Kracher Cuvée Beerenauslese | 2004 | BURGENLAND, AUSTRIA

★★★ $ $ $ (375 ml) Luxury for a relatively low price; Kracher brings flavors of baked apricot, zingy lemon curd and mixed spice flavors to this complex Beerenauslese.

Louis Guntrum Penguin Silvaner Eiswein | 2004 |
RHEINHESSEN, GERMANY
★★★ $ $ $ $ (375 ml) Pure, fresh-squeezed flavors of grapefruit dominate this rare, very fine German ice wine.

Nederburg Special Late Harvest | 2005 |
WESTERN CAPE, SOUTH AFRICA
★ $ Hints of honey, flowers and bitter herb flavors accent this bright, lemony South African bargain.

Paul Jaboulet Aîné Le Chant des Griolles | 2003 |
MUSCAT DE BEAUMES-DE-VENISE, FRANCE
★★ $ $ $ A soft and smooth expression of citrus, flower and spice. Pour this with fresh fruit tarts.

Peller Estates Riesling Icewine | 2004 |
NIAGARA PENINSULA, CANADA
★★★ $ $ $ $ (375 ml) This tastes more tropical than Canadian, with flavors of juicy pineapple infused by smoke.

Pierre Soulez Château de Chambourceau Chevalier Buhard Doux | 2002 | **SAVENNIÈRES ROCHE AUX MOINES, FRANCE**
★★★ $ $ $ Fresh and succulent grapefruit flavors take on an aristocratic air with precious notes of truffles and smoke.

Prinz von Hessen Johannisberger Klaus Riesling Beerenauslese | 2004 | **RHEINGAU, GERMANY**
★★★★ $ $ $ $ (375 ml) Attention-grabbing wine for its rare flavor balance of marzipan, pineapple, mushroom, smoke and peach.

Royal Tokaji Essencia | 1999 | **TOKAJI, HUNGARY**
★★★★ $ $ $ $ (500 ml) Spectacular, one-of-a-kind wine. Laden with sublime flavors of honey, apricot and smoke, this is so intensely thick, it required six and a half years to ferment.

---

star producers
white dessert wines

best value
1 Elderton (Australia)
2 Errazuriz (Chile)
3 Long Vineyards (California)
4 Samos Winery (Greece)
5 Weiss (Austria)

best of the best
1 Brown Brothers (Australia)
2 Château d'Yquem (France)
3 Kracher (Austria)
4 Royal Tokaji (Hungary)
5 Weingut Robert Weil
   (Germany)

Rutherglen Estates Muscat | NV | **RUTHERGLEN, AUSTRALIA**
★ ★ ★ $ $ (375 ml) Rutherglen Muscats are gems. This chestnut-colored wine is no exception, with raisin, maple and oregano.

Standing Stone Vineyards Vidal Ice | 2004 |
FINGER LAKES, NEW YORK
★ ★ $ $ (375 ml) The Finger Lakes region offers something different here, with earthy, mushroom and spicy baked-quince flavors.

Velich Welschriesling Trockenbeerenauslese | 2001 |
NEUSIEDLERSEE, AUSTRIA
★ ★ ★ ★ $ $ $ $ (375 ml) Sultry, exotic wine that seduces with smooth apricot and marzipan flavors sprinkled with toasted coconut and a flourish of dry, savory herb and spice.

Villa La Selva Vigna del Papa | 2001 |
VIN SANTO DEL CHIANTI, ITALY
★ ★ ★ ★ $$$ (500 ml) Vin Santo at a high level, with notes of toasted pecan and praline.

red dessert wines

Port and Madeira might be the best known, but they are far from the only red dessert wines. From France to Italy, California to Australia, you'll find noteworthy sweet reds in styles ranging from light and bubbly to chocolaty rich.

Red Dessert Wines Grapes & Styles

Grenache is the base of two fortified wines from Roussillon in southern France, Banyuls and Maury. From northeastern Italy comes the relatively lighter Recioto della Valpolicella, the sweet sibling of bittersweet Amarone (see p. 105). Italy also produces sweet wines from red Muscat Blanc à Petits Grains (Moscato Rosa) and Brachetto, which is a charming red equivalent to sparkling Moscato d'Asti. California and Australia make sweet late-harvest and Port-style wines from a range of grape varieties.

BEST PAIRINGS Banyuls and Maury are some of the only wines that pair with chocolate. Recioto della Valpolicella is delicious with ripe peaches marinated in Amaretto. Serve Brachetto with berries. Port-style wines from California and Australia can be paired with blue cheese and walnuts.

red dessert wine recommendations

Domaine de la Casa Blanca | 2004 | **BANYULS, FRANCE**
★★★ $ $ Suave Banyuls with chewy tannin beautifully smoothed out by ripe berry, orange and spice flavors. This is ideal for chocolate.

Domaine de La Rectorie Le Muté sur Grains de La Rectoire | 2004 | **BANYULS, FRANCE**
★★★ $ $ (500 ml) Red berry, black earth and bitter chocolate flavors saturate this earthy, tannic, medium-sweet wine.

Domaine des Schistes | 2004 | **MAURY, FRANCE**
★★★ $ Marvelously sappy, yet nicely structured, sweet wine from Maury, this balances thick berry and spice flavors with velvety but firm tannin.

Domaine du Mas Blanc Rimage La Coume | 2004 | **BANYULS, FRANCE**
★★★★ $ $ $ $ (375 ml) Charming Banyuls with assertive flavors of wild berry matched by musk, herb and earth notes.

Hardys Whiskers Blake Classic Tawny | NV | **SOUTH EASTERN AUSTRALIA**
★★ $ Tawny-styled Aussie similar to Port for a very good price.

M. Chapoutier | 2003 | **BANYULS, FRANCE**
★★★ $ $ $ (500 ml) Berry flavors are infused with an entrancing medley of honeysuckle, fresh ground pepper and ginger.

Quady's Starboard | 1996 | **AMADOR COUNTY, CALIFORNIA**
★★ $ $ $ Ten years old and doing fine, this California Port is made from Portuguese grapes and offers both complexity and brute power.

Stone Hill Winery Port | 2003 | **HERMANN, MISSOURI**
★ $ $ (500 ml) It seems unlikely, but Missouri can make delicious Port-style wines. This is full of pleasing berry and savory spice.

Tsantali Cellar Reserve 5 Year Oak Aged | NV | **MAVRODAPHNE OF PATRAS, GREECE**
★★ $ (500ml) Sweet, balanced wine with lots of savory notes in the form of musky earth.

grape varieties

There are thousands of different grape varieties, but only about twenty dominate American wine racks. Many are grown worldwide, while others are specific to a certain place. Here's a short guide to the most common varieties along with wines that provide excellent examples of each grape's typical characteristics.

cabernet franc

Cabernet Franc adds spicy pepper and bright red cherry flavors to Bordeaux red wines, but it stars in France's Loire Valley, where it makes light, spicy reds. California and Long Island also make some good examples.

Château Figeac Premier Grand Cru | 2003 |
★★★ $ $ $ $ | P. 38
Jean-Maurice Raffault Les Galuches | 2004 | ★★ $ $ | P. 62
Schneider Roanoke Point | 2003 | ★★★ $ $ $ | P. 221

cabernet sauvignon

Cabernet Sauvignon is revered for its cedary black currant flavors bolstered by tannin. It finds its best expression in the reds of Bordeaux and California's Napa Valley, although stellar examples are made worldwide.

Château Brane-Cantenac Grand Cru | 2003 |
★★★ $ $ $ | P. 37
Duckhorn Vineyards Monitor Ledge Vineyard | 2002 |
★★★★ $ $ $ $ | P. 180
Estancia Keyes Canyon Ranches | 2003 | ★ $ | P. 180
Peñalolen | 2003 | ★★ $ $ | P. 251
Sequoia Grove | 2002 | ★★★ $ $ $ | P. 184

chardonnay

Chardonnay grows almost everywhere. It reaches its apex in France's Burgundy, where it makes elegant, mineral-laden whites. Elsewhere it is responsible for full-bodied, fruit-driven wines, toasty Champagnes and dessert wines.

Domaine François et Antoine Jobard Poruzots | 2004 |
★★★★ $ $ $ | P. 46

Domaine Serene Dijon Clones Etoile Vineyard
| 2003 | ★★★★ $ $ | P. 205

Jean-Marc Brocard Montmains | 2004 | ★★★ $ $ $ | P. 44

Ramey Ritchie Vineyard | 2003 | ★★★★ $ $ $ $ | P. 170

Yering Station | 2004 | ★★★ $ $ | P. 225

chenin blanc

Chenin Blanc's lush fruit and high acidity make for some of
France's greatest wines, like the Loire Valley's full-bodied,
long-aging dry whites, dessert elixirs and sparklers. South
Africa and California also make lighter but eminently enjoyable examples.

Cederberg | 2005 | ★★ $ | P. 254

Domaine des Baumard Clos du Papillon | 2003 |
★★★ $ $ $ | P. 58

Dry Creek Vineyard | 2005 | ★★ $ | P. 175

Huet Clos du Bourg Sec | 2004 | ★★★ $ $ $ | P. 58

Thierry Germain Domaine des Roches Neuves L'Insolite
| 2004 | ★★★ $ $ | P. 58

gewürztraminer

Pink-skinned Gewürztraminer offers flamboyant flavors
ranging from honeysuckle to lychee, apricot, mineral and
spice. It's especially important in the white wines of Germany and Alsace. New York and California are also responsible for some excellent versions.

Darting Dürkheimer Nonnengarten Kabinett | 2004 |
★★★ $ $ | P. 145

Handley | 2005 | ★★ $ $ | P. 175

Standing Stone Vineyards | 2005 | ★★★ $ $ | P. 218

Trimbach Cuvée des Seigneurs de Ribeaupierre
| 2000 | ★★★★ $ $ $ | P. 31

Wolfberger | 2004 | ★★ $ $ | P. 31

grenache/garnacha

The fresh, spicy cherry flavors of Grenache are essential to many southern French red wines, such as Châteauneuf-du-Pape and Côtes-du-Rhône. Spanish winemakers rely heavily on Grenache (Garnacha, in Spanish), particularly in Priorat. It is also important in Sardinia (where it's called Cannonau) and shows up in California and Australia.

Beckmen Vineyards Estate | 2004 | ★★ $ $ | P. 200
Domaine Rabasse Charavin | 2003 | ★★ $ $ | P. 70
E. Guigal | 2003 | ★★ $ $ | P. 71
Francesc S. Bas Cellars de la Cartoixa Montgarnatx | 2002 | ★★★ $ $ $ | P. 125
Shingleback | 2004 | ★★ $ $ | P. 234

malbec

Malbec is the signature red wine grape of Argentina, where it is full of lush dark berry fruits and chocolate flavors. It's no longer important in Bordeaux, its place of origin, but dominates in the French region of Cahors, where it's called Auxerrois, and shows up in the Loire Valley, California, Australia and Chile.

Clos La Coutale | 2003 | ★★ $ | P. 81
Don Miguel Gascón | 2004 | ★ $ | P. 245
Georges Vigouroux Pigmentum | 2004 | ★★ $ | P. 81
La Posta del Viñatero Pizzella Family Vineyard | 2004 | ★★★ $ $ | P. 246
Punto Final Reserva | 2004 | ★★★ $ | P. 247

marsanne

Most at home in France's Rhône Valley, the white wine grape Marsanne is prized for its honey flavors and full body. Good versions are found in California and Australia. It often appears as part of a blend with Roussanne.

Domaine Courbis | 2004 | ★★ $ $ | P. 65
Domaine des Martinelles | 2004 | ★★ $ $ | P. 65
M. Chapoutier De l'Orée | 2003 | ★★★★ $ $ $ $ | P. 65
Yering Station M.V.R. | 2004 | ★★★ $ $ | P. 227

merlot

With its plum and chocolate flavors, Merlot is one of the world's most popular grapes, and is responsible for some of the world's greatest red wines, such as those from Bordeaux's Pomerol and Washington State. Terrific examples are also made in California and northeastern Italy.

Château Corbin Grand Cru | 2003 | ★★★ $ $ | P. 37
Château La Conseillante | 2003 | ★★★★ $ $ $ $ | P. 39
Clos du Bois Reserve | 2003 | ★★ $ $ | P. 188
Duckhorn Vineyards Estate Grown | 2003 |
★★★★ $ $ $ $ | P. 188
Leonetti Cellar | 2004 | ★★★★ $ $ $ $ | P. 214

muscat

All Muscat, both red and white, bursts with fragrant flavors such as honeysuckle, orange blossom and musk. It's found throughout the world, most famously in Italy as Moscato and in Spain as Moscatel, as well as in Alsace, southern France, Greece, California and Australia.

Bodegas Gutiérrez de la Vega Casta Diva Cosecha Miel
| 2004 | ★★★ $ $ $ | P. 281
Domaine Ostertag Fronholz | 2004 | ★★★ $ $ $ | P. 32
Paul Jaboulet Aîné Le Chant des Griolles | 2003 |
★★ $ $ $ | P. 283

nebbiolo

Nebbiolo achieves glory in Italy's Piedmont region, where its cherry, tar and tobacco flavors define the long-lived reds of Barolo and Barbaresco. Vintners outside Italy work with Nebbiolo, too, particularly in California and Australia.

Borgogno Riserva | 1999 | ★★★★ $ $ $ $ | P. 86
Clendenen Family Vineyards Bricco Buon Natale | 2001 |
★★★★ $ $ $ | P. 200
L.A. Cetto Private Reserve | 2000 | ★★★ $ $ | P. 260
Parusso | 2003 | ★★ $ $ $ | P. 90
Poderi Luigi Einaudi | 2002 | ★★★ $ $ $ $ | P. 87

pinot blanc

Alsace, California and Italy make wines from Pinot Blanc (also called Pinot Bianco), but this white wine grape is most important in Austria, where, under the name Weiss-burgunder, it takes on richer flavors with more character than the typical medium-bodied, mild-flavored versions.

Alois Lageder | 2004 | ★★★ $ | P. 102

Elk Cove Vineyards | 2005 | ★★ $$ | P. 205

Marc Kreydenweiss Les Charmes Kritt | 2004 |
★★★ $$ | P. 28

Trimbach | 2004 | ★★ $ | P. 28

pinot gris/pinot grigio

In Alsace and Oregon, Pinot Gris produces full-bodied, nutty white wines. All over Italy, where it is called Pinot Grigio, the grape makes light, brisk whites. The grape also performs well in California.

Benton-Lane | 2005 | ★★★ $$ | P. 204

Domaine Ostertag Barriques | 2004 | ★★★ $$$ | P. 29

**Domaine Weinbach Clos des Capucins Cuvée
Ste. Catherine** | 2004 | ★★★★ $$$$ | P. 29

Giovanni Puiatti Le Zuccole Isonzo del Friuli | 2004 |
★★ $ | P. 103

Ponzi Vineyards | 2005 | ★★★ $$ | P. 205

pinot noir

Called the heartbreak grape, Pinot Noir is difficult to grow and make. Done well, Pinot Noir is incredibly seductive, with aromas of roses, smoke, red fruits and earth. The red wines of Burgundy are regarded as its ultimate expression, but excellent Pinot Noir comes from Australia, California, the Loire Valley, New York, New Zealand and Oregon.

Felton Road Block 5 | 2004 | ★★★ $$$$ | P. 240

Nicolas Potel Vieilles Vignes | 2004 | ★★★ $$$ | P. 50

Saintsbury Brown Ranch | 2003 | ★★★ $$$$ | P. 192

Sokol Blosser | 2003 | ★★★ $$$ | P. 208

riesling

Riesling can make white wines of incredible complexity with high acidity and lots of mineral flavors, in styles that range from bone-dry to sumptuously sweet. Riesling is made all around the world, but the best are from Alsace, Germany, Austria, Australia and New York. Many can age for decades.

Domaine Marcel Deiss Beblenheim | 2004 | ★★★ $ $ | P. 30
Dr. Thanish Berncasteler Doctor Spätlese | 2004 |
★★★★ $ $ $ | P. 140
Georg Breuer Berg Schlossberg | 2004 |
★★★★ $ $ $ $ | P. 140
Grosset Polish Hill | 2005 | ★★★★ $ $ $ | P. 226
Hermann J. Wiemer | 2004 | ★★★★ $ $ | P. 218

roussanne

Roussanne is at home in the northern Rhône, where its nutty, unctuous flavors are often combined with Marsanne for the white wines of Crozes-Hermitage, Hermitage and St-Joseph. It's grown in California, with some good results.

Domaine Courbis | 2004 | ★★ $ $ | P. 65
Domaine des Martinelles | 2004 | ★★ $ $ | P. 65
Doyenne | 2004 | ★★★★ $ $ $ | P. 211
M. Chapoutier De l'Orée | 2003 | ★★★★ $ $ $ $ | P. 65

sangiovese

Sangiovese is an important grape in Italy, where it is prized for its red cherry and leather flavors and high acidity. It is most common in Tuscany, where it makes most of the red wines of Chianti and many of the exalted Super-Tuscans. California also grows the grape.

Badia a Coltibuono Riserva | 2000 | ★★★★ $ $ $ | P. 93
Castello Banfi | 2003 | ★★ $ $ $ | P. 96
Kuleto Estate Family Vineyards | 2002 | ★★★ $ $ | P. 201
La Doga | 2004 | ★★ $ $ | P. 98
Terrabianca Croce Riserva | 2001 | ★★★ $ $ $ | P. 95

sauvignon blanc

Sauvignon Blanc is at its best in the lemony, herbaceous white wines of France's Sancerre and Pouilly-Fumé, but New Zealand examples, with flavors of grapefruit and grass, have become wildly popular, too. California, Austria and South Africa make excellent Sauvignon Blancs as well.

Concha y Toro Terrunyo | 2005 | ★ ★ ★ $ $ | P. 249

Craggy Range Winery Te Muna Road Vineyard | 2005 | ★ ★ ★ ★ $ $ | P. 238

Daniel Chotard | 2004 | ★ ★ ★ $ $ | P. 60

Jean Tatin Domaine du Tremblay | 2004 | ★ ★ $ $ | P. 61

Mason | 2004 | ★ ★ ★ $ $ | P. 173

semillon

The second of Bordeaux's great whites after Sauvignon Blanc, Semillon serves as the primary component of the region's luxurious, sweet Sauternes. It also appears on its own or blended with Sauvignon Blanc to make some great, full-bodied dry wines in Bordeaux and Australia.

Elderton Botrytis | 2005 | ★ ★ ★ $ $ | P. 282

Kaesler Old Vine | 2004 | ★ ★ ★ $ | P. 227

Keith Tulloch | 2005 | ★ ★ ★ $ $ | P. 227

L'Ecole No. 41 Fries Vineyard | 2004 | ★ ★ ★ $ $ | P. 211

syrah/shiraz

Typically full-bodied and tannic with berry, pepper and smoky flavors, Syrah makes reds of power and finesse. Its most renowned domain is the Rhône Valley, but California's Central Coast, Washington State and Australia, where it's called Shiraz, also make impressive versions.

Chateau Reynella Basket Pressed | 2003 | ★ ★ ★ $ $ $ | P. 230

Clarendon Hills Liandra | 2003 | ★ ★ ★ ★ $ $ $ $ | P. 230

J.M. Gerin Champin Le Seigneur | 2004 | ★ ★ ★ ★ $ $ $ $ | P. 66

Qupé Bien Nacido Hillside Estate | 2002 | ★ ★ ★ ★ $ $ $ | P. 194

Yann Chave Le Rouvre | 2004 | ★ ★ ★ $ $ $ | P. 66

tempranillo

Grown throughout Spain, Tempranillo is best known as the grape responsible for Rioja's reds. Tempranillo tends to give spicy aromas, full, red fruit flavors and medium body.

Allende | 2003 | ★ ★ ★ $ $ | P. 121
Dare | 2003 | ★ ★ ★ ★ $ $ $ | P. 200
Pesquera Crianza | 2003 | ★ ★ ★ $ $ $ | P. 123
R. López de Heredia Viña Tondonia Reserva | 1998 |
★ ★ ★ $ $ $ | P. 122

viognier

The basis of many of the famed white wines of France's northern Rhône Valley, Viognier has become a favorite in California for its lush peach, citrus and floral flavors.

Cougar Crest Winery | 2005 | ★ ★ ★ $ $ | P. 211
E. Guigal | 2004 | ★ ★ ★ $ $ $ | P. 65
JM | 2005 | ★ ★ ★ $ $ | P. 211
Viognier de Campuget Cuvaumas Cuvée Prestige | 2005 |
★ ★ $ $ | P. 74

zinfandel

California's own red grape (by way of Croatia), Zinfandel assumes many forms, from off-dry pale rosés and quaffable spaghetti reds to full-bodied, tannic wines with blackberry and spice flavors. Zinfandel also makes thick Port-style dessert wines.

Cline Big Break | 2004 | ★ ★ ★ $ $ $ | P. 196
Foppiano | 2002 | ★ ★ $ | P. 197
Joseph Swan Vineyards Stellwagen Vineyard | 2002 |
★ ★ ★ ★ $ $ | P. 197
Limerick Lane Collins Vineyard | 2004 | ★ ★ ★ ★ $ $ $ | P. 197
Robert Biale Vineyards Black Chicken | 2004 |
★ ★ ★ ★ $ $ $ | P. 198

bargain wine finder

Great wine does not have to be expensive. Often, it is more rewarding to drink an outstanding bottle for which you would gladly have paid more. When making recommendations for this Guide, good value was a key consideration. Following is an index of many different wines whose quality (★) to price ($) ratio makes them exceptional values and worth stocking up on.

Whites

★★★★ $ $

Chateau Ste. Michelle & Dr. Loosen Eroica Riesling, Columbia Valley, Washington State, p. 210

Craggy Range Winery Te Muna Road Vineyard Sauvignon Blanc, Martinborough, New Zealand, p. 238

Hermann J. Wiemer Dry Riesling, Finger Lakes, New York, p. 218

Inama Vigneto du Lot Soave Classico, Veneto, Italy, p. 103

Jean Reverdy et Fils La Reine Blanche, Sancerre, France, p. 60

Kalin Cellars Semillon, Livermore Valley, California, p. 176

Luis Pato Vinha Formal, Beiras, Portugal, p. 133

★★★★ $

Domaine Tselepos Moscofilero, Mantinia, Greece, p. 154

★★★ $

Alois Lageder Pinot Bianco, Alto Adige, Italy, p. 102

Anselmi San Vincenzo, Veneto, Italy, p. 102

Bodegas Bretón Loriñon, Rioja, Spain, p. 121

Chamard Estate Reserve Chardonnay, Connecticut, p. 218

Champalou Sec, Vouvray, France, p. 57

Château de la Fessardière Climat, Muscadet, France, p. 59

Crios de Susana Balbo Torrontés, Cafayate Valley, Argentina, p. 244

Davis Bynum Fumé Blanc, Russian River Valley, California, p. 172

DiStefano Sauvignon Blanc, Columbia Valley, Washington State, p. 211

Domaine de la Pépière Muscadet sur Lie, Sèvre-et-Maine, France, p. 59

Domaine de Pellehaut Harmonie de Gascogne, Vin de Pays des Côtes de Gascogne, France, p. 80

Domaine La Croix Belle Le Champ des Lys, Vin de Pays des Côtes de Thongue, France, p. 74

Domaine La Haute Févrie Muscadet sur Lie, Sèvre-et-Maine, France, p. 59

Domaine Pichot Domaine Le Peu de la Moriette, Vouvray, France, p. 58

Dry Creek Vineyard Fumé Blanc, Sonoma County, California, p. 172

The Eyrie Vineyards Pinot Blanc, Oregon, p. 205

Garcés Silva Amayna Sauvignon Blanc, San Antonio/Leyda Valley, Chile, p. 249

Grans-Fassian Trittenheimer Riesling Kabinett, Mosel-Saar-Ruwer, Germany, p. 140

Gritsch Mauritiushof Axpoint Federspiel, Wachau, Austria, p. 147

Houghton Semillon/Sauvignon Blanc, Western Australia, p. 226

Kaesler Old Vine Semillon, Barossa Valley, Australia, p. 227

Kuentz-Bas Tradition Riesling, Alsace, France, p. 30

La Lot Vigneti delle Dolomiti Pinot Grigio, Alto Adige, Italy, p. 103

Leth Steinagrund Lagenreserve, Donauland, Austria, p. 148

Martin Schaetzel Vieilles Vignes Pinot Blanc, Alsace, France, p. 28

Monarchia Cellars Zen, Eger, Hungary, p. 159

Pierre Luneau-Papin Clos des Allées Muscadet sur Lie, Sèvre-et-Maine, France, p. 59

Royal Tokaji Furmint, Tokaji, Hungary, p. 160

Vinum Cellars White Elephant, California, p. 177

von Buhl Maria Schneider Medium-Dry Riesling, Pfalz, Germany, p. 143

Rosés

★★★ $

Bonny Doon Vineyard Vin Gris de Cigare Rosé, California, p. 178

Verdad Rosé, Arroyo Grande Valley, California, p. 178

Wölffer Rosé, The Hamptons, New York, p. 219

Reds

★★★★ $ $

Joseph Swan Vineyards Stellwagen Vineyard Zinfandel, Sonoma Valley, California, p. 197

Louis Jadot Château des Lumières, Morgon, France, p. 55

Marcel Lapierre, Morgon, France, p. 55

Orphéus Etna, Sicily, Italy, p. 117

Tenuta Cocci Grifoni Vigna Messieri Rosso Piceno Superiore, Marche, Italy, p. 112

★★★★ $

Frédéric Mabileau Les Rouillères, St-Nicolas de Bourgueil, France, p. 62

★★★ $

Château Bouscassé, Madiran, France, p. 80

Château des Erles Cuvée des Ardoises, Fitou, France, p. 75

Fontanafredda Eremo Barbera e Nebbiolo, Langhe, Italy, p. 90

Jean-Paul Brun Terres Dorées L'Ancien Vieilles Vignes, Beaujolais, France, p. 55

Pikes Luccio, Clare Valley, Australia, p. 234

Producteurs Plaimont Les Vignes Retrouvées, Côtes de St-Mont, France, p. 81

Punto Final Reserva Malbec, Perdriel, Argentina, p. 247

Sella & Mosca Riserva Cannonau di Sardegna, Sardinia, Italy, p. 117

top wine websites

Nearly everything has a website—and increasingly these days, blogs—devoted to it, and wine is no exception. Listed here are a dozen informative wine websites that might raise your sipping to a whole new level.

www.allamericanwineries.com
A comprehensive winery and vineyard guide for locating producers in every U.S. state.

www.burgundy-report.com & www.burghound.com
Two fountains of wisdom and opinion for Burgundy lovers.

www.wineloverspage.com
Robin Garr's collection of wine reviews, commentary and an outstanding range of wine-related links.

www.wine-searcher.com & www.winezap.com
Find obscure bottles and compare prices worldwide.

www.jancisrobinson.com
One of the world's most admired critics offers her insights, and the complete text of her Oxford Companion to Wine.

www.erobertparker.com
Massive database of articles and wine reviews from the world's most influential—and controversial—wine critic.

www.winealert.com
Track down hard-to-find bottles and learn to pronounce their names with a sound-clip pronunciation guide.

www.localwineevents.com & www.wineevents-calendar.com
Find a local wine tasting or plan a wine-oriented vacation.

www.practicalwinery.com
Learn how wine is made from the science of grape-growing to the techniques winemakers use in the cellar.

reliable importers

Not sure which bottle to choose? Look for the importer's name on the front or back label. The following importers, grouped by specialty, consistently offer excellent wines, available nationally, that are among the best of their type.

Australia
The Australian Premium Wine Collection, Domaine Select Wine Estates, Epic Wines, Epicurean Wines, The Grateful Palate, Old Bridge Cellars, Paterno Wines International

Austria
Domaine Select Wine Estates, Terry Theise Estate Selections, Vin Divino, Wine Monger

France
European Cellars, Kermit Lynch Wine Merchant, Kysela Père et Fils, Louis/Dressner Selections, North Berkeley Imports, Robert Chadderdon, Robert Kacher Selections, Rosenthal Wine Merchant, VOS Selections, Wilson Daniels

Germany
Classical Wines, Rudi Wiest Selections, Terry Theise Estate Selections, Valckenberg

Italy
Domaine Select Wine Estates, Empson USA, Marc de Grazia Selections, Montecastelli Selections, Paterno Wines International, Vias Imports, Vin Divino, Winebow

Portugal
Aidil Wines & Liquors, Broadbent Selections, Signature Imports, Tri-Vin Imports

South Africa
Broadbent Selections, Cape Classics, Vineyard Brands

Spain
Classical Wines, De Maison Selections, Eric Solomon Selections/European Cellars, Europvin, Jorge Ordoñez

index

a

Abacela Albariño, Southern Oregon, 204

Abbazia Santa Anastasia Montenero, Sicily, 116

Abbazia Santa Anastasia Sinestesìa, Sicily, 114

Abeja Cabernet Sauvignon, Columbia Valley, 212

Abeja Chardonnay, Washington State, 210

Acacia Chardonnay, Carneros, 167

A. Clape Le Vin des Amis, Vin de Table de France, 65

Adega de Monção Muralhas de Monção, Vinho Verde, 132

Adelsheim Caitlin's Reserve Chardonnay, Willamette Valley, 204

Adelsheim Elizabeth's Reserve Pinot Noir, Willamette Valley, 206

Adobe Guadalupe Kerubiel, Guadalupe Valley, 260

A. & F. Boudin La Chantemerle, Chablis, 44

Alain Jaume Grande Garrigue, Vacqueyras, 69

Alba de Bretón, Rioja, 121

Alban Vineyards Reva Syrah, Edna Valley, 193

Albarossa Salice Salentino, Apulia, 116

Albemarle Rosé, Virginia, 219

Alderbrook Old Vine Zinfandel, Dry Creek Valley, 196

Alderbrook Pinot Noir, Russian River Valley, 190

Alenza Gran Reserva, Ribera del Duero, 123

Alitus Reserva, Ribera del Duero, 123

Allegrini Palazzo della Torre, Veneto, 106

Allegrini Soave, Veneto, 102

Allende, Rioja, 121

Alois Lageder Lagrein, Alto Adige, 106

Alois Lageder Pinot Bianco, Alto Adige, 102

Alpha Estate Xinomavro, Amyndeon, 155

Alquézar Moristel, Somontano, 125

Altaïr, Cachapoal Valley, 250

Altamura Cabernet Sauvignon, Napa Valley, 179

Altesino Rosso di Altesino, Tuscany, 99

A Mano Primitivo, Apulia, 116

Amity Vineyards Late Harvest Riesling, Willamette Valley, 281

Amity Vineyards Riesling, Willamette Valley, 204

Amity Vineyards Schouten Single Vineyard Pinot Noir, Willamette Valley, 206

Anne Amie Hawks View Vineyard Pinot Noir, Willamette Valley, 206

Annie's Lane Copper Trail Shiraz/ Grenache/Mourvèdre, Clare Valley, 233

Anselmi San Vincenzo, Veneto, 102

Antech Cuvée Elégance Brut, Blanquette de Limoux, 267

Anton Bauer Best of 04 Chardonnay & Welschriesling, Donauland, 149

Anton Bauer Ried Wagram Cuvée No. 9, Donauland, 150

Antonopoulos Vineyards Adoli Ghis, Pátras, 154

Araldica La Luciana, Gavi, 84

Aramis The Governor Syrah, McLaren Vale, 230

Aranleón Solo, Utiel-Requena, 128

Arboleda Merlot, Colchagua Valley, 250

Archery Summit Arcus Estate Pinot Noir, Willamette Valley, 206

Aresti A Gewürztraminer, Curicó Valley, 249

Argiano, Brunello di Montalcino, 95

Argiolas Is Argiolas Vermentino di Sardegna, Sardinia, 114

Argiolas Turriga Isola dei Nuraghi, Sardinia, 116

Arnaldo-Caprai Grecante Grechetto dei Martani, Umbria, 110

Arnaldo-Caprai Rosso Montefalco, Umbria, 111

Arrogant Frog Ribet Red, Vin de Pays d'Oc, 75

Artur Steinmann Pastorius Sommerhäuser Ölspiel Silvaner, Franken, 145

Artur Steinmann Pastorius Sommerhäuser Steinbach Riesling, Franken, 139

Atalon Merlot, Napa Valley, 188

Au Bon Climat Hildegard, Santa Maria Valley, 175

Au Bon Climat Knox Alexander Pinot Noir, Santa Maria Valley, 190

Au Bon Climat Unity Nuits-Blanches au Bouge Chardonnay, Santa Maria Valley, 167

Augusta Winery Chambourcin, Missouri, 220

Avinyó Reserva Brut, Cava, 269

A to Z Pinot Gris, Oregon, 204

A to Z Pinot Noir, Oregon, 206

b

Babcock Black Label Cuvee Syrah, Central Coast, 193

Babcock Grand Cuvee Pinot Noir, Santa Rita Hills, 190

Babcock Pinot Grigio, Santa Rita Hills, 175

Babcock's Big Fat Pink Shiraz, Santa Barbara County, 178

Badia a Coltibuono Riserva, Chianti Classico, 93

Baglio di Pianetto Ficiligno, Sicily, 114

Barbadillo Eva Cream Sherry, 274

Bargetto Dry Gewurztraminer, Santa Cruz Mountains, 175

Bargetto La Vita, Santa Cruz Mountains, 200

Bargetto Pinot Noir, Santa Cruz Mountains, 190

Barnett Vineyards Cabernet Sauvignon, Spring Mountain District, 179

Barnett Vineyards Sangiacomo Vineyard Chardonnay, Carneros, 167

Baron de Ley Finca Monasterio, Rioja, 121

Barone Ricasoli Castello di Brolio, Chianti Classico, 93

Baron Knyphausen Estate Riesling, Rheingau, 139

Baron Philippe de Rothschild Mouton Cadet, Bordeaux, 36

Baron von Heyl Estate Riesling, Rheinhessen, 139

Barossa Valley Estate E & E Black Pepper Shiraz, Barossa Valley, 230

Bassermann-Jordan Deidesheimer Paradiesgarten Riesling Kabinett, Pfalz, 139

Beaulieu Vineyard Cabernet Sauvignon, Rutherford, 179

Beauvignac Syrah Rosé, Vin de Pays d'Oc, 74

Beckmen Vineyards Estate Grenache, Santa Maria Valley, 200

Beckmen Vineyards Purisima Mountain Vineyard Sauvignon Blanc, Santa Ynez Valley, 172

Beckman Vineyards Purisima Mountain Vineyard Syrah, Santa Ynez Valley, 193

Bellavista Gran Cuvée Satèn, Franciacorta, 268

Belle Glos Clark & Telephone Vineyard Pinot Noir, Santa Maria Valley, 190

Bellenda Extra Dry, Prosecco di Conegliano Valdobbiadene, 268

Benton-Lane First Class Pinot Noir, Willamette Valley, 206

Benton-Lane Pinot Gris, Willamette Valley, 204

Beringer Alluvium Blanc, Knights Valley, 175

Beringer Private Reserve Cabernet Sauvignon, Napa Valley, 179

Bernard Baudry Franc de Pied, Chinon, 61

Bernard Magrez La Passion d'une Vie, Côtes du Roussillon, 75

Bernardus Marinus, Carmel Valley, 186

Bertani Duè Uvè, Veneto, 102

Bethel Heights Vineyard Estate Grown Pinot Noir, Willamette Valley, 207

Bethel Heights Vineyard Pinot Gris, Oregon, 204

Betts & Scholl Riesling, Eden Valley, 226

Bieler Père et Fils Sabine Rosé, Vin de Pays des Maures, 77

Big House Red, California, 200

Binomio Montepulciano d'Abruzzo, Abruzzi, 111

Bisol Jeio Brut, Prosecco, 268

Black Star Farms A Capella Riesling Ice Wine, Old Mission Peninsula, 281

Black Star Farms Arcturos Pinot Gris, Old Mission Peninsula, 218

Black Star Farms Arcturos Pinot Noir, Leelanau Peninsula, 220

Blandy's 5 Year Rich Alvada Madeira, 278

Blason d'Issan, Margaux, 36

Bocce Zinfandel, California, 196

Bodegas Bretón Loriñon, Rioja, 121

Bodegas Campante Gran Reboreda, Ribeiro, 127

Bodegas Gutiérrez de la Vega Casta Diva Cosecha Miel Muscat, Alicante, 281

Bodegas Gutiérrez de la Vega Viña Ulises Crianza, Alicante, 128

Bodegas Hidalgo La Gitana Manzanilla Sherry, 274

Bodegas Hidalgo La Gitana Pastrana Manzanilla Pasada Sherry, 274

Bodegas Nieto Senetiner Limited Edition Bonarda, Mendoza, 245

Bodegas Toro Albalá Don PX Gran Reserva Sherry, 274

Bonny Doon Vineyard Il Circo La Donna Cannone, Ruché di Castagnole Monferrato, 89

Bonny Doon Vineyard Il Circo La Funambola, Erbaluce di Caluso, 84

Bonny Doon Vineyard Le Cigare Blanc, California, 175

Bonny Doon Vineyard Vin Gris de Cigare, California, 178

Borghese Barrel Fermented Chardonnay, North Fork of Long Island, 218

Borgogno Riserva, Barolo Classico, 86

Boroli Villero, Barolo, 86

Boscarelli, Vino Nobile di Montepulciano, 97

Bottega Vinaia Lagrein, Trentino, 106

Boutari Kallisti, Santorini, 154

Boutari Skalani, Archanes, 155

Bouvet Saphir Brut, Saumur, 267

Bowen Estate Shiraz, Coonawarra, 230

Brassfield Estate Vineyard Pinot Grigio, Clear Lake, 175

Braunstein Mitterjoch Zweigelt, Burgenland, 150

Bricco Mondalino, Barbera del Monferrato Superiore, 88

Broadbent Colheita Madeira, 278

Broadbent Rainwater Madeira, 278

Broglia La Meirana, Gavi, 85

Brunel Frères Château St-Roch, Lirac, 69

Bruno Giacosa, Roero Arneis, 85

Bruno Paillard Première Cuvée Rosé Brut, 266

Bruno Porro Vigna Ribote, Dolcetto di Dogliani, 88

Buil & Giné Extra Brut, Cava, 269

Buil & Giné Giné Rosat, Priorat, 124

Buil & Giné Nosis Verdejo, Rueda, 127

Buil & Giné Pleret, Priorat, 125

Bulletin Place Cabernet Sauvignon, South Eastern Australia, 228

Bunnell Family Cellar Boushey-McPherson Vineyard Syrah, Yakima Valley, 212

Bunnell Family Cellar Roza Bergé Vineyard Gewürztraminer, Yakima Valley, 210

Buty Rediviva of the Stones, Walla Walla Valley, 212

Byington Bates Ranch Vineyard Cabernet Sauvignon, Santa Cruz Mountains, 179

Byron Pinot Noir, Santa Maria Valley, 190

C

Cabreo La Pietra Chardonnay, Tuscany, 91

Cadence Ciel du Cheval Vineyard, Red Mountain, 212

Cadiz Monastrell/Cabernet, Valencia, 128

Cakebread Cellars Chardonnay, Napa Valley, 168

Cakebread Cellars Merlot, Napa Valley, 188

Calera Chardonnay, Mt. Harlan, 168

Calera Reed Vineyard Pinot Noir, Mt. Harlan, 190

Callaghan Vineyards Claire's, Sonoita, 220

Callanans Road Chardonnay, Victoria, 224

Callanans Road Pinot Noir, Mornington Peninsula, 233

Camaraderie Cellars Cabernet Franc, Washington State, 213

Cambria Bench Break Vineyard Pinot Noir, Santa Maria Valley, 190

Cambria Katherine's Vineyard Chardonnay, Santa Maria Valley, 168

Camerano Cannubi San Lorenzo, Barolo, 86

Camigliano, Brunello di Montalcino, 95

Camille Giroud, Santenay, 47

Campo al Mare, Bolgheri, 99

Campo Ardosa, Douro, 133

Campo di Sasso Insoglio del Cinghiale, Tuscany, 99

Can Blau, Montsant, 125

Can Feixes Chardonnay, Penedès, 124

Canonbah Bridge Drought Reserve Shiraz, Western Plains, 230

Ca'ntele Riserva Salice Salentino, Apulia, 116

Cantina dell'Alunno Sagrantino di Montefalco, Umbria, 111

Caparzo La Caduta, Rosso di Montalcino, 95

Caparzo Riserva, Brunello di Montalcino, 96

Cape Mentelle Cabernet Sauvignon, Margaret River, 228

Cape Mentelle Sauvignon Blanc/ Semillon, Margaret River, 226

Carpe Diem Firepeak Vineyard Chardonnay, Edna Valley, 168

Cartuxa, Alentejo, 132

Casa Castillo Monastrell, Jumilla, 128

Casa de Piedra Vino de Piedra, Ensenada, 260

Casa dos Zagalos Reserva, Alentejo, 133

Casa Ermelinda Freitas Dona Ermelinda, Palmela, 134

Casa Ferreirinha Reserva, Douro, 134

Casa Lapostolle Clos Apalta, Colchagua Valley, 250

Casa Marin Lo Abarca Hills Pinot Noir, San Antonio Valley, 250

Casa Nuestra Dry Chenin Blanc, Napa Valley, 175

Casa Santos Lima Palha-Canas, Estremadura, 134

Casa Silva Quinta Generación, Colchagua Valley, 249

Cascina Bongiovanni, Barolo, 86

Castell Frenzy Müller-Thurgau Trocken, Franken, 145

Castello Banfi, Brunello di Montalcino, 96

Castello Banfi, Rosso di Montalcino, 96

Castello Banfi Excelsus Sant'Antimo, Tuscany, 99

Castello Banfi San Angelo Pinot Grigio, Tuscany, 91

Castello dei Rampolla, Chianti Classico, 93

Castello del Terriccio Con Vento, Tuscany, 91

Castello di Bossi Berardo Riserva, Chianti Classico, 93

Castello di Corbara Cabernet Sauvignon Lago di Corbara, Umbria, 111

Castello di Meleto, Chianti Classico, 93

Catena Cabernet Sauvignon, Mendoza, 245

Catena Chardonnay, Mendoza, 244

Catherine & Pierre Breton Trinch!, Bourgueil, 61

Cave de Rasteau Tradition, Côtes-du-Rhône Villages Rasteau, 69

Cave Spring CSV Riesling, Niagara Peninsula, 259

Ca'Viola Vilot, Dolcetto d'Alba, 88

Cavit Collection Vigneti delle Dolomiti Teroldego, Alto Adige, 106

Caymus Vineyards Cabernet Sauvignon, Napa Valley, 180

Ceàgo Vinegarden Del Lago Chardonnay, Mendocino, 168

Cederberg Chenin Blanc, Cederberg, 254

Cellier des Dauphins Prestige, Côtes-du-Rhône, 69

Cellier des Dauphins Prestige Rosé, Côtes-du-Rhône, 68

Cenit Crianza, Tierra del Vino de Zamora, 128

Ceretto Asij, Barbaresco, 86

Ceretto Blange' Arneis, Langhe, 85

Cesani, Vernaccia di San Gimignano, 91

Chalk Hill Sauvignon Blanc, Chalk Hill, 172

Chalone Vineyard Estate Grown Chardonnay, Chalone, 168

Chamard Estate Reserve Chardonnay, Connecticut, 218

Champalou Sec, Vouvray, 57

Charles Heidsieck Brut Champagne, 264

Charles Hours Cuvée Marie, Jurançon Sec, 79

Charles Joguet Cuvée Terroir, Chinon, 62

Charles Viénot Chaînes Carteaux, Nuits St-Georges Premier Cru, 47

Château Angélus Premier Grand Cru, St-Émilion, 36

Château Batailley Grand Cru, Pauillac, 36

Château Bellevue Claribes, Bordeaux, 36

Château Beychevelle, St-Julien, 36

Château Bonnet, Entre-Deux-Mers, 35

Château Bouissel Classic, Fronton, 80

Château Bouscassé, Madiran, 80

Château Brane-Cantenac Grand Cru, Margaux, 37

Château Cadillac Club Merlot, Bordeaux, 37

Château Caronne Ste-Gemme Cru Bourgeois, Haut-Médoc, 37

Château Chasse-Spleen, Moulis-en-Médoc, 37

Château Clarke, Listrac-Médoc, 37

Château Corbin Grand Cru, St-Émilion, 37

Château Coufran Cru Bourgeois, Haut-Médoc, 37

Château Coutet Premier Cru, Sauternes-Barsac, 281

Château d'Aqueria Rosé, Tavel, 68

Château d'Auvernier, Neuchâtel, 158

Château d'Epiré, Savennières, 57

Château de Beauregard Les Cras, Pouilly-Fuissé, 52

Château de Candale, Haut-Médoc, 37

Château de Chantegrive, Graves, 35

Château de Cugat Cuvée Première, Bordeaux Supérieur, 37

Château de Jau, Muscat de Rivesaltes, 281

Château de la Fessardière Climat, Muscadet, 59

Château de la Gardine (red), Châteauneuf-du-Pape, 69

Château de la Gardine (white), Châteauneuf-du-Pape, 68

Château de la Ragotière (Black Label) Muscadet sur Lie, Sèvre-et-Maine, 59

Château de la Saule, Montagny Premier Cru, 51

Château de la Terrière Vieilles Vignes Cuveé Jules de Souzy, Brouilly, 54

Château de Lascaux, Coteaux du Languedoc, 74

Château de la Vieille Tour, Bordeaux Supérieur, 37

Château de Lussac, Lussac-St-Émilion, 38

Château de Peña C Réserve, Côtes du Roussillon Villages, 75

Château de Pennautier, Cabardès, 75

Château de Pibarnon, Bandol, 77

Château de Pibarnon Rosé, Bandol, 77

Château de Pourcieux Rosé, Côtes de Provence, 77

Château de Roquefort Corail Rosé, Côtes de Provence, 77

Château de Roquefort Les Mûres, Côtes de Provence, 77

Château de Sancerre, Sancerre, 60

Château de Ségriès Rosé, Tavel, 68

Château des Erles Cuvée des Ardoises, Fitou, 75

Château des Tours Réserve, Vacqueyras, 69

Château du Cèdre Le Prestige, Cahors, 80

Château du Donjon Grande Tradition, Minervois, 75

Château du Haut Caillou, Canon-Fronsac, 38

Château du Juge, Premières Côtes de Bordeaux, 38

Château Ferry Lacombe Cuvée Lou Cascaï Rosé, Côtes de Provence, 77

Château Figeac Premier Grand Cru, St-Émilion, 38

Château Fuissé Charmes, Morgon, 54

Château Fuissé Le Clos, Pouilly-Fuissé, 52

Château Gravas, Sauternes, 281

Château Haut Selve, Graves, 39

Château Haut-Surget, Lalande de Pomerol, 39

Château Kefraya, Bekaa Valley, 163

Château Kefraya La Dame Blanche, Bekaa Valley, 162

Château Labat, Haut-Médoc, 39

Château La Bourrée, Côtes de Castillon, 39

Château La Conseillante, Pomerol, 39

Château Lafon-Rochet Grand Cru, St-Estèphe, 39

Château La Gaffelière Premier Grand Cru, St-Émilion, 39

Château Lagrange Grand Cru, St-Julien, 39

Château Lagrange Les Arums de Lagrange, Bordeaux, 35

Château La Louvière, Pessac-Léognan, 35

Château Lamothe de Haux, Bordeaux, 35

Château La Nerthe, Châteauneuf-du-Pape, 68

Château La Pierrière, Côtes de Castillon, 39

Château La Roque, Coteaux du Languedoc, 74

Château Lascombes Grand Cru, Margaux, 39

Château Lastours, Gaillac, 81

Château La Tour Carnet Grand Cru, Haut-Médoc, 39

Château Latour-Martillac Grand Cru, Pessac-Léognan, 35

Château Lestrille Capmartin, Bordeaux Supérieur, 40

Château Lynch-Bages Grand Cru, Pauillac, 40

Château Lyonnat, Lussac-St-Émilion, 40

Château Malartic-Lagravière Grand Cru, Pessac-Léognan, 40

Château Montus Sec, Pacherenc du Vic-Bilh, 79

Château Musar Hochar Père et Fils, Bekaa Valley, 163

Château Ollieux Romanis Cuvée Classique, Corbières, 75

Château Pérenne, Premières Côtes de Blaye, 35

Château Peyros Greenwich 43N, Madiran, 81

Château Phélan Ségur, St-Estèphe, 40

Chateau Reynella Basket Pressed Shiraz, McLaren Vale, 230

Château Rousselle Cru Bourgeois, Côtes de Bourg, 40

Château Sainte-Marie, Entre-Deux-Mers, 35

Château Smith Haut Lafitte Grand Cru, Pessac-Léognan, 35

Chateau Ste. Michelle & Dr. Loosen Eroica Riesling, Columbia Valley, 210

Chateau Ste. Michelle Indian Wells Merlot, Columbia Valley, 213

Château Ste. Roséline (red), Côtes de Provence, 78

Château Ste. Roséline (white), Côtes de Provence, 77

Château St-Estève d'Uchaux Jeunes Vignes Viognier, Côtes-du-Rhône, 68

Chateau St. Jean Cinq Cépages Cabernet Sauvignon, Sonoma County, 180

Château St-Jean d'Aumières, Coteaux du Languedoc, 75

Chateau St. Jean Pinot Noir, Sonoma County, 190

Chateau St. Jean Robert Young Vineyard Chardonnay, Alexander Valley, 168

Château Suduiraut Premier Cru, Sauternes, 281

Château Tour de Mirambeau, Bordeaux, 35

C.H. Berres Impulse Riesling, Mosel-Saar-Ruwer, 139

C.H. Berres Ürziger Würzgarten Riesling Kabinett, Mosel-Saar-Ruwer, 139

Chehalem Reserve Dry Riesling, Willamette Valley, 204

Chehalem 3 Vineyard Pinot Noir, Willamette Valley, 207

Chimney Rock Cabernet Sauvignon, Stags Leap District, 180

Chono Cabernet Sauvignon, Central Valley, 250

Christmann Idig Riesling, Pfalz, 139

Churchill's Vintage Port, 276

Cima Vigneto Candia Alto, Candia dei Colli Apuani, 91

Claiborne & Churchill Pinot Gris, Arroyo Grande Valley, 175

Claiborne & Churchill Twin Creeks Pinot Noir, Edna Valley, 190

Clarendon Hills Kangarilla Grenache, Clarendon, 233

Clarendon Hills Liandra Syrah, Clarendon, 230

Clearview Estate Winery Unwooded Chardonnay, Hawkes Bay, 239

Clendenen Family Vineyards Bricco Buon Natale Nebbiolo, Santa Maria Valley, 200

Cline Big Break Zinfandel, Contra Costa County, 196

Clinton Vineyards Seyval Naturel, Hudson River, 270

Clos de la Roilette, Fleurie, 54

Clos de l'Hermitage, Côtes-du-Rhône, 69

Clos du Bois Cabernet Sauvignon, Sonoma County, 180

Clos du Bois Chardonnay, North Coast, 168

Clos du Bois Marlstone, Alexander Valley, 186

Clos du Bois Reserve Merlot, Alexander Valley, 188

Clos Du Val Cabernet Sauvignon, Napa Valley, 180

Clos Du Val Chardonnay, Carneros, 168

Clos La Coutale, Cahors, 81

Clos Lapeyre, Jurançon Sec, 79

Clos Pegase Mitsuko's Vineyard Pinot Noir, Carneros, 191

Clos Roche Blanche Gamay, Touraine, 62

Clos Ste. Magdeleine, Cassis, 77

Cloudy Bay Pinot Noir, Marlborough, 240

Cloudy Bay Te Koko Sauvignon Blanc, Marlborough, 238

Cobos Malbec, Mendoza, 245

Cogno Bricco dei Merli, Barbera d'Alba, 88

Col d'Orcia Banditella, Rosso di Montalcino, 96

Coldstream Hills Reserve Chardonnay, Yarra Valley, 224

Coldstream Hills Sauvignon Blanc, Yarra Valley, 226

Colli Ripani Centauro Ripano Sangiovese, Marche, 112

Colosi (red), Sicily, 116

Colosi (white), Sicily, 114

Columbia Crest Grand Estates Chardonnay, Columbia Valley, 210

Columbia Crest Reserve Syrah, Columbia Valley, 213

Col Vetoraz Brut, Prosecco di Valdobbiadene, 268

Comtesse Thérèse Russian Oak Chardonnay, North Fork of Long Island, 218

Concannon Limited Release Petite Sirah, Central Coast, 200

Concha y Toro Private Reserve Late Harvest Sauvignon Blanc, Maule Valley, 281

Concha y Toro Terrunyo Sauvignon Blanc, Casablanca Valley, 249

Condé Cabernet Sauvignon, Stellenbosch, 256

Conde de Valdemar Gran Reserva, Rioja, 121

Conterno Fantino, Barolo, 87

Conterno Fantino Mon Pra', Langhe, 89

Conti Costanti, Brunello di Montalcino, 96

Conti Formentini Collio Pinot Grigio, Friuli–Venezia Giulia, 102

Contini Nieddera Valle del Tirso, Sardinia, 116

Conundrum, California, 175

Cooperative Cephalonia San Gerassimo Robola, Cephalonia, 154

Cooper Mountain Vineyards Faces Pinot Noir, Willamette Valley, 207

Cooper Mountain Vineyards Old Vines Pinot Gris, Willamette Valley,

Corison Cabernet Sauvignon, Napa Valley, 180

Cortenova Pinot Grigio delle Venezie, Veneto, 102

Corte Sant'Alda Vigne di Mezzane Soave, Veneto, 102

Cortes de Cima, Alentejo, 134

Cossart Gordon 5 Year Bual Madeira, 278

Cougar Crest Winery Viognier, Walla Walla Valley, 211

Cousiño-Macul Finis Terrae, Maipo Valley, 251

Craggy Range Winery Gimblett Gravels Vineyard Merlot, Hawkes Bay, 241

Craggy Range Winery Te Muna Road Vineyard Sauvignon Blanc, Martinborough, 238

Crichton Hall Chardonnay, Napa Valley, 168

Crichton Hall Vineyard Merlot, Napa Valley, 188

Crios de Susana Balbo Syrah/Bonarda, Mendoza, 245

Crios de Susana Balbo Torrontés, Cafayate Valley, 244

Cusumano Benuara Nero d'Avola/ Syrah, Sicily, 116

d

Daheuiller Domaine des Varinelles, Saumur-Champigny, 62

Dalla Valle Vineyards Cabernet Sauvignon, Napa Valley, 180

Damianitza Uniqato Rubin, Trakia, 160

Damijan Prelit, Venezia Giulia, 106

Damijan Ribolla Gialla, Venezia Giulia, 102

Damilano, Dolcetto d'Alba, 88

Dancing Man Rare Meritage, Maribor, 159

Daniel Chotard, Sancerre, 60

Danjean-Berthoux Clos du Cras Long, Givry Premier Cru, 51

d'Arenberg The Coppermine Road Cabernet Sauvignon, McLaren Vale, 228

Dare Tempranillo, Napa Valley, 200

Darting Dürkheimer Nonnengarten Gewürztraminer Kabinett, Pfalz, 145

Dashe Cabernet Sauvignon, Alexander Valley, 180

Dashe Todd Brothers Ranch Old Vines Zinfandel, Alexander Valley, 196

Davis Bynum Fumé Blanc, Russian River Valley, 172

Davis Bynum Limited Edition Chardonnay, Russian River Valley, 168

Davis Bynum Lindleys' Knoll Pinot Noir, Russian River Valley, 191

Deakin Estate Cabernet Sauvignon, Victoria, 229

Dehesa La Granja Selección, Tierra del Vino de Zamora, 128

Delaforce Colheita Port, 276

Delamotte Blanc de Blancs Brut Champagne, 264

Delas Les Bessards, Hermitage, 65

DeLille Cellars Chaleur Estate, Columbia Valley, 211

DeLille Cellars Harrison Hill, Yakima Valley, 213

De Martino Gran Familia Cabernet Sauvignon, Maipo Valley, 251

Deutz Classic Brut Champagne, 264

Devil's Lair, Margaret River, 233

Diamond Creek Gravelly Meadow Cabernet Sauvignon, Napa Valley, 180

Diebolt-Vallois Cuvée Prestige Blanc de Blancs Brut Champagne, 264

DiStefano Sauvignon Blanc, Columbia Valley, 211

DiStefano Syrah R, Columbia Valley, 213

Dolce, Napa Valley, 281

Domaine A. et P. de Villaine, Bouzeron, 51

Domaine Bernard Morey et Fils, Beaune Grèves Premier Cru, 46

Domaine Bernard Morey et Fils Clos St-Jean, Chassagne-Montrachet Premier Cru, 47

Domaine Bouchard Père & Fils Le Corton, Corton Grand Cru, 48

Domaine Bourillon Dorléans La Coulée d'Argent Vieilles Vignes Sec, Vouvray, 57

Domaine Carneros By Taittinger Le Rêve Blanc de Blancs Brut, Carneros, 270

Domaine Chanson Clos des Fèves, Beaune Premier Cru, 48

Domaine Chanson Les Caradeux, Pernand-Vergelesses Premier Cru, 46

Domaine Charles Audoin, Marsannay, 46

Domaine Charles Audoin Les Favières, Marsannay, 48

Domaine Chofflet-Valdenaire Clos de Choué, Givry Premier Cru, 51

Domaine Christian Moreau Père & Fils Vaillon, Chablis Premier Cru, 44

Domaine Courbis (red), St-Joseph, 66

Domaine Courbis (white), St-Joseph, 65

Domaine d'Ardhuy Les Combottes, Côte de Beaune Villages, 49

Domaine de Bellivière Le Rouge-Gorge, Coteaux du Loir, 62

Domaine de Cassan Cuvée St-Christophe, Côtes-du-Rhône Villages Beaumes-de-Venise, 69

Domaine de Chatenoy (red), Menetou-Salon, 62

Domaine de Chatenoy (white), Menetou-Salon, 60

Domaine de Font-Sane, Gigondas, 69

Domaine de Grangeneuve Vieilles Vignes, Coteaux du Tricastin, 70

Domaine de la Casa Blanca, Banyuls, 285

Domaine de la Chanteleuserie Cuvée Alouettes, Bourgueil, 62

Domaine de la Croix Senaillet, St-Véran, 52

Domaine de la Madone Le Perreon, Beaujolais-Villages, 54

Domaine de la Mordorée La Reine des Bois, Châteauneuf-du-Pape, 70

Domaine de la Noblaie Les Chiens-Chiens, Chinon, 58

Domaine de la Pépière Muscadet Sur Lie, Sèvre-et-Maine, 59

Domaine de la Pigeade, Muscat de Beaumes-de-Venise, 281

Domaine de la Rectorie Le Muté sur Grains de la Rectoire, Banyuls, 285

Domaine de la Salette, Vin de Pays des Côtes de Gascogne, 80

Domaine de l'Ecu Expression de Granite Muscadet sur Lie, Sèvre-et-Maine, 59

Domaine de Nizas Rosé, Coteaux du Languedoc, 74

Domaine de Pellehaut Harmonie de Gascogne, Vin de Pays des Côtes de Gascogne, 80

Domaine de Roally, Mâcon-Montbellet, 52

Domaine des Baumard Clos de Ste-Catherine, Coteaux du Layon, 281

Domaine des Baumard Clos du Papillon, Savennières, 58

Domaine des Martinelles, Crozes-Hermitage, 65

Domaine des Schistes, Maury, 285

Domaine Diochon Cuveé Vieilles Vignes, Moulin-à-Vent, 55

Domaine du Banneret, Châteauneuf-du-Pape, 70

Domaine du Granit Cuvée Tradition, Moulin-à-Vent, 55

Domaine du Gros Noré, Bandol, 78

Domaine du Mas Blanc Rimage La Coume, Banyuls, 285

Domaine du Meix-Foulot (red), Mercurey Premier Cru, 51

Domaine du Meix-Foulot (white), Mercurey, 51

Domaine du Tariquet Chenin/Chardonnay, Vin de Pays des Côtes de Gascogne, 80

Domaine du Vieux Pressoir, Saumur, 267

Domaine du Vieux Télégraphe, Châteauneuf-du-Pape, 70

Domaine Etxegaraya, Irouleguy, 81

Domaine François et Antoine Jobard Poruzots, Meursault, 46

Domaine Gachot-Monot, Côte de Nuits Villages, 49

Domaine Gerovassiliou Malagousia, Epanomi, 154

Domaine Grand Veneur, Châteauneuf-du-Pape, 70

Domaine Henri Gouges Les Chênes Carteaux, Nuits-St-Georges Premier Cru, 49

Domaine La Croix Belle Le Champ des Lys, Vin de Pays des Côtes de Thongue, 74

Domaine La Haute Févrie Muscadet sur Lie, Sèvre-et-Maine, 59

Domaine La Millière Cuvée Unique Merlot, Vin de Pays de Vaucluse, 70

Domaine Le Briseau Kharaktêr, Jasnières, 58

Domaine Leflaive Les Folatières, Puligny-Montrachet Premier Cru, 46

Domaine Louise-Fabry Naoudoy, Corbières, 74

Domaine Louis Moreau Les Clos Chablis Grand Cru, 44

Domaine Lucien Boillot & Fils Les Caillerets, Volnay, 49

Domaine Maestracci E Prove (red), Calvi, 81

Domaine Maestracci E Prove (white), Calvi, 80

Domaine Manoir du Carra, Beaujolais-Villages, 55

Domaine Marcel Deiss Beblenheim Riesling, Alsace, 30

Domaine Marcel Deiss Engelgarten, Alsace, 32

Domaine Mercouri Cava, Letrinon, 155

Domaine Michel Brock Cuvée Cécile, Sancerre, 60

Domaine Monte de Luz Syrah, San Jose, 260

Domaine Ostertag Barriques Pinot Gris, Alsace, 29

Domaine Ostertag Fronholz Muscat, Alsace, 32

Domaine Paul Autard, Châteauneuf-du-Pape, 70

Domaine Paul Blanck Rosenbourg Riesling, Alsace, 30

Domaine Paul Blanck Vieilles Vignes Pinot Auxerrois, Alsace, 32

Domaine Pichot Domaine Le Peu de la Moriette, Vouvray, 58

Domaine Piron & Lafont Quartz, Chénas, 55

Domaine Ponsot Cuvée Vieilles Vignes, Clos de la Roche Grand Cru, 49

Domaine Rabasse Charavin, Côtes-du-Rhône Villages Cairanne, 70

Domaines Barons de Rothschild (Lafite) Los Vascos Reserve Cabernet Sauvignon, Colchagua, 251

Domaines Barons de Rothschild (Lafite) and Nicolas Catena Caro, Mendoza, 245

Domaine Serene Dijon Clones Etoile Vineyard Chardonnay, Willamette Valley, 205

Domaine Serene Evenstad Reserve Pinot Noir, Willamette Valley, 207

Domaine Spiropoulos, Mantinia, 154

Domaine Tempier, Bandol, 78

Domaine Tselepos Moscofilero, Mantinia, 154

Domaine Vincent Delaporte Chavignol, Sancerre, 60

Domaine Weinbach Clos des Capucins Cuvée Ste. Catherine Pinot Gris, Alsace, 29

Domaine Weinbach Clos des Capucins Cuvée Théo Riesling, Alsace, 30

Domaine Zind-Humbrecht Clos Windsbuhl Gewurztraminer, Alsace, 31

Domaine Zind-Humbrecht Herrenweg de Turckheim Pinot Gris, Alsace, 29

Domaine Zind-Humbrecht Vendanges Tardives Brand Riesling, Alsace, 282

Domäne Wachau Terrassen Grüner Veltliner Federspiel, Wachau, 147

Dominio de Tares Bembibre, Bierzo, 128

Dominique Cornin Mâcon-Chânes Les Serreudières, Mâcon-Villages, 52

Dominus, Napa Valley, 186

Domus Aurea Cabernet Sauvignon, Upper Maipo Valley, 251

Doña Paula Estate Cabernet Sauvignon, Luján de Cuyo, 245

Doña Paula Los Cardos Sauvignon Blanc, Tupungato, 244

Don Miguel Gascón Malbec, Mendoza, 245

Doro Princic Collio Tocai Friulano, Friuli–Venezia Giulia, 103

Dos Cabezas La Montaña, Arizona, 220

Dow's Fine Ruby Port, 276

Dow Vale Do Bomfim Reserva Douro, 135

Doyenne Roussanne, Columbia Valley, 211

Dr. Bürklin-Wolf Wachenheimer Rechbächel Riesling, Pfalz, 140

Dr. Konstantin Frank Rkatsiteli, Finger Lakes, 218

Dr. Thanisch Berncasteler Doctor Riesling Spätlese, Mosel-Saar-Ruwer, 140

Dry Creek Vineyard Dry Chenin Blanc, Clarksburg, 175

Dry Creek Vineyard Fumé Blanc, Sonoma County, 172

Dry Creek Vineyard Heritage Zinfandel, Sonoma County, 197

Duckhorn Vineyards Estate Grown Merlot, Napa Valley, 188

Duckhorn Vineyards Monitor Ledge Vineyard Cabernet Sauvignon, Napa Valley, 180

Duckhorn Vineyards Sauvignon Blanc, Napa Valley, 172

Dunham Cellars Syrah, Columbia Valley, 213

e

Easton Estate Bottled Zinfandel, Shenandoah Valley, 197

Edizione Pennino Zinfandel, Rutherford, 197

Edmeades Zinfandel, Mendocino County, 197

E. Guigal, Condrieu, 65

E. Guigal, Côtes-du-Rhône, 68

E. Guigal, Gigondas, 70

El Coto Crianza, Rioja, 121

El Coto Rosé, Rioja, 121

El Nido, Jumilla, 128

Elderton Botrytis Semillon, Riverina, 282

Elderton Command Single Vineyard Shiraz, Barossa, 231

Elk Cove Vineyards Pinot Blanc, Willamette Valley, 205

Emery Mountain Slopes Athiri, Rhodes, 154

Emilio Moro, Ribera del Duero, 123

Encostas do Lima Medium Dry, Vinho Verde, 132

Engelbrecht Els Vineyards, Western Cape, 256

Erath La Nuit Magique Pinot Noir, Willamette Valley, 207

Errazuriz Late Harvest Sauvignon Blanc, Casablanca Valley, 282

Errazuriz Viñedo Chadwick, Maipo Valley, 251

Errazuriz Wild Ferment Chardonnay, Casablanca Valley, 249

Erwin Sabathi Klassik Sauvignon Blanc, Southern Styria, 149

Estancia Keyes Canyon Ranches Cabernet Sauvignon, Paso Robles, 180

Estancia Meritage, Paso Robles, 186

Et Fille Palmer Creek Vineyards Pinot Noir, Oregon, 207

Etienne Sauzet Hameau de Blagny, Puligny-Montrachet Premier Cru, 46

Etude Pinot Noir, Carneros, 191

Eugénio de Almeida E.A., Alentejo, 132

Eyrie Vineyards Pinot Blanc, Oregon, 205

Eyrie Vineyards Reserve Pinot Noir, Willamette Valley, 207

f

Failla Phoenix Ranch Syrah, Napa Valley, 193

Fairview Pinotage, Coastal Region, 256

Faiveley, Latricières-Chambertin Grand Cru, 49

Faiveley Domaine de la Croix Jacquelet, Montagny, 51

Faiveley Georges Faiveley Chardonnay, Bourgogne, 46

Faiveley La Framboisiere, Mercurey, 51

Falesco Montiano, Lazio, 112

Fantinel Vigneti Sant'Helena Refosco dal Peduncolo Rosso Grave, Friuli–Venezia Giulia, 106

Far Niente Cabernet Sauvignon, Oakville, 181

Far Niente Chardonnay, Napa Valley, 169

Farnese Farneto Valley Trebbiano d'Abruzzo, Abruzzi, 110

Fassati Salarco Riserva, Vino Nobile di Montepulciano, 97

Fattoria del Cerro, Vino Nobile di Montepulciano, 97

Fattoria La Valentina Spelt Montepulciano d'Abruzzo, Abruzzi, 112

Fattoria Nicodemi Trebbiano d'Abruzzo, Abruzzi, 110

Faustino V Reserva, Rioja, 122

Fazi Battaglia Arkezia Muffo di San Sisto, Marche, 282

Fazi Battaglia Verdicchio dei Castelli di Jesi Classico, Marche, 110

Feather Cabernet Sauvignon, Columbia Valley, 213

Felipe Rutini Apartado, Mendoza, 245

Felton Road Block 5 Pinot Noir, Central Otago, 240

Féraud-Brunel, Côtes-du-Rhône Villages Cairanne, 71

Ferreira Quinta do Porto 10 Year Tawny Port, 276

Fess Parker Ashley's Vineyard Chardonnay, Santa Rita Hills, 169

Fess Parker Rodney's Vineyard Syrah, Santa Barbara County, 193

Feudi di San Gregorio Falanghina Sannio, Campania, 114

Feudi di San Marzano Sessantanni Old Vines Primitivo di Manduria, Apulia, 116

Final Cut Ballandown Vineyard Shiraz, Langhorne Creek, 231

Finca El Portillo Sauvignon Blanc, Valle de Uco, 244

Finca Sandoval, Manchuela, 128

Firesteed Pinot Noir, Oregon, 207

Fisher Vineyards Coach Insignia Cabernet Sauvignon, Napa Valley, 181

Fleming Jenkins Madden Ranch Syrah, Livermore Valley, 194

Fleming Jenkins Syrah Rosé, San Francisco Bay, 178

Foley Rancho Santa Rosa Chardonnay, Santa Rita Hills, 169

Foley Rancho Santa Rosa Pinot Noir, Santa Rita Hills, 191

Foley Rancho Santa Rosa Syrah, Santa Rita Hills, 194

Fonseca 40 Year Tawny Port, 276

Fontanafredda Eremo Barbera e Nebbiolo, Langhe, 90

Foppiano Vineyards Bacigalupi Vineyard Petite Sirah, Russian River Valley, 200

Foppiano Vineyards Merlot, Russian River Valley, 188

Foppiano Zinfandel, Dry Creek Valley, 197

Foradori Teroldego Rotaliano, Trentino, 106

Foris Pinot Gris, Rogue Valley, 205

Foundry Viognier, Coastal Region, 254

Four Graces Pinot Blanc, Willamette Valley, 205

Four Graces Reserve Pinot Noir, Willamette Valley, 207

Four Sisters Chardonnay, South Eastern Australia, 224

Fox Creek Short Row Shiraz, McLaren Vale, 231

Fox Creek Vixen, McLaren Vale, 271

Foxes Island Chardonnay, Marlborough, 239

Foxes Island Sauvignon Blanc, Marlborough, 238

Fra Guerau Rosé, Montsant, 125

Francesc S. Bas Cellars de la Cartoixa Montgarnatx, Priorat, 125

Francine et Olivier Savary, Chablis, 44

Francis Coppola Diamond Collection Black Label Claret Cabernet Sauvignon, California, 181

Francis Coppola Diamond Collection Green Label Syrah-Shiraz, California, 194

François Chidaine Les Bournais, Montlouis-sur-Loire, 58

Frankland Estate Isolation Ridge Vineyard Shiraz, Frankland River, 231

Franz Haas Manna Vigneti delle Dolomiti, Alto Adige, 103

Franz Hirtzberger Singerriedel Riesling Smaragd, Wachau, 148

Frédéric Mabileau Les Rouillères, St-Nicolas de Bourgueil, 62

Frédéric Magnien Seuvrées, Gevrey-Chambertin, 49

Freemark Abbey Bosché Cabernet Sauvignon, Napa Valley, 181

Frei João Reserva, Bairrada, 135

Freixenet Cordon Negro Brut, Cava, 269

Fritz Haag Riesling, Mosel-Saar-Ruwer, 140

Frontier Red Lot No.51, California, 200

Frühwirth Scheurebe, Styria, 150

F. Tinel-Blondelet L'Arret Buffatte, Pouilly-Fumé, 60

g

Gai'a Estate, Neméa, 155

Gai'a Thalassitis, Santorini, 154

Garcés Silva Amayna Sauvignon Blanc, San Antonio/Leyda Valley, 249

Garciarevalo Casamaro, Rueda, 127

Gaston Chiquet Tradition Brut Champagne Premier Cru, 264

Georg Breuer Berg Schlossberg Riesling, Rheingau, 140

Georg Breuer Charm Riesling, Rheingau, 140

Georges Gardet Cuvée St-Flavy Brut Champagne, 265

Georges Vigouroux Pigmentum Malbec, Vin de Pays du Lot, 81

Geyser Peak Winery Block Collection River Road Ranch Sauvignon Blanc, Russian River Valley, 172

Geyser Peak Winery Reserve Cabernet Sauvignon, Alexander Valley, 181

Giacomo Marengo, Le Tornaie, 93

Giant Steps Chardonnay, Yarra Valley, 224

Giovanni Puiatti Le Zuccole Isonzo del Friuli Pinot Grigio, Friuli–Venezia Giulia, 103

Girard Chardonnay, Russian River Valley, 169

Girlan Patricia Pinot Noir, Alto Adige, 106

Girlan San Martino Pinot Bianco, Alto Adige, 103

Glen Carlou Chardonnay, Paarl, 254

Glen Carlou Syrah, Paarl, 256

Goats Do Roam, Western Cape, 256

Goats Do Roam in Villages, Western Cape, 254

Goldeneye Pinot Noir, Anderson Valley, 191

Golden Hill Chardonnay, Maribor, 159

Gonzalez Byass Apóstoles Palo Cortado Muy Viejo Sherry, 274

Gonzalez Byass Tio Pepe Palomino Extra Dry Fino Sherry, 274

Gordon Brothers Family Vineyards Tradition, Columbia Valley, 213

Gosset Grande Réserve Brut Champagne, 265

Graff Wehlener Sonnenuhr Riesling Kabinett, Mosel-Saar-Ruwer, 140

Grans-Fassian Trittenheimer Riesling Kabinett, Mosel-Saar-Ruwer, 140

Grant Burge Barossa Vines Shiraz, Barossa, 231

Grant Burge Cameron Vale Cabernet Sauvignon, Barossa, 229

Grant Burge Nebuchadnezzar, Barossa, 233

Grant Burge Thorn Riesling, Eden Valley, 226

Green Point Chardonnay, Yarra Valley, 224

Green Point Shiraz, Victoria, 231

Greg Norman Estates Shiraz, Limestone Coast, 231

Grgich Hills Cabernet Sauvignon, Napa Valley, 181

Grgich Hills Chardonnay, Napa Valley, 169

Grgich Hills Fumé Blanc, Napa Valley, 173

Gritsch Mauritiushof Axpoint Grüner Veltliner Federspiel, Wachau, 147

Grosset Polish Hill Riesling, Clare Valley, 226

Gruet Brut, New Mexico, 270

Gruet Cuvée Gilbert Gruet Pinot Noir, New Mexico, 220

Gsellmann & Gsellmann Beerenauslese, Burgenland, 282

Gsellmann & Gsellmann Pinot Noir, Burgenland, 150

Gunderloch Jean-Baptiste Riesling Kabinett, Rheinhessen, 141

Gypsy Dancer Gary & Christine's Vineyard Pinot Noir, Oregon, 207

h

Hall Sauvignon Blanc, Napa Valley, 173

Hamilton Russell Vineyards Chardonnay, Walker Bay, 254

Hamilton Russell Vineyards Pinot Noir, Walker Bay, 254

Handley Brut, Anderson Valley, 270

Handley Estate Vineyard Chardonnay, Anderson Valley, 169

Handley Gewürztraminer, Anderson Valley, 175

Handley Handley Vineyard Sauvignon Blanc, Dry Creek Valley, 173

Handley Zinfandel, Mendocino County, 197

Hanna Bismark Mountain Vineyard Zinfandel, Sonoma Valley, 197

Hanna Cabernet Sauvignon, Sonoma County, 181

Haras de Pirque Estate Cabernet Sauvignon, Maipo Valley, 251

Hardys Whiskers Blake Classic Tawny, South Eastern Australia, 285

Harlan Estate, Napa Valley, 186

Heart of Darkness, Madiran, 81

Heathcote Estate Shiraz, Heathcote, 231

Hedges CMS, Columbia Valley, 211

Hedges Family Estate Three Vineyards, Red Mountain, 213

Henri Badoux Aigle Les Murailles, Aigle, 158

Herdade Do Esporão Vinha da Defesa, Alentejo, 135

Hermann J. Wiemer Dry Riesling, Finger Lakes, 218

Hermann J. Wiemer Select Late Harvest Johannisberg Riesling, Finger Lakes, 282

Hess Select Cabernet Sauvignon, California, 181

Hewitson Mermaids Muscadel, Barossa Valley, 226

Hewitson Old Garden Mourvèdre, Barossa Valley, 233

Hexamer Meddersheimer Rheingräfenberg Quarzit Riesling, Nahe, 141

Högl Ried Bruck Viessling Riesling Smaragd, Wachau, 148

Hogue Merlot, Columbia Valley, 213

Hogue Reserve Chardonnay, Columbia Valley, 211

Holy-Field Vineyard & Winery Cynthiana, Kansas, 220

Honig Bartolucci Vineyard Cabernet Sauvignon, Napa Valley, 181

Honig Sauvignon Blanc, Napa Valley, 173

Hope Estate Verdelho, Hunter Valley, 226

Houghton Semillon/Sauvignon Blanc, Western Australia, 226

Huet Clos du Bourg Sec, Vouvray, 58

Hugel et Fils Gentil, Alsace, 32

Hugel et Fils Hugel Gewurztraminer, Alsace, 31

Hugues Beaulieu Picpoul de Pinet, Coteaux du Languedoc, 74

Huguet Gran Reserva Brut Nature, Cava, 269

i

Il Brecciarolo Rosso Piceno Superiore, Marche, 112

Il Feuduccio Ursonia Montepulciano d'Abruzzo, Abruzzi, 112

Il Molino di Grace, Chianti Classico, 93

Il Piccolo Borgo, Chianti Classico, 93

Il Podere dell'Olivos Teroldego, Central Coast, 200

Il Poggione, Rosso di Montalcino, 96

I'M Chardonnay, Sonoma County, 169

I'M, Napa Valley, 178

Inama Vigneto du Lot Soave, Classico Veneto, 103

Indaba Shiraz, Western Cape, 256

Indis Chardonnay, Western Australia, 225

Inniskillin Oak Age Vidal Ice Wine, Niagara Peninsula, 282

Innocent Bystander Shiraz/Viognier, Victoria, 231

IO Syrah, Santa Barbara County, 194

Iris Hill Pinot Noir, Oregon, 207

Iron Horse Blanc de Blanc LD, Sonoma County/Green Valley, 270

Isenhower River Beauty Syrah, Horse Heaven Hills, 213

Isenhower Snapdragon, Columbia Valley, 211

Ivo Skaramuca Vineyard Dingac, Peljesac Peninsula, 160

j

Jackson-Triggs Proprietors' Grand Reserve Sauvignon Blanc, Okanagan Valley, 259

Jackson-Triggs Proprietors' Reserve Vidal Icewine, Niagara Peninsula, 282

Jacky Blot Domaine de la Taille aux Loups Rémus Sec, Montlouis-sur-Loire, 58

Jade Mountain La Provençale, California, 200

Jaillance Cuvée Impériale Tradition, Clairette de Die, 267

Jamesport Sarah's Hill Pinot Noir, North Fork of Long Island, 220

Jean-Claude Bessin Vieilles Vignes, Chablis, 44

Jean-Claude Boisset Les Charmes, Chambolle-Musigny Premier Cru, 49

Jean Ginglinger Cuvée George Pinot Blanc, Alsace, 28

Jean Ginglinger Riesling, Alsace, 30

Jean-Luc Colombo Les Forots, Côtes-du-Rhône, 71

Jean-Luc Colombo Les Ruchets, Cornas, 66

Jean-Marc Brocard Montmains, Chablis Premier Cru, 44

Jean-Maurice Raffault Les Galuches, Chinon, 62

Jean-Paul & Benoit Droin Les Clos, Chablis Grand Cru, 45

Jean-Paul Brun Terres Dorées L'Ancien Vieilles Vignes, Beaujolais, 55

Jean Reverdy et Fils La Reine Blanche, Sancerre, 60

Jean Tatin Domaine du Tremblay, Quincy, 61

Jean Thévenet et Fils Domaine Emilian Gillet Quintaine, Viré-Clessé, 52

Jermann Capo Martino, Venezia Giulia, 103

Jermann Mjzzu Blau & Blau, Venezia, 106

J. & H.A. Strub Niersteiner Riesling Kabinett, Rheinhessen, 141

J. Hofstätter Lagrein, Alto Adige, 106

J.L. Chave Selection Offerus, St-Joseph, 66

J. Lohr Los Osos Merlot, Paso Robles, 188

J.L. Wolf Villa Wolf Pinot Gris, Pfalz, 145

J.M. Boillot, St-Aubin Premier Cru, 46

J.M. Boillot Grésigny, Rully Premier Cru, 51

J.M. Gerin Champin Le Seigneur, Côte-Rôtie, 66

JM Tre Fanciulli, Columbia Valley, 214

JM Viognier, Columbia Valley, 211

Joffré e Hijas Reserva Merlot, Valle de Uco, 246

Joh. Jos. Prüm Wehlener Sonnenuhr Riesling Kabinett, Mosel-Saar-Ruwer, 141

Jordan Cabernet Sauvignon, Alexander Valley, 181

Jordan Chardonnay, Russian River Valley, 169

José Maria da Fonseca Periquita, Terras Do Sado, 135

Joseph Drouhin, Moulin-à-Vent, 55

Joseph Drouhin Clos des Mouches, Beaune Premier Cru, 49

Joseph Drouhin Domaine de Vaudon, Chablis, 45

Joseph Drouhin Véro Pinot Noir, Bourgogne, 49

Joseph Moda Cabernet Sauvignon/ Merlot, McLaren Vale, 233

Joseph Phelps Vineyards Cabernet Sauvignon, Napa Valley, 181

Joseph Phelps Vineyards Le Mistral, Monterey County, 201

Joseph Sparkling Red, Adelaide, 271

Joseph Swan Vineyards Côtes du Rosa, Russian River Valley, 201

Joseph Swan Vineyards Stellwagen Vineyard Zinfandel, Sonoma Valley, 197

Joseph Swan Vineyards Trenton Estate Vineyard Pinot Noir, Russian River Valley, 191

Josmeyer Le Dragon Riesling, Alsace, 30

J. Vidal Fleury, Côtes du Ventoux, 71

k

Kaesler The Bogan Shiraz, Barossa Valley, 231

Kaesler Old Vine Semillon, Barossa Valley, 227

Kaesler Stonehorse Grenache/Shiraz/ Mourvèdre, Barossa Valley, 234

Kahina, Guerrrouane, 163

Kalin Cellars Cuvee LD Chardonnay, Sonoma County, 169

Kalin Cellars Semillon, Livermore Valley, 176

Kanu Sauvignon Blanc, Stellenbosch, 254

Karlsmühle Kaseler Nies'chen Riesling Kabinett, Mosel-Saar-Ruwer, 141

Karyda, Náoussa, 155

Kathryn Kennedy Cabernet Sauvignon, Santa Cruz Mountains, 182

Kathryn Kennedy Winery Sauvignon Blanc, California, 173

Katnook Estate Odyssey Cabernet Sauvignon, Coonawarra, 229

Katnook Estate Prodigy Shiraz, Coonawarra, 231

Keith Tulloch Semillon, Hunter Valley, 227

Kendall-Jackson Grand Reserve Cabernet Sauvignon, Sonoma/Napa Counties, 182

Kendall-Jackson Grand Reserve Chardonnay, Monterey/Santa Barbara Counties, 169

Kendall-Jackson Vineyard Estates Taylor Peak Merlot, Bennett Valley, 188

Kendall-Jackson Vintner's Reserve Riesling, California, 176

Kendall-Jackson Vintner's Reserve Syrah, California, 194

Kendall-Jackson Vintner's Reserve Zinfandel, California, 197

Kenwood Sauvignon Blanc, Sonoma County, 173

King Estate Pinot Noir, Oregon, 208

Kir-Yianni Ramnista, Náoussa, 155

Klein Constantia Mme. Marlbrook, Constantia, 254

Kollwentz Föllikberg Zweigelt, Burgenland, 150

Kongsgaard Chardonnay, Napa Valley, 169

Königschaffhausen Flaneur, Baden, 145

Kozlovic Malvazija, Istria, 159

Kracher Cuvée Beerenauslese, Burgenland, 282

Kracher Pinot Gris Trocken, Burgenland, 150

Krug Brut Champagne, 265

Krug Rosé Brut, 266

Kuentz-Bas Blanc, Alsace, 32

Kuentz-Bas Tradition Riesling, Alsace, 30

Kuleto Estate Family Vineyards Rosato di Sangiovese, Napa Valley, 178

Kuleto Estate Family Vineyards Sangiovese, Napa Valley, 201

Kuleto Estate Family Vineyards Syrah, Napa Valley, 194

Kumeu River Pinot Gris, Kumeu, 239

Kumeu River Village Pinot Noir, Kumeu, 240

Kunde Estate Magnolia Lane Sauvignon Blanc, Sonoma Valley, 173

Kunde Estate Winery Reserve Cabernet Sauvignon, Sonoma Valley, 182

Kupe by Escarpment Pinot Noir, Marlinborough, 240

l

Labouré-Roi, Gevrey-Chambertin, 50

Labouré-Roi, Puligny-Montrachet, 46

L.A. Cetto Private Reserve Nebbiolo, Guadalupe Valley, 260

La Crema Pinot Noir, Anderson Valley, 191

La Doga, Morellino di Scansano, 98

Lafazanis Roditis, Peloponnese, 154

Lagaria Chardonnay, Venezia, 103

Lail Vineyards J. Daniel Cuvée Cabernet Sauvignon, Napa Valley, 182

La Lot Vigneti delle Dolomiti Pinot Grigio, Alto Adige, 103

La Massa, Tuscany, 99

Lanciola Le Masse di Greve, Chianti Classico, 93

Lanciola Riccionero Pinot Nero, Tuscany, 99

Langlois-Château Brut, Crémant de Loire, 267

Langlois-Château Château de Fontaine-Audon, Sancerre, 61

La Posta del Viñatero Pizzella Family Vineyard Malbec, La Consulta, 246

La Sansonnière La Lune, Anjou, 58

La Scolca Black Label, Gavi, 85

La Spinetta, Barbaresco, 87

L. Aubry Fils Brut Champagne Premier Cru, 265

Laurent Miquel Nord Sud Viognier, Vin de Pays d'Oc, 74

Laurent-Perrier Grand Siècle Brut Champagne, 265

La Vieille Ferme Rosé, Côtes du Ventoux, 69

Leasingham Bin 7 Riesling, Clare Valley, 227

Le Clos du Caillou Cuvée Unique Vieilles Vignes, Côtes-du-Rhône, 71

L'Ecole No. 41 Fries Vineyard Semillon, Washington State, 211

L'Ecole No. 41 Pepper Bridge Vineyard Apogee, Walla Walla Valley, 214

Leeuwin Estate Art Series Riesling, Margaret River, 227

Le Galantin, Bandol, 78

Leitz Dragonstone Riesling, Rheingau, 141

Leo Hillinger Hill 1, Burgenland, 151

Leo Hillinger Small Hill White, Burgenland, 150

Leonetti Cellar Merlot, Columbia Valley, 214

Le Salette Valpolicella Classico, Veneto, 107

Les Héritiers du Comte Lafon Les Maranches, Mâcon-Uchizy, 53

Les Trois Domaines Blanc, Guerrouane, 162

Les Trois Domaines Rouge, Guerrouane, 163

Leth Steinagrund Lagenreserve Grüner Veltliner, Donauland, 148

Leth Wagramterrassen Lagenreserve Riesling, Wagram/Donauland, 148

Limerick Lane Collins Vineyard Zinfandel, Russian River Valley, 197

Lincourt Chardonnay, Santa Barbara County, 170

Livio Felluga Terre Alte Colli Orientali del Friuli, Friuli–Venezia Giulia, 103

Lockwood Vineyard Cabernet Sauvignon, Monterey, 183

Lolonis Heritage Vineyards Petros, Redwood Valley, 201

Long Flat Shiraz, Barossa, 232

Loosen Bros. Dr. L Riesling, Mosel-Saar-Ruwer, 141

Louis-Claude Desvignes Javernières, Morgon, 55

Louis Guntrum Oppenheimer Sackträger Riesling Spätlese Trocken, Rheinhessen, 141

Louis Guntrum Penguin Silvaner Eiswein, Rheinhessen, 283

Louis Jadot, Nuits-St-Georges, 50

Louis Jadot Château des Lumières, Morgon, 55

Louis Roederer Premier Brut Champagne, 265

Louis Tête, Brouilly, 55

Luca Chardonnay, Altos de Mendoza, 244

Lucien Albrecht Cuvée Balthazar Pinot Blanc, Alsace, 28

Lucien Albrecht Cuvée Henri Riesling, Alsace, 30

Lucien Crochet La Croix du Roy, Sancerre, 62

Luis Pato Vinha Barrosa Vinha Velha, Beiras, 135

Luis Pato Vinha Formal, Beiras, 133

Lulu B. Syrah, Vin de Pays d'Oc, 75

Lungarotti Torre di Giano Bianco di Torgiano, Umbria, 110

Lungarotti Vigna Monticchio Rubesco Riserva Torgiano, Umbria, 112

Lupicaia, Tuscany, 99

Lustau East India Solera Sherry, 274

Lustau Los Arcos Dry Amontillado Sherry, 274

m

Macari Estate Merlot, North Fork of Long Island, 220

Machherndl Steinwand Grüner Veltliner Smaragd, Wachau, 148

Maghie Cellars Merlot, Red Mountain, 214

Magrez-Fombrauge Grand Cru, St-Émilion, 40

Main Divide Pinot Noir, Canterbury, 240

Malivoire Pinot Gris, Niagara Peninsula, 259

Malivoire Pinot Noir, Niagara Peninsula, 261

Mandra Rossa Nero d'Avola, Sicily, 116

Man Vintners Chenin Blanc, Coastal Region, 254

Mapema Tempranillo, Mendoza, 246

Marcarini Ciabot Camerano, Barbera d'Alba, 88

Marcel Lapierre, Morgon, 55

Marchese Carlo Guerrieri Gonzaga San Leonardo Vigneti delle Dolomiti, Alto Adige, 107

Marchesi de' Frescobaldi Castello di Nipozzano Mormoreto, Tuscany, 99

Marchesi de' Frescobaldi Castello di Nipozzano Vigneto Montesodi, Chianti Rùfina, 93

Marchesi di Barolo Madonna di Como, Dolcetto d'Alba, 88

Margaine Brut Champagne Premier Cru, 265

Marc Kreydenweiss Kastelberg Le Château Riesling Grand Cru, Alsace, 30

Marc Kreydenweiss Les Charmes Kritt Pinot Blanc, Alsace, 28

Markham Vineyards Cabernet Sauvignon, Napa Valley, 183

Marqués de Cáceres, Rioja, 121

Marqués de Cáceres Reserva, Rioja, 122

Marqués de Cáceres Rosé, Rioja, 121

Marqués de Griñon Petit Verdot, Dominio de Valdepusa, 128

Marquis Philips Sarah's Blend, South Eastern Australia, 234

Martha Clara Vineyards Estate Reserve Cabernet Sauvignon, North Fork of Long Island, 220

Martha Clara Vineyards Five-O, North Fork of Long Island, 218

Martin Schaetzel Kaefferkopf Granit Riesling, Alsace, 30

Martin Schaetzel Vieilles Vignes Pinot Blanc, Alsace, 28

Mas de Daumas Gassac, Vin de Pays de l'Hérault, 74

Mas de Gourgonnier, Les Baux de Provence, 78

Mas Estela Quindals, Empordà, 125

Mas Marçal, Catalonia, 125

Maschio M Spago, Prosecco del Veneto, 268

Masi Serego Alighieri Vaio Armaron Amarone della Valpolicella, Veneto, 107

Mason Sauvignon Blanc, Napa Valley, 173

Mastroberardino Nova Serra Greco di Tufo, Campania, 114

Mastroberardino Radici Riserva Taurasi, Campania, 116

Matanzas Creek Winery Merlot, Bennett Valley, 188

Matanzas Creek Winery Sauvignon Blanc, Sonoma County, 173

Matetic EQ Syrah, San Antonio, 251

Matheus Piesporter Goldtröpfchen Riesling Kabinett, Mosel-Saar-Ruwer, 141

Matthews, Columbia Valley, 214

Matthews Klipsun Vineyard Sauvignon Blanc, Red Mountain, 211

Matua Valley Pinot Noir, Marlborough, 240

Maximin Grünhäuser Herrenberg Riesling Kabinett, Mosel-Saar-Ruwer, 142

Mayacamas Vineyards Cabernet Sauvignon, Mt. Veeder, 183

Maysara Jamsheed Pinot Noir, McMinnville, 205

Maysara Pinot Gris, McMinnville, 205

Mazzocco Reserve Cabernet Sauvignon, Dry Creek Valley, 183

M. Chapoutier, Banyuls, 285

M. Chapoutier De l'Orée, Hermitage, 65

M. Chapoutier La Bernardine, Châteauneuf-du-Pape, 71

M. Chapoutier Les Granits, St-Joseph, 66

M. Cosentino Ol' Red, California, 201

M. Cosentino Syrah, California, 194

Melini Laborel Riserva, Chianti Classico, 94

Melipal Malbec, Mendoza, 247

Melis, Priorat, 125

Meridian Pinot Noir, Central Coast, 191

Merry Edwards Meredith Estate Pinot Noir, Sonoma Coast, 191

Merryvale Beckstoffer Vineyards Vineyard X Cabernet Sauvignon, Oakville, 183

Merryvale Juliana Vineyards Sauvignon Blanc, Napa Valley, 173

Métisse, Napa Valley, 186

Metiusco Salento, Apulia, 115

Michel Bouzereau et Fils Les Grands Charrons, Meursault, 47

Michel Colin-Deléger & Fils, Chassagne-Montrachet, 47

Michele Chiarlo, Gavi, 85

Michele Laluce Zimberno Aglianico del Vulture, Basilicata, 117

Michel Redde La Moynerie, Pouilly-Fumé, 61

Michel Tête Domaine du Clos du Fief, Juliénas, 55

Michel Thomas Silex, Sancerre, 61

Michel Torino Don David Reserve Torrontés, Cafayate Valley, 244

Miles Mossop Wines Saskia, Coastal Region, 254

Miner The Oracle, Napa Valley, 186

Miner Syrah, Napa Valley, 194

Miner Wild Yeast Chardonnay, Napa Valley, 170

Mionetto Cartizze, Prosecco di Valdobbiadene, 268

Mirabile Insolia, Sicily, 115

Moccagatta Bric Balin, Barbaresco, 87

Moët & Chandon Dom Pérignon Oenothèque Brut Champagne, 265

Moët & Chandon White Star Champagne, 265

Monarchia Cellars Zen, Eger, 159

Mönchhof Mosel Slate Riesling Spätlese, Mosel-Saar-Ruwer, 142

Mongeard-Mugneret, Fixin, 50

Montecastro, Ribera del Duero, 123

Montecillo, Rioja, 121

Montes Alpha Chardonnay, Casablanca Valley, 249

Montes Purple Angel, Colchagua Valley, 251

Monte Velho, Alentejo, 133

Montinore Estate Gewürztraminer, Willamette Valley, 205

Mont Marçal Extremarium Brut, Cava, 269

Morey-Blanc, St-Aubin Premier Cru, 47

Morgadío Albariño, Rías Baixas, 127

Morgan Double L Vineyard Chardonnay, Santa Lucia Highlands, 170

Morgan Double L Vineyard Pinot Noir, Santa Lucia Highlands, 191

Moroder Rosso Conero, Marche, 112

Mounthes Le Bihan Vieillefont, Côtes-de-Duras, 81

Mount Langi Ghiran Billi Billi Shiraz, Victoria, 232

Mount Langi Ghiran Pinot Gris, Victoria, 227

Mount Pleasant Vignoles, Missouri, 218

Mount Riley Sauvignon Blanc, Marlborough, 238

Mount Veeder Winery Reserve, Napa Valley, 186

Movia Veliko (red), Goriska Brda, 161

Movia Veliko (white), Goriska Brda, 159

Mumm Napa DVX, Napa Valley, 270

Murphy-Goode Merlot, Alexander Valley, 188

Murphy-Goode Sarah Block Cabernet Sauvignon, Alexander Valley, 183

Murphy-Goode Wild Card Claret, Alexander Valley, 186

Murrieta's Well Meritage, Livermore Valley, 176

Musar Cuvée Blanc, Bekaa Valley, 162

n

Naiades Verdejo, Rueda, 127

Neckenmarkt Blaufränkisch, Burgenland, 151

Nederburg Shiraz, Western Cape, 256

Nederburg Special Late Harvest, Western Cape, 283

Neil Ellis Chardonnay, Stellenbosch, 254

Nelms Road Merlot, Columbia Valley, 214

Newton Forrest Estate Cornerstone Cabernet/Merlot/Malbec, Hawkes Bay, 241

Nicholas Cole Cellars Camille, Columbia Valley, 214

Nickel & Nickel Suscol Ranch Merlot, Napa Valley, 189

Nicodemi Notàri Montepulciano d'Abruzzo, Abruzzi, 112

Nicolas Feuillatte Cuvée 225 Brut Champagne, 265

Nicolas Joly Clos de la Coulée de Serrant, Savennières, 58

Nicolas Potel Vieilles Vignes, Volnay, 50

Nine Stones Shiraz, Hilltops, 232

Nitída Semillon, Durbanville, 255

Nobilo Icon Pinot Gris, Marlborough, 239

Nora da Neve, Rías Baixas, 127

o

Oak Knoll Vintage Reserve Pinot Noir, Willamette Valley, 208

Oakville Ranch Cabernet Sauvignon, Napa Valley, 183

O. Fournier B Crux, Valle de Uco, 247

Olivier Leflaive, Puligny-Montrachet, 47

Opus One, Napa Valley, 186

Origine Marcel Hemard Brut Champagne Premier Cru, 265

Ornellaia Le Volte, Tuscany, 99

Orphéus Etna, Sicily, 117

Osborne 10 RF Oloroso Medium Sherry, 274

Osborne 10 Year Tawny Port, 276

Osoyoos Larose Le Grand Vin, Okanagan Valley, 261

Ostatu Reserva, Rioja, 122

P

Pago de Valdoneje Mencia, Bierzo, 129

Palacio de Fefiñanes Albariño, Rías Baixas, 127

Palazzone Terre Vineate Orvieto Classico, Umbria, 110

Palladio, Brunello di Montalcino, 96

Palladio, Rosso di Montalcino, 96

Panther Creek Freedom Hill Vineyard Pinot Noir, Willamette Valley, 208

Parusso Nebbiolo, Langhe, 90

Parusso Piani Noce, Dolcetto d'Alba, 88

Pasanau Finca La Planeta, Priorat, 125

Pascal Jolivet Le Château du Nozay, Sancerre, 61

Patianna Organic Vineyards Fairbairn Ranch Syrah, Mendocino, 194

Patton Valley Vineyard Pinot Noir, Willamette Valley, 208

Paul Hobbs Cabernet Sauvignon, Napa Valley, 183

Paul Hobbs Chardonnay, Russian River Valley, 170

Paul Jaboulet Aîné Le Chant des Griolles, Muscat de Beaumes-de-Venise, 283

Paul Jaboulet Aîné Les Cèdres, Châteauneuf-du-Pape, 71

Paumanok Cabernet Sauvignon, North Fork of Long Island, 220

Paumanok Chenin Blanc, North Fork of Long Island, 218

Pecchenino San Luigi, Dolcetto di Dogliani, 88

Pedestal Merlot, Columbia Valley, 214

Peju Province Cabernet Franc, Napa Valley, 186

Peju Province Cabernet Sauvignon, Napa Valley, 183

Peller Estates Riesling Icewine, Niagara Peninsula, 283

Peñalolen Cabernet Sauvignon, Maipo Valley, 251

Penfolds Bin 407 Cabernet Sauvignon, South Australia, 229

Penfolds Koonunga Hill Cabernet/Merlot, South Eastern Australia, 234

Penfolds Magill Estate Shiraz, South Australia, 232

Peninsula Ridge Estates Winery Vintners Private Reserve Chardonnay, Niagara Peninsula, 259

Penley Estate Reserve Cabernet Sauvignon, Coonawarra, 229

Penny's Hill Red Dot Shiraz, McLaren Vale, 232

Pepi Chardonnay, California, 170

Perrin & Fils Les Christins, Vacqueyras, 71

Perrin Réserve Rosé, Côtes-du-Rhône, 69

Pesquera Crianza, Ribera del Duero, 123

Peter Lehmann Clancy's, Barossa, 234

Peter Michael Winery Le Moulin Rouge Pinot Noir, Santa Lucia Highlands, 191

Peter Michael Winery Les Pavots, Knights Valley, 187

Peter Michael Winery Ma Belle-Fille Chardonnay, Sonoma County, 170

Pfeffingen Dry Riesling, Pfalz, 142

Philippe Faury, Côte-Rôtie, 66

Philippe Pacalet, Pommard, 50

Pieropan Calvarino Soave Classico, Veneto, 103

Pierre Luneau-Papin Clos des Allées Muscadet sur Lie, Sèvre-et-Maine, 59

Pierre Morey, Bourgogne, 50

Pierre Soulez Château de Chambourceau Chevalier Buhard Doux, Savennières Roche aux Moines, 283

Pierrette et Marc Guillemot-Michel Quintaine, Mâcon-Villages, 53

Pighin Collio Pinot Grigio, Friuli–Venezia Giulia, 104

Pike & Joyce Pinot Gris, Adelaide Hills, 227

Pikes Luccio, Clare Valley, 234

Pine Ridge Cabernet Sauvignon, Rutherford, 183

Pink Zeppelin, Paso Robles, 178

Piper-Heidsieck Cuvée Rare Champagne, 265

Piping Shrike Shiraz, Barossa Valley, 232

Plaisir de Merle Sauvignon Blanc, Coastal Region, 255

Planeta La Segreta, Sicily, 115

Plozner Grave del Friuli Tocai Friulano, Friuli–Venezia Giulia, 104

PlumpJack Reserve Cabernet Sauvignon, Oakville, 183

Poças 20 Year Tawny Port, 276

Pöckl Zweigelt, Burgenland, 151

Podere Il Caio, Umbria, 112

Podere Il Caio Grechetto, Umbria, 110

Poderi Colla Costa Bruna, Barbera d'Alba, 89

Poderi Foglia Concabianco Roccamonfina, Campania, 115

Poderi Luigi Einaudi, Barolo, 87

Poderi Luigi Einaudi Vigna Tecc, Dolcetto di Dogliani, 89

Poet's Leap Riesling, Columbia Valley, 211

Poggio Antico Altero, Brunello di Montalcino, 96

Poggio Bertaio Stucchio Sangiovese, Umbria, 112

Pol Roger Brut Champagne, 266

Pommery Brut Royal Champagne, 266

Ponzi Vineyards Pinot Gris, Willamette Valley, 205

Ponzi Vineyards Pinot Noir, Willamette Valley, 208

Potel-Aviron, Morgon Côte du Py, 55

Prager Hinter der Burg Grüner Veltliner Federspiel, Wachau, 148

Primo Estate La Biondina, Adelaide, 227

Prinz von Hessen Riesling, Rheingau, 142

Prinz von Hessen Johannisberger Klaus Riesling Beerenauslese, Rheingau, 283

Prinz von Hessen Winkeler Hasensprung Erstes Gewächs Riesling, Rheingau, 142

Pro Nobis, Ruché di Castagnole Monferrato, 90

Producteurs Plaimont Colombelle, Vin de Pays des Côtes de Gascogne, 80

Producteurs Plaimont Les Vignes Retrouvées, Côtes de St-Mont, 81

Punto Final Reserva Malbec, Perdriel, 247

q

Quady's Starboard, Amador County, 285

Quinta das Baceladas Single Estate, Beiras, 135

Quinta da Terrugem Single Estate, Alentejo, 135

Quinta de Cabriz Colheita Seleccionada, Dão, 133

Quinta do Crasto Late Bottled Vintage Port, 277

Quinta do Crasto Old Vines Reserva, Douro, 135

Quinta do Noval Vintage Port, 277

Qupé Bien Nacido Block Eleven Reserve Chardonnay, Santa Maria Valley, 170

Qupé Bien Nacido Hillside Estate Syrah, Santa Maria Valley, 194

Qupé Los Olivos Cuvée, Santa Ynez Valley, 201

r

Raats Family Wines Original Unwooded Chenin Blanc, Coastal Region, 255

Rabbit Ridge Syrah, Paso Robles, 194

Rabbit Ridge Westside Zinfandel, Paso Robles, 197

Rainer Wess Wachauer Riesling, Wachau, 149

Ramey Ritchie Vineyard Chardonnay, Russian River Valley, 170

Ramos Pinto Vintage Port, 277

Ramsay Merlot, Napa Valley, 189

Ram's Leap Semillon/Sauvignon Blanc, Western Plains, 227

Rancho Zabaco Reserve Sauvignon Blanc, Russian River Valley, 173

Rancho Zabaco Stefani Vineyard Zinfandel, Dry Creek Valley, 198

Rare Wine Co. Historic Series Special Reserve Charleston Sercial Madeira, 278

Ravenswood Dickerson Zinfandel, Napa Valley, 198

Red Knot Shiraz, McLaren Vale, 232

Red Zeppelin Bear Valley Ranch & O'Neill Vineyards Syrah, Central Coast, 195

Reguengo de Melgaço Alvarinho, Vinho Verde, 133

Reichsgraf von Kesselstatt RK Riesling, Mosel-Saar-Ruwer, 142

Renato Ratti Marcenasco, Barolo, 87

Renato Ratti Ochetti, Nebbiolo d'Alba, 90

René Barbier Mediterranean White, Catalonia, 124

Rex Hill Maresh Vineyard Pinot Noir, Oregon, 208

Ricardo Santos La Madras Vineyard Malbec, Mendoza, 247

Rideau Vineyard Iris Estate Viognier, Santa Ynez Valley, 176

Rideau Vineyard Reserve Chardonnay, Santa Barbara County, 170

Ridge Lytton Springs Zinfandel, Dry Creek Valley, 198

Ridge Monte Bello, Santa Cruz Mountains, 187

Rijckaert En Pottes Vieilles Vignes, Mâcon-Montbellet, 53

Riverside by Foppiano Cabernet Sauvignon, California, 184

R. López de Heredia Viña Tondonia Reserva (red), Rioja, 122

R. López de Heredia Viña Tondonia Reserva (white), Rioja, 121

Robert Biale Vineyards Black Chicken Zinfandel, Napa Valley, 198

Robert Biale Vineyards Thomann Station Petite Sirah, Napa Valley, 201

Robert-Denogent Les Pommards, St-Véran, 53

Robert Gilliard Dôle des Monts, Valais, 158

Robert Gilliard Les Murettes Fendant, Valais, 158

Robert Mondavi Winery Reserve Cabernet Sauvignon, Napa Valley, 184

Robert Mondavi Winery Reserve Chardonnay, Carneros, 170

Robert Mondavi Winery To Kalon Vineyard Reserve Fumé Blanc, Napa Valley, 173

Robert Sinskey Vineyards Abraxas Vin de Terroir, Carneros, 176

Robert Sinskey Vineyards Merlot, Carneros, 189

Robert Sinskey Vineyards Pinot Noir, Carneros, 192

Robert Sinskey Vineyards RSV SLD Estate Cabernet Sauvignon, Stags Leap District, 184

Rocca delle Macìe Riserva, Chianti Classico, 94

Rocca di Castagnoli, Chianti Classico, 94

Rochioli Pinot Noir, Russian River Valley, 192

Rochioli Sauvignon Blanc, Russian River Valley, 174

Roederer Estate Brut, Anderson Valley, 270

Roland Lavantureux, Chablis, 45

Romariz Vintage Port, 277

Rosemount Estate GSM, McLaren Vale, 234

Rosemount Estate Hill of Gold Chardonnay, Mudgee, 225

Rosenblum Cellars Monte Rosso Vineyard Reserve Zinfandel, Sonoma Valley, 198

Rosenblum Cellars Pickett Road Petite Sirah, Napa Valley, 201

Rosenblum Cellars Rominger Vineyard Syrah, Yolo County, 195

Rotllan Torra Amadís, Priorat, 125

RoxyAnn Pinot Gris, Oregon, 205

Royal Tokaji Essencia, Tokaji, 283

Royal Tokaji Furmint, Tokaji, 160

Rudd Cabernet Sauvignon, Oakville, 184

Rudd Sauvignon Blanc, Napa Valley, 174

Rudi Pichler Wösendorfer Hochrain Grüner Veltliner Smaragd, Wachau, 148

Ruffino Riserva Ducale Oro Riserva, Chianti Classico, 94

Rusack Reserve Chardonnay, Santa Maria Valley, 170

Rusack Reserve Pinot Noir, Santa Rita Hills, 192

Rusack Syrah, Santa Barbara County, 195

Russiz Superiore Col Disôre Collio, Friuli–Venezia Giulia, 104

Russiz Superiore Collio Merlot, Friuli–Venezia Giulia, 108

Rutherford Hill Cabernet Sauvignon, Napa Valley, 184

Rutherford Hill Merlot, Napa Valley, 189

Rutherglen Estates Muscat, Rutherglen, 284

Ryan Patrick Vineyards Rock Island Red, Columbia Valley, 214

S

Sagelands Vineyard Four Corners Merlot, Columbia Valley, 214

Saia Nero d'Avola, Sicily, 117

Saintsbury Brown Ranch Chardonnay, Carneros, 171

Saintsbury Brown Ranch Pinot Noir, Carneros, 192

Salentein Syrah, Alto Valle de Uco, 247

Salmon Run Meritage, New York, 220

Sanctum Shiraz, Western Cape, 256

Sandhill Cabernet Sauvignon, Red Mountain, 214

Sandrone, Barbera d'Alba , 89

San Fabiano Conti, Chianti, 94

Sanford Pinot Noir, Santa Rita Hills, 192

Santadi Cala Silente Vermentino di Sardegna, Sardinia, 115

Santadi Terre Brune Carignano del Sulcis Superiore, Sardinia, 117

Santa Maria La Palma Aragosta Vermentino di Sardegna, Sardinia, 115

Santi Solane Ripasso Valpolicella Classico Superiore, Veneto, 108

San Vicente Tempranillo, Rioja, 122

Sartarelli Verdicchio dei Castelli di Jesi Classico, Marche, 110

Sauvignon Republic Cellars Sauvignon Blanc, Russian River Valley, 174

Scharffenberger Brut, Mendocino County, 270

Schiopetto Collio Pinot Bianco, Friuli–Venezia Giulia, 104

Schloss Johannisberger Estate Riesling Spätlese Trocken, Rheingau, 142

Schloss Saarstein Riesling Spätlese, Mosel-Saar-Ruwer, 142

Schloss Wallhausen Two Princes Riesling, Nahe, 142

Schlumberger Cuvée Klimt Brut, Vienna, 271

Schneider Roanoke Point Cabernet Franc, North Fork of Long Island, 221

Schramsberg Brut Rosé, Napa/Mendocino/Sonoma/Marin Counties, 270

Scilio Rubé, Sicily, 115

S.C. Pannell Shiraz/Grenache, McLaren Vale, 234

Screwed, McLaren Vale, 227

Seavey Cabernet Sauvignon, Napa Valley, 184

Sebastiani Secolo, Sonoma County, 187

Sebastiani Zinfandel, Sonoma County, 198

Seghesio Family Vineyards Old Vine Zinfandel, Sonoma County, 198

Seghesio Family Vineyards Omaggio, Sonoma County, 201

Segura Viudas Creu de Lavit Xarel-lo, Penedès, 124

Segura Viudas Mas d'Aranyó Tempranillo Reserva, Penedès, 125

Segura Viudas Reserva Heredad Brut, Cava, 269

Seis de Luberri, Rioja, 122

Selbach Dry Riesling (Fish Label), Mosel-Saar-Ruwer, 142

Selene Hyde Vineyards Sauvignon Blanc, Carneros, 174

Sella & Mosca Riserva Cannonau di Sardegna, Sardinia, 117

Señorío de Cuzcurrita, Rioja, 122

Sequel Syrah, Columbia Valley, 215

Sequoia Grove Cabernet Sauvignon, Napa Valley, 184

Sequoia Grove Chardonnay, Carneros, 171

Sergio Zenato Lugana, Veneto, 104

Serveaux Carte d'Or Brut Champagne, 266

Shafer Cabernet Sauvignon, Napa Valley, 184

Shafer Red Shoulder Ranch Chardonnay, Carneros, 171

Shannon Ridge Barbera, Lake County, 201

Shannon Ridge Syrah, Lake County, 195

Shannon Ridge Zinfandel, Lake County, 199

Shardana Valli di Porto Pino, Sardinia, 117

Shaw and Smith M3 Vineyard Chardonnay, Adelaide Hills, 225

Shaw and Smith Sauvignon Blanc, Adelaide Hills, 227

Sherwood House Vineyards Merlot, North Fork of Long Island, 221

Shingleback Cabernet Sauvignon, McLaren Vale, 229

Shingleback Grenache, McLaren Vale, 234

Shoestring Vineyard & Winery Sangiovese, Santa Ynez Valley, 202

Sigalas, Santorini, 154

Silverado Vineyards Limited Cabernet Sauvignon, Napa Valley, 184

Silverado Vineyards Merlot, Napa Valley, 189

Silverado Vineyards Sangiovese, Napa Valley, 202

Silverado Vineyards Vineburg Chardonnay, Carneros, 171

Simi Cabernet Sauvignon, Alexander Valley, 184

Simonsig Chenin Blanc, Stellenbosch, 255

Sincerity Merlot/Cabernet Sauvignon, Colchagua, 251

Skouras Saint George, Neméa, 155

Snoqualmie Vineyards Reserve Merlot, Columbia Valley, 215

Sokol Blosser Evolution 9th Edition, America, 205

Sokol Blosser Pinot Noir, Dundee Hills, 208

Soléna Domaine Danielle Laurent Pinot Noir, Willamette Valley, 209

Soléna Pinot Gris, Oregon, 205

Spalletti, Chianti, 94

Speri Amarone della Valpolicella Classico, Veneto, 108

Spice Route Malabar, Swartland, 256

Spice Route Viognier, Swartland, 255

Spiropoulos Ode Panos Brut, Peloponnese, 271

Spottswoode Cabernet Sauvignon, St. Helena, 184

Spreitzer Hattenheimer Wisselbrunnen Riesling Spätlese Trocken, Rheingau, 143

Spring Mountain Vineyard Elivette Reserve, Napa Valley, 187

Spy Valley Sauvignon Blanc, Marlborough, 238

Staglin Family Vineyard Cabernet Sauvignon, Rutherford, 185

Staglin Family Vineyard Stagliano Sangiovese, Rutherford, 202

Standing Stone Vineyards Gewurztraminer, Finger Lakes, 218

Standing Stone Vineyards Pinnacle, Finger Lakes, 221

Standing Stone Vineyards Vidal Ice, Finger Lakes, 284

Stark Syrah, Stellenbosch, 256

St. Francis Winery Red, Sonoma County, 202

Stoller Chardonnay, Dundee Hills, 205

Stone Hill Winery Norton, Hermann, 221

Stone Hill Winery Port, Hermann, 285

Stone Hill Winery Vidal Blanc, Missouri, 219

Stonehaven Winemaker's Selection Shiraz, South Australia, 232

Stoneleigh Riesling, Marlborough, 239

Stonestreet Merlot, Alexander Valley, 189

Stony Hill Chardonnay, Napa Valley, 171

Stony Hill Gewurztraminer, Napa Valley, 176

Straccali, Chianti, 94

Strauss Welschriesling, Southern Styria, 150

Strozzi Titolato, Vernaccia di San Gimignano, 91

St. Supéry Élu, Napa Valley, 187

St. Supéry Limited Edition Dollarhide Cabernet Sauvignon, Napa Valley, 185

St. Supéry Virtú, Napa Valley, 176

Stuhlmuller Vineyards Estate Chardonnay, Alexander Valley, 171
Suavia Soave Classico, Veneto, 104
Swanson Pinot Grigio, Napa Valley, 176

t

Tablas Creek Vineyard Esprit de Beaucastel, Paso Robles, 176
Tablas Creek Vineyard Mourvèdre, Paso Robles, 202
Tahbilk Cabernet Sauvignon, Nagambie Lakes, 229
Taittinger Comtes de Champagne Brut Rosé, 266
Takler Heritage Cuvée, Szekszard, 161
Talbott Cuvée Cynthia Chardonnay, Monterey County, 171
Taltarni Brut Taché, Victoria/Tasmania, 271
Tamarack Cellars Firehouse Red, Columbia Valley, 215
Tamás Estates Barbera, Livermore Valley, 202
Tapestry Chardonnay, McLaren Vale, 225
Tasca d'Almerita Rosso del Conte Contea di Sclafani, Sicily, 117
Taurino Notarpanaro Salento, Apulia, 117
Taylor Fladgate Vintage Port, 277
Tedeschi Amarone della Valpolicella Classico, Veneto, 108
Tempus Alba Preludio Acorde # 1 Reserve, Mendoza, 247
Tenimenti Angelini San Leonino, Chianti Classico, 94
Tenimenti Angelini Trerose, Vino Nobile di Montepulciano, 98
Tenimenti Angelini Val di Suga, Brunello di Montalcino, 96
Tenimenti Ruffino Ludola Nuova, Vino Nobile di Montepulciano, 98
Tenuta Cocci Grifoni Vigna Messieri Rosso Piceno Superiore, Marche, 112
Tenuta di Arceno Arcanum III, Tuscany, 99
Tenuta di Nozzole La Forra Riserva, Chianti Classico, 95
Tenuta di Nozzole Le Bruniche Chardonnay, Tuscany, 91
Tenuta San Guido Sassicaia, Bolgheri, 100
Tenuta Sette Ponti Oreno, Tuscany, 100
Tenute Cisa Asinari dei Marchesi di Gresy Martinenga, Barbaresco, 87
Terrabianca Campaccio Riserva, Tuscany, 100
Terrabianca Croce Riserva, Chianti Classico, 95
Terraces Cabernet Sauvignon, Napa Valley, 185
Terraces Zinfandel, Napa Valley, 199

Terra dei Re Divinus Aglianico del Vulture, Basilicata, 117
Terra Noble Gran Reserva Carmenère, Maule Valley, 251
Terra Rosa Old Vine Malbec, Mendoza, 247
Terra Valentine Wurtele Vineyard Cabernet Sauvignon, Spring Mountain District, 185
Terrazas de los Andes Reserva Chardonnay, Mendoza, 244
Terredora Di Paolo Terre di Dora Fiano di Avellino, Campania, 115
Terre Rouge Enigma, Sierra Foothills, 176
Terre Rouge High Slopes Syrah, Sierra Foothills, 195
Teruzzi & Puthod Terre di Tufi, Tuscany, 91
Thelema Cabernet Sauvignon, Stellenbosch, 256
Theo Minges Gleisweiler Hölle Scheurebe Spätlese, Pfalz, 145
Theo Minges Gleisweiler Hölle Riesling Spätlese, Pfalz, 145
Thierry et Pascale Matrot Les Chevalières, Meursault, 47
Thierry Germain Domaine des Roches Neuves L'Insolite, Saumur, 58
Thierry Germain Domaine des Roches Neuves Terres Chaudes, Saumur-Champigny, 62
Thomas Fogarty Pinot Noir, Santa Cruz Mountains, 192
Tibor Gal Egri Bikavér, Eger, 161
Tibor Gal Egri Chardonnay, Eger, 160
Tiefenbrunner Chardonnay, Alto Adige, 104
Tikal Patriota, Mendoza, 247
Tir Na N'og Old Vines Grenache, McLaren Vale, 234
Tokara, Stellenbosch, 257
Torii Mor Olson Estate Vineyard Pinot Noir, Dundee Hills, 209
Torre Quarto Bottaccia Nero di Troia, Apulia, 117
Torresella Chardonnay, Veneto, 104
Torres Viña Sol, Penedès, 124
Toscolo Riserva, Chianti Classico, 95
Tour des Gendres, Bergerac Sec, 80
Tramin Pinot Grigio, Alto Adige, 104
Trapiche Broquel Cabernet Sauvignon, Mendoza, 247
Treana Mer Soleil Vineyard Marsanne/Viognier, Central Coast, 177
Trefethen Cabernet Franc, Oak Knoll District, 187
Trefethen Chardonnay, Oak Knoll District, 171
Trefethen Dry Riesling, Oak Knoll District, 177

Trefethen Halo Cabernet Sauvignon, Oak Knoll District, 185

Trefethen Merlot, Oak Knoll District, 189

Trentadue Winery La Storia Petite Sirah, Alexander Valley, 202

Trentadue Winery La Storia Zinfandel, Alexander Valley, 199

Trevor Jones Boots Grenache, South Australia, 234

Trimbach Cuvée des Seigneurs de Ribeaupierre Gewurztraminer, Alsace, 31

Trimbach Pinot Blanc, Alsace, 28

Trimbach Réserve Personnelle Pinot Gris, Alsace, 29

Trivento Golden Reserve Malbec, Mendoza, 247

Trouillard Extra Sélection Brut Champagne, 266

Tsantali Cellar Reserve 5 Year Oak Aged, Mavrodaphne of Patras, 285

Tsantali Rapsani Réserve, Epilegmenos, 155

Tuck's Ridge Pinot Noir, Mornington Peninsula, 234

Turley Dusi Vineyard Zinfandel, Paso Robles, 199

Txomin Etxaniz, Getariako Txakolina, 127

Tyrrell's Wines Reserve Chardonnay, Hunter Valley, 225

U, V

Urban Uco Malbec/Tempranillo, Valle de Uco, 247

Valdinera Sontuoso, Nebbiolo d'Alba, 90

Valley of the Moon Pinot Blanc, Sonoma County, 177

Valley of the Moon Syrah, Sonoma County, 195

Valmar Cabernet Sauvignon, Baja California, 261

Valmiñor Albariño, Rías Baixas, 127

Valsacro, Rioja, 122

Vega Sindoa Cabernet Sauvignon/Tempranillo, Navarra, 129

Vega Sindoa Rosé, Navarra, 127

Velich Welschriesling Trockenbeerenauslese, Neusiedlersee, 284

Veramonte Primus, Casablanca Valley, 251

Verdad, Arroyo Grande Valley, 178

Verdad Ibarra-Young Vineyard Albariño, Santa Ynez Valley, 177

Verdad Tempranillo/Syrah/Grenache, Santa Barbara County, 202

Vértice, Douro, 135

Vértice Reserva Bruto, Douro, 271

Veuve Clicquot Ponsardin Brut Rosé, 266

Viader Syrah, Napa Valley, 195

Vicentini Agostino Terre Lunghe Soave, Veneto, 104

Vietti Castiglione, Barolo, 87

Vigne Regali L'Ardì, Dolcetto d'Acqui, 89

Vilafonté Series M, Paarl, 257

Villa Bucci Riserva Verdicchio dei Castelli di Jesi Classico, Marche, 110

Villa La Selva Selvamaggio Cabernet Sauvignon, Tuscany, 100

Villa La Selva Vigna del Papa, Vin Santo del Chianti, 284

Villa Maria Cellar Selection Cabernet Sauvignon/Merlot, Hawkes Bay, 241

Villa Maria Reserve Sauvignon Blanc, Clifford Bay, 238

Villa Russiz Collio Sauvignon, Friuli–Venezia Giulia, 104

Villa Sparina Montej, Monferrato, 85

Viña Ijalba Graciano, Rioja, 122

Viña Sastre Pago de Santa Cruz, Ribera del Duero, 123

Vincent Dureuil-Janthial En Guesnes, Rully, 51

Vincent Girardin La Fussière, Maranges Premier Cru, 50

Vincent Girardin Vieilles Vignes, Puligny-Montrachet, 47

Viñedo de los Vientos Angel's Cuvée Blanc de Bianco, Atlantida, 259

Viñedo de los Vientos Tannat, Atlantida, 261

Viñedos de Nieva Pasil Pie Franco Verdejo, Rueda, 127

Vineyard 48 Reserve Merlot, North Fork of Long Island, 221

Vini Cabernet Sauvignon, Sliven, 161

Vinum Cellars The Scrapper Cabernet Franc, El Dorado County, 187

Vinum Cellars White Elephant, California, 177

Viognier de Campuget Cuvaumas Cuvée Prestige, Vin de Pays du Gard, 74

Vittoria Contini Bonacossi Trefiano, Carmignano, 98

von Buhl Armand Riesling Kabinett, Pfalz, 143

von Buhl Maria Schneider Medium-Dry Riesling, Pfalz, 143

von Hövel Oberemmeler Hütte Riesling Kabinett, Mosel-Saar-Ruwer, 144

von Othegraven Maria v. O. Riesling, Mosel-Saar-Ruwer, 144

Voss Estate Riesling, Martinborough, 239

Vylyan Villanyi Pinot Noir, Villany, 161

W

Walter Dacon C'est Syrah Beaux, Columbia Valley, 215

Warre's Quinta da Cavadinha Vintage Port, 277

Warwick Estate Old Bush Vines Pinotage, Stellenbosch, 257

Warwick Estate Professor Black Sauvignon Blanc, Simonsberg-Stellenbosch, 255

Waterbrook Cabernet Sauvignon, Columbia Valley, 215

Wattle Creek Shiraz, Alexander Creek, 195

Weinert Carrascal, Mendoza, 247

Weingut Ch. W. Bernhard Frei-Laubersheimer Fels Gewürztraminer Spätlese, Rheinhessen, 145

Weingüter Wegeler Rüdesheimer Berg Rottland Riesling Spätlese, Rheingau, 144

Weingut Johann Donabaum Offenberg Riesling Smaragd, Wachau, 149

Weingut Knoll Loibenberg Grüner Veltliner Smaragd, Wachau, 148

Weingut Knoll Schütt Riesling Smaragd, Wachau, 149

Weingut Münzberg Weisser Burgunder Kabinett Trocken, Pfalz, 145

Weingut Robert Weil Estate Dry Riesling, Rheingau, 144

Weingut Schloss Lieser Riesling Kabinett, Mosel-Saar-Ruwer, 144

Wente Vineyards Charles Wetmore Reserve Cabernet Sauvignon, Livermore Valley, 185

Westside White, Central Coast, 177

Wild Horse Cabernet Sauvignon, Paso Robles, 185

Wild Horse Pinot Noir, Central Coast, 192

Willakenzie Estate Triple Black Slopes Pinot Noir, Willamette Valley, 209

Willamette Valley Vineyards Estate Vineyard Pinot Noir, Willamette Valley, 209

Wishing Tree Unoaked Chardonnay, Western Australia, 225

Wolfberger Brut Rosé, Crémant d'Alsace, 267

Wolfberger Gewurztraminer, Alsace, 31

Wolf Blass Platinum Label Shiraz, Adelaide Hills, 232

Wölffer Brut, The Hamptons, 270

Wölffer Premier Cru Merlot, The Hamptons, 221

Wölffer Rosé, The Hamptons, 219

Woodenhead Buena Tierra Vineyard Pinot Noir, Russian River Valley, 192

Woodenhead Martinelli Road Vineyard Old Vine Zinfandel, Russian River Valley, 199

Woodward Canyon Estate, Walla Walla Valley, 215

Woop Woop Chardonnay, South Eastern Australia, 225

Y

Yabby Lake Vineyard Pinot Noir, Mornington Peninsula, 235

Yann Chave Le Rouvre, Crozes-Hermitage, 66

Yellow Hawk Cellar Barbera, Columbia Valley, 215

Yering Station Chardonnay, Yarra Valley, 225

Yering Station M.V.R., Yarra Valley, 227

Yering Station Reserve Pinot Noir, Yarra Valley, 235

Yonna, Campo de Borja, 129

Yves Leccia Domaine d'E Croce, Patrimonio, 80

Z

Zantho St. Laurent, Burgenland, 151

Zardetto Zeta, Prosecco Conegliano, 268

Zilliken Butterfly Medium-Dry Riesling, Mosel-Saar-Ruwer, 144

Zlatan Plavac Grand Cru, Hvar, 161

Zonte's Footstep Cabernet/Malbec, Langhorne Creek, 235

Zonte's Footstep Shiraz/Viognier, Langhorne Creek, 232